WHERE DID THE TRACKS GO: FOLLOWING RAILROAD GRADES IN THE ADIRONDACKS

Michael Kudish, Ph.D.
Professor, Division of Forestry
Paul Smith's College
Paul Smiths, New York

Where Did The Tracks Go:
Following Railroad Grades in The Adirondacks

Library of Congress Cataloging in Publication Data

Kudish, Michael, 1943-
    Where did the tracks go.

    Bibliography: p.
    Includes index.
    1. Railroads — New York (State) — Adirondack Mountains —
History. I. Title.
TF25.A35K83   1985   385'.09747'5   84-23191
ISBN 0-918517-00-1
ISBN 0-918517-01-X (pbk.)

TURTLE POND ROAD
SARANAC LAKE, NEW YORK 12983

A Division of M & M Publications and Sails, Ltd.

Table
Of Contents

Table Of Maps

Chapter IV: New York Central Adirondack Division

Chapter V: Carthage & Adirondack RR and Cranberry Lake Railroad

Addendum

ACKNOWLEDGEMENTS

People who have written books and articles on Adirondack regional railroads are acknowledged in the Bibliography, but what about people who have assisted this writer in other ways? By opening their private collections for examination? By donating timetables and other information? By sharing exploration of rights-of-way in the field? By lengthy discussions? There are many people in this category but the following stand out and are acknowledged here: Christopher Brescia and Fred Baker of Saranac Lake, Luke Wood of Gabriels, and Alan Thomas of West Thornton, New Hampshire.

The Paul Smith's College Lands Department (Fred Klein, Stanley Ingison, Thomas McCartney) and Dean William Rutherford of the Forestry Division have permitted me free access to and use of their priceless collection of old U.S.G.S. 15-minute quadrangles. The Paul Smith's College Library Staff (Theodore Mack and Neil Surprenant) have been more than cooperative in allowing me to turn their historic Adirondack-Smith collection upside down. James Bailey, Plattsburgh City Historian, has resolved some of the complex puzzles in that area. Betty Jane Forrester typed the manuscript. Thomas Wilson has done a superb job in drafting the maps. Dr. Murray Heller has encouraged this volume from its very beginning and has provided many suggestions in improving the manuscript.

—Michael Kudish

Preface

Need For This Volume

Where did the tracks go? This is a frequent question asked by Adirondack visitors and residents alike attempting to locate the many abandoned (and some still existing) railroad rights-of-way. There are many references available on the subject — books, articles, photographs, and old maps are in profusion, but all are widely-scattered. No one has yet compiled and synthesized all this material into one convenient volume. There are three primary aims for this reference work: (1) to locate precisely on topographic maps the rights-of-way, (2) to date the opening and abandonment of the lines, and (3) to provide a variety of references so that one can easily obtain much more detail on these lines than can possibly be offered in this work.

In studying the railroads, one learns also about the industries which the railroads served — both passenger and freight — and this leads to a fuller, richer, more interdisciplinary appreciation of the Adirondack past. In effect, this is a tour guide of the Adirondack railroads as viewed from a train window — better yet, looking out the door of the last coach and watching the tracks spin out behind you, switch-by-switch, industry-by-industry. Since the railroads touched nearly every industry, such a tour will give us a representative idea of what activities took place in this region during the last one-hundred to one hundred-twenty-five years. We will look at passenger service (summer tourists, tuberculosis patients, year-round local people, wealthy camp owners) and freight shipped in and out of the Adirondacks such as products from pulp and papermills, sawmills, charcoal kilns, iron mines, gravel and sand pits and tanneries.

What This Volume Does Not Do

The great bulk of railroad history books and articles traditionally dwell on the detailed mechanical operations of the locomotives. There is no need to duplicate such material as engine specifications here, as references on the subject are more than adequate. Also, many railroad history books appear to be built around spectacular photographs of speeding locomotives, of wrecks or other extraordinary occurrences, without much organization or internal structure; references to photographs instead of the photographs themselves are presented in this volume. This is not a "coffee table" picture book to be casually browsed; it is a reference work describing the ordinary, day-to-day operation of the railroads, arranged with geographic precision in order that the rights-of-way can be located in the field.

This volume is set by geographic boundaries and does not include railroads which operate or operated in areas peripheral to the Adirondacks. The Delaware and Hudson Mainline follows the eastern boundary of the Adirondacks for some distance, but is not wholly located in the Adirondacks; secondly, much has been written on the Mainline so that any detail here would be redundant. The Ogdensburgh and Lake Champlain Railroad (later a division of the Rutland) is only mentioned in this volume because it connected with several of the Adirondack Lines, and detail is available in other works. Railroads lying wholly within the St. Lawrence Valley are omitted, as are lines which entered from the Mohawk Valley to the south.

This volume does not include detailed business, political, or social history, since much information is already provided in other references.

There has been little research on the part of this writer done directly in preparation for this work! All the reference materials used in preparation had been informally accumulated over a decade without any initial aim in compiling them into a book. Some of these materials were come upon by chance, while many others were given to the author by those who know of his interest. The book idea came much later, in 1981, at the suggestion of Dr. Murray Heller.

It is the hope of this writer that this book will encourage many readers to explore these old railroad rights-of-way *in the field*. There are many miles which this writer has not had time to personally examine. There is still much joy and excitement to be gained in the discovery and solution of railroad location puzzles! It is better for one to reconstruct history now than decades from now as remnants become more obscure.

Knowing that there are gaps and errors in the details, this writer will greatly appreciate additions and corrections which will bring this great puzzle closer to solution.

Commentary

The reasons for the decline of railroad service in the United States are numerous and have been described many times elsewhere. Another helpless, unrealistic, sentimental plea to restore service of a bygone age and bring back the past is not in order here, but some commentary may not be out of place. The fuel-consumption efficiency of the railroad may restore some service on a small scale in the future if fossil fuel costs become prohibitive for less fuel-efficient vehicles. To have a major restoration of railroad service, a major change in attitude or philosophy on the part of most Americans is necessary; this will take time — perhaps decades. Most young people today are not against railroads, they are merely without railroads; they have not ridden on trains, shipped freight on them, nor watched them with awe-inspiring fascination.

To this writer, railroads are not only fuel-efficient, they are aesthetically pleasing (the most sublime of human inventions are the railroad and the fugue) and safe (safe if well-maintained and run right!). Highway traffic is so subject to accidents because it is mostly random and without an overall plan; one driver does not know what the other is doing nor when another vehicle will suddenly appear. On a well-run railroad, all meets and passes are planned in advance by dispatchers and nothing is left to chance.

Introduction

How Material Is Gathered

Hiking Railroad Grades:

One way of gathering material on abandoned railroads is to walk the old grades. Several of us interested in railroad history in the Paul Smiths-Saranac Lake area (Chris Brescia and Fred Baker especially) began a project in 1976 of hiking most of the local rights-of-way in order to locate sidings, industrial spurs, yards, switches, servicing facilities, and the like. We developed detailed field notes.

Topographic Maps:

United States Geological Survey topographic quadrangles are extremely useful in locating railroad beds, especially the older 15-minute sheets at a scale of 1/62,500 published from the 1890s through the 1930s. The newer 7½ minute sheets at a scale of 1/24,000 published from the 1940s through the present are also helpful.

One must use caution, however, in using these quadrangles to determine precise track plans of yards. The topographic sheets do no more than to suggest yards and give only an approximate track plan. In those instances in which topographic quadrangles constitute my only evidence, I have stated so on the maps.

Topographic sheets may miss a short-lived railroad because these maps are published so many years apart. For example, the 1922 Childwold and 1902–1903 St. Regis Quadrangles were published before Bay Pond Inc. built their logging railroad in 1924. Obviously, the maps cannot possibly show the line. Bay Pond Inc. abandoned the railroad in 1932. The next quadrangles were published in 1953 (St. Regis 15-minute) and in 1970 (Augerhole Falls 7½-minute), long after the line was abandoned, and also thus do not show it. Another example is the Paul Smith's Electric Railway. It was built in 1906 and abandoned between 1930 and 1932. The first Saranac Lake Quadrangle was published in 1902, before the Railway. The second Saranac Lake Quadrangle was done in 1953, after the Railway. Hence, neither Quadrangle shows the Railway! Some logging spurs were in use only two or three years before the tracks were removed and laid somewhere else.

In a few places, a series of elevation benchmarks strung out in a line often at regular intervals of about a mile way out "in the middle of nowhere" may suggest an old grade. Check the steepness of the imaginary line or truck trail connecting these benchmarks: railroads rarely ascended or descended grades of more than 3 or 4% (although some logging lines could double that). I have two examples of such strings of benchmarks which, as I had confirmed later, were indeed old railroad grades! One was a Brooklyn Cooperage branch on the 1919 Nicholville Quadrangle between Blue (Azure) Mountain and the St. Lawrence County Line (see page 73). Another is on the Cranberry Lake (1916–1919) and Stark (1920–1921) Quadrangles between Newton Falls and Newbridge (see page 127).

Highways may be built upon old railroad grades. Be suspicious that a railroad could have been present where the highway is straight for long distances (a mile or more) or has large-radius curves; be especially suspicious where the highway climbs at very gentle grades not exceeding 3 or 4%. An example is Lake Colby Drive in Saranac Lake (Route 86) in front of the General Hospital; it follows the D&H Chateaugay Railroad Branch. Note how straight Highways 3 and 30 are about a mile west of their junction near Wawbeek and heading toward Tupper Lake; this is a spur of the old Brooklyn Cooperage. The highway from St. Regis Falls to Duane (number 99) follows in part the old Everton Railroad from the Falls to Everton. Highways with steep hills (5 to 12%) and tight curves do not follow old railroad lines.

Maps Other Than Topographic Quadrangles:

The New York State Department of Environmental Conservation and its predecessor organizations (New York State Forest Commission, 1885–1894; N.Y. State Forest, Fish and Game Commission, 1895–1910; N.Y. State Conservation Commission, 1911–1926; N.Y. State Conservation Department, 1927–1970) published periodically Adirondack Land Maps. The older ones were published every several years showing State Lands acquired within the Adirondack Park. Some of these maps show the logging branches as well as the main lines. An example is the Brooklyn Cooperage trackage east and west of Meno on the New York & Ottawa Railroad in the 1910–1920 era.

In examining maps printed before about 1890, when the U.S. Geological Survey began to publish topographic quadrangles, we must depend on maps which lack the elevation contours. Some of these *do* show railroads and branch lines, for example the Beers' county atlases.

Photographs:

Photographs published in books and articles are very useful in determining track plans and types of equipment used. When I have come across photographs, I have listed the book (or article) and page number as a reference, arranged station-by-station. Unpublished photographs can also be very useful, for example those by Alan Thomas who intensely observed operations here in the 1950s.

Timetables:

Old timetables, both public and employees', offer a variety of data. Timetables indicate when each station was first placed into service and when the trains no longer stopped there. One must have a complete set of timetables to determine this dating accurately; an incomplete set of timetables such as mine can only approximate the period that a station was in service. For example, often I have listed timetable dates when a station or water tower has been listed, such as 1910 and 1913 on page 89. This merely indicates my timetables, not a discontinuation of service in the years between. Timetables also inform us if and when a station name was changed; there were many: Fulton Chain Sta.-Thendara, Carter-Clearwater, Sabattis-Long Lake West, Pleasant Lake-Mt. Arab, Paul Smith's Station-Gabriels, Lake Kushaqua-Stonywold, Saranac Junction-Lake Clear Junction, White Lake-Woodgate, Horseshoe-American Legion, Bog

Lake-Robinwood are some changes I've noted.

Old timetables offer station mileages from a zero or base point, the employees' 'tables usually listing them to the nearest one-hundredth of a mile (52.8 feet). Elevations are occasionally also listed, but one must use caution here; the New York Central Railroad exaggerated the elevation of Lake Placid Station as 2000 feet, when it actually is 1736. Elevations must be checked on the topographic quadrangles.

Passenger timetables may inform us of the nature of the passenger equipment. The origins and destinations of sleeping cars are given, as are diners. Most trains carried coaches, and a few carried parlor or lounge cars.

Employees' timetables offer capacities of passing sidings in numbers of freight cars, and locations of water, fueling, and other facilities. Employees' timetables often give clues to the class of locomotives used.

Timetables give us an idea of the speed of trains since we know how long (in minutes) it took for each train to travel the measured distance between stations.

In some instances when I had no employees' timetable available, I was able to determine indirectly the existence of a passing siding by using a public passenger timetable. If two trains were scheduled to be at the same station at the same time but traveling in opposite directions, there must have been a passing siding there, as all the Adirondack lines were single-track.

Books and Articles:

A wide variety of reference books and articles of variable quality was used in preparing this manuscript. The format for this book (parallel text and strip maps) is based on the books of Manville B. Wakefield, who illustrated his own works with marvelously clear maps. The very carefully-researched and finely-detailed articles by William Gove and Richard Palmer have served as the mainstay for information on the logging branches. Henry Harter's book, *The Fairy Tale Railroad* is of Gove and Palmer caliber but describes a whole division. Peripheral to the Adirondacks is the work of Jim Shaughnessy on the Delaware and Hudson and Rutland Railroads — massive books, but not concentrating on the Adirondack Region.

Some books have no indices, and this writer had to index them in order to use them more efficiently. Examples are Harter, Collins, and Simmons. Gardner not only lacked an index but pagination! I had to number Gardner's pages in order to cite him here! Many books lack ample detailed maps showing precise location of lines; I hope that this volume will not be criticized for this kind of shortcoming.

Several sources are available on abandoned railroad grades in New York State. Nielsen (1970) is the least complete, offering mostly *periods* of years (an approximation) for abandonment dates instead of the year of abandonment, and a rough, small-scale map. The New York State Department of Transportation (1974), Real Property Division, published an Inventory of Abandoned Railroads Rights of Way; it is more complete than Nielsen, offers descriptions of the old grades, but no maps. Palmer's (1979) is the most complete, although it lacks descriptions of grades and maps. Weitzman's (1980, pp. 2–40) book is most general geographically (covering the whole United States), but has excellent illustrations of signals, rails, switches, bridges, ties, locomotives, and other wayside structures.

Unraveling Complexities And Subtleties:

Station name changes have been mentioned earlier; one must know that a single station had different names at different times. In a number of instances, the name of the railroad itself was changed, especially following reincorporation after bankruptcy. An example is the Northern Adirondack Railroad which became the Northern New York Railroad, then the New York and Ottawa, and finally the Ottawa Division of the New York Central Railroad. The Chateaugay Railroad for less than a year became the Chateaugay and Lake Placid immediately before becoming the Chateaugay Branch of the Delaware and Hudson. A third example is the Northern New York Railroad, which became, in turn, the Ogdensburg Railroad, the Ogdensburg and Lake Champlain Railroad, the Central Vermont Railroad, and finally the Ogdensburg Division of the Rutland Railroad.

In a few cases two different railroads had the *same name*, but fortunately not at the same time. The Fulton Chain Railroad (1888–1892) ran from Moose River to Minnehaha; the second Fulton Chain Railroad (1896–1932) ran from Fulton Chain Station to Old Forge. The first Northern New York Railroad (1848–1858) ran from Rouses Point to Ogdensburg; the second Northern New York Railroad (1895–1897) ran from Moira to Tupper Lake. The Adirondack Company's Railroad (1865–1889) ran from Saratoga Springs to North Creek; the Adirondack Railway (1979 and 1980) with a very similar but not identical name ran from Remsen to Lake Placid.

Ownership changes, especially in saw-

mills, can be very confusing as one is not aware at first that only a single mill site is involved. Tupper Lake breaks all records for this kind of thing: Hurd's, Shepard and Morse, Ducey et al, Norwood Manufacturing Company, Santa Clara Lumber Company, and finally Elliott's Mangle Roller Plant were all on one site! Hobson's Mill became the Sherman (or Sisson) Mill and ultimately was acquired by Oval Wood Dish Company. U.S. Bobbin and Shuttle Company became Jamestown Adirondack Corporation. A Brooklyn Cooperage mill was later owned by Tupper Lake Chemical, with the Draper Corporation building later on the same site. In some instances a mill burned down and another was built on the same site by the same or another company. More specifically referring to railroads, an example is Kinsley Lumber Co. selling to Baker Brother at Tekene. Oval Wood Dish Company's logging railroads at Kildare became Sisson-White's.

In three instances, a railroad had been abandoned and the rails removed, with another company relaying the track on the old right-of-way at a later date! The Everton Railroad (1886–ca. 1898) between St. Regis Falls and Everton was rebuilt by the Brooklyn Cooperage Company (1904–1920). Mac-a-Mac Corporation (1912–1920) built a line from Brandreth Station to Brandreth Lake, while Whitney Industries used much of the old line from 1936 to 1939. The Higbie Lumber Company (1902–1919) built a railroad from Newton Falls to Newbridge (The Newton Falls and Northern Railroad), and later the grade was used by the Hanna Mining Company in the early 1940s. How's this for complexity?

Some railroads had trackage rights over other railroad's lines. The New York Central had trackage rights from 1893 through 1946 to run its trains between Saranac Lake and Lake Placid on Delaware and Hudson tracks. The reverse occurred between 1940 and 1946 when the D&H trains used New York Central tracks between Plumadore and Saranac Lake via Lake Clear Junction. Brooklyn Cooperage had trackage rights over the New York and Ottawa as did the Oval Wood Dish Company trains.

Track plans at industries and yards constantly changed as did needs. One can locate differing yet correct maps of sidings at stations published years apart. In Saranac Lake, Tupper Lake, and Lake Placid, I have presented maps showing track plans at different stages in the history of these villages.

The Text:

The Text includes a variety of information: Mileage is from a zero point on each line. For the Chateaugay and Ausable Forks Branches of the Delaware and Hudson, it is Plattsburgh. For the Adirondack Company's Railroad to North Creek, it is Saratoga Springs. For the New York Central Adirondack Division it is Herkimer, but Moira on the Ottawa Division, and Carthage on the Carthage and Adirondack Branch. On the Grasse River Railroad it is Childwold Station.

Elevations are in feet above mean sea level taken from U.S.G.S. topographic quadrangles. Sometimes the older 15-minute and the newer 7½-minute maps disagree as more modern survey methods refine the earlier data. I have tried to use the most recent elevation data.

Years of operation for a station are estimated as best as possible from this writer's incomplete timetable collection. If there are doubts, they will be stated, either with a range of possible years or a "ca.".

Chapters II (Branch Lines off the D & H mainline) and V (N. Y. Central Carthage and Adirondack Branch) are less detailed than the lines in Chapters I, III, and IV. The reason for this is simply the writer's lack of familiarity with these lines, little field-checking, and less printed materials available. Still, it is thought better to include less detail on these lines than none at all in this volume.

References are cited thusly: Author(s) names are given first with the year of publication in parenthesis, e.g., Gove (1978). Where specific page numbers are important in locating facts, they follow the year of publication, e.g., Harter (1979, p. 226). Footnotes are not used. At the end of this volume is a Bibliography listing the authors or publishing organizations alphabetically.

The Maps:

Maps are drawn at four different levels of detail:
- #1. One overall map on the following page which shows locations of all the lines and branches covered in this volume. The purpose of this map is to allow the reader a glance at the whole Adirondacks, with less clutter of detail.
- #2. A map of each of the lines in Chapters I, II, and IV (Chateaugay Railroad, New York & Ottawa, and Adirondack Division, respectively) showing all branches and major references on a single sheet. These #2 level maps are on a larger scale than the level #1 map but cover a smaller area.
- #3. Local maps along each line and

branch at a scale of 1/62,500 (about one inch equals one mile). The vast bulk of the maps are these level #3 maps, with the railroads drawn in bold face ink on 15-minute U.S.G.S. topographic quadrangles.
- #4. Level #4 maps are superdetailed large-scale maps of smaller areas of intense activity such as the yards at Malone, Tupper Lake, Saranac Lake, and Lake Placid.

The 15-minute quadrangles were chosen for the level #3 maps because the railroads can be shown in relation to topography in addition to roads and streams. Some clutter exists in these topographic maps, but I feel that this is the best manner of presentation. Palmer (1973) in his work on the Peg-Leg Railroad and Clark (1974) on the A.A. Low Railroad at Horseshoe use topographic maps very effectively.

Ideally, in this book there would be one page of text on the left side and the corresponding level #3 map on the right side. This would facilitate reading the text and viewing the appropriate locator map. Unfortunately, this cannot be done with any degree of consistency because some areas require lengthy descriptive text and little map. Other areas require detailed maps and little descriptive text. Under these conditions, I have attempted to match text and maps as best as possible. This format is used effectively in Lobeck's *Things Maps Don't Tell Us* (1956, 1964).

Another spatial problem in this volume involves placement of the branchlines. There are two possibilities. The first is to add the branch line to the text of the mainline at the junction point. Unfortunately, this interrupts the trend of thought along the main line. The second possibility is to hold the branch line maps and text until the end of the chapter, as an addendum to the mainline text and maps; in this way the mainline text and maps are uninterrupted. I have decided on an inconsistent solution! The smaller branches, with little text and appearing wholly on the map with the mainline, are placed at the junction point. The larger branches with long text and separate maps are placed at the end of the chapter; examples of the latter case are the Raquette Lake and Grasse River Railways.

Note that the orientation of the level #3 maps (1/62,500 scale topographic quadrangles) is variable. North is not always at the top. Look for north arrows on each map for orientation. Some maps are obliquely shown, in order to present the greatest mileage of track in the smallest space.

When a branch has been drawn onto a non-topographic map by other authors (primarily Gove), I have had to do some approximating

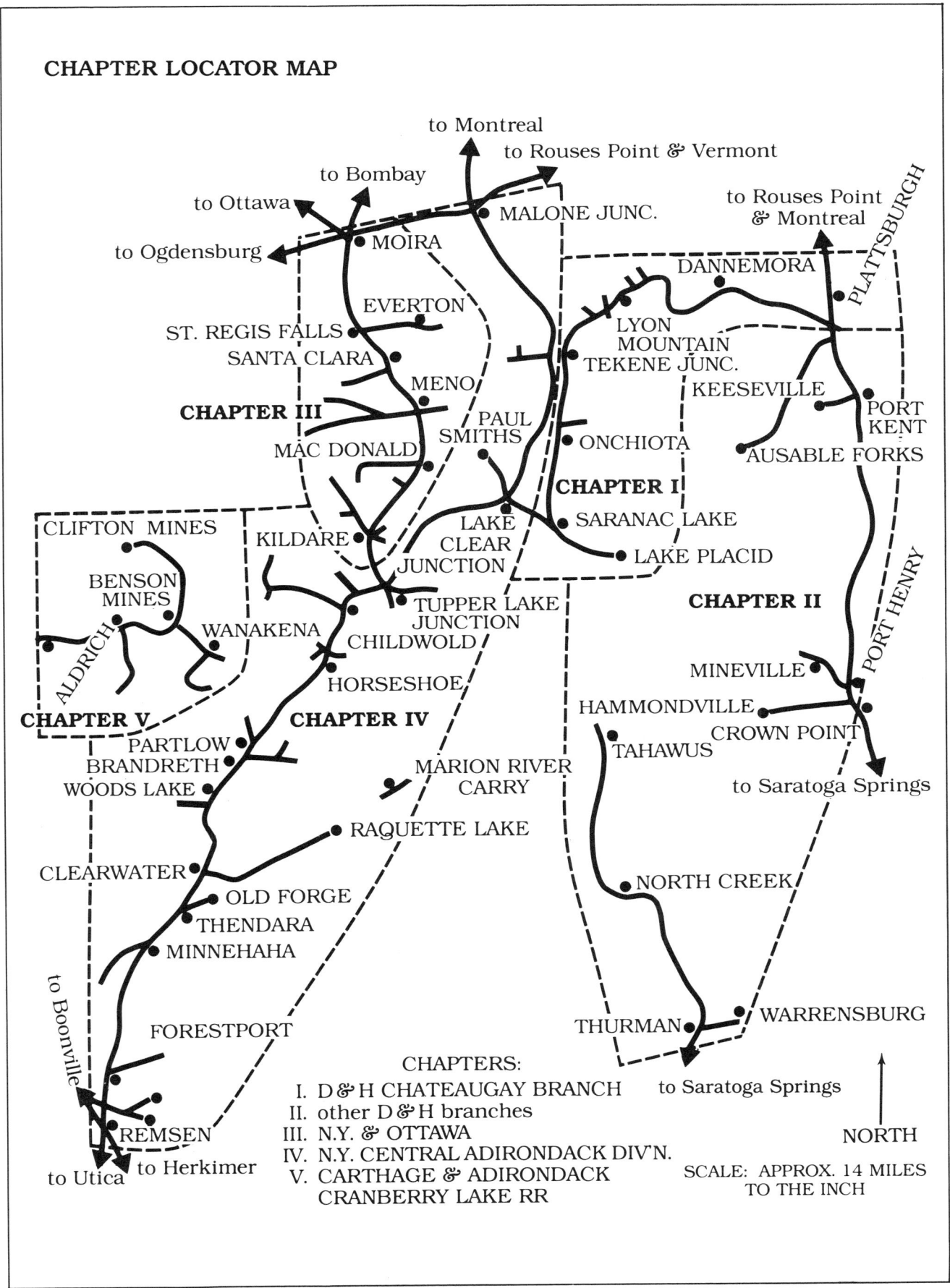

CHAPTER LOCATOR MAP

to Montreal
to Rouses Point & Vermont
to Bombay
to Ottawa
to Ogdensburg
to Rouses Point & Montreal
PLATTSBURGH
MALONE JUNC.
MOIRA
DANNEMORA
EVERTON
ST. REGIS FALLS
SANTA CLARA
LYON MOUNTAIN
TEKENE JUNC.
KEESEVILLE
MENO
PORT KENT
CHAPTER III
PAUL SMITHS
ONCHIOTA
AUSABLE FORKS
MAC DONALD
CHAPTER I
CLIFTON MINES
KILDARE
LAKE CLEAR JUNCTION
SARANAC LAKE
LAKE PLACID
BENSON MINES
CHAPTER II
ALDRICH
WANAKENA
TUPPER LAKE JUNCTION
CHILDWOLD
PORT HENRY
CHAPTER V
HORSESHOE
MINEVILLE
CHAPTER IV
HAMMONDVILLE
CROWN POINT
PARTLOW
BRANDRETH
WOODS LAKE
MARION RIVER CARRY
TAHAWUS
to Saratoga Springs
CLEARWATER
RAQUETTE LAKE
OLD FORGE
THENDARA
MINNEHAHA
NORTH CREEK
to Boonville
FORESTPORT
THURMAN
WARRENSBURG

CHAPTERS:
I. D & H CHATEAUGAY BRANCH
II. other D & H branches
III. N.Y. & OTTAWA
IV. N.Y. CENTRAL ADIRONDACK DIV'N.
V. CARTHAGE & ADIRONDACK CRANBERRY LAKE RR

to Saratoga Springs

NORTH

SCALE: APPROX. 14 MILES TO THE INCH

REMSEN
to Utica
to Herkimer

in order to transfer the branch to a topographic map. Examples are the North Tram and spurs off the Grasse River, the Mac-a-Mac Railroad at Brandreth, the International Paper Company spur at Woods Lake, and the Rich Lumber Company near Wanakena.

Track Symbols on Maps:

Note that standard procedure in presenting track schematics (plans) is that *a single line represents one track, not one rail.* Hence, on the following maps in this book:

On U.S.G.S. topographic quadrangles and on most other maps which show a combination of railroads, rivers, highways, contours, powerlines, political boundaries, etc., a railroad track is shown as a line with cross ties (see below). However, maps which involve railroad track schematics almost exclusively (maps published in railroad history books or by the drafting departments of railroads themselves) show the railroad track as a line lacking cross ties (see below); on the latter maps there is no confusion with highway, powerline, boundary symbols, etc. The latter representation is chosen here, with highways shown as dotted lines and rivers as wavy lines.

Single Track vs. Double Track:

Building two-track railroads is more expensive than constructing single-track lines because the two-track right-of-way must be wider: hence, wider cuts and fills. Two-track lines also cost more to maintain, but they do have the advantage of permitting heavy traffic to flow more freely. Two-track lines create fewer delays and bottlenecks.

All lines within the Adirondacks were built as single track because the number of trains per day could be accommodated on a single track. Besides, the cost per mile of railroad construction in hilly or mountainous regions such as ours was great enough for one track, let alone for two. The Delaware and Hudson's Chateaugay Branch in the summer of 1908 (the peak railroad era) oper-

ated only four passenger trains daily in each direction plus the freights. The New York and Ottawa had only two passenger trains daily each way plus the freights in its peak years 1909 and 1912. Even the busy New York Central Adirondack Division had only six passenger and two freight trains daily each way in 1910 through 1915; on weekends and holidays, some passenger trains ran in several sections but still the single track was adequate.

Passing Sidings:

To accommodate such trains on single track lines, passing sidings were built at fairly regular intervals, about every five to seven miles, usually at or near stations. These sidings were double-ended, that is, they connected to the maintrack at both ends so that trains could enter or leave freely from either end without having to run in reverse. Passing sidings could, of course, allow fast trains to overtake slow trains traveling in the same direction (passes); trains using a passing siding in opposite directions are called meets.

Stub Tracks and Team Tracks:

In addition to passing sidings, at most stations single-ended stub (dead-end) sidings were built for the loading and unloading of freight cars. It would have been poor judgment to load or unload such cars while they were spotted (placed) on the main track or passing sidings, because traffic would be delayed; could you imagine a crowd of restless passengers in a hurry to get to their hotel waiting for a freight car to be loaded with lumber up ahead?

Some stub tracks served specific industries, while others served businesses which lacked their own stub tracks. In the latter case, the stub tracks were called "team tracks" because teams of horses with wagons in tow would pull up alongside the freight car to load or unload it.

Sometimes two or more industries shared

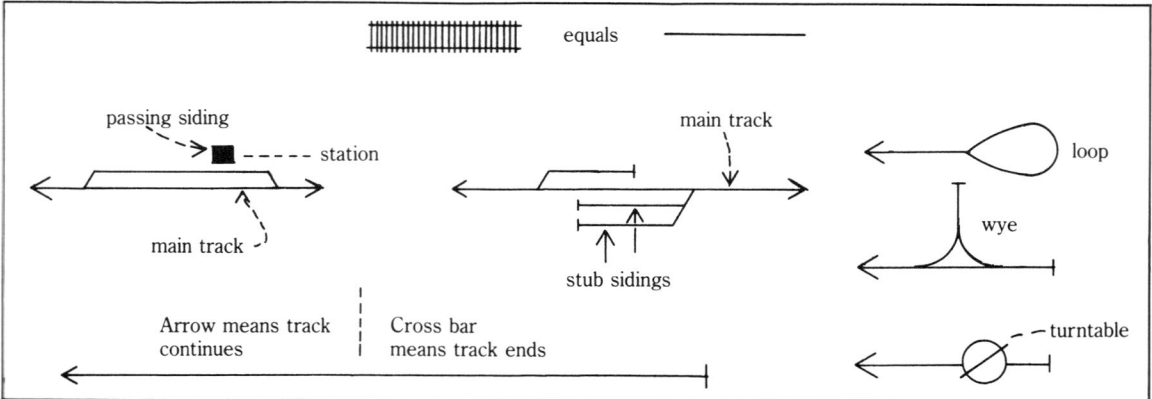

the same stub track. In a few cases where industries and team tracks were especially busy, the sidings were double-ended very much like a passing siding. Some wealthy camp-owners had not only their own private cars but also stubs to lay them up on!

Turning of Steam Locomotives:

Although most freight and passenger cars were double-ended and did not require turning around at the end of a run, steam locomotives had to be turned. Steam locomotives could run in reverse for short distances, but it was not wise to run them so for long distances (diesel locomotives are double ended and need not be turned). There were three ways of turning a steam locomotive: (1) a loop track, such as at Raquette Lake Station, (2) a wye (pronounced as the letter "y") and (3) a turntable. The wye principle works just as in turning an automobile around in a narrow driveway off a highway; such triangular track patterns were found at Saranac Lake, Lake Clear Junction, and Tupper Lake. Turntables occupied the least space and were often associated with round houses or engine sheds; turntables existed at Lake Placid, Malone Junction, and Fulton Chain Station.

Runaround Tracks:

At route terminals, such as Lake Placid, it was necessary to move the locomotive to the opposite end of the train in order for the train to later depart from the terminal. Although the diesels did not need to be turned, they *did* need to be uncoupled from and run alongside their train on a parallel track in order to be coupled on to the rear of the train. Such a parallel track in terminals, actually a form of passing siding, is called a runaround track. Steam locomotives in Lake Placid "escaped" from their trains using the runaround, but in addition had to be turned on the turntable.

Crossovers vs. Crossings:

A crossover is a track that connects two parallel tracks, allowing a train to pass from one track to the other. A crossing is simply two or more tracks crossing each other without any means of allowing a train to pass from one to another; crossings can also imply highway crossings.

Interchange Tracks:

At junctions of two or more railroads, connecting tracks permitting trains to pass from one railroad to another are called interchange tracks. These are often associated with crossings, forming hypotenuses of triangles. Such interchange tracks were locat-

ed at Tupper Lake Junction (between the Adirondack and Ottawa Divisions) and at Malone Junction (between the Adirondack Division and the Rutland), usually with yards nearby.

Yards and Engine Servicing Facilities:

A yard is a series of parallel tracks used for the storage of cars or for the making-up or breaking-up of trains. Large yards were located at Tupper Lake Junction and Malone Junction. Smaller ones were at Lake Placid, Saranac Lake, Lake Clear Junction, Conifer, Remsen, Moira, and Thendara. The larger and middle-sized yards had engine servicing facilities such as coal, water, and oiling stations, and repair shops. Water towers were scattered along the lines at more remote stations as well.

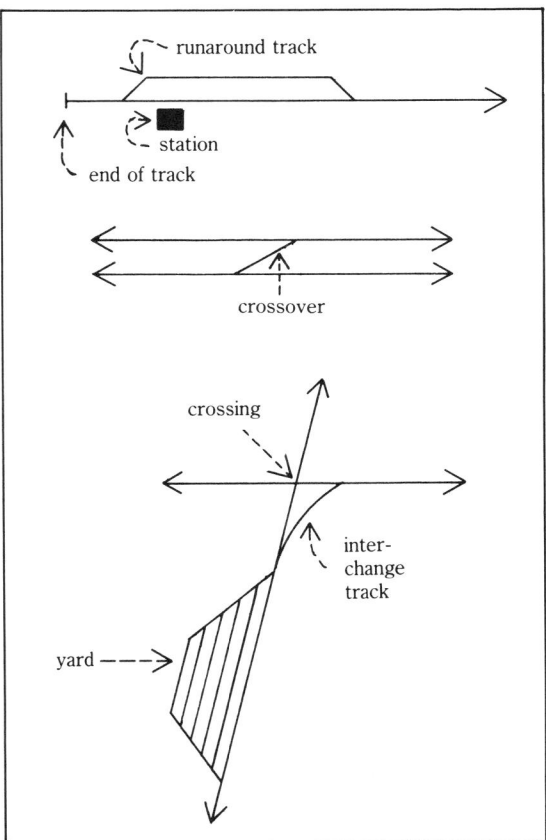

Glossary

Standard, Narrow, and Dual Gauge:

Almost all railroads in North America since the beginning of the Twentieth Century have been standard-gauged so that locomotives and cars can be easily interchanged. The distance between the inner sides of the rails is 4 feet, 8½ inches; this gauge dates back to early Nineteenth-Century Britain when stagecoach wheels were this far apart. The first railroad passenger cars were stagecoaches equipped with flanged wheels; although railroad cars grew in size and were altered in form, the distance between the wheels and rails remained the same.

Narrow gauge lines were built in North America primarily in the 19th Century in hilly or mountainous areas. Narrow gauge meant narrow cuts and fills and smaller radius curves for smaller trains: hence less expense and easier construction. The most frequent narrow gauge was 3 feet between the inner sides of the rails; Adirondack area examples were the Chateaugay Branch of the Delaware and Hudson from 1878 through 1903, the Crown Point Iron Company's Railroad from 1874 through 1893, and the Herkimer, Newport, and Poland.

Narrow gauge railroads presented a problem when connections were made with standard-gauged lines, such as at Plattsburgh from 1878 through 1903; here, freight cars had to be unloaded and then reloaded, while passengers were forced to change trains.

Dual gauge lines required elaborate switches. The Saranac and Lake Placid, opening in 1893 between these two villages, was dual gauge until the D&H standard-gauged in 1903. Hence, for the ten miles there was three-rail track, but NOT with the center rail equidistant between the outer ones. Both the New York Central and the D&H Chateaugay shared a common rail as shown in the diagram below:

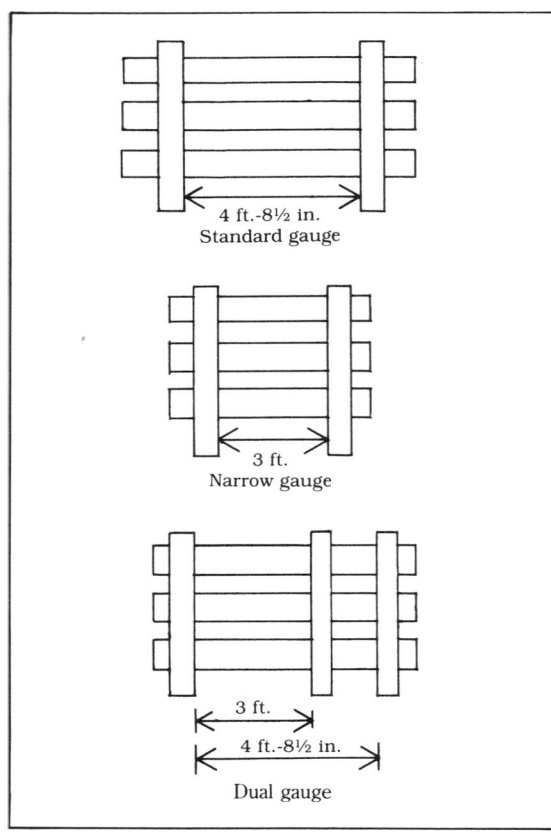

4 ft.-8½ in.
Standard gauge

3 ft.
Narrow gauge

3 ft.
4 ft.-8½ in.
Dual gauge

Doubling the Hill vs. Doubleheading:

When upgrades were so steep that the locomotive power provided could not ascend with its train, the hill was often doubled. That is, the train was split in half at the base of the grade and the front half hauled up the hill. At the summit, the cars were cut off on a siding and the engine backed down on its own. At the base, the second half of the train was then hauled up the hill and reunited with the first half at the summit. With particularly long trains, the cars had to be divided into three segments. Doubling was common-place on the grade between Cadyville and Dannemora, and sometimes occurred between White Lake (Woodgate) and Otter Lake, and between Carter Station (Clearwater) and Big Moose.

Doubleheading means placing two locomotives at the head of the train, when a single engine was inadequate to haul the weight up the grades. Adirondack Division trains were often double-headed to make the two grades mentioned in the above paragraph, as well as the grade between Ray Brook and Lake Placid. In extreme cases, trains could be triple-headed and/or with a pusher engine coupled on the rear.

Union Station:

A union station served a union of two or more railroads, as opposed to serving a single railroad. Union stations existed at Lake Placid and at Malone Junction; Childwold Station on the Adirondack Division and on the Grasse River Railroad could also be considered a union station.

Jackworks and Barnhart Log Loaders:

Jackworks were places where railroad flat cars were loaded or unloaded into bodies of water such as rivers or lakes. Conveyor belts (escalator-like devices) caught on to the logs and hauled them up or down the ramp.

The best photo of a jackworks which I have seen appears in Gove (1981, page 12). Most logging railroads had jackworks, especially if softwood (pine and spruce) logs were cut (hardwood logs barely float downstream because of their greater specific gravity). Paul Smith's Electric Railway had a jackworks on Lower St. Regis Lake where logs were unloaded in winter from the flat cars and piled up on the ice; when the lake thawed, the logs were floated down to the sawmill.

The most common log-loader was the steam-powered Barnhart. Because it was a small crane that ran on rails along the tops of flatcars, it could load or unload a series of cars without any uncoupling, coupling, or shuffling. If the crane were secured permanently to a single car, then flat cars would have to be constantly uncoupled, coupled, and shuffled around to be loaded or unloaded! The best photos of a Barnhart Log Loader are in Hyde (1974, pp. 31 and 34).

Pulp Mill, Paper Mill, and Rossed Pulp Plant:

A pulp mill produces only pulp from logs, an intermediate product. Pulp must then be shipped to a paper mill for finishing into paper. Paper mills most often include a pulp mill and thus can perform the complete operation. Rossed pulp plants such as at Underwood and nearby Tupper Lake Junction only removed the bark from the pulpwood logs; the logs were then sent to Piercefield to be made into paper.

Classes of Steam and Diesel Locomotives serving the Adirondacks

(see chart on pp. 14 and 15)

Locomotives which served the Adirondacks can be divided into three main groups, with each group containing a number of classes. The three main groups are: rod steam locomotives, geared steam locomotives, and diesel-electric locomotives.

Rod steam locomotives were the most familiar kind as they hauled passenger trains and freight trains on main lines and main branches. The "rods" are the nearly-horizontal bars which connected the pistons with the driving wheels. Steam rod locomotives are classified according to the number of wheels, from a system devised by Frederic M. Whyte in 1900 (Weitzman, 1980, pages 16 and 17); the class consists of three numbers separated by hyphens. The first number of Whyte's System refers to the small pilot wheels directly behind the "cowcatcher". There are two pilot wheels (one axle) in most freight locomotives, four (two axles) in most passenger locomotives and none in yard switching engines; exceptions do exist. The second number of Whyte's System refers to the large driving powered wheels (connected to the pistons via rods); small locomotives have four drivers (two axles), medium-sized locomotives have six (three axles), while large locomotives have eight (four axles). More modern steam locomotives may have ten drivers, and others have the drivers in two sets; the sets can rotate independently so that the long engines can negotiate curves (the latter are called articulated locomotives). The third number of Whyte's System refers to the trailing wheels under the firebox and/or cab, usually zero, two (one axle) or four (two axles).

In the Adirondacks, the earliest rod steam engines were of the 4-4-0 American Standard class, the zero referring to an absence of trailing wheels under the cab in these predominantly passenger engines. After about 1890, when trains increased in weight, larger 4-6-0 class engines were introduced; these were called Ten-wheelers. About 1910 or 1915, still heavier passenger trains required still heavier Pacifics, class 4-6-2.

Freights were hauled by Moguls (2-6-0) and by Consolidations (2-8-0), although Mikados (2-8-2) did run on the Adirondack Division. In the years just prior to dieselization, the New York Central ran freight Pacifics (4-6-2). Locomotives with eight drivers were absent from Adirondack railroads, although some DID operate on the Delaware and Hudson Mainline and on the Rutland.

Switching in yards was accomplished by small locomotives with neither pilot nor trailing wheels (0-4-0, 0-6-0, 0-8-0), although road engines such as Moguls, Consolidations, and Mikados also performed these tasks.

Geared steam locomotives ran exclusively on the logging railroads and were built to hold back heavy loads down steep hills and run at low speeds. Usually, the sawmill was in the valley near a river and the logging area on the hillsides above, in most cases necessitating a downgrade for loaded log trains. Empty flat cars were easily hauled up the steep grades, sometimes as much as six or eight percent. Shay locomotives were invented by a gentleman of the same name in Michigan in the 1880s; these unusual engines had on one side of the boiler small vertical pistons which turned a horizontal crankshaft that ran the length of the engine and tender. The small driving wheels were attached to the crankshaft by means of gears, hence making it difficult to "run away" on downgrades; the engine would literally have to *slide* down the tracks to "run away".

Other geared locomotives were Climaxes (with pistons held at an odd 45° angle with the horizontal) and Heislers.

Diesel-electric locomotives became common and replaced steam locomotives in the late 1940s and early 1950s. The most common diesels to run on the Adirondack Division were Alco (American Locomotive Company) road switchers, models ##2 and 3, called RS-2 and RS-3, respectively. These were used for both freight and passenger service through 1972 when the Penn-Central abandoned the line. The Adirondack Railway in 1979 and 1980 also used Alco RS-2s and RS-3s, one with six-wheeled trucks designated "RSC-3". The through freight "banana train" from Utica to Montreal in the

CLASSES OF STEAM LOCOMOTIVES IN THE GREATER
ADIRONDACK REGION: This chart is not intended to be complete.

NYC = New York Central   **D&H = Delaware and Hudson**   **RUT = Rutland**
Numbers refer to individual locomotive road numbers

MOSTLY FREIGHT LOCOMOTIVES
A. Number of wheels in leading or pilot truck directly behind the "cowcatcher" is TWO (2)

B. Number of Driver Wheels ➞	FOUR (4)	SIX (6)	EIGHT (8)	TEN (10)

C. Number of wheels in trailing truck under cab ↓
 	
NONE (0)
	2-4-0	2-6-0 MOGULS
		
		NYC Class E:
		  1900s & 5100s
		D&H Class C:
		  300s
		Grasse River:
		  60s
			2-8-0
			CONSOLIDATIONS
			NYC Class G:
			  2200s
			D&H Class E:
			  700s to 1200s
			RUT: 20s &
			  2000s
				2-10-0
				DECAPODS
				NYC Class Z

TWO (2)	2-4-2
	COLUMBIAS
		2-6-2
		PRAIRIES
			2-8-2 MIKADOS
			NYC Class H5:
			  1300s, 1800s
			  & 5100s
			RUT: 30s
				2-10-2
				BULLMOOSE

FOUR (4)	2-4-4	2-6-4	2-8-4 BERKSHIRES	2-10-4 TEXAS
SIX (6)		2-6-6 NYC Class D 2-6-6-0 (Articulated) NYC Class H.		

SWITCHERS
Number of wheels in leading or pilot truck directly behind the "cowcatcher" is ZERO (0)

0-4-0 Marion River Carry	0-6-0 NYC Class B D&H Class B1 to B4	0-8-0 NYC Class U D&H Class B5 to B7	0-10-0 NYC Class M
		0-8-8-0 SWITCHER MALLET (ARTICULATED) NYC Class NU D&H Class H	

NY&O = New York and Ottawa

<table>
<tr><td colspan="5">MOSTLY PASSENGER LOCOMOTIVES
A. Number of wheels in leading or pilot truck directly behind the "cowcatcher" is FOUR (4)</td></tr>
<tr><td>B. Number of Driver Wheels →</td><td>FOUR (4)</td><td>SIX (6)</td><td>EIGHT (8)</td><td>TEN (10)</td></tr>
<tr><td>C. Number of wheels in trailing truck under cab ↓</td><td></td><td></td><td></td><td></td></tr>
<tr><td>NONE (0)</td><td>4-4-0
AMERICAN STANDARD
NYC Class C: 400s, 900s, & 1600s
D&H Class G: 100s & 300s
RUT & NY&O: 700s, 800s, 900s & 40s</td><td>4-6-0
TEN-WHEELER
NYC Class F: 800s, 2000s, 2100s
D&H Class D: 500s
RUT: 70s</td><td>4-8-0
TWELVE WHEELER
Raquette Lake Railway #2</td><td>4-10-0
MASTODON</td></tr>
<tr><td>TWO (2)</td><td>4-4-2
ATLANTIC
NYC Class I</td><td>4-6-2
PACIFIC*
NYC Class K3n: 4700s
NYC Class K11c: 4400s 4500s, 3000s, & 3100s

NYC Class K11b: 4400s
D&H Class P: 600s</td><td>4-8-2
MOUNTAIN
NYC
Class L:
MOHAWKS</td><td>4-10-2</td></tr>
<tr><td>FOUR (4)</td><td>4-4-4</td><td>4-6-4
HUDSON
NYC Class J
5400s

4-6-6-4
CHALLENGER
D&H Class J: 1500s
(Articulated)</td><td>4-8-4
NORTHERN
NYC
Class S:
NIAGARAS
6000s
D&H Class K: 300s</td><td>4-10-4</td></tr>
</table>

*Note: Some NYC Class K Pacific locomotives were also used in freight service.

1950s also used Alco FA and FB units (not considered switchers), the B units being cabless.

Those smaller lines which survived into the diesel era (such as the Grasse River Railroad) used small industrial switchers. The Adirondack Railway had one in 1979–1980 for maintenance trains.

Of course, the Chateaugay Branch, the New York and Ottawa, and the Cranberry Lake Railroad closed before the diesel era. In contrast, the D&H Ausable Forks and Dannemora Branches, which survived until 1981, had D&H modern diesels serving them. Likewise, Conrail runs modern engines to Newton Falls.

Dating Old Maps

Frequently I come across old maps which are not dated. It is fun to see how close I can come to determining the year of publication by examining the railroads on the map. Here are three examples:

An acquaintance from Virginia sent me a New York Central Railroad map which includes other connecting railroads in the northeastern states. The D&H mainline is shown through from Albany to Montreal, but the Chateaugay Branch to Dannemora is not shown; the former was completed in 1875 and the latter in 1879. Thus, the map dates from the period 1876 to 1878, provided that the New York Central Railroad kept up-to-date on the inclusion of new lines and branches.

Dr. Murray Heller has in his office an undated map. It shows the Saranac Lake and Lake Placid Railroad into Lake Placid which opened in 1893. It shows the D&H Ausable Branch joining the mainline at Plattsburgh rather than at South Junction; the junction relocation was completed in 1894. Thus the map dates from a very brief period in late 1893 or early 1894.

Dr. Heller has another undated map entitled "Resort Map of the Adirondacks, New York", issued by the Century Company and the New York Central Railroad, printed by the Matthews-Northrup Works of Buffalo, Cleveland, and New York. Logging railroads are normally not included on such maps, but lines having public passenger and freight service are. First, I look for the most recent line or branch built; this map shows the Grasse River Railroad, built in 1913. The map dates from 1913 or later. Second, I look for the first line or branch to be abandoned; this map still shows the Keeseville, Ausable Chasm, and Lake Champlain, abandoned in 1924. The map dates from 1924 or earlier. My conclusion, combining the 1913 or later knowledge with the 1924 or earlier, brackets the year of publication between late 1913 and early 1924.

TIME LINE: Comparison of dates of opening and abandonment

Modified from C. Francis Belcher's *Logging Railroads of the White Mountains* (New Hampshire), 1980, Appalachian Mountain Club, page 5. This is a novel and efficient method of presenting dates of operation. A dashed line is used here if the line were abandoned in stages.

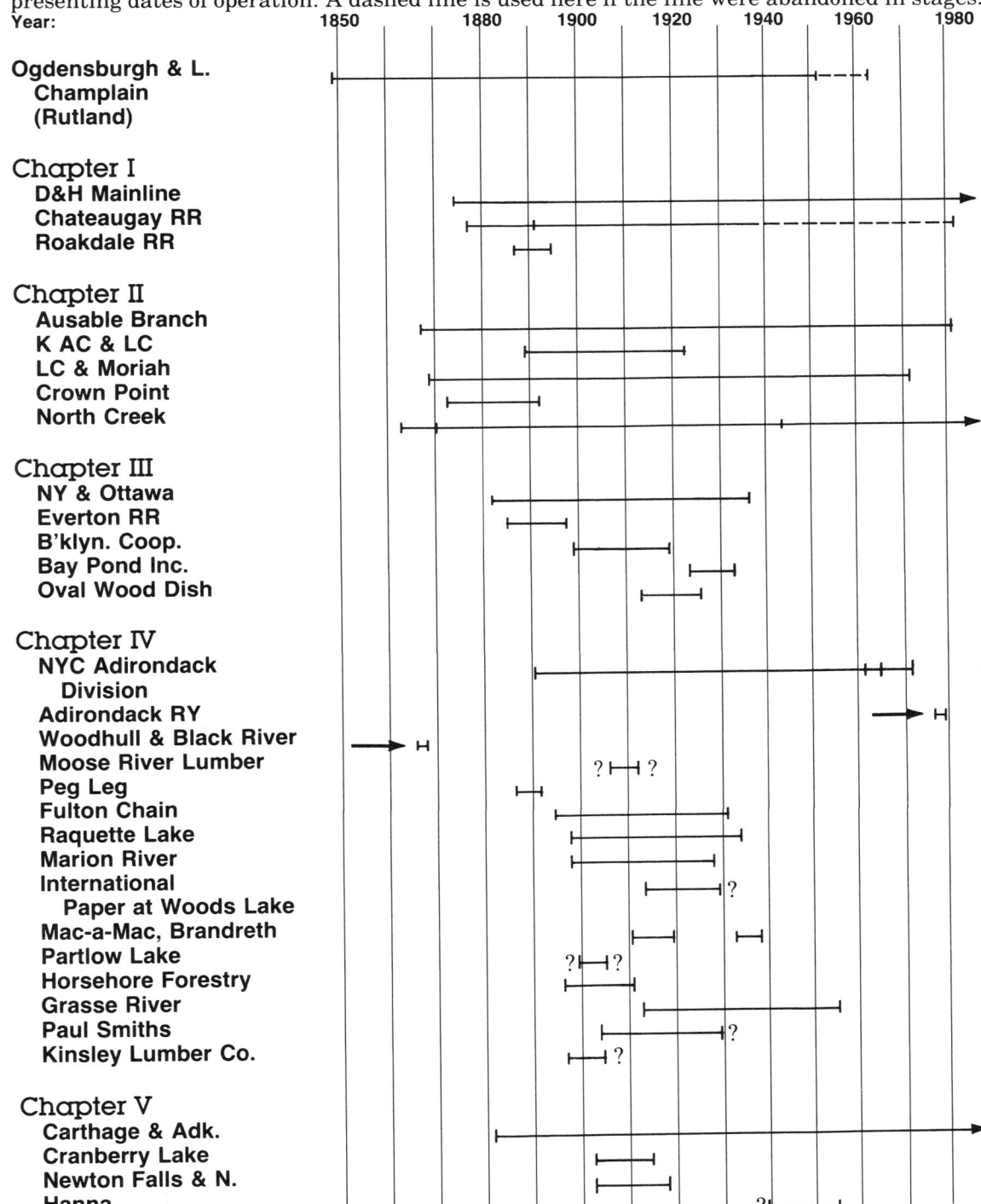

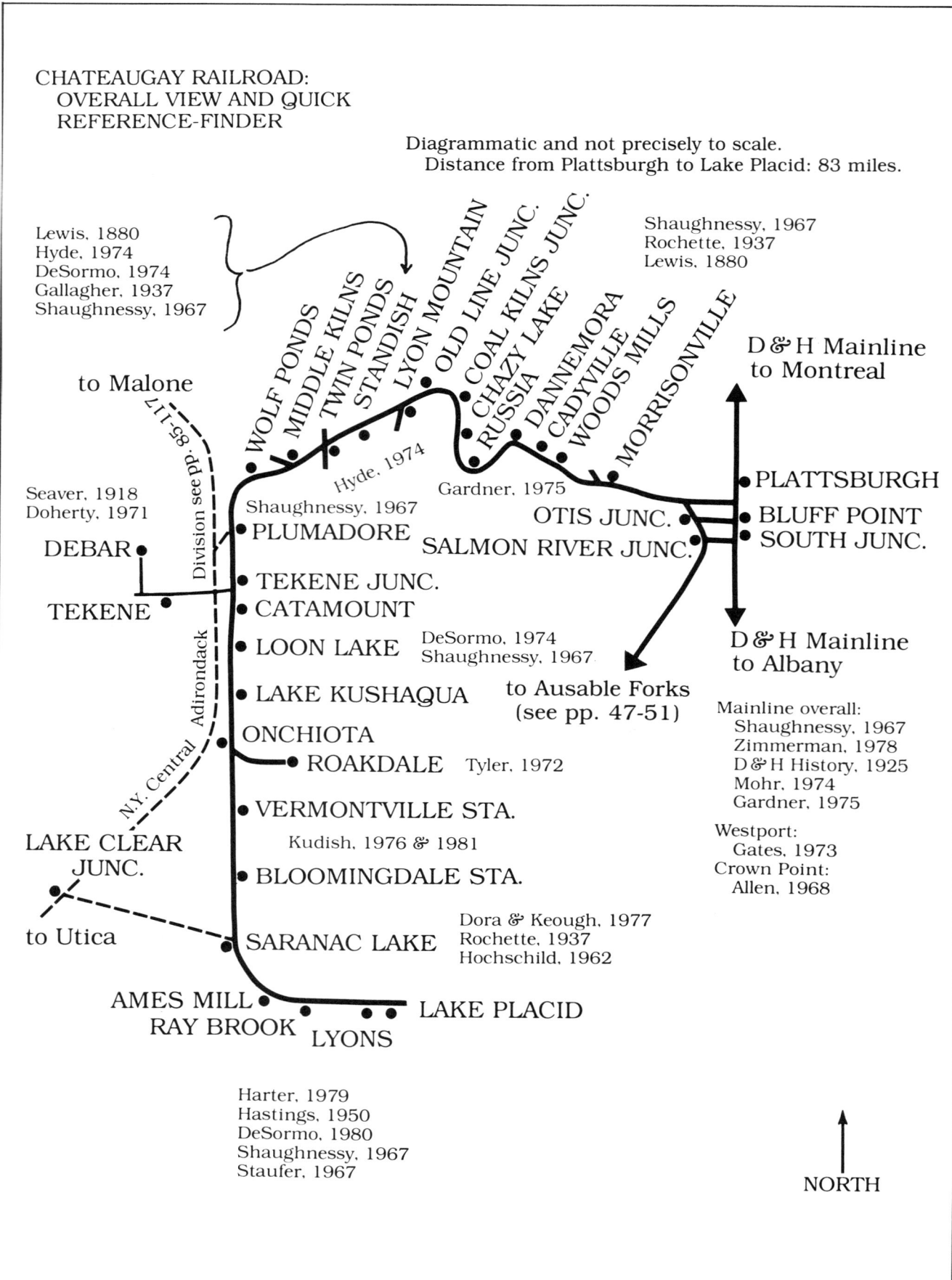

CHATEAUGAY RAILROAD:
   OVERALL VIEW AND QUICK
   REFERENCE-FINDER

Diagrammatic and not precisely to scale.
   Distance from Plattsburgh to Lake Placid: 83 miles.

Lewis, 1880
Hyde, 1974
DeSormo, 1974
Gallagher, 1937
Shaughnessy, 1967

WOLF PONDS
MIDDLE KILNS
TWIN PONDS
STANDISH
LYON MOUNTAIN
OLD LINE JUNC.
COAL KILNS JUNC.
CHAZY LAKE
RUSSIA
DANNEMORA
CADYVILLE
WOODS MILLS
MORRISONVILLE

Shaughnessy, 1967
Rochette, 1937
Lewis, 1880

to Malone

Division see pp. 85-117

Hyde, 1974

Gardner, 1975

D & H Mainline
to Montreal

Seaver, 1918
Doherty, 1971

Shaughnessy, 1967

PLUMADORE

OTIS JUNC.

SALMON RIVER JUNC.

PLATTSBURGH
BLUFF POINT
SOUTH JUNC.

DEBAR

TEKENE JUNC.
CATAMOUNT

N.Y. Central   Adirondack

TEKENE

LOON LAKE

DeSormo, 1974
Shaughnessy, 1967

D & H Mainline
to Albany

LAKE KUSHAQUA

to Ausable Forks
(see pp. 47-51)

ONCHIOTA

ROAKDALE   Tyler, 1972

Mainline overall:
   Shaughnessy, 1967
   Zimmerman, 1978
   D & H History, 1925
   Mohr, 1974
   Gardner, 1975

VERMONTVILLE STA.

Kudish, 1976 & 1981

Westport:
   Gates, 1973
Crown Point:
   Allen, 1968

LAKE CLEAR
JUNC.

BLOOMINGDALE STA.

to Utica

Dora & Keough, 1977
Rochette, 1937
Hochschild, 1962

SARANAC LAKE

AMES MILL
RAY BROOK   LAKE PLACID
         LYONS

Harter, 1979
Hastings, 1950
DeSormo, 1980
Shaughnessy, 1967
Staufer, 1967

NORTH

Chapter I

The Chateaugay Railroad

Introduction and Summary

Between November 16 and 29, 1875, the Delaware and Hudson mainline opened from Port Henry to Plattsburgh; this permitted through trains to operate from Albany to Montreal for the first time. The line from Plattsburgh to Montreal via Mooers had been in service since 1852. Much has been written on the D&H mainline (Shaughnessy, 1967; Zimmerman, 1978; D&H History, 1925; Gardner, 1975; Mohr, 1974; Transportation Lines map of the D&H, 1973 Sesquicentennial), the Plattsburgh area (Lewis, 1880; Plattsburgh Press-Republican, August 6, 1974), the Westport area (Gates, 1973; Saranac Lake Daily Enterprise, August 6, 1974), and the Crown Point Iron Company's Railroad (Allen, 1968). When passenger service through Plattsburgh was reinstated in 1974, the D&H in cooperation with the New York State Department of Transportation published a booklet on the "Adirondack" and likewise did Amtrak in 1975. To avoid duplication of all this material available on the mainline, I will include in this work information regarding only the Chateaugay Railroad.

On May 20, 1878, the Plattsburgh and Dannemora Railroad was organized by the State of New York to connect the State Prison at Dannemora with the recently-completed D&H mainline. Construction was completed on the narrow three-foot gauge to Dannemora by December, 1878, but the locomotives and cars were not delivered until the next year. The junction point for the narrow gauge was *Plattsburgh*, not Bluff Point and not South Junction.

Between May 15 and 20, 1879, the Chateaugay Railroad was incorporated, took over the Plattsburgh and Dannemora, and began extending the line on June 8, 1879, from Dannemora to the Chateaugay Ore Bed east of Lyon Mountain. The track reached the first mine shaft on December 6, 1879, and eleven days later the first regularly-scheduled freight train left Plattsburgh for the Ore Bed; it returned on December 18, 1879, to Plattsburgh with a load of ore. Transfer of the ore from the narrow gauge to standard-gauge mainline D&H cars at Plattsburgh was necessary until 1903 (see page 20). Great detail on the construction of the line to Lyon Mountain is offered in Lewis (1880, pages 309–312). The 1925 D&H History (pages 625–626) mentions that the line was completed and opened to Lyon Mountain, slightly west of the Ore Bed, by March 30, 1880, and extended to Standish in 1885 along with the construction of the blast furnace. Loon Lake was reached on November 15, 1886, and Saranac Lake on December 5, 1887; the reasons for the extension to Loon Lake and beyond will be made apparent on page 33.

The Saranac and Lake Placid Railroad was organized on June 13, 1890. When the line was completed between Saranac Lake and Lake Placid on August 1, 1893, it consisted of three rails to accommodate both the narrow gauge Chateaugay Railroad equipment and the standard-gauged Adirondack & St. Lawrence equipment (the A. & St. L. had arrived in Saranac Lake on July 15, 1892). The Saranac and Lake Placid trackage will be included in this chapter since the line between these two points was, between 1903 and 1946, under full D&H control; the New York Central (abbreviated NYC) had only trackage rights.

The D&H in 1901 began to assume greater and greater control of the Chateaugay Railroad and the Saranac and Lake Placid Railroad. In 1902, standard-gauging began, with the elimination of some curves and relocation of track in some places; the junction was moved from Plattsburgh to Bluff Point, 3.3 miles to the south. By July 29, 1903, the entire line from Plattsburgh to Lake Placid was under full control of the D&H and standard-gauged; it was the Chateaugay Branch of the D&H.

In 1940, the segment between Plumadore and Saranac Lake, which, for the bulk of its length, closely paralleled the NYC Adirondack Division, was abandoned. A connection was built at Plumadore so that D&H trains could use NYC trackage from there to Lake Clear Junction and then to Saranac Lake (Shaughnessy, 1967, p. 355). On November 1, 1946, D&H trains ceased operating to Lake Placid, and the remaining trackage from Plumadore back to Lyon Mountain was abandoned. The final 9.1 miles of track between Saranac Lake and Lake Placid was sold to the NYC. Construction of the Air Force base at Plattsburgh in 1955 caused a second relocation of the junction: from Bluff Point southward 1.2 miles to South Junction. Can you imagine what would have happened if this 1955 relocation were not made? There would have been a grade crossing on the runway!

In June, 1966, the Chateaugay Branch was abandoned further from Lyon Mountain to Dannemora (Hyde, 1974, p. 170). Finally, in August and September of 1981, the last remaining trackage of the Chateaugay (and, ironically, also the first built!) was removed from Dannemora to Otis Junction.

The mileages of the following sequential description of stations are along the standard-gauged line, 1903–1955, with the Plattsburgh passenger station as milepost 0.00.

Station Descriptions

Plattsburgh Station, *0.00 mile. Elevation 118 feet above sea level (twenty-three feet above Lake Champlain).*

Little attempt is made here to describe this busy railroading center on the D&H mainline. It is necessary to call the reader's attention to two points, however, as they involve also the Cheateaugay Railroad. First, Plattsburgh was the junction for the narrow-gauge Chateaugay from 1878 through 1903. Second, during this period, trestles were operated to transfer bulk commodities such as iron ore, iron, wood pulp, coal, sand, gravel, etc., from narrow-gauge cars to standard-gauge cars and vice versa (Lewis, 1880, p. 311). The hopper car to be emptied was pushed onto the

trestle, and its contents dumped into the empty hopper of a different gauge waiting beneath the trestle.

PHOTOS: Shaughnessy (1967, pp. 152, 155, 294, 423).

At 0.3 mile south of Plattsburgh Station, a spur, connecting with the mainline via a wye, headed west for 0.7 mile crossing the Saranac River as shown on the 1893 Plattsburgh Quadrangle. According to James Bailey, Plattsburgh City Historian, the spur served several industries in the 1902–1909 era including the Plattsburgh Foundry and Machine Shop and the D&H Railroad Foundry on the west side of the River; on the east side of the River were the Plattsburgh Electric, Heat, and Power Plant and the sheds for the Plattsburgh Traction Company trolleys (1897–1925). By 1956, the spur terminated before crossing the River.

"Plattsburgh Junction", *0.7 mile. Elevation 136 feet.*

I have taken the liberty to name a few unnamed strategic places simply for convenience, hence the name in quotes. In 1868, the railroad from Montreal to Plattsburgh was extended to Ausable River Station. Seven years later, in 1875, the mainline opened from Port Henry to Plattsburgh. The junction between the Ausable River Station line and the mainline was originally here at "Plattsburgh Junction"; the Ausable line thus became a branch. When the Chateaugay Railroad opened in 1878, its trains also used this junction with the mainline. In 1894, the Ausable Branch was relocated to join the mainline at South Junction (see Chapter II, Part I), so that from 1894 to 1903 only Chateaugay trains joined the mainline at "Plattsburgh Junction". After the Chateaugay was standard-gauged in 1903, it was also relocated, but the junction with the mainline became Bluff Point. Thus after 1903, "Plattsburgh Junction" ceased to exist as a junction, except for a short stub 0.4 mile long (shown on the 1939–1956 Plattsburgh Quadrangle); this stub terminated at U.S. Highway 9 at a point I have named "Chateaugay Junction".

"Chateaugay Junction", *1.1 miles. Elevation 165 feet.*

Again, I have taken the liberty to name a place. In 1878, the Chateaugay Railroad was built from this point on the Ausable Branch. In 1894, the Ausable Branch trains ceased running through here because of the relocation to South Junction, but Chateaugay trains operated through here until 1903.

Chronological Development of Plattsburgh Area Railroads

Not to scale. Approximate north is at the top.

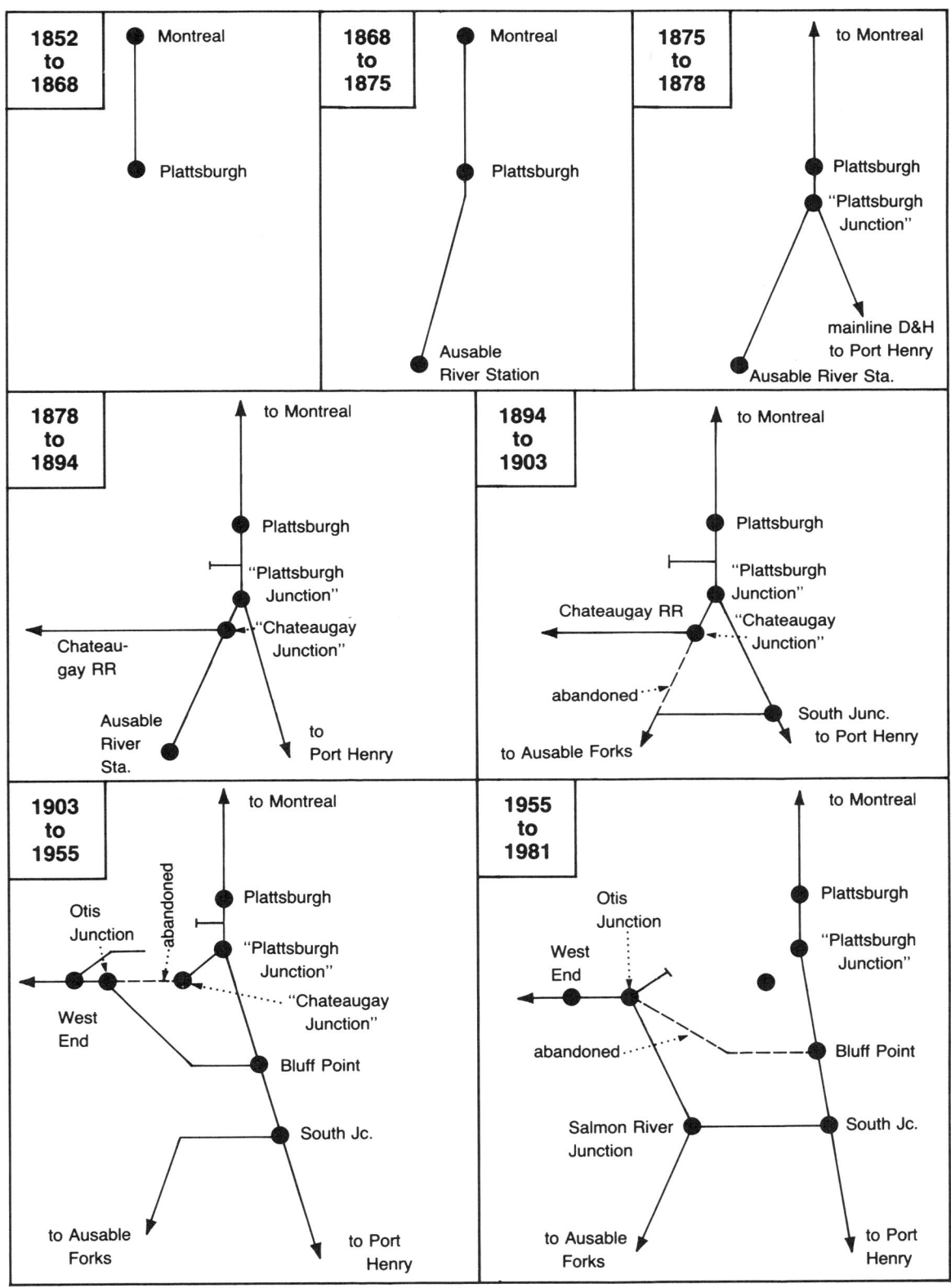

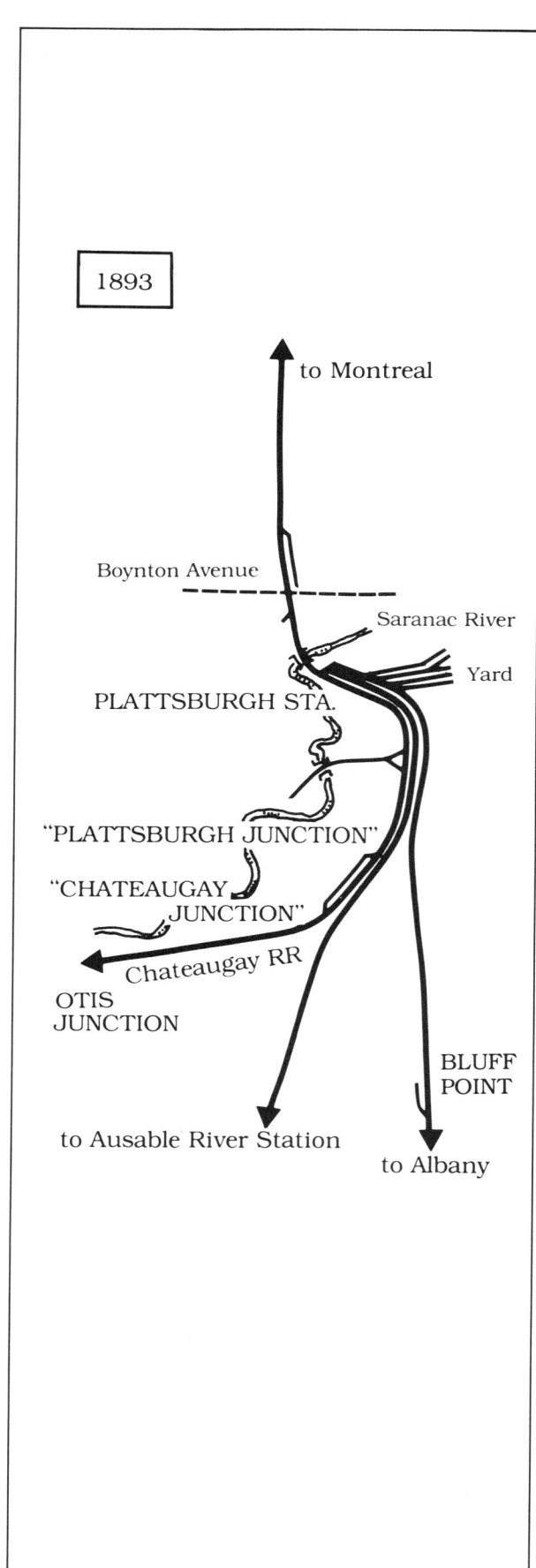

1893

to Montreal

Boynton Avenue

Saranac River

Yard

PLATTSBURGH STA.

"PLATTSBURGH JUNCTION"

"CHATEAUGAY JUNCTION"

Chateaugay RR

OTIS
JUNCTION

BLUFF
POINT

to Ausable River Station

to Albany

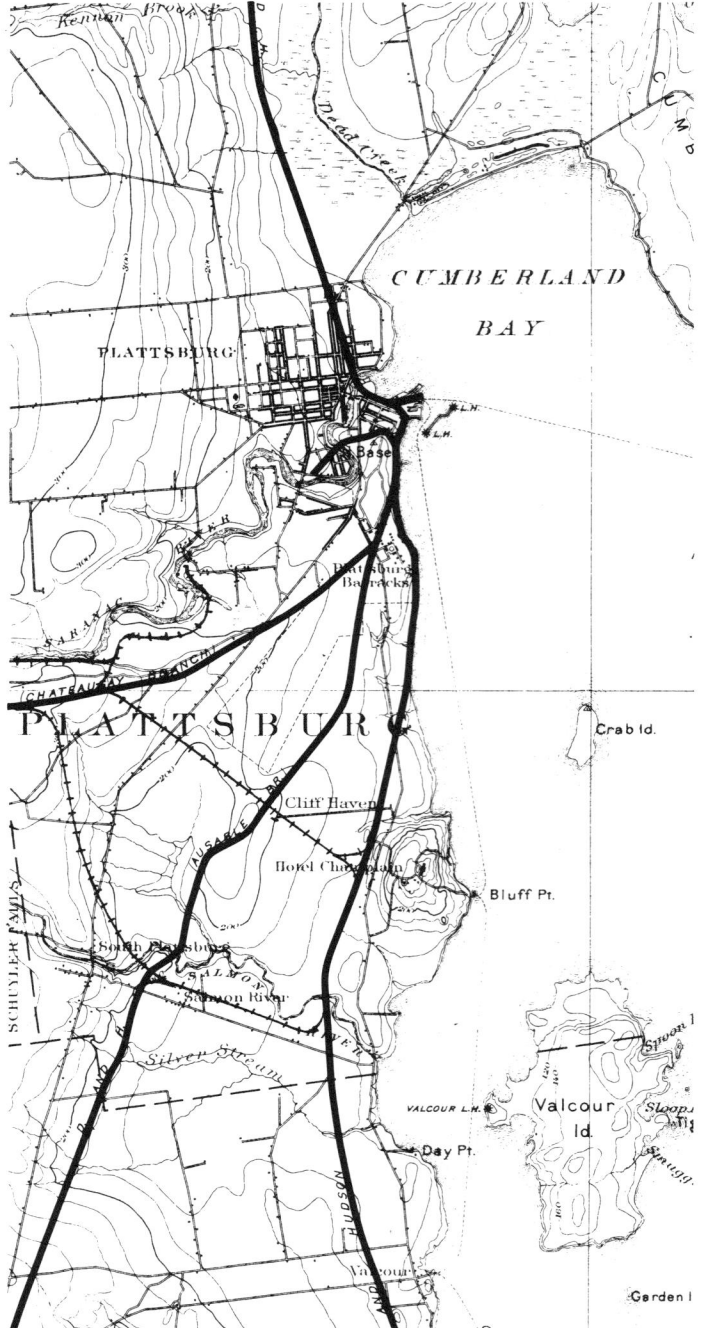

CUMBERLAND
BAY
PLATTSBURG
Base
Plattsburg Barracks
SARANAC
CHATEAUGAY BRANCH
PLATTSBURG
Crab Id.
Cliff Haven
AUSABLE BR.
Hotel Champlain
Bluff Pt.
South Plattsburg
Salmon River
Silver Stream
VALCOUR L.H.
Valcour Id.
Sloop Bay
Day Pt.
Valcour
Garden Id.
CHAMPLAIN
HUDSON
DELAWARE
SCHUYLER FALLS
Dead Creek
Kennan Brook
Woodruff Pond
CUMBERLAND
Spoon Bay

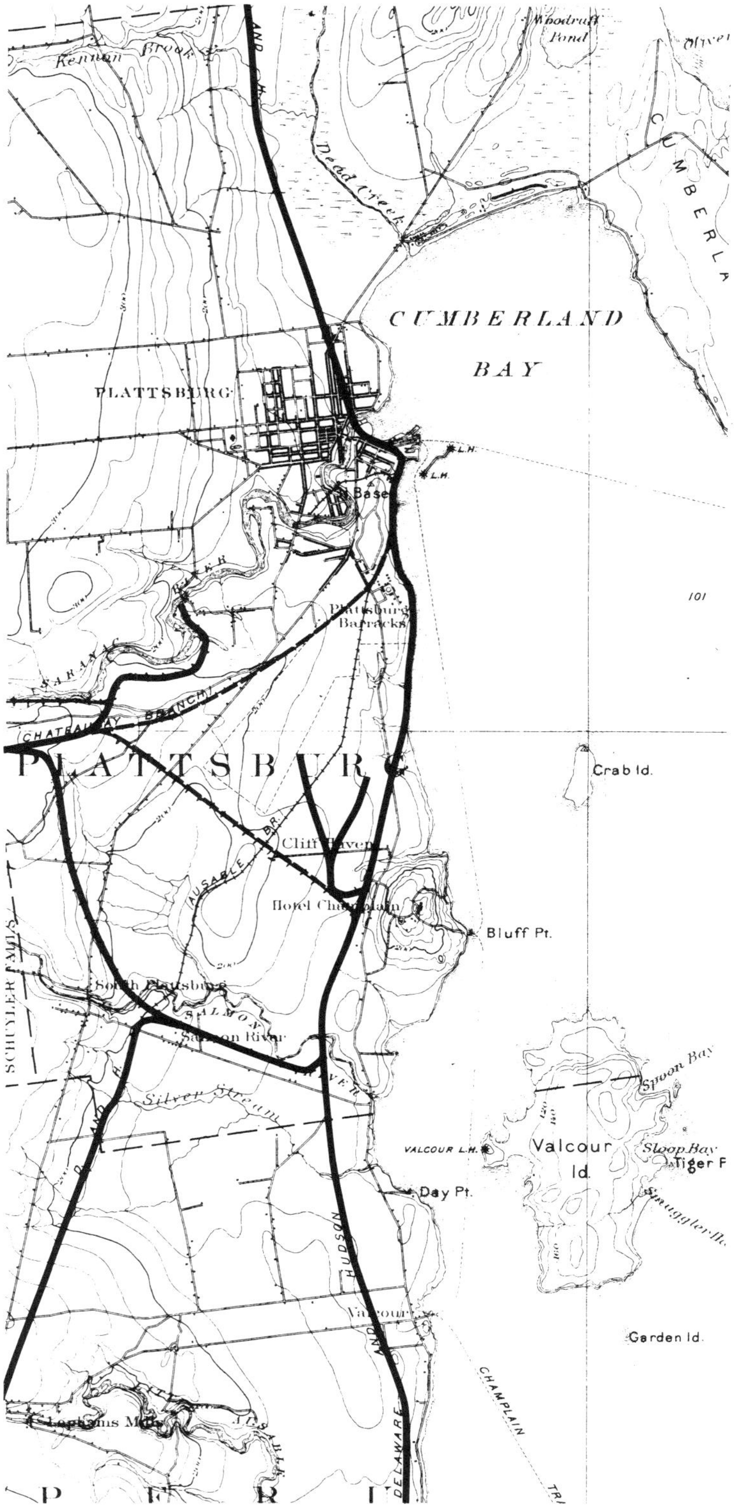

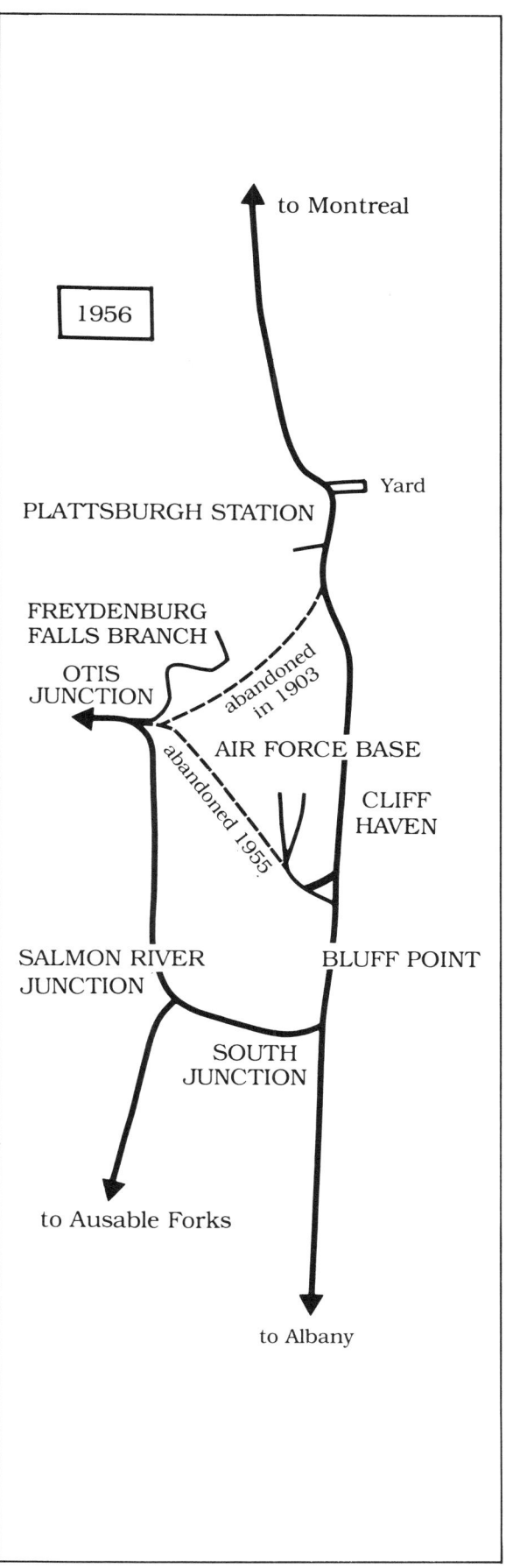

1956
to Montreal
Yard
PLATTSBURGH STATION
FREYDENBURG FALLS BRANCH
OTIS JUNCTION
abandoned in 1903
AIR FORCE BASE
abandoned 1955
CLIFF HAVEN
SALMON RIVER JUNCTION
BLUFF POINT
SOUTH JUNCTION
to Ausable Forks
to Albany

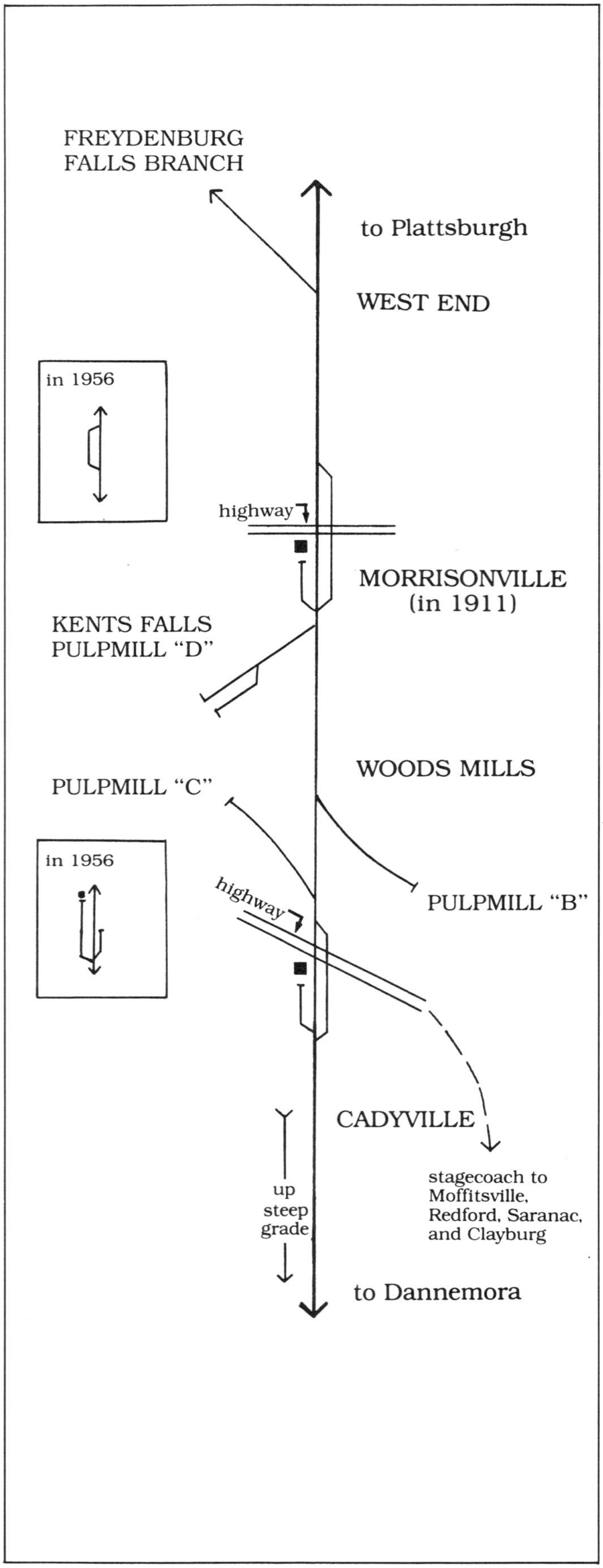
FREYDENBURG
FALLS BRANCH
to Plattsburgh
WEST END
in 1956
highway
MORRISONVILLE
(in 1911)
KENTS FALLS
PULPMILL "D"
WOODS MILLS
PULPMILL "C"
in 1956
highway
PULPMILL "B"
CADYVILLE
stagecoach to
Moffitsville,
Redford, Saranac,
and Clayburg
up
steep
grade
to Dannemora

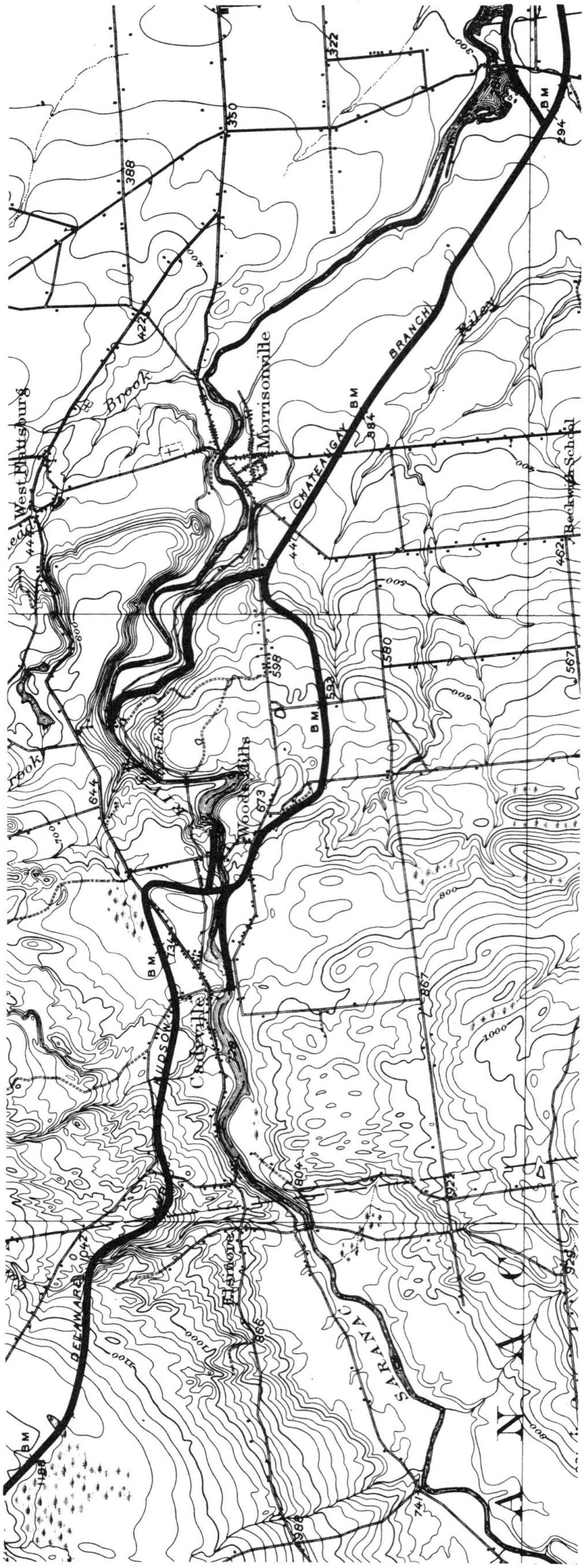
Morrisonville
CHATEAUGAY
BRANCH
Riley
Brook
Woods Mills
Cadyville
HUDSON
DELAWARE
SARANAC

Cliff Haven, *2.88 miles. Elevation 135.*

Prior to standard-gauging of the Chateaugay, only D&H mainline and Ausable Branch trains stopped here. But after 1903, and certainly in 1912 and 1916 as the timetables show, Chateaugay trains stopped here, too. The timetable of September 24, 1916, no longer lists Cliff Haven as a Chateaugay stop.

Bluff Point, *3.36 miles. Elevation 143.*

Located here was the junction of the Chateaugay Branch from 1903 through 1955. 1927 timetables still show Chateaugay trains as stopping here, but they no longer did in 1932. Remnants of the Branch still exist today as freight spurs into the Air Force Base, but they no longer cross the runway!

PHOTOS: *Gardner (1975, page 91) has a photo of the station.*

Shaughnessy (1967, pages 280 and 281) offers pictures of the Hotel Champlain atop Bluff Point.

The D&H mainline timetable of June 21, 1908, advertises the Hotel Champlain and presents a drawing on page 14.

Shaughnessy (1967), page 422 shows a coaling tower at South Junction.

Mohr (1974) has a photo of Hotel Champlain and trolley cars at Cliff Haven.

Otis Junction, *6.2 miles. Elevation 303.*

From 1903 through 1955, Chateaugay Branch trains crossed what is now the runway of the Air Force Base. But after 1955, Chateaugay Branch trains were rerouted around the south end of the runway via South Junction and up the Ausable Forks Branch for 1.3 miles; here, near South Plattsburgh, a new segment of track was built 2.4 miles long around the west side of the runway and up the grade to connect with the track coming in from Morrisonville and West End at Otis Junction. The new junction near South Plattsburgh with the Ausable Forks Branch was called Salmon River Junction.

West End, *7.24 miles. Elevation 294.*

Here, the 1911 Dannemora and the 1939 Plattsburgh Quadrangles indicate a spur, about 3.6 miles long, descending along the south bank of the Saranac River to an industry at Underwood Avenue. The Dannemora 1954 and Plattsburgh 1956 Quadrangles show that the junction for this spur had been moved from West End to Otis Junction, shortening the spur to a length of about 2.4 miles.

According to James Bailey, Plattsburgh City Historian, this spur, in 1916 called the Freydenburg Falls Branch, served the Maine Paper Comany Mill (built about 1880) and the American Carbide Company in the 1909 era. Before standard-gauging of the Chateaugay Railroad in 1903, both narrow and standard-gauged tracks served these industries. In 1984, the spur serves the Imperial Wallpaper Mill.

Morrisonville, *10.42 miles. Elevation 410.*

The earliest timetable in my collections showing this as a station stop is dated 1889, and the latest 1932; passenger trains no longer stopped here in 1942. The 1911 Dannemora Quadrangle indicates a passing siding 0.3 mile long on the south side and a stub track 0.1 mile long on the north. The 1956 Dannemora Quadrangle shows only a passing siding, 0.4 mile long and on the north.

The 1911 Dannemora Quadrangle also shows, 0.3 mile west of the Station, a 1.7 mile-long spur heading north to the Saranac River. According to Baker (1970, p. 54) and James Bailey (personal communication), the industry served was the International Paper Company's Pulp Mill "D", running in 1909 and in 1913. Pulp was made into flat sheets and shipped by rail to the paper mills at Fort Edward, Glens Falls, and Corinth. By 1922, the mill had closed and had been converted into a hydro-electric power house.

Woods Mills, *13.1 miles. Elevation 718.*

This was never a station stop. However, from here two spurs, shown on the 1911 Dannemora Quadrangle, diverged. One spur headed for 0.6 mile west (upstream) along the south side of the Saranac River to the International Paper Company's Pulp Mill "B", abandoned but still standing in 1913 (Baker, 1970, p. 54). The other spur headed for 0.4 mile east (downstream) along the River's north bank to the International Paper Company's Pulp Mill "C", still running in 1913. By 1922, both Mills 'B" and "C" had been abandoned and converted into hydroelectric powerhouses (Baker, 1950, p. 54). James Bailey confirms the existence of the pulp mills. The 1956 Dannemora Quadrangle no longer shows these spurs.

PHOTOS: *A photograph of the trestle over the Saranac River at this point is shown on page 159 of Shaughnessy (1967).*

Baker (1970) offers a photo of the trestle facing page 15.

Cadyville, *14.03 miles. Elevation 729.*

Cadyville was a station stop probably for the entire life of the Chateaugay; at least the

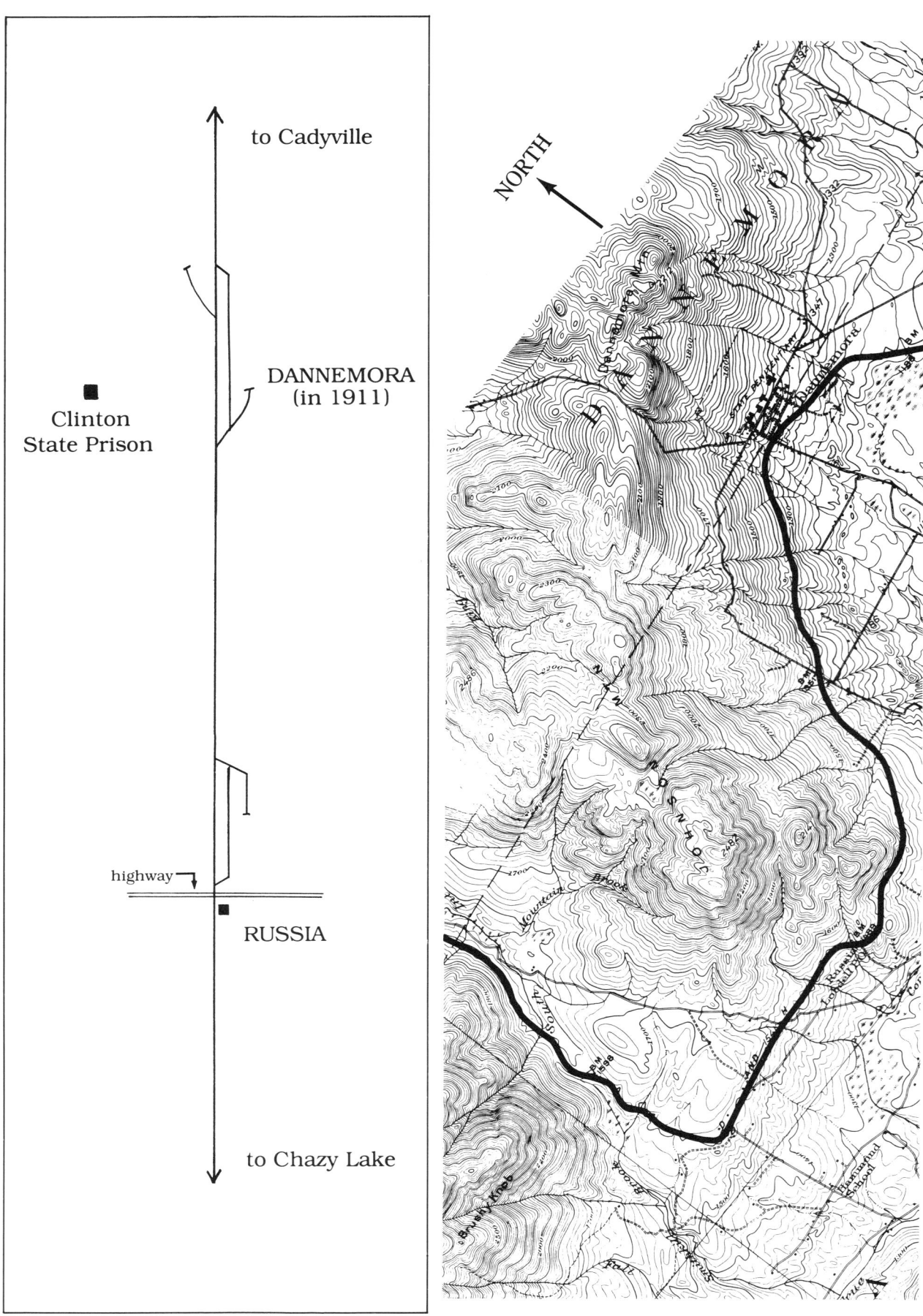

to Cadyville

Clinton
State Prison

DANNEMORA
(in 1911)

highway

RUSSIA

to Chazy Lake

NORTH

timetables from June 24, 1889, through June 6, 1948, indicate this. The timetables dated June 22, 1896, and June 25, 1899, note stagecoach connections for Moffitsville, Redford, Saranac (not Saranac Lake), and Clayburg.

A passing siding and a dead-end stub track are shown on thee 1911 Dennemora Quadrangle. From Cadyville, the line steeply ascended toward Dannemora. According to Rochette (1937), the most-inclined mile climbed 169 feet, equivalent to 3.2%; trains had to be doubled on this hill (see p. 12) using the sidings at Cadyville and at Dannemora. The 5.58 miles between Cadyville and Dannemora necessitated an ascent of 627 feet, averaging 1.1%. Rochette also notes that for several years prior to 1903, three-rail, dual-gauge track ran from Plattsburgh to Cadyville.

Dannemora, *19.61 miles. Elevation 1356.*

Like Cadyville, Dannemora was a station for the entire life of the Chateaugay; my 1889 and 1948 timetables establish this fact.

The original purpose of this line out of Plattsburgh in 1878 (see page 19) was to serve the prison here at Dannemora, bringing in coal and supplies. Dannemora was the terminus of the line from December 1878 to December 1879.

Both the 1891 and 1896 timetables indicated that trains in opposite directions passed here, suggesting a passing siding. The 1911 Dannemora Quadrangle proves the existence of that siding: 0.25-mile-long on the south side. This siding was also used when trains were doubled on the hill out of Cadyville (see above paragraph on Cadyville). In addition, the 1911 Quadrangle shows two short stub sidings; perhaps these stubs were used for laying up the hopper cars loaded with coal for heating the State Prison.

PHOTO: Gardner (1975), page 93) shows the station with two tracks in the foreground.

Russia (Lobdell Post Office or Saranac Station), *24.25 miles. Elevation 1489.*

Lewis (1890) informs us that when the line first opened, the station was called "Saranac Station," as it was only a few miles north of the community of the same name (Saranac is NOT to be confused with Saranac Lake!). The timetable of December 10, 1890, already lists the stop as Russia. Trains were still stopping here on October 1, 1927, but had ceased by September 25, 1932.

The timetable of June 25, 1899, indicates that two trains running in opposite directions passed at Russia, suggesting a passing siding. A glance and quick measurement of the 1911 Dannemora Quadrangle reveals the siding as 0.15 mile long. The siding was still here on November 1, 1942, as the employees' timetable even states its capacity: 18 cars!

Chazy Lake, *30.30 miles. Elevation 1665.*

Timetables from 1899 through 1932 show a stop here, but service had been discontinued by 1942. June 22, 1896 timetables denote that a steamer met trains at the station and crossed to the north end of the Lake for the Chazy Lake House.

A siding is suggested on the September 24, 1916 timetable as two trains passed here. Gardner (1975) confirms the siding with two trains passing:

PHOTO: Gardner (1975), page 64.

Coal Kilns Junction, *ca. 31.5 miles. Elevation 1683.*

This point, never a station, is shown on an 1895 Stoddard map.

Bradley Pond Station (Old Line Junction), *34.58 miles. Elevation 1710.*

From here, a 1.1-mile-long branch northwest to Bradley Pond (elevation 1630) diverged, as shown on the 1911 Lyon Mountain Quadrangle. This spur is still shown on the 1953 Adirondack Land Map (New York State Conservation Department), as the only spur near the Lyon Mountain terminus. The employees' timetable of November 1, 1942, lists Old Line Junction but not as a station stop. Apparently, this was never listed as a stop on any passenger timetable.

Lyon Mountain, *36.32 miles. Elevation 1753.*

Lyon Mountain was the temporary terminus for the period 1880 to 1885, so that it had facilities for the servicing and turning of trains. Lewis (1880, p. 312) describes a trip made over the new line in December, 1879, from Plattsburgh to Lyon Mountain. On Separator Brook was an engine house with two pits for housing locomotives, a machine shop, and a carpentry shop to repair and build engines and do car work. Above the depot and shops, Lewis (1880) continues, was a side track upon which the mined rock with its impurities was brought up in railroad cars; the cars were then emptied by gravity into a separator and roasting kilns, the ore finally washed and reloaded into empty cars below to be hauled to Plattsburgh. Of course, this was before the blast furnace at Standish was opened in 1885.

Hyde (1974, pp. 156–165) offers a fine overview of the history of the Lyon Mountain iron

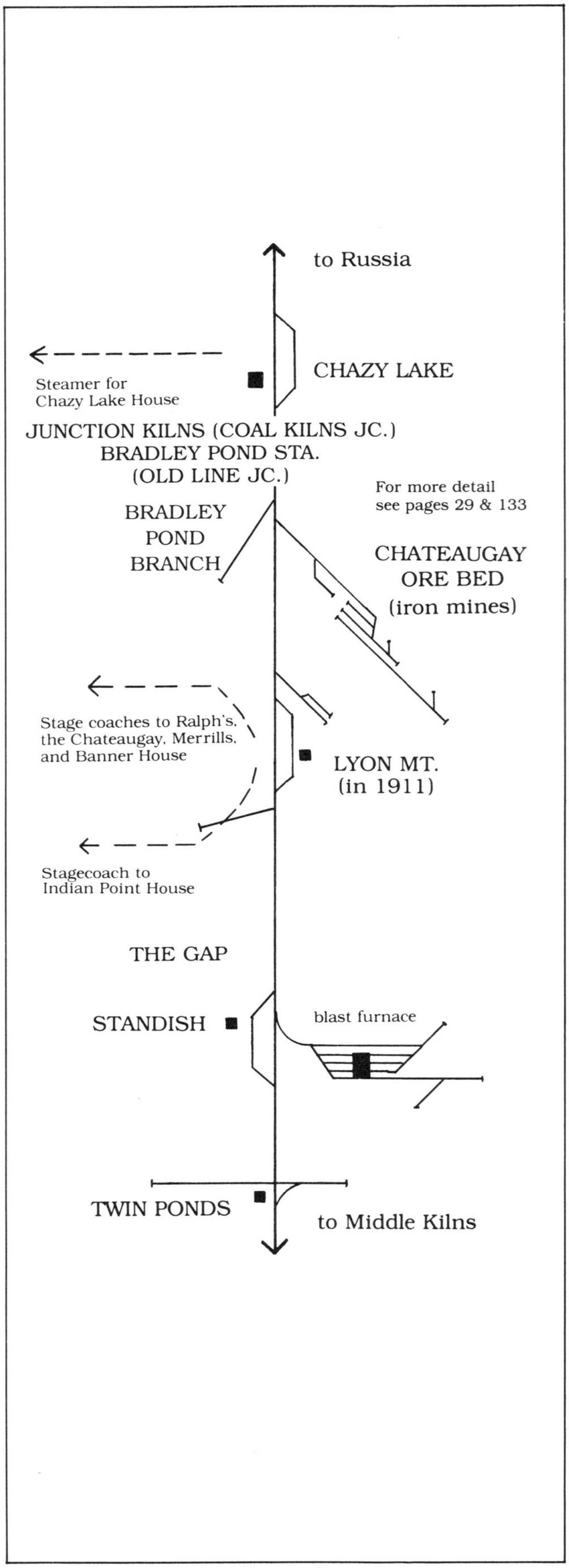

to Russia
CHAZY LAKE
Steamer for
Chazy Lake House
JUNCTION KILNS (COAL KILNS JC.)
BRADLEY POND STA.
(OLD LINE JC.)
For more detail
see pages 29 & 133
BRADLEY
POND
BRANCH
CHATEAUGAY
ORE BED
(iron mines)
Stage coaches to Ralph's,
the Chateaugay, Merrills,
and Banner House
LYON MT.
(in 1911)
Stagecoach to
Indian Point House
THE GAP
STANDISH
blast furnace
TWIN PONDS
to Middle Kilns

CHAZY LAKE
BRANCH
Lyon Mountain
Separator
Brook
Brandy
Standish
UPPER CHATEAUGAY
CLINTON CO
FRANKLIN CO
NORTH

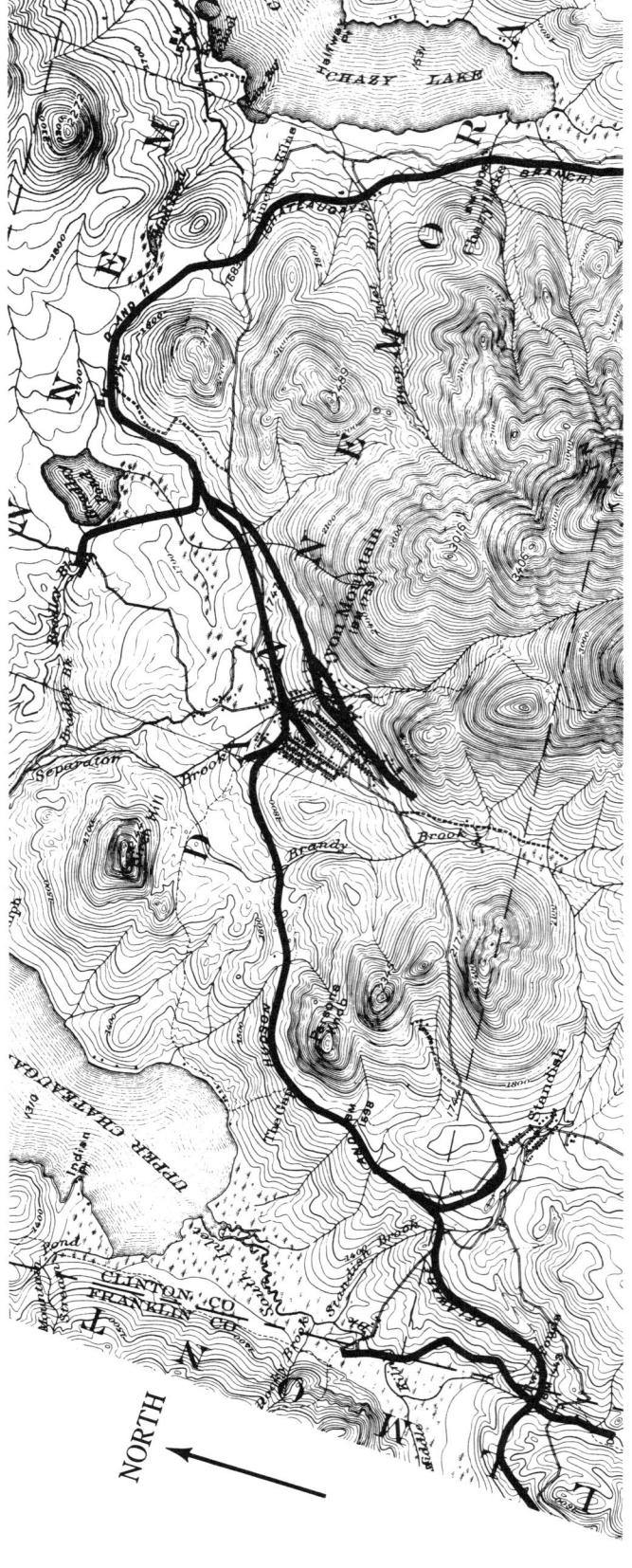

mines, beginning well before the Chateaugay Railroad era. Prior to 1880, the ore was brought down from the mines by wagon to the south shore of Chateaugay Lake, then loaded on a barge. At the north end of the Lake was the huge Belmont Forge (photo, Hyde, p. 159). From here, the ore was loaded once again on wagons and transported to Chateaugay Station on the Ogdensburg and Lake Champlain Railroad, the nearest station to Lyon Mountain after 1849. What a difference in shipping the ore out was made in 1880 when the Chateaugay Railroad arrived at Lyon Mountain! See also Cootey, Hoit and Hoy (1973) on the Forge on Chateaugay Lake.

Hyde (1974, p. 156) notes a turntable at the bank of Separator Brook.

The 1911 Lyon Mountain Quadrangle shows the approximate track plan, with eleborate trackwork going up (southeast) to the iron mines reaching a maximum elevation of 1950 feet; this trackwork diverged from the main track at a point about 1.5 miles east of the depot. Four-tenths of a mile west of the depot, a small spur ¼ mile long diverged off the the north and dropped to an elevation of

1720 feet. When the D&H took full control of the line in 1903 and standard-gauged it, Hyde (1974, p. 165) says that the railroad facilities were greatly increased.

The approximate track plan in 1965 (Lyon Mountain 7½ Minute Quadrangle) was quite reduced compared to the older 1911 map; this is to be expected, as the mines shut down in June, 1966, along with the railroad. Track plans of the Lyon Mountain area are shown here on the bottom of this page.

Lyon Mountain was a station on the Chateaugay Railroad from the time it opened in 1880 through at least September 26, 1948; at this recent date, trains were still running between Lyon Mountain and Plattsburgh. The timetable of October 3, 1896, indicates two trains passing here, requiring a passing siding.

Stagecoach connections at Lyon Mountain station were made in the seasons of 1896 and 1899 for a series of hotels along the Chateaugay Lakes: Ralph's, The Chateaugay, Merrill's, Indian Point House, and Banner House.

The 1889 timetable lists connecting times for Chateaugay Lake but does not specify

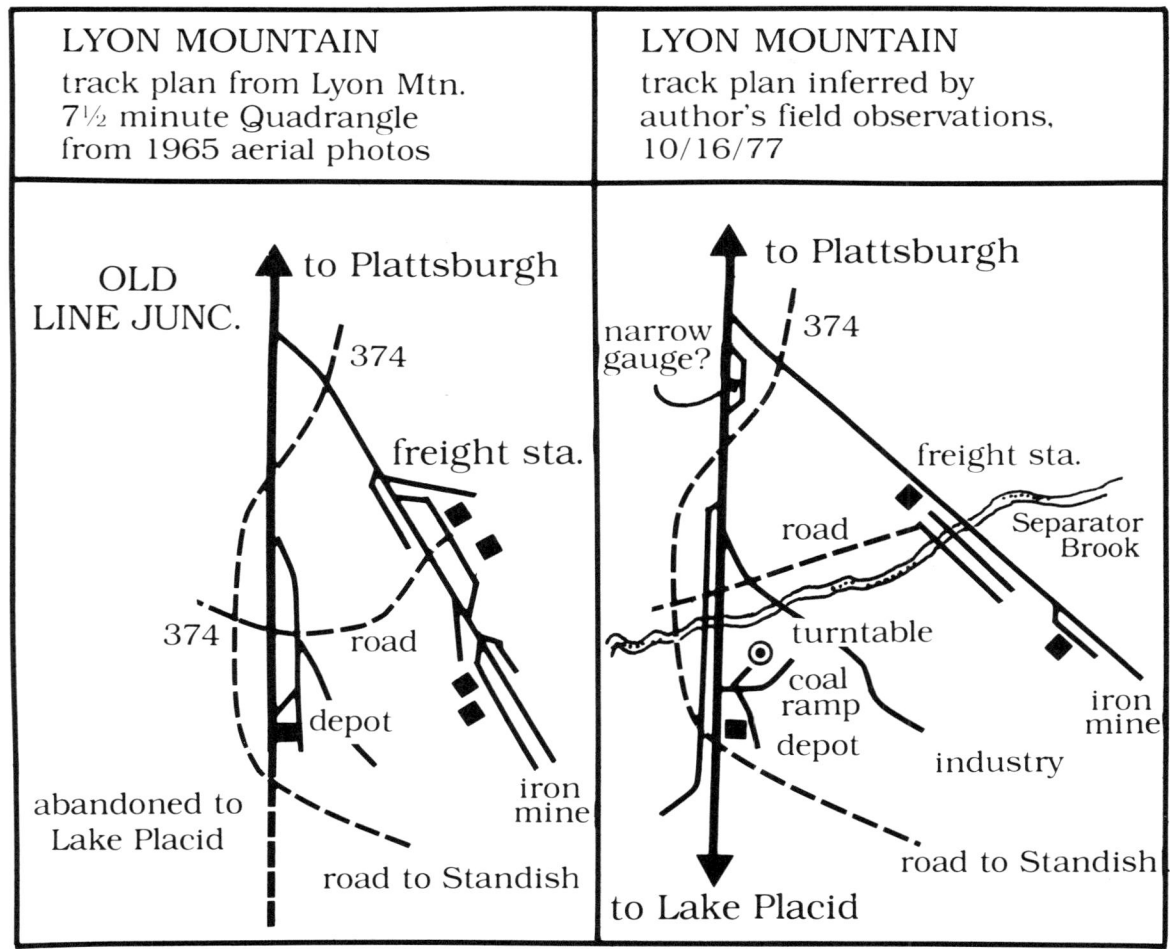

| LYON MOUNTAIN track plan from Lyon Mtn. 7½ minute Quadrangle from 1965 aerial photos | LYON MOUNTAIN track plan inferred by author's field observations, 10/16/77 |

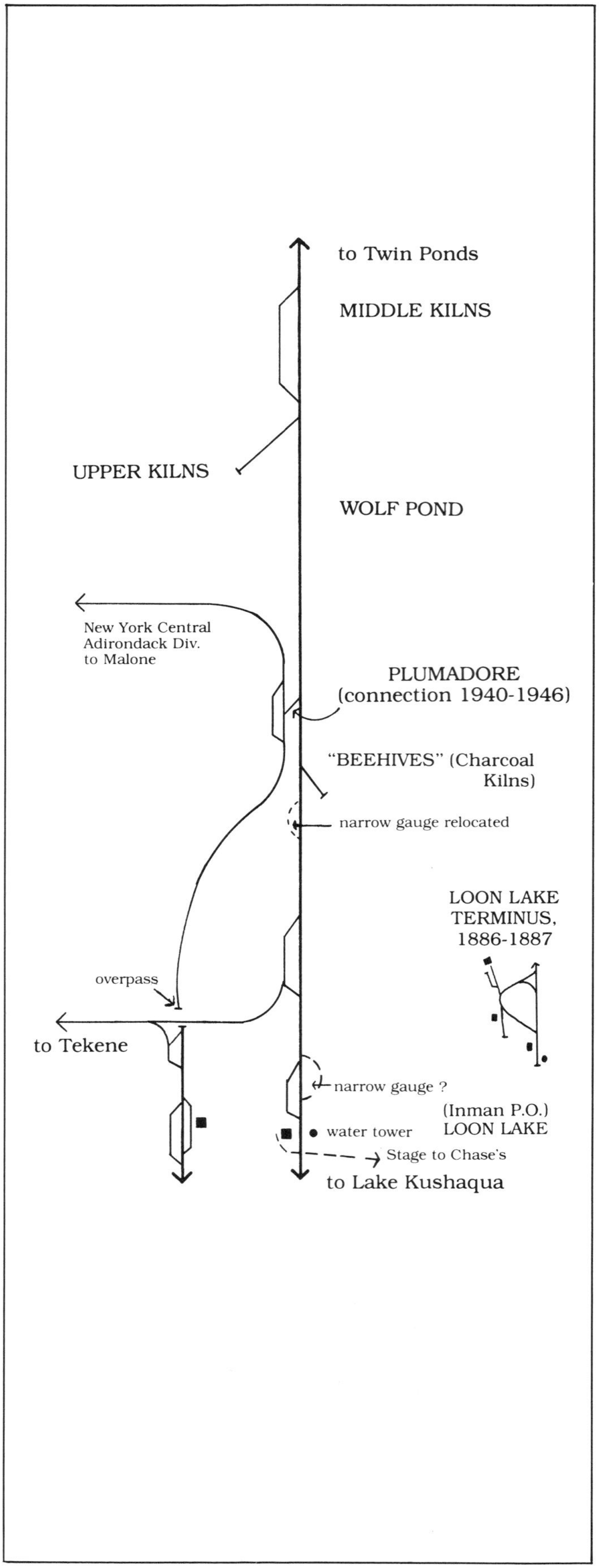

to Twin Ponds
MIDDLE KILNS
UPPER KILNS
WOLF POND
New York Central
Adirondack Div.
to Malone
PLUMADORE
(connection 1940-1946)
"BEEHIVES" (Charcoal
Kilns)
narrow gauge relocated
LOON LAKE
TERMINUS,
1886-1887
overpass
to Tekene
narrow gauge ?
(Inman P.O.)
LOON LAKE
water tower
Stage to Chase's
to Lake Kushaqua

NORTH
Wolf Pond
Plumadore
Duck Pond
Tekene

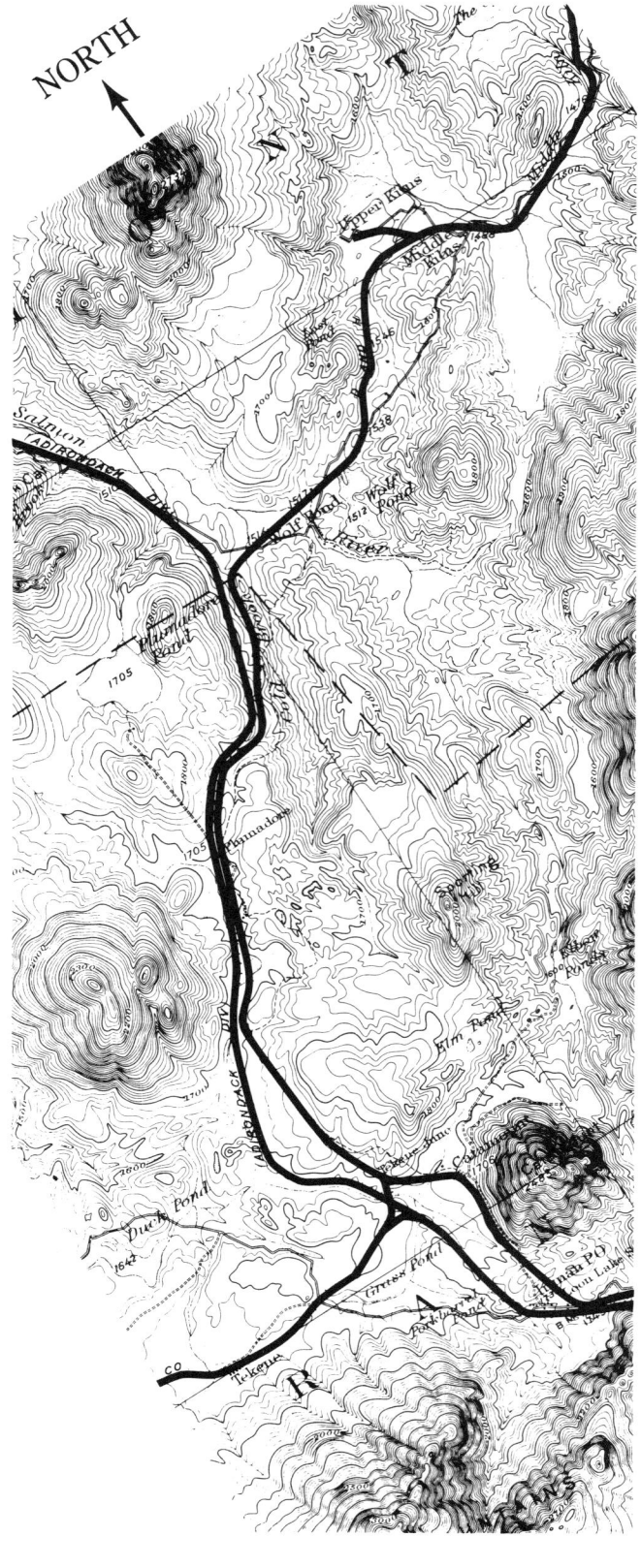

hotels. DeSormo (1974) has a chapter on the Banner House on Lower Chateaugay Lake, pages 79–83.

PHOTOS: *A photograph showing the depot, passenger train, two narrow gauge tracks, and yard trackage in the background will be found in Shaughnessy (1967), page 165; the same photo appears in Mohr (1974).*

At our Paul Smith's College Library, we have an old photograph (undated, unfortunately) showing the trestle at Lyon Mountain.

Hyde (1974) presents a series of photos of Lyon Mountain, but with railroad facilities only sometimes in the background; they appear on pages 163, 168, 170, 172.

Hyde (1974) also includes a photo of the Belmont Forges at the outlet of the Chateaugay Lakes on page 159.

Standish, *39.95 miles. Elevation 1575.*

Less than a mile east of Standish Station, the 1911 Lyon Mountain Quadrangle shows a place called "The Gap, elevation 1598", possibly indicating a cut along the Chateaugay Railroad.

The railroad opened to Standish in 1885, but the first timetable I have listing the community as a stop is 1890. Trains were still stopping here in January, 1943, ceasing in 1946.

The 1911 Quadrangle also shows a passing siding 0.2 mile long, with a branch on the other (south)side leading 0.9 mile to the blast furnace, with the tracks climbing to an elevation of 1670 feet. The blast furnace produced pig iron (iron in bars or ingots) which decreased transportation costs since pig iron is less bulky than ore.

PHOTOS: *Shaughnessy (1967, page 158) includes a picture of the Standish Hotel and General Store (doubling probably as the station) with two tracks alongisde; the train is narrow gauge.*

Hyde (1974, page 164) presents a picture of the blast furnace taken about 1930 with five tracks of hopper cars in the foreground.

Details on the geology of the Chateaugay Ore Bed and Lyon Mountain mines will be found in Gallagher (1937).

Twin Ponds, *41.79 miles. Elevation 1443.*

Twin Ponds appears as a station stop on timetables from 1908 through 1932 but not on 1899 and not in 1942.

From Twin Ponds, a branch headed 0.3 mile to the south, and another branch 1.5 miles to the north; the latter northerly branch terminated at Middle Kilns Brook (elevation 1315) not far from the south end of Upper Chateaugay Lake. These branches are indicated on the 1911 Lyon Mountain Quadrangle.

Middle Kilns, *44.76 miles. Elevation 1488.*

Like Twin Ponds, Middle Kilns appears as a station stop on timetables from 1908 through 1932, but not 1899 or earlier, and not 1942 or later.

The 1899 timetable does, however, suggest that two trains passed here, roughly midway between Loon Lake and Lyon Mountain, although Middle Kilns is not listed; a siding is suggested. Verification appears in the 1942 employees' timetable where a siding is noted with a capacity of thirty-one cars.

Upper Kilns Junction, *45.1 miles. Elevation 1490.*

From here, a spur 0.4 mile long diverged to the northwest. This Junction was never a station stop.

Wolf Pond, *47.23 miles. Elevation 1514.*

This was a station during the period 1908 throug 1942, but not in 1899 and not in 1943. The 1912 and 1916 timetables list the stop as "Wolf Ponds" in the plural!

Plumadore, *50.26 miles. Elevation 1705.*

Timetables from 1908 through 1932 show Plumadore as a station stop, but not 1899 nor 1942. On Page 29 of the November 1, 1942, employees' timetable, there is an entry:

"A connection to the New York Central Railroad has been made at a point 4600 feet south of milepost 49, north of Plumadore, to a point 236 feet south of milepost 50, to be known as Plumadore Junction, and for location purpose, a sign board will be located 2000 feet north of The New York Central Railroad clearance point at Plumadore Junction . . ."

According to Shaughnessy (1967, p. 355), this connection was built in 1940 so that the segment from Plumadore to Saranac Lake could be abandoned.

In effect, the D&H Railroad trackage duplicated the Central's, and the D&H could eliminate maintenance costs on the segment. D&H Chateaugay Branch trains ran on the Central's tracks via Lake Clear Junction until 1946. The now-abandoned crossover connection is plainly visible when one hikes the rights-of-way at Plumadore.

If one examines old maps, from the period 1892 through 1940, the closely parallel trackage of the D&H and the New York Central Railroads becomes very obvious between

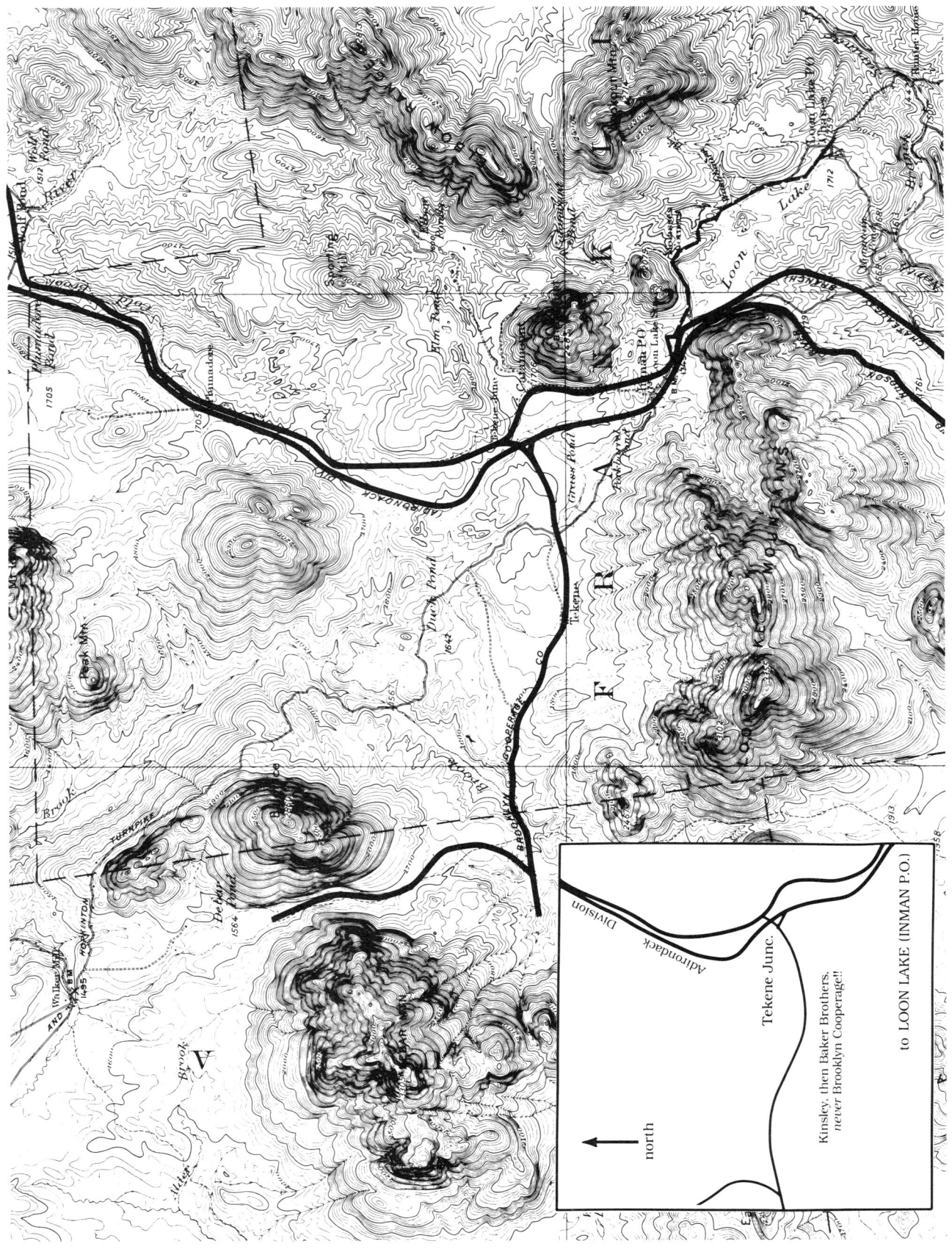

Plumadore and Onchiota. Could the maps be in error? Surely, there must have been but one railroad here! No, there were two! In the earlier years, the two railroads competed, but in later years the relation was more of cooperation.

"The Beehives", *ca. 50.5 miles. Elevation 1705.*

About one quarter of a mile south of Plumadore, while hiking the D&H Railroad right-of-way on November 5, 1978, our party found some puzzling artifacts. On the east side of the former track was a cut in the glacial outwash sands — a cut large enough to include a spur track; why would anyone make such a large excavation unless a track were to be placed through it? We followed the cut and soon came out into a flat area with tie impressions still in the ground — definite evidence of a spur siding. Along this siding were five circular foundations, about 18 feet in diameter, made of bricks set in mortar. These ring-like foundations were largely overgrown, and we scratched our heads trying to figure out what they were. Then we remembered the photographs in Hyde (1974, pp. 109 and 168) of "beehive-type" charcoal kilns. Now, things were beginning to fit together! Why was the Chateaugay Railroad extended past Standish so hurriedly after 1885 towards Plumadore and Loon Lake? Charcoal! The blast furnace at Standish required vast quantities of charcoal for fuel, and charcoal required hardwood timber. That is why there were so many short branches along the Chateaugay (Coal Kilns Junction, Old Line Junction, Twin Ponds, Upper Kilns Junction, Tekene Junction) — logging spurs to get the hardwoods out of the woods! Even the very names of the places attest to charcoal: Coal Kilns Junction, Middle Kilns, Upper Kilns!

What an opportunity for model railroaders who are seeking to recreate in miniature a fairly small area with a tremendous diversity of railroading activities. Picture this and duplicate it in your living room or basement or attic:

(1) Ore trains from the Lyon Mountain mines to the Standish blast furnace;

(2) Trains carrying iron ingots (pig iron or iron bars) from Standish to Plattsburgh;

(3) Logging trains carrying hardwood timber to the charcoal kilns;

(4) Trains carrying charcoal from the kilns to the blast furnace;

(5) Local freights delivering supplies for Lyon Mountain Village;

(6) Passenger, mail, and express trains: Plattsburgh to Lake Placid.

Unfortunately, with all the hardwood logging occurring in the area, much slash (unwanted tree tops and branches) was left in the woods near the tracks; during dry spells especially in spring and fall, cinders from passing locomotives set fire to the woods. A great portion of the thousands upon thousands of acres which burned in the Adirondacks in 1903 and 1908 was caused by locomotives. Maps of the New York State Forest Commission (1891), New York State Conservation Commission (1916), and by Suter (1903) show the extent of these fires; most of the major burns follow railroad rights-of-way! For details on the fires closer to the Paul Smith's area (Onchiota to Saranac Lake along the Chateaugay Railroad), see Kudish (1976 and 1981). The Plumadore area along the Chateaugay is no exception; the woods look as if they had been severely burned.

Just south of milepost 51, one can still see where the old narrow gauge swung out to the west in a sharp curve, and where the newer, standard gauge line was rebuilt on a curve with a much gentler radius.

Tekene Junction, *52.66 miles. Elevation 1700.*

One of the logging railroad branches diverged here, but this little line had a most complex history. According to Seaver (1918, p. 363), and Doherty (1971, p. 13) the Kinsley Lumber Co. about 1896 built a line west from the New York Central Railroad (not the D&H Railroad) 1.8 miles to Tekene; from here the track continued west for another 2.8 miles, with a branch 2.5 miles long touching the south shore of Debar Pond. Seaver says that the line was for hauling timber and pulpwood. The 1902-1906 Loon Lake Quadrangle *incorrectly* labels this Kinsley line as Brooklyn Cooperage; Brooklyn Cooperage had all their operations near and along the New York and Ottawa from Tupper Lake to St. Regis Falls and Everton, not here.

Palmer's unpublished notes in the reference Library at the Adirondack Museum in Blue Mountain Lake dates construction of the Kinsley in 1898, two years later than Seaver's estimate. Palmer then states that the Kinsley Lumber Co. sold the line to the Baker Brothers of Plattsburgh. Apparently, the Bakers were tied in with The D&H Railroad, not The New York Central Railroad. So, in order to get the forest products out of the woods and on to the D&H line, the Baker Brothers with the D&H Railroad had to build a connection from the logging railroad to the Chateaugay Branch; this necessitated a junction built on the Chateaugay, and a bridge over the intervening New York Central Railroad Adirondack Division track. Our hiking party, on November 6, 1976, was

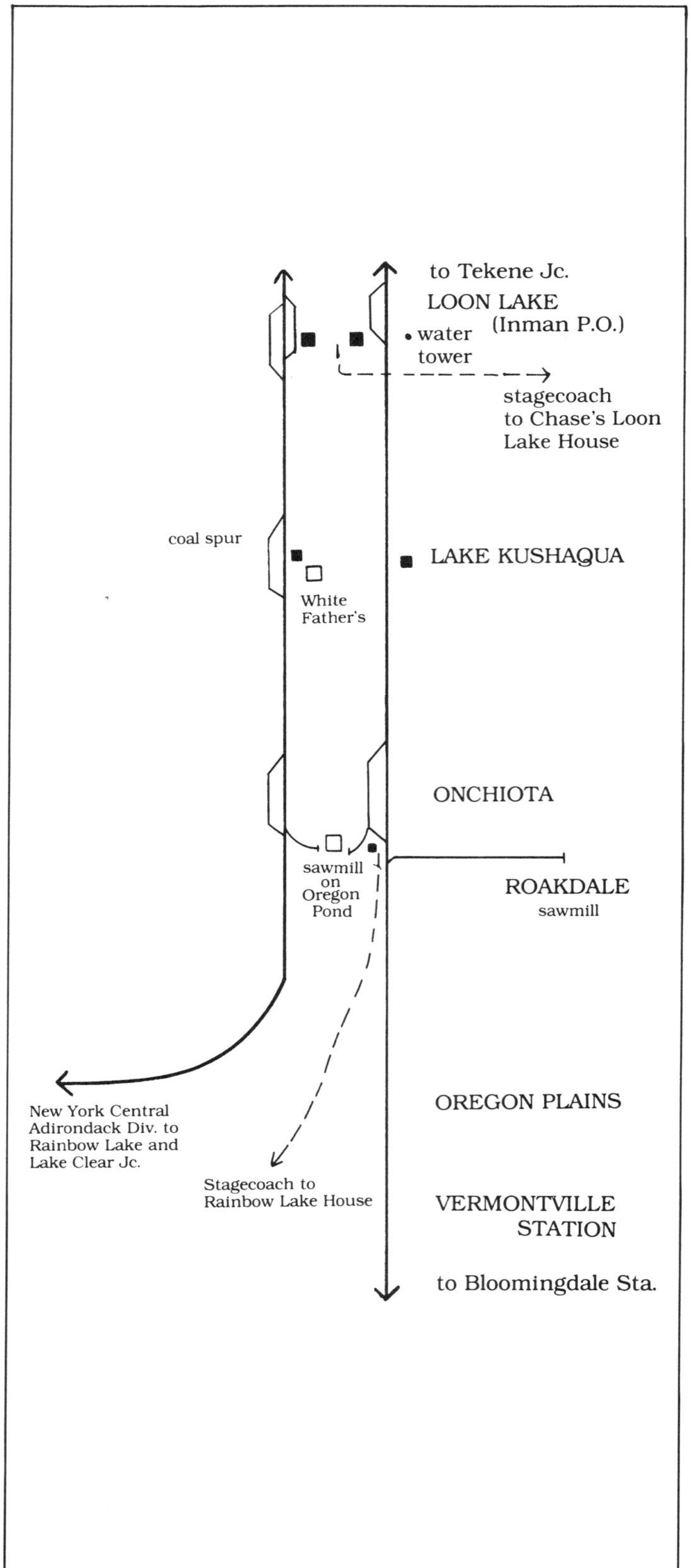

to Tekene Jc.
LOON LAKE
(Inman P.O.)
water
tower
stagecoach
to Chase's Loon
Lake House
coal spur
LAKE KUSHAQUA
White
Father's
ONCHIOTA
sawmill
on
Oregon
Pond
ROAKDALE
sawmill
New York Central
Adirondack Div. to
Rainbow Lake and
Lake Clear Jc.
OREGON PLAINS
Stagecoach to
Rainbow Lake House
VERMONTVILLE
STATION
to Bloomingdale Sta.

Inman P.O.
Loon Lake Sta.
Lake Kushaqua
Mountain Pond
Little Hope Pond
Hope Pond
Buck Pond
Roakdale
Oregon Pond
Onchiota
Square Pond
Vermontville Sta.
F R A N

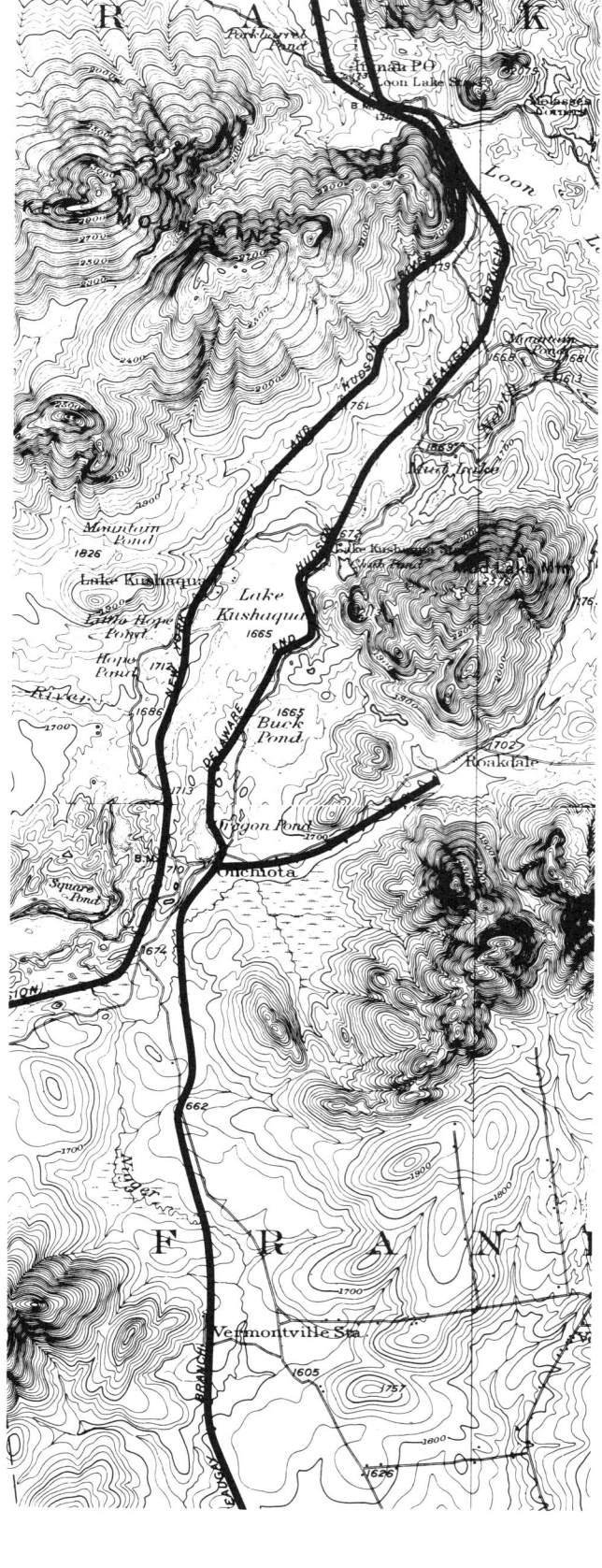

amazed at the sheer size of the concrete bridge abutments which were still standing. The bridge was long gone, as were the tracks, but the massive structures loomed out of the marsh as a pair of gigantic parentheses around the Niagara Mohawk power line (now occupying the old NYC right-of-way). A cornerstone revealed the year of construction: 1903 — the same year that The D&H Railroad standard-gauged the Chateaugay!

Seaver tells us more about the logging line. The D&H Railroad had hopes of extending the Tekene Branch past Debar Pond west to St. Regis Falls or Santa Clara or Everton, where it could connect with and acquire the New York and Ottawa Railroad. The D&H Railroad never did extend the Tekene Branch past Debar Pond, nor did it ever acquire Hurd's old line; ironically, the competing New York Central Railroad took over The New York and Ottawa Railroad in 1906. Seaver notes that the Tekene Branch had been abandoned a while when he wrote in 1918; my guess is that The D&H Railroad and Baker Brothers dropped it in 1906 or shortly after, when the Central gained control of Hurd's old line.

The timetable of June 21, 1908, shows that two trains passed in opposite directions here, requiring a passing siding at Tekene Junction. This is the only timetable in my file which actually lists the Junction as a station stop.

Catamount, *53.2 miles. Elevation 1710.*

The map shows this as a place-name (1902–1906 Loon Lake Quadrangle), but no timetable ever listed it as a station.

Loon Lake (Inman Post Office), *54.42 miles. Elevation 1730.*

Loon Lake was the temporary terminus for the Chateaugay from November 15, 1886 (when the line arrived) to December 4, 1887 (when it opened to Saranac Lake). During this one year period, stagecoaches from Paul Smith's Hotel met the trains here. Ray McKnight has supplied me with a track plan which he suspects existed at Loon Lake while it was a terminus during the winter of 1886-1887; I have duplicated his map here on page 30.

Loon Lake was a station stop for nearly the entire life of the Chateaugay, from 1886 through June 16, 1946. Of course, from 1940 to 1946, The D&H Railroad trains were stopping at The New York Central Railroad station across the highway, not any longer at the D&H Railroad station. Timetables from 1889 through 1899 indicate stagecoach connections to the Loon Lake House (Chase's)

three miles away; much detail is available on this major Adirondack hotel in DeSormo (1974, pp. 43–54). In 1896 and 1899, timetables inform us that trains passed here in opposite directions, necessitating a passing siding.

Travel recommendations in the first Paul Smith's Electric Railway timetable of August 20, 1906, suggest that people from Plattsburgh board The D&H Railroad trains for Loon Lake. Here, passengers walked across the road to The New York Central Railroad station and waited for the southbound to take them to Lake Clear Junction. At Lake Clear Junction, the Paul Smith's electric railway car could be boarded for the remaining 6½ mile journey to the Hotel. In the afternoon or evening, the return trip could be made. In other words, for many years Loon Lake served as a transfer point for passengers on both railroads.

PHOTOS: Shaughnessy (1967) offers several photos of Loon Lake Station on pages 159, 162, and 165. A water tower appears in one of the photos, and its foundation is still visible on the ground today.

Lake Kushaqua (Round Pond), *58.20 miles. Elevation 1675.*

The earliest timetable I have shows this as a station in 1890, but the name is Round Pond, not Lake Kushaqua. The 1896 timetable calls it Lake Kushaqua and service continued through at least 1932. By 1942, trains were no longer stopping here, and, of course, at this time, were on the Central's track.

Onchiota (Rainbow), *60.78 miles. Elevation 1690.*

This station was called Rainbow on the earlier timetables (1889 through 1896), but by 1899 the name was Onchiota. Trains still stopped here in 1932 but not in 1942. The 1891 timetable informs us that two trains passed here, requiring a passing siding. Stagecoaches from the Rainbow Lake House, 4 miles to the southwest, met trains here in 1896 and in 1899, according to timetable maps.

Helen Escher Tyler (1972), in a chapter entitled "A Train's Last Run" describes the nearly two-mile long narrow gauge railroad that connected the sawmill at Roakdale with Onchiota. She does not offer the date of construction, but it must have been 1887 or later, *following* the opening of the Chateaugay; a sawmill operator like Roak, wanting to get his lumber to market, would not build a railroad line to Onchiota *without* a connection to a larger railroad. Tyler *does* tell us that the

to Vermontville Sta.
BLOOMINGDALE
STATION
Stagecoach to
Paul Smiths
Stagecoach to
Crystal Springs House
in Bloomingdale
Stagecoach to
Rice's House in
Lake Clear
Bloomingdale Bog
PECK'S CORNERS
Fuel oil
Latours
SARANAC LAKE
see detail on
pgs. 38, 39
Adirondack
Bottled Gas
Will Rogers
Hospital
86
narrow gauge
relocated
1915 wreck on 90° curve
AMES MILLS
to Ray Brook

Brook
Bloomingdale Sta.
Harrietstown
HUDSON
Pecks
Corners
Colby Pond
Mt Pisgah
Trudeau
Baker Mt
SARANAC
LAKE
Moody Pond
Lake
Flower
Algonquin
Moose
Kiwassa Lake
Oseetah Lake
Ray Pond
Ames Mills
ESSEX CO.
FRANKLIN CO.

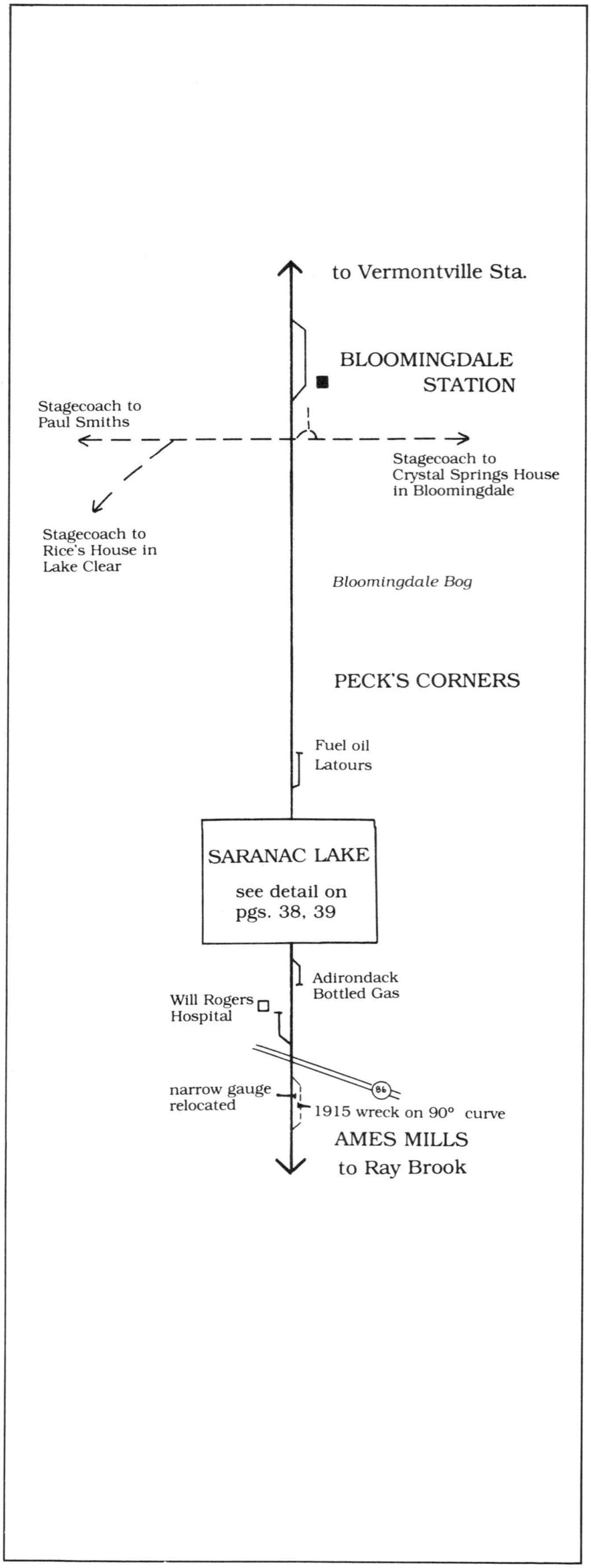

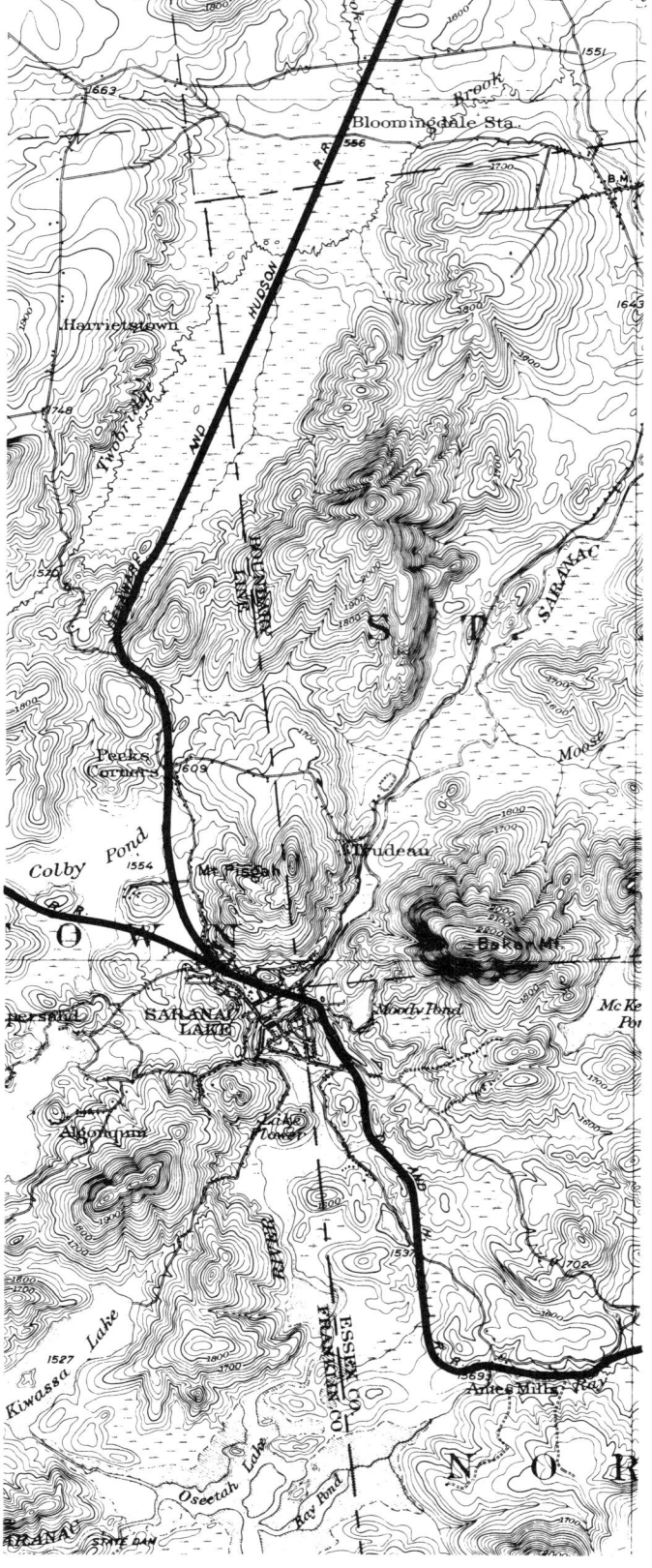

Roakdale line shut down several months before November 4, 1895. The sawmill was then moved to the south shore of Oregon Pond in Onchiota; Roak sold the mill to Baker and Odell of Plattsburgh who ran it until 1913 or 1914.

This sawmill on Oregon Pond, which lay between The D&H Railroad and the NYC, was served by both railroads (although not necessarily simultaneously) since old railroad grades converge upon it from two directions. South of Onchiota, the D&H Railroad and NYC tracks diverged.

Vermontville Station, *64.31 miles. Elevation 1610.*

This station is listed on timetables dated 1890 through 1932. Trains could not have stopped here after 1940, as this segment of track was abandoned and the NYC was three miles to the west. Chateaugay trains stopped not in the hamlet of Vermontville, but 2½ miles to the west. In the vicinity of Vermontville Station, also called Oregon Plains, extensive fire damage in 1903 occurred (see Kudish, Flora II, 1981). Tyler (1969) has written detail on the history of the community of Vermontville.

Bloomingdale Station, *66.61 miles. Elevation 1550.*

Bloomingdale Station was located one-and-three-quarters miles west of the center of Bloomingdale Village. Trains stopped at this station from the time that the Chateaugay opened to Saranac Lake on December 5, 1887, through at least 1932 and probably until 1940.

Stages from Paul Smith's Hotel, instead of travelling all the way to Loon Lake as they had since December of 1886, needed come only the seven miles to Bloomingdale Station. When Paul Smith opened his electric railway on August 20, 1906, regularly-scheduled stagecoach service ceased; however an on-call conveyance service persisted at least through 1908: "Private conveyance for Paul Smith's can be secured promptly on telegraphing advice to Paul Smith's Hotel Company" stated the June 21, 1908, D&H Railroad timetable. Maps accompanying the 1896 and 1899 Chateaugay timetables announced connections by stage to the Crystal Springs House in Bloomingdale and Rice's House in Lake Clear.

A 0.15-mile-long passing siding can be discerned on the 1902 Saranac Quadrangle. In fact, trains passed here according to the 1912 timetable. Tyler (1968, pp. 21–25) describes a family moving with all their belongings, including domesticated animals, from Bloomingdale, and loading up a boxcar on the siding here.

South of Bloomingdale Station, the Chateaugay Railroad crossed the great Bloomingdale Bog for three miles on an embankment; this Bog, incidentally, is one of my favorite places to botanize. In fact, along the abandoned right-of-way occur three species of plants which I have found nowhere else in the Paul Smith's Flora area!!

Saranac Lake, *72.99 miles. Elevation 1550.*

Approaching Saranac Lake, the Chateaugay Railroad right-of-way from Peck's Corners (Trudeau Road) at 71.3 miles to Keene Street at 72.5 miles is now called Lake Colby Drive (State Highway 86). Upper Broadway, which parallels the Drive on the east, was the original turnpike. The construction skill of the railroad crews in 1887 can be seen in noting how level and straight Lake Colby Drive is!

At 71.9 miles, just south of the Saranac Lake General Hospital, was a siding that served some fuel storage tanks — possibly LaTour's, a local firm; these tanks were removed as recently as 1975. This segment of track, as has been mentioned many times before, was abandoned in 1940; however, I have heard that for several years after that, a dead-end spur persisted from Saranac Lake Junction at 72.7 miles north to this siding. I have no documentation to confirm this, but the 1955 Saranac Lake Quadrangle, based on 1953 aerial photos, shows Lake Colby Drive. Thus, if this spur persisted after 1940, it did not last until 1953. My guess is that the abandoned date was 1946, along with the D&H Railroad service into Saranac Lake and Lake Placid.

At 72.7 miles was Saranac Lake Junction. Here at Cedar Street, the New York Central Railroad track came in from Lake Clear and paralleled the D&H Railroad track into the Station. Since two railroads shared the same station, this depot was a union station — that is, a station of a union of two or more railroads.

Saranac Lake was the temporary terminus for the Chateaugay from December 5, 1887, through August 1, 1893. A map in the Franklin County Clerk's Office in Malone shows the track plan during this time, complete with depot, freight house, engine house, and turning wye (see map, page 38). The 1902 Saranac Quadrangle also shows this wye, but the scale is so small that it is difficult to see. Rochette (1937) describes the station as he pulled the first train into it in 1887.

Railroad history after 1892 in Saranac Lake becomes somewhat complicated. On July 16, 1892, the Adirondack & St. Law-

SARANAC LAKE TRACK SCHEMATICS

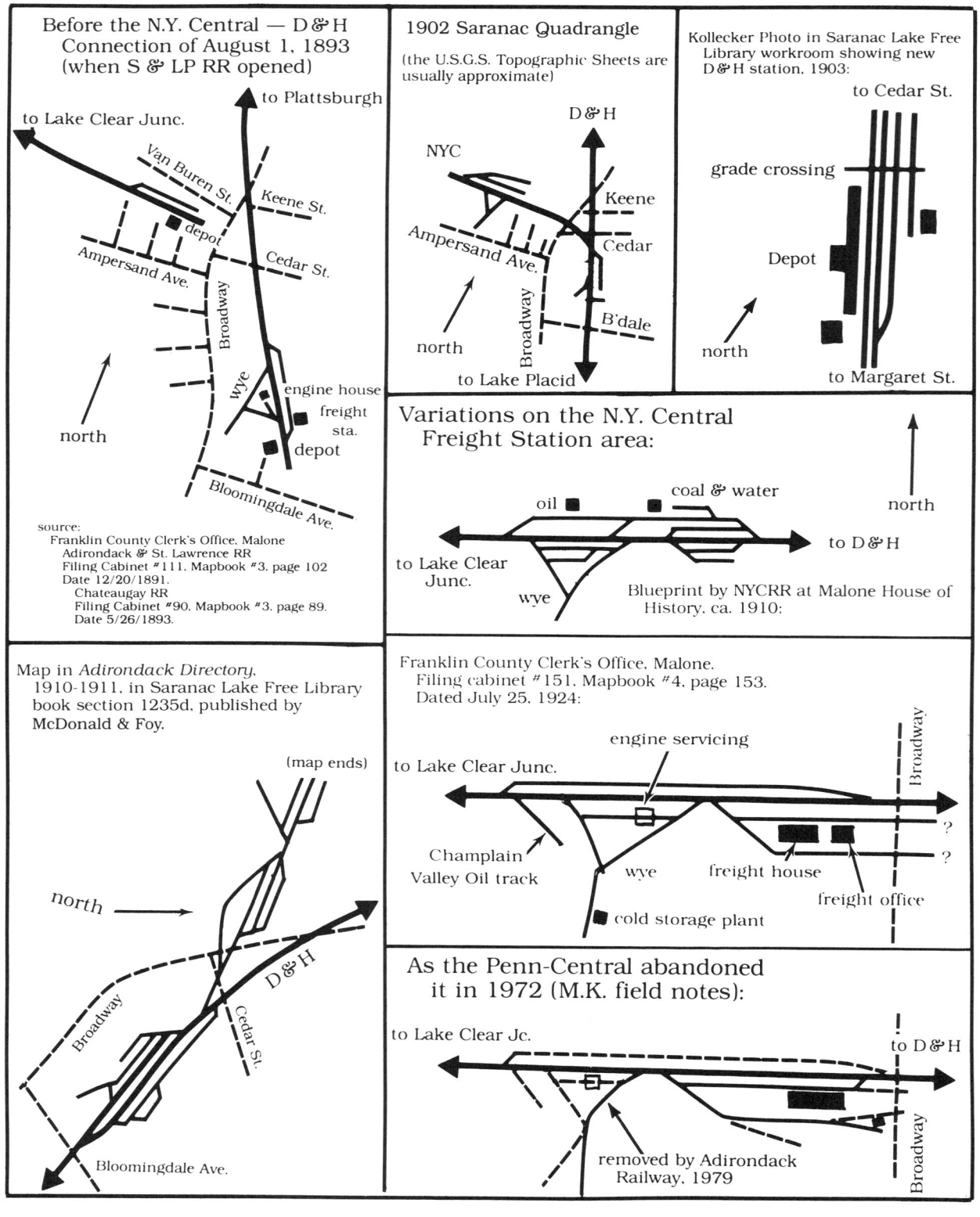

Before the N.Y. Central — D & H Connection of August 1, 1893 (when S & LP RR opened)

to Lake Clear Junc.

to Plattsburgh

Van Buren St.

Keene St.

depot

Cedar St.

Ampersand Ave.

Broadway

wye

north

engine house

freight sta.

depot

Bloomingdale Ave.

source:
Franklin County Clerk's Office, Malone
  Adirondack & St. Lawrence RR
  Filing Cabinet #111, Mapbook #3, page 102
  Date 12/20/1891.
    Chateaugay RR
  Filing Cabinet #90, Mapbook #3, page 89.
  Date 5/26/1893.

1902 Saranac Quadrangle

(the U.S.G.S. Topographic Sheets are usually approximate)

D & H

NYC

Keene

Cedar

Ampersand Ave.

Broadway

north

B'dale

to Lake Placid

Kollecker Photo in Saranac Lake Free Library workroom showing new D & H station, 1903:

to Cedar St.

grade crossing

Depot

north

to Margaret St.

Variations on the N.Y. Central Freight Station area:

oil

coal & water

north

to Lake Clear Junc.

to D & H

wye

Blueprint by NYCRR at Malone House of History, ca. 1910:

Map in *Adirondack Directory*, 1910-1911, in Saranac Lake Free Library book section 1235d, published by McDonald & Foy.

(map ends)

north

D & H

Broadway

Cedar St.

Bloomingdale Ave.

Franklin County Clerk's Office, Malone. Filing cabinet #151, Mapbook #4, page 153. Dated July 25, 1924:

Broadway

engine servicing

to Lake Clear Junc.

?

?

Champlain Valley Oil track

wye

freight house

freight office

cold storage plant

As the Penn-Central abandoned it in 1972 (M.K. field notes):

to Lake Clear Jc.

to D & H

Broadway

removed by Adirondack Railway, 1979

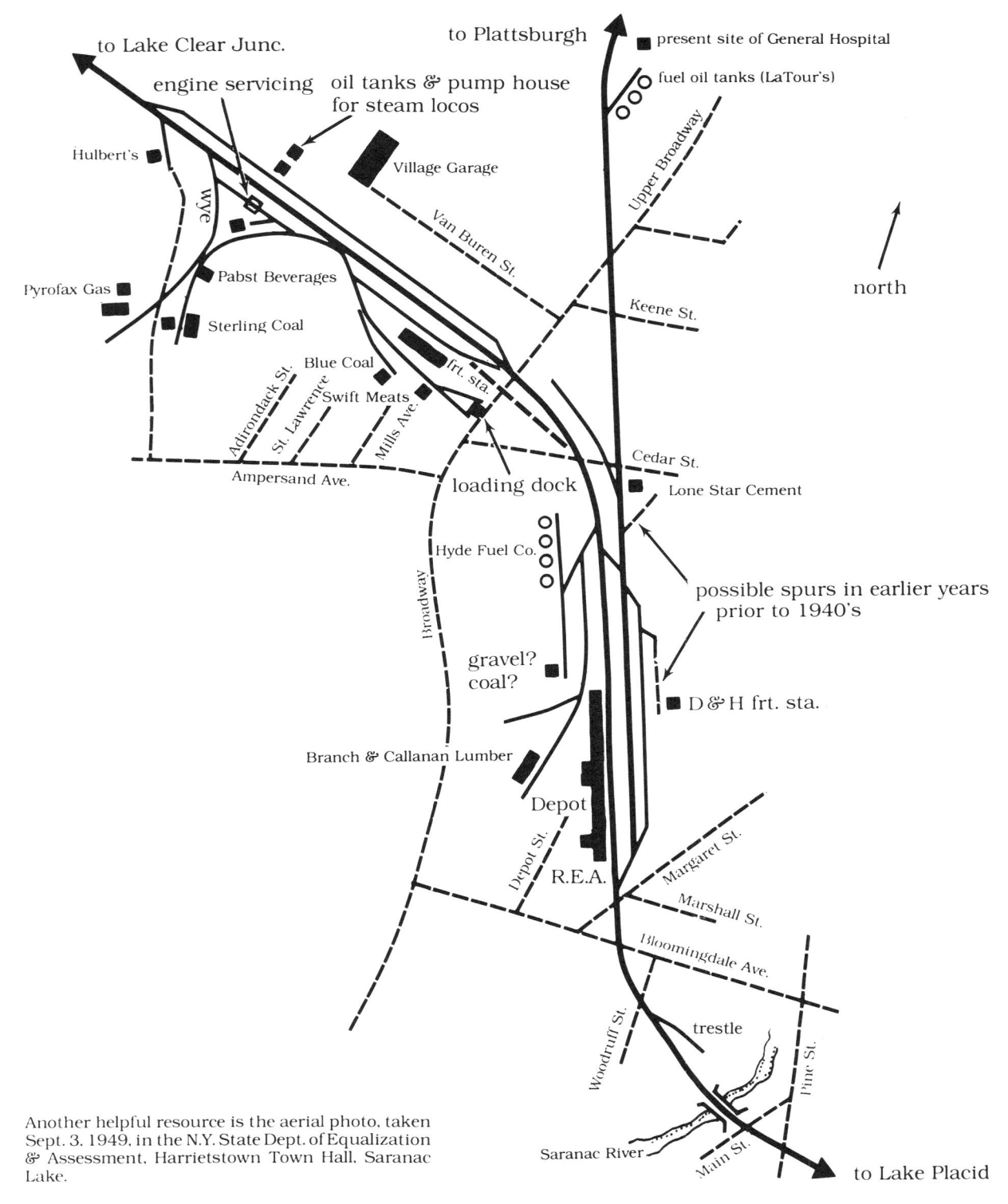

SARANAC LAKE TRACK
SCHEMATIC COMPOSITE

(detail obtained by recent field work, 1971-1980, combined with old photos and maps)

to Lake Clear Junc.

engine servicing

oil tanks & pump house for steam locos

to Plattsburgh

present site of General Hospital

fuel oil tanks (LaTour's)

Hulbert's

Village Garage

Upper Broadway

WYE

Van Buren St.

north

Pyrofax Gas

Pabst Beverages

Sterling Coal

Keene St.

Adirondack St.

Blue Coal

St. Lawrence

Swift Meats

Mills Ave.

frt. sta.

Cedar St.

Ampersand Ave.

loading dock

Lone Star Cement

Hyde Fuel Co.

Broadway

possible spurs in earlier years prior to 1940's

gravel? coal?

D & H frt. sta.

Branch & Callanan Lumber

Depot

Depot St.

R.E.A.

Margaret St.

Marshall St.

Bloomingdale Ave.

Woodruff St.

trestle

Pine St.

Saranac River

Main St.

to Lake Placid

Another helpful resource is the aerial photo, taken Sept. 3, 1949, in the N.Y. State Dept. of Equalization & Assessment, Harrietstown Town Hall, Saranac Lake.

rence Railroad (soon to become the Adirondack Division of The New York Central Railroad) opened to Saranac Lake from Lake Clear (see page 85 for details). The A & St. L. Railroad depot was separate from the Chateaugay's initially; the former was located just west of the Broadway crossing, where Big D (a building supply retail store) is at present. Later this depot became the NYC freight station.

In 1890, the Saranac and Lake Placid Railroad was organized and began constructing an extension of the Chateaugay from Saranac Lake to Lake Placid. This extension opened August 1, 1893, to Lake Placid and accommodated both Chateaugay and The New York Central Railroad trains. At this time that the Chateaugay was narrow-gauged and the NYC standard-gauged. To resolve this dilemma, the Saranac and Lake Placid was built as dual-gauge track — that is three-rail track; but the track did *not* look like a Lionel model railroad 0-gauge track because the middle rail on the S&LP was off-center. The first rail was shared by both railroads. The second rail was three feet from the first and used by Chateaugay trains. The third rail was four feet eight and one-half inches from the first rail and used by the NYC. Can you imagine the complexity of the switches? The only contemporary situation I can think of that approximates this is the Mount Washington Cog Railway in New Hampshire, where the middle cog creates extraordinarily complex switches. Of course, Chateaugay and NYC trains could not interchange cars until the Chateaugay standard-gauged in 1903.

When the S&LP opened on August 1, 1893, the NYC built a connection with the Chateaugay at Cedar Street. A photo in Hochschild (1962, p. 12) shows the original wooden Saranac Lake depot in the 1890s with NYC trains already using it. The present station was built by the D&H Railroad in 1903.

In the summer of 1896, Chateaugay trains passed at Saranac Lake, requiring a narrow-gauge passing siding. This siding was standard-gauged in 1903. D&H Railroad trains passed again here in 1912.

The track plan during the peak years of operation (1910 to 1920 era) as can best be reconstructed, is shown on page 38. When The Penn Central Railroad abandoned its freight operations in the spring of 1972, the track plan at that time is presented also on page 38. Many of the industrial sidings in Saranac Lake were served by the NYC instead of the D&H Railroad, and some were served by both probably.

Near the Union Station were at least six freight spurs, one to unload coal or gravel,

two to the Branch and Callanan Lumber Company, one to the Hyde Fuel Company, and two to the D&H Railroad freight house. The two firms mentioned are locally owned and still in business. A seventh possible freight siding could have existed at the Junction at Cedar Street, but I have no positive evidence. Since many passenger trains passed here, there were two tracks in front of the Station.

A host of hotels sent stagecoaches and other conveyances to Union Station. Before the S&LP Railroad was opened, only four points were listed for Saranac Lake in the 1889 timetable: Ray Brook House, Lake Placid, Saranac Inn and Cascade Lake. However, by 1896 and 1899 the timetables and accompanying maps listed many more: Algonquin, Miller's, Ampersand Hotel, DelMonte, Berkley, Riverside Inn, and Edgewater Inn. In addition to the charcoal and iron industry which kept the D&H Railroad operating further north, the passenger business at the south end of the line also must have been of significance. Great detail on these hotels and others is available in *Summers on the Saranacs* by DeSormo (1980).

Abandonments began with the D&H Railroad in 1946, followed by The New York Central Railroad passenger service on April 24, 1965, and The Penn Central Railroad freight service in the spring of 1972. The D&H Railroad freight house was removed between 1954 and 1965.

PHOTOS of Saranac Lake Station:

Shaughnessy (1967), pp. 166, 190, 278. Page 166 shows dual gauge.

Dora and Keough (1977) pp. 89, 90.

DeSormo (1974), p. 113.

Gardner (1975), p. 91.

Hochschild (1962), p. 12.

Harter (1979), p. 67 (this is same photo as in DeSormo), P. 68, p. 75.

Saranac Lake Daily Enterprise: 4/9/72, 4/28/76, April 22–25, 1965.

Adirondack Advertiser: 9/14/77, 9/21/77, 5/31/78, 6/7/78 (the June 7, 1978, photo is the same as that in DeSormo & Harter).

Robbins (1975) p. 26 (same photo as in Hochschild).

Staufer (1967), p. 73.

Remains of an old trestle behind the present Belvidere Restaurant on Bloomingdale Avenue suggest a siding; this is substantiated by an aerial photo, page 92 in Dora and Keough (1977) taken of Saranac Lake Village in the 1930s. This siding might have facilitated the delivery of coal and/or gravel, and would be at about milepost 73.2.

The next siding, at 74.0 miles, served the Adirondack Bottled Gas Company and was in use with huge tank cars until 1972. This siding was located just south of the River Street grade crossing.

A fellow railroad historian, Chris Brescia, noticed, about 1978, evidence of a siding into the Will Rogers Hospital area at about milepost 74.9. We could not find any documented evidence about this long-abandoned siding, the industry it served, nor the dates of operation. When new ties were installed in preparation for The Adirondack Railway operations in 1979, much of the evidence of the old siding was destroyed.

Ames Mill, *76.5 miles. Elevation 1570.*

This was never a station, but is shown on some old turn-of-the-century maps and the 1902 Saranac Quadrangle. Even a map in the 1908 D&H Railroad timetable shows Ames Mill. What kind of mill was here and whether or not a railroad siding served it are unknown.

PHOTO: Harter (1979, p. 68) shows a wreck which occurred around 1915 probably on the big 90° curve just northwest of Ames Mill.

Ray Brook, *77.30 miles. Elevation 1575.*

Ray Brook served The D&H Railroad trains from 1893 through 1946, and The New York Central Railroad trains (passenger) until 1965. On the north side of the track west of the Station was a stub track to spot (leave) occasional freight cars. South of the track, alongside the heating plant for the old sanatorium (now Camp Adirondack — a New York State prison), were two dead-end sidings on which coal hoppers were set. These latter two sidings were in use through the spring of 1972, when The Penn Central Railroad abandoned freight service. In fact, when a washout down the line toward Utica prevented a locomotive from reaching Ray Brook and hauling away the last remaining hopper cars, these railway cars had to be trucked away by flatbed trailer over the highways to Potsdam! I am sorry that I did not see this most unusual and entertaining movement through Saranac Lake! The trucks had to be removed from the railway cars for clearance purposes along the highways, and put back on again in Potsdam where the hoppers were re-railed on The Penn Central Railroad tracks. The Adirondack Railway in 1979, removed the two coal sidings.

An employees' timetable of November 1, 1942, by The D&H Railroad lists Ray Brook Siding at 77.9 miles and with a capacity of 24 cars. An article in the Lake Placid News, June 30, 1977, featuring Tony Moreno, the agent at Ray Brook, stated: "That was the year (1932) the railroad put in a spur and siding at our station and dead trains laid in here overnight to accommodate the anticipated (Olympics) crowds that might be coming and going."

PHOTOS: The Lake Placid News, June 30, 1977, shows Ray Brook Station in the 1920s with agent Tony Moreno in front.

Hastings (1950), page 25 shows the upgrade to the east.

Harter (1979), page 69.

Saranac Lake Daily Enterprise, April 9, 1972.

Lyons, *82.1 miles. Elevation 1742.*

Although never a station stop, this locality is shown on a map included in The D&H Railroad June 21, 1908 timetable.

Here, where the Old Military Road crosses the track, was a siding serving Adirondack Bottled Gas and Raeoil Corporation, both local firms; huge tank cars filled with bottled gas were unloaded here as recently as 1972. Chris Brescia informed me that northeast of the crossing, where the firemens' training ground is today, several tracks were temporarily laid to hold the overflow passenger cars during the 1932 Winter Olympics in Lake Placid — a second Ray Brook Siding. This needs confirmation.

Lake Placid (Newman Post Office), *82.71 miles. Elevation 1736.*

Last stop! As previously noted, both The Chateaugay Railroad and The New York Central Railroad trains began operating to and from here August 1, 1893. The D&H Railroad service ceased in 1946, The New York Central Railroad passenger in 1965, and freight in 1972. When The D&H Railroad pulled out in 1946 they sold the 9.1 miles of track from Saranac Lake to the NYC.

This terminus included a passenger station with a runaround track, three additional passenger car storage tracks, a freight house track, two spurs for coal delivery, a turntable built in 1916, an engine house, and a gravel-sand trestle (see map, page 43). The track plan from 1965 to 1972, as The Penn Central Railroad eliminated service is shown also on page 43. I photographed the old turntable in 1965, but it was gone by 1971. An employees' timetable of The New

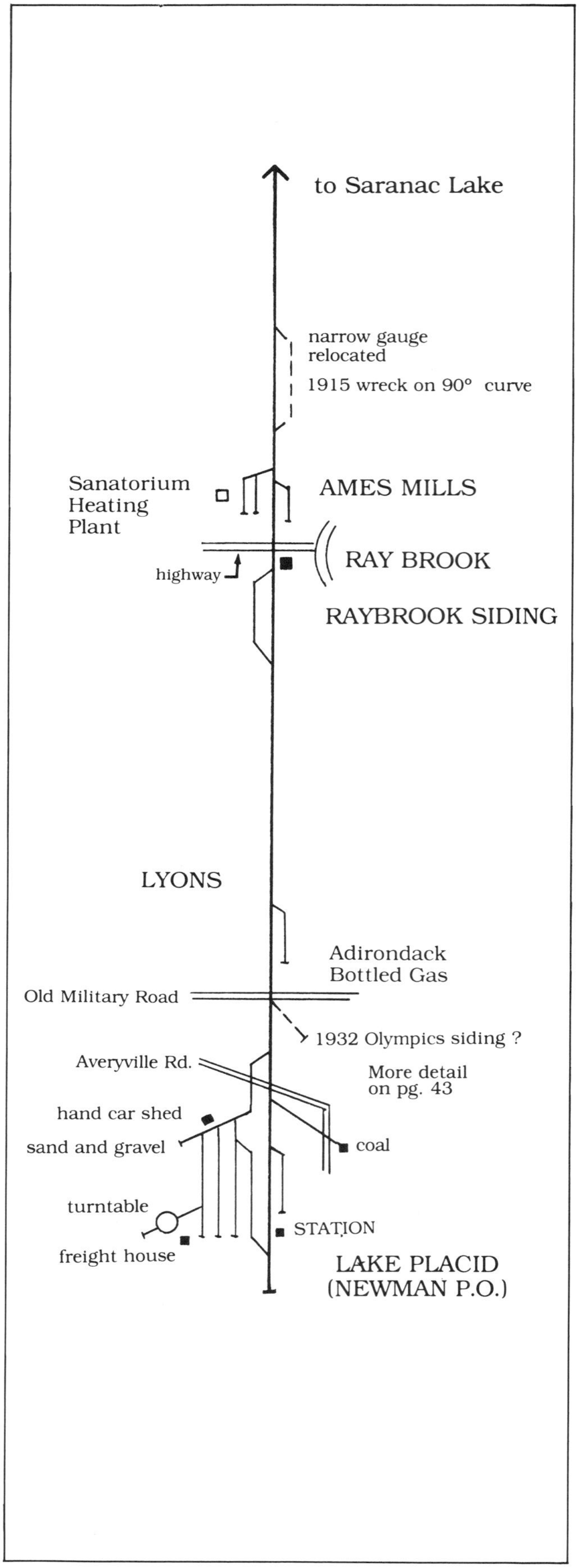

to Saranac Lake
narrow gauge
relocated
1915 wreck on 90° curve
Sanatorium
Heating
Plant
AMES MILLS
highway
RAY BROOK
RAYBROOK SIDING
LYONS
Adirondack
Bottled Gas
Old Military Road
1932 Olympics siding ?
Averyville Rd.
More detail
on pg. 43
hand car shed
sand and gravel
coal
turntable
STATION
freight house
LAKE PLACID
(NEWMAN P.O.)

Oseetah Lake
Ray Pond
RIVER
ESSEX CO
FRANKLIN CO
Ray Brook
Mirror Lake
Lake Placid
Newman
Whiteface
PLACID

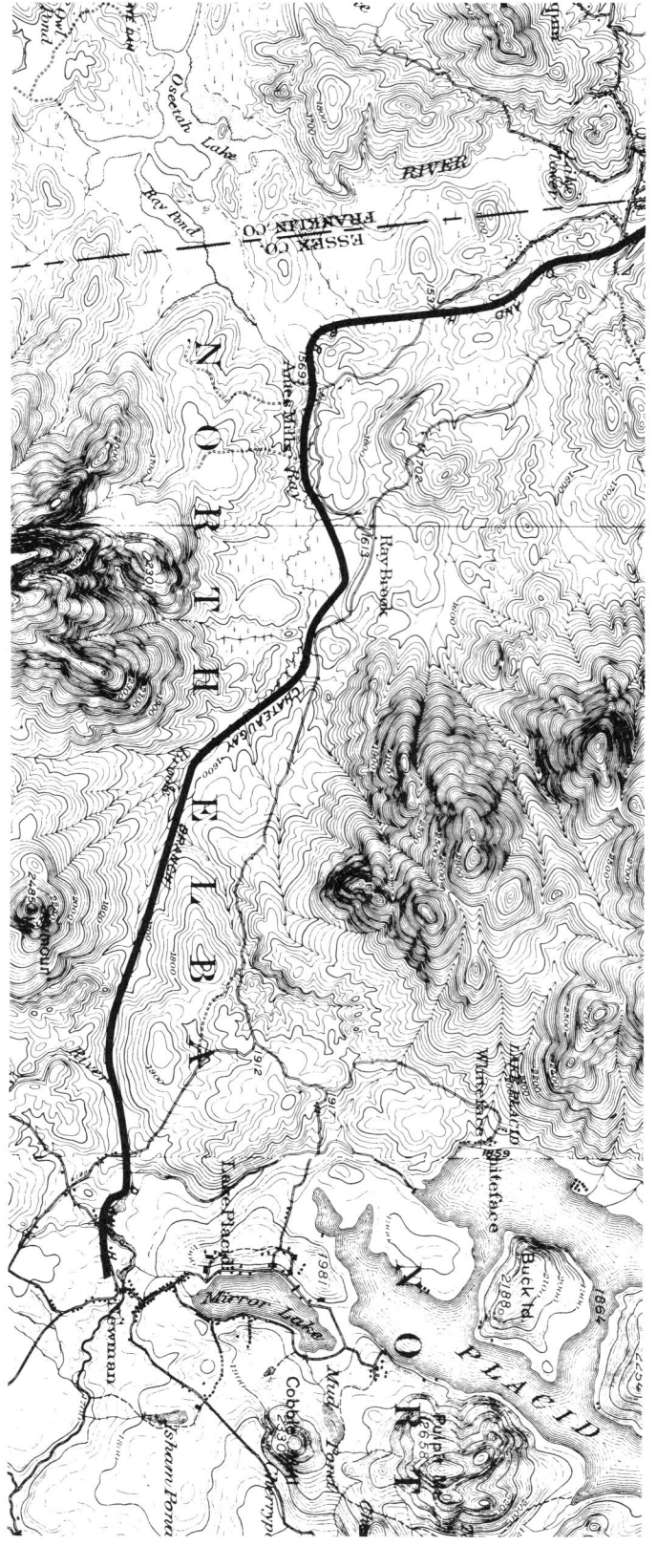

LAKE PLACID YARD

From 1950 (Hasting's photos) and Kudish's 1965 field notes   July 15, 1965 (Kudish field notes) as New York Central began to remove trackage   July, 1975 (Kudish field notes after Penn-Central abandonment)

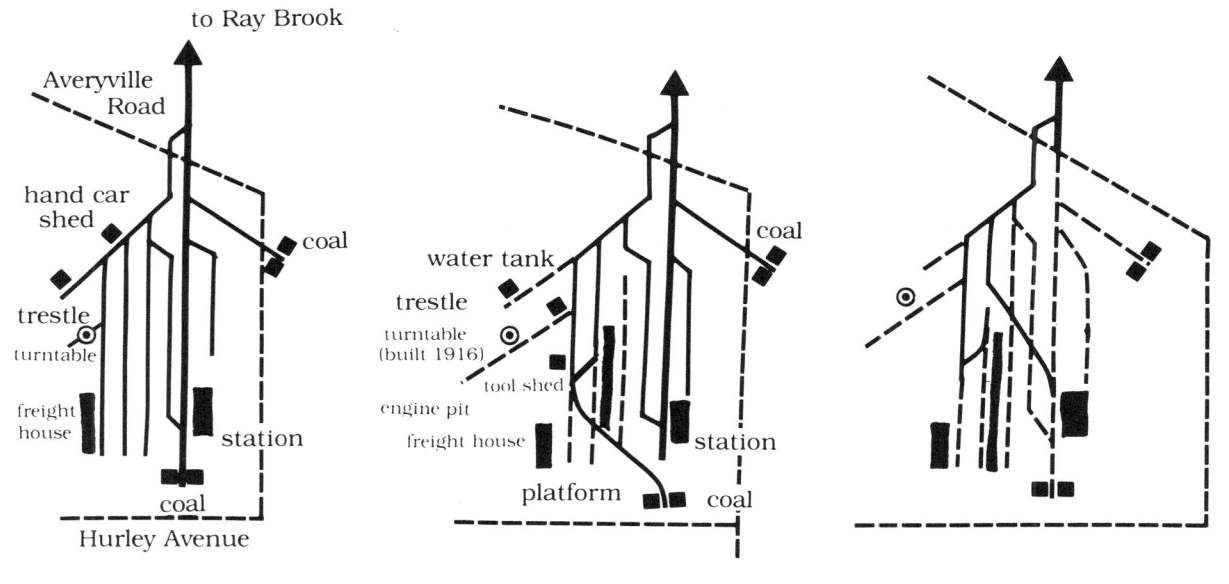

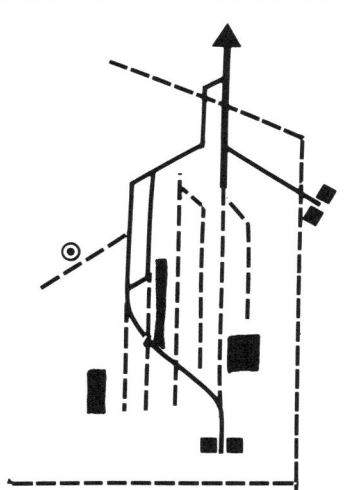

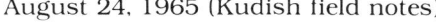

August 24, 1965 (Kudish field notes)

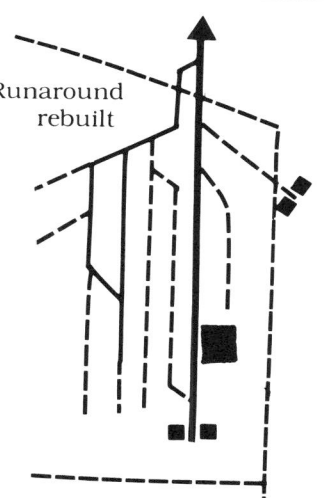

Adirondack Railway, June 14, 1980

43

York Central Railroad dated September 30, 1951, noted that only steam locomotive watering facilities were here at that time; the nearest diesel watering facilities were at Lake Clear.

PHOTOS: Hastings (1950), page 22, 26.

> *Lake Placid News, November 16, 1978, shows a picture of a steam-powered train entering Lake Placid. Track is standard-gauged, hence post-1903.*

> *Harter (1979), pages 69, 71, 75, 166 (the photo of the turntable on page 71 is my own, taken in July, 1965). P. 69 shows dual-gauge.*

> *Shaughnessy (1967), page 166 (top).*

Timetable Operation

Rochette (1937) informs us that during the period that The Chateaugay Railroad terminated at Lyon Mountain (1880-1885), there were four passenger trains and three freights each way daily between Lyon Mountain and Plattsburgh.

Summer timetables of 1889 and 1891 indicate two round trips daily between Plattsburgh and Saranac Lake with an additional one-way run early in the morning from Lyon Mountain to Plattsburgh. In winter, during this period, service was reduced to one round trip daily between Plattsburgh and Saranac Lake (December, 1890) and one round trip daily between Lyon Mountain and Plattsburgh.

In the summer of 1893, the line was extended to Lake Placid from Saranac Lake, and a timetable of The Saranac and Lake Placid Railroad dated December, 1893, shows two round trips daily between these points.

By the summer seasons of 1896 and 1899, three round trips were run daily between Plattsburgh and Lake Placid, although the number was decreased to two for the autumn and winter.

As determined indirectly from connections shown on the August 20, 1906, Paul Smith's Railway timetable, there were still three trains daily each way between Plattsburgh and Lake Placid. By 1908, the summer schedule exhibits an all-time frequency maximum for the Chateaugay Branch: four trains daily each way between Plattsburgh and Lake Placid.

A summer timetable of 1912 shows the number of round trips between Plattsburgh and Lake Placid down to three daily, only one of them running on Sunday.

The autumn, 1916, timetable revealed two round trips daily between Plattsburgh and Lake Placid, one of them running on Sun-

days. By the autumn of 1927, the number of round trips daily between Plattsburgh and Lake Placid was reduced to one, with a supplemental round trip daily between Standish and Plattsburgh. By September, 1932, the supplemental Standish-Plattsburgh run was eliminated.

In the autumn of 1942, one train daily each way operated between Plattsburgh and Lake Placid. At this time (between 1940 and 1946), this train was run over The New York Central Railroad trackage from Plumadore to Saranac Lake via Lake Clear Junction. A photo in Shaughnessy (1967, p. 278) suggests that this train was mixed (i.e., freight and passenger combined).

Service to Lake Placid on The D&H Railroad ceased on November 1, 1946; however, as recently as September 26, 1948, one passenger train was still running daily (except Sunday) each way between Lyon Mountain and Plattsburgh, stopping at Cadyville and Dannemora.

Throughout the period 1908 to 1946 (and most probably between 1903 and 1908 as well), additional trains were run by The New York Central Railroad over Delaware and Hudson Railroad trackage between Saranac Lake, Ray Brook, and Lake Placid; these trains originated in Utica or shuttled from Lake Clear Junction (see chapter IV).

Running times between Plattsburgh and Saranac Lake (73 miles) averaged three hours and five minutes in 1891. Between Plattsburgh and Lake Placid (83 miles), running times averaged about three and one-half hours in 1896 and 1899. By 1908, one express made the trip in two hours and twenty-five minutes, but locals averaged about three hours. In the 1940s, when The D&H Railroad trains were rerouted via Lake Clear Junction, one way-running times between Plattsburgh and Lake Placid increased to four hours or even slightly over four hours (there was another reason probably for this lethargic trip — see following section on The Chateaugay Railroad equipment)!

Chateaugay Equipment

There is a detailed roster in Shaughnessy (1967, p. 470) of the narrow-gauge Chateaugay Railroad locomotives with photographs of several of them. There were fourteen in all.

Four of these were of the 4-4-0 wheel arrangement, primarily used in passenger service. Three of these are photographed in Shaughnessy:

> #10 "Loon Lake" on page 165 at Loon Lake.
> #11 "St. Regis" on page 159 at Loon Lake, and on page 167.

#12 "Mirror Lake" on page 161 and on page 162 at Loon Lake.

The photo of this engine on page 165 at Lyon Mountain is duplicated in Mohr (1974).

Nine of these were of the 2-6-0 wheel arrangement (Moguls), primarily used in freight service. Two of these are photographed in Shaughnessy:

No. 8 "Dannemora" on page 159 at Cadyville (Woods Mills).

No. 4 "Thomas Dickson" on page 158 at Standish.

The fourteenth engine was an 0-4-0 switcher.

The Saranac and Lake Placid Railroad had its own engines for some time. No. 1, a Ten-wheeler or 4-6-0, is shown on page 166 in Shaughnessy.

As for railroad cars of the narrow-gauge Chateaugay Railroad, some of these appear in the Shaughnessy photos coupled to the locomotives.

A boxcar appears on page 159 at Cadyville (Woods Mills).

A round-roof baggage-express car appears on page 159 at Loon Lake. This or another identical car appears on page 158 at Standish.

A round-roof baggage car appears on page 165 at Loon Lake.

A standard-roof baggage-express car appears on page 162 at Loon Lake.

Coaches appear on page 165 at Loon Lake and Lyon Mountain (two of them). One of the coaches appears on page 162 at Loon Lake. It is not possible to determine how many coaches The Chateaugay Railroad had: at least two and probably many more.

A combine appears on page 159 at Loon Lake.

President McKinley came by narrow-gauge Chateaugay Railroad to Saranac Lake in 1897, and he is shown on the vestibule of a coach in Shaughnessy (page 190).

One car that looks like a combination RPO (Railway post office)-baggage appears on page 165 at Lyon Mountain, repeated on Mohr (1974).

Parlor cars were run over the line between Plattsburgh and Lake Placid, according to the timetables of 1896 and 1899. Diners and sleepers only were in service along the main line out of Plattsburgh until standard-gauging.

Once standard-gauging was completed in 1903, mainline The D&H Railroad equipment could run over The Chateaugay Branch Railroad and did. This included through Pullman sleeping cars from New York and through coaches on express trains, according to the 1908 timetable. Rochette (1937) mentions running passenger trains in 1908 over the line with four cars maximum; if he had more than that, he'd need a helper engine on the hill out of Cadyville! Rochette also ran freight trains: "Each morning they made one trip from Plattsburgh to Dannemora with coal and other freight for the prison, returning with any empty cars that might be on hand. On the second trip they went through to Lyon Mountain with perhaps fifteen empty seven-ton-capacity cars for the Chateaugay Iron plant. At Morrisonville or Cadyville they stopped to cut the train into sections of four or five cars each for the laborious climb up Dannemora Hill, which even now rises 169 feet to the mile, doubling the hill as many times as was necessary to get the entire train to the summit."

In 1912, the timetable lists buffet-sleeping cars and parlor cars through to New York City.

Mr. Thomas Kyle, a former New York Central Railroad employee, told me that in the 1940s, The D&H Railroad ran mixed trains into Lake Placid over The New York Central Railroad. Having freight cars on the same train dragged out the running time to over 4 hours and discouraged passenger use. The mixed train is confirmed by a photo in Shaughnessy (p. 278) with Consolidation #999, a 2-8-0. Another photo of a D&H Railroad standard-gauged engine is on page 166; it is No. 3 "Lake Placid," a 4-4-0, photographed at Saranac Lake with a D&H Railroad boxcar.

Years after standard-gauging, Rochette (1937) notes the use of 900 and 1000 class engines on The Chateaugay Railroad Branch. According to Shaughnessy's roster, these were Consolidations (2-8-0).

Chapter II

Branches Off The D&H Mainline

Part I — Ausable Forks Branch Of The D&H Railroad

Construction

The construction history of this branch is far more involved and fascinating than I ever imagined! It was built from Plattsburgh to the Ausable River *before* the mainline through Port Kent. Shaughnessy (1967, p. 137) states that in 1866, the Whitehall and Plattsburgh was organized to build a railroad between these two points; construction began at both ends, from Plattsburgh south toward the Ausable River and from Ticonderoga north to Port Henry (the Whitehall-Ticonderoga segment was built later). The idea was to avoid the rugged cliffs along Lake Champlain especially around Willsboro by constructing a line *inland* between Port Henry and Plattsburgh. The Ausable River — Port Henry inland route never materialized, leaving the Plattsburgh — Ausable River segment "hanging" without a through-route function.

Construction from Plattsburgh to the Ausable River was completed in the latter part of 1868 (Shaughnessy, 1967, p. 137), although The D&H Railroad Map, published in 1973, indicates completion of the line to the Ausable River in 1869–1870. The terminus was called "Point of Rocks" or "Rogers" or "Ausable River Station." Maps showing construction appear on pages 153 and 164 of Shaughnessy (1967). The line became the Ausable Branch of The D&H Railroad in 1875, and was extended 2.7 miles upstream in 1894 to Ausable Forks.

Relocation of the junction with the mainline from Plattsburgh (which I named "Plattsburgh Junction" in Chapter I, page 20) to South Junction occurred in 1894, and lengthened the line by 0.9 mile. Shaugh-nessy (1967, p. 202) states the reason for the junction relocation: not enough room in downtown Plattsburgh for yard and storage tracks, and to get the line off the military reservation. The military reservation much later became the U.S. Air Force Base, with runway construction beginning in 1955–1956, forcing further relocation of The Chateaugay Railroad Branch (see Chapter I, pp. 20 and 25).

The following list of stations and industries includes mileages after the 1894 junction relocation to South Junction. For mileages prior to 1894, estimate 0.9 mile less from Salmon River Junction to Ausable River Station.

Plattsburgh Station, *0.0 mile. Elevation 118 feet.*

"Plattsburgh Junction," *0.7 mile. Elevation 136 feet.*

At this point the Ausable Branch trains diverged from The D&H Railroad mainline from 1875 through 1894, and Chateaugay Branch trains from 1878 through 1903.

Cliff Haven, *2.88 miles. Elevation 135.*

Bluff Point, *3.36 miles. Elevation 143.*

At this point the Chateaugay Branch diverged from The D&H Railroad mainline from 1903 through 1955.

South Junction, *4.6 miles. Elevation 147.*

This Junction was built in 1894 as a relocation of the north end of the Ausable Branch off the military reservation.

Salmon River Junction, *6.1 miles. Elevation 170.*

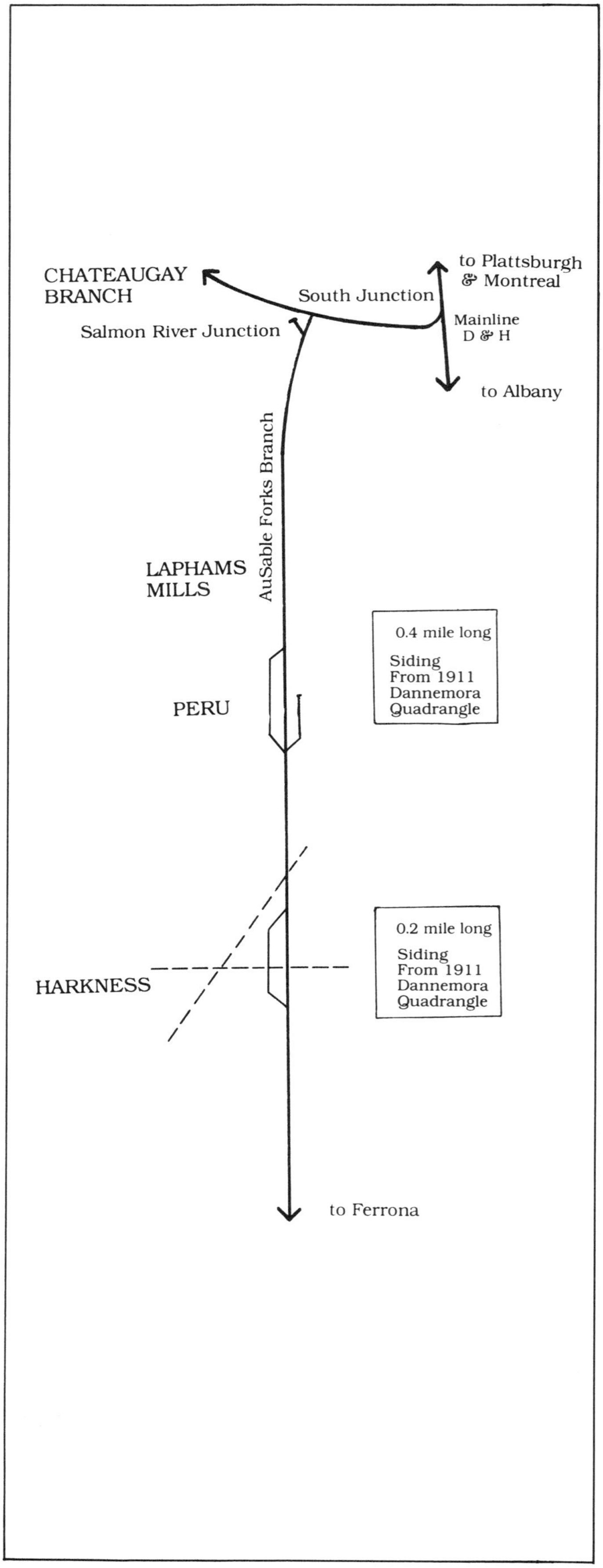

CHATEAUGAY
BRANCH
South Junction
to Plattsburgh
& Montreal
Salmon River Junction
Mainline
D & H
to Albany
AuSable Forks Branch
LAPHAMS
MILLS
0.4 mile long
Siding
From 1911
Dannemora
Quadrangle
PERU
0.2 mile long
Siding
From 1911
Dannemora
Quadrangle
HARKNESS
to Ferrona

Silver Stream
Peru
Spaulding
Harkness
Ausable
Calkins School
Delaware and Hudson

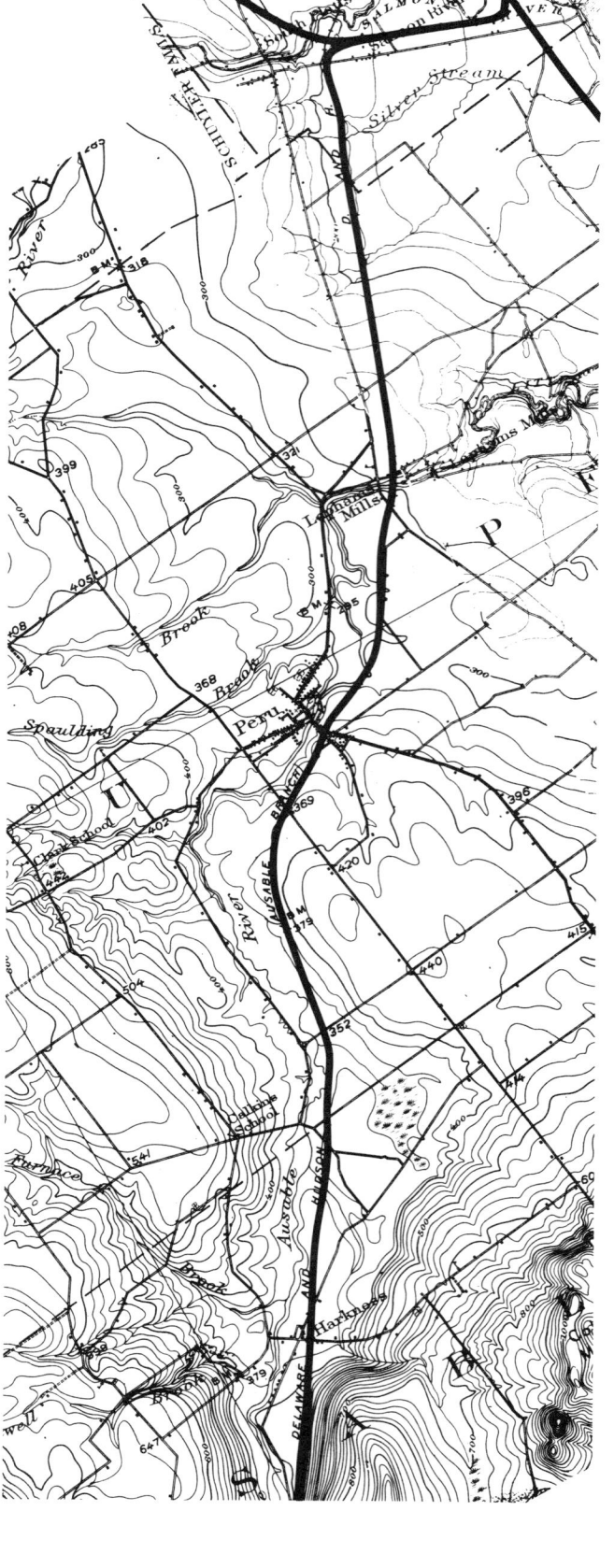

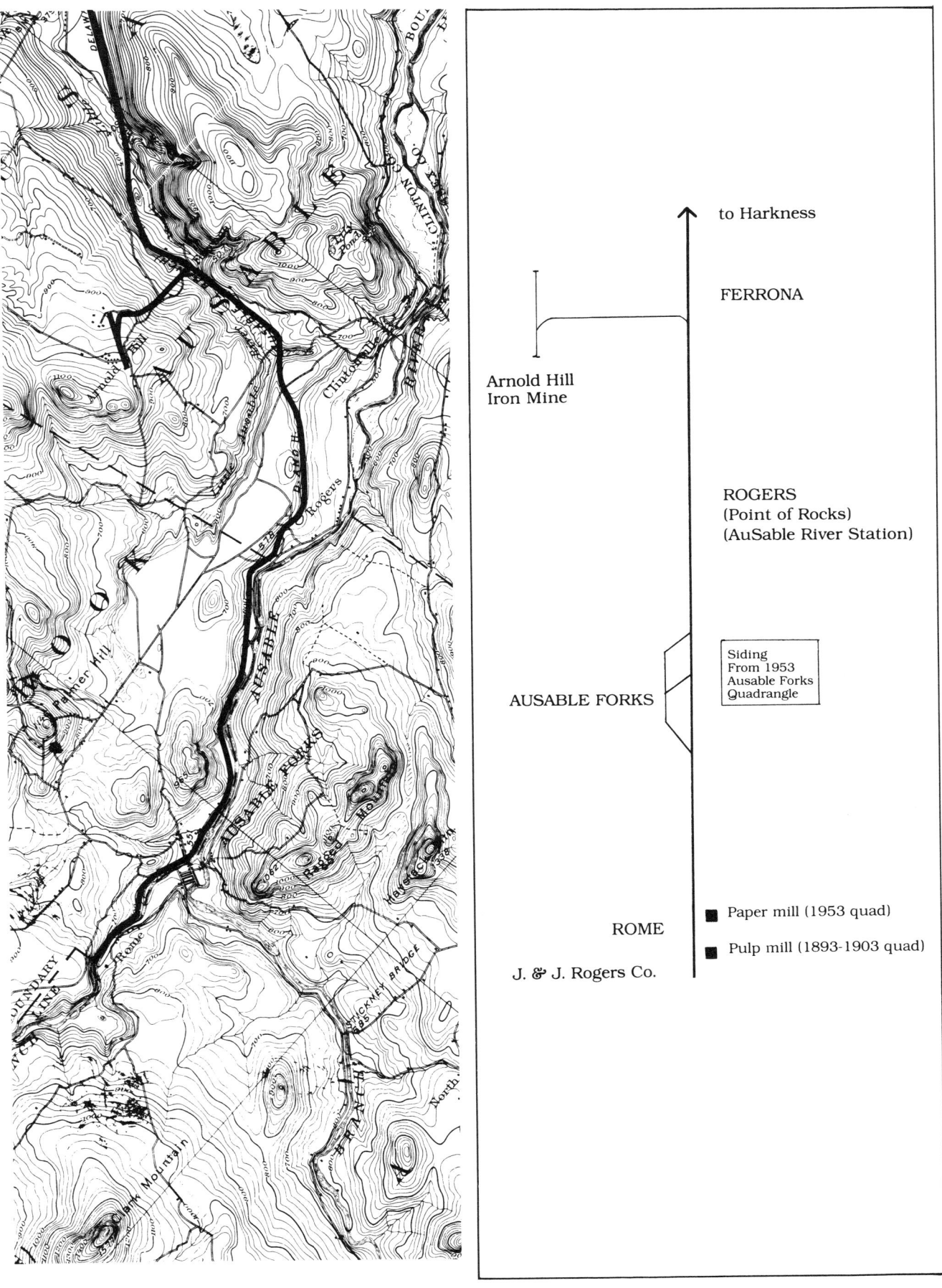

to Harkness

FERRONA

Arnold Hill
Iron Mine

ROGERS
(Point of Rocks)
(AuSable River Station)

Siding
From 1953
Ausable Forks
Quadrangle

AUSABLE FORKS

ROME

■ Paper mill (1953 quad)

■ Pulp mill (1893-1903 quad)

J. & J. Rogers Co.

At this point the Chateaugay Branch diverged after its 1955 relocation off the Air Force Base runway.

Lapham's Mills, *8.8 miles. Elevation 306.*

The original name for this point was **Bartonville Station.**

Peru, *10.9 miles. Elevation 348.*

Sidings are shown on the map on pages 48 and 132 as they appear on the 1911 Dannemora Quadrangle.

Harkness, *15.2 miles. Elevation 375.*

Sidings are shown as they appear on the 1911 Dannemora Quadrangle.

Arnold (Ferrona), *17.9 miles. Elevation 507.*

Timetables from 1870 through 1875 name this stop "Ferrona," but by 1908 it had become "Arnold." The 1893–1903 Ausable Quadrangle indicates a railroad spur heading up to the Arnold Hill iron mine, but note the steepness of this grade: some 500 feet in 1.2 miles! No railroad could manage this 7.9% grade; the only possibility is an inclined or cog railway. Perhaps some geared logging locomotives could ascend a 7.9% grade, but this wasn't a logging spur. Probably, by the time the 1953 Ausable Forks Quadrangle was surveyed, the Arnold Hill iron mine railroad had been long abandoned. James Rogers III (owner of radio station WNBZ in Saranac Lake, personal communication) informs me that there was indeed an inclined railway, narrow gauge with two tracks. Loaded ore cars were let down on one track to Ferrona from the iron mine while empties were drawn up as a counterweight on the other track.

Ausable River Station (Point of Rocks or Rogers), *20.8 miles. Elevation 578.*

This was the terminus from about 1868 through 1894 (see p. 47).

Ausable Forks, *23.5 miles. Elevation 551.*

In 1894, the Ausable Branch was extended to here. The 1953 Ausable Forks Quadrangle indicates the sidings as shown here on pages 49 and 132. The three grade crossings within one-half mile of each other along Route 9N east of town and the track running down the middle of the street were an unusual sight as late as 1981!

J & J Rogers Company, *24.7 miles. Elevation 600.*

The 1893 Ausable Quadrangle, revised in 1903, shows an extension 1.2 miles up the West Branch Ausable River to the J&J Rogers Company pulp mill, built in 1893 (A. Smith, 1980, and James Rogers III, personal communication); the hamlet on the 1893–1903 map for the vicinity around the pulp mill is "Rome." In 1901 or shortly thereafter, the J&J Rogers Company built a paper mill (A. Smith, 1980, and James Rogers III, personal communication); the 1953 Ausable Forks Quadrangle shows the track terminating at the paper mill 0.5 mile from the Forks.

Timetable Operation

On May 6, 1870 (Shaughnessy, 1964, p. 31), there were two round trips daily, originating in Plattsburgh, one in the morning and one in the afternoon. One round trip, with mail and passengers, required a running time one-way of an hour. The second round trip required 90 minutes, as it was mixed (both freight and passenger), also one way.

By December 9, 1872 (Shaughnessy, 1964, p. 43), the service was similar except that one-way running times had been lengthened to 100 minutes passenger and 120 minutes mixed.

Shaughnessy (1967, p. 151) includes a November, 1875, timetable indicating but one round trip daily, originating in Plattsburgh in the morning.

Timetables from 1908 (June 21) through 1927 (October 1) show similar service: two round trips daily originating at Plattsburgh, one in the early morning and the second in the mid-afternoon. Running times one way were 45 to 65 minutes. There was no Sunday service. One change did occur between the timetable of September 3, 1912 and the timetable of September 24, 1916 (the latter published in Gardner (1975, p. 81); Bluff Point and Cliff Haven no longer were stops by 1916.

The index to a Spring, 1933, *Official Guide* notes that Peru and Ausable Forks had freight service only, suggesting that passenger service was discontinued on the Ausable Forks Branch sometime between 1927 and 1933.

Photographs, Equipment, And Closure

Oddly, I have not come across any photographs of the Ausable Branch printed in any of the Adirondack railroad history books and articles.

Equipment, since the Branch was standard-gauged and connected with The D&H

Railroad mainline, could be shared with the mainline.

Freight service terminated only very recently at the time of this writing. My sources indicate that the tracks were removed from about Lapham's Mills to Ausable Forks in August or September 1981.

Part II — Keeseville, Ausable Chasm, And Lake Champlain Railroad Company

The Keeseville, Ausable Chasm, and Lake Champlain Railroad Company was a separately-owned line only 5.6 miles long, and apparently never became a branch of The D&H Railroad with which it connected at Port Kent. The Annual Report of the New York State Board of Railroad Commissioners (1893, p. 293) tells us that the line was chartered April 4, 1889, and began operations May 26, 1890. By the detail in the Annual Report, one would guess that the line originally opened with steam power, although it soon became electrified. Palmer (1979) lists February 1, 1911, as the last of the electric operation, the line reverting back to steam power until its closure in 1924 (Shaughnessy, 1967, p. 203).

Gardner (1975, p. 10) includes a timetable of June 26, 1916. There were seven round trips daily to meet the boats of the Champlain Transportation Company and The D&H Railroad trains, and three on Sunday. Trips initiated at Keeseville, and required a running time one-way of 20 minutes for the 5.6 miles. Thus a single train shuttling back and forth could provide all the passenger service. Ausable Chasm station was located 4.3 miles from Port Kent, or 1.3 miles from the Keeseville terminal.

The D&H Railroad timetable (Gardner, 1975, p. 83) shows connections only at Port Kent for Ausable Chasm — five daily each way and none on Sunday as of September 3, 1912. My D&H Railroad timetable of June 21, 1908, also indicates connections only to Ausable Chasm, five of them daily each way and 3 on Sunday. Two of the seven round trips daily were to meet boats only, as was in 1916, and also probably in 1912.

There are several photos available on the KAC&LC Railroad. Gardner (1975, p. 11) depicts two scenes of the 158-foot-high cantilever bridge over the Ausable Chasm. The first shows a Mogul No. 1 with a sloping-rear tender pulling (backwards) a single open-vestibule combine. The second shows another steam locomotive (with tender as a single unit) pulling a short mixed train. On page 203 of Shaughnessy (1967), is a close up of No. 1 at The D&H Railroad Colonie shops for repairs in 1913.

Part III — Lake Champlain And Moriah

This 7.66-mile long mining line joined what is now The D&H Railroad mainline at Port Henry and ascended nearly 1400 feet towards Moriah Center and Mineville to serve several iron mines. The D&H Railroad 1973 Map says that the opening date is *ca.* 1870. The Annual Report of the New York State Board of Railroad Commissioners (1893, p. 305) states that the line was chartered on December 4, 1867, and offers details on the equipment, income and expenses; the steepest grades were 250 feet to the mile (fortunately, the ore cars loaded went down!). Passenger service in 1892 existed, but I have never seen a timetable.

The Whitehall and Plattsburgh Railroad was chartered in 1866, and was built northward from Ticonderoga toward Port Henry beginning in 1868 (Shaughnessy, 1967, pp. 139 and 164), reaching Port Henry in 1870. The Lake Champlain and Moriah Railroad must have connected with it almost immediately, if both railroads were opened in 1870.

Oddly enough, the first through train from Whitehall to Port Henry did not occur until November 30, 1874 (Shaughnessy, 1967, p. 147 since the Whitehall-Ticonderoga section was built several years later than the Ticonderoga-Port Henry section! The Whitehall and Plattsburgh Railroad merged with the Montreal and Plattsburgh Railroad on February 25, 1873 (Shaughnessy, p. 144), becoming The New York and Canada Railroad Company. The NY&C built the Whitehall-Ticonderoga segment, and soon was merged under the parent company, The Delaware and Hudson Railroad.

The Witherbee Sherman Corporation had developed the mines about 1880, according to Hyde (1974, p. 154), and built the last blast furnaces at Port Henry; pig iron was shipped to Troy by rail and barge. The Republic Steel Corporation bought the operation in the late 1930s. The D&H Railroad 1973 Map notes that the segment from Port Henry to Switchback (Moriah Center) was purchased in 1972, but it is difficult to determine whether the purchase was *by* or *from* The D&H Railroad; for the segment from Switchback to Mill Number 7, The D&H Railroad obtained trackage rights in 1972 from Republic Steel Corportion.

I have not yet come across photographs or descriptions of the railroading operations from Port Henry to the mines.

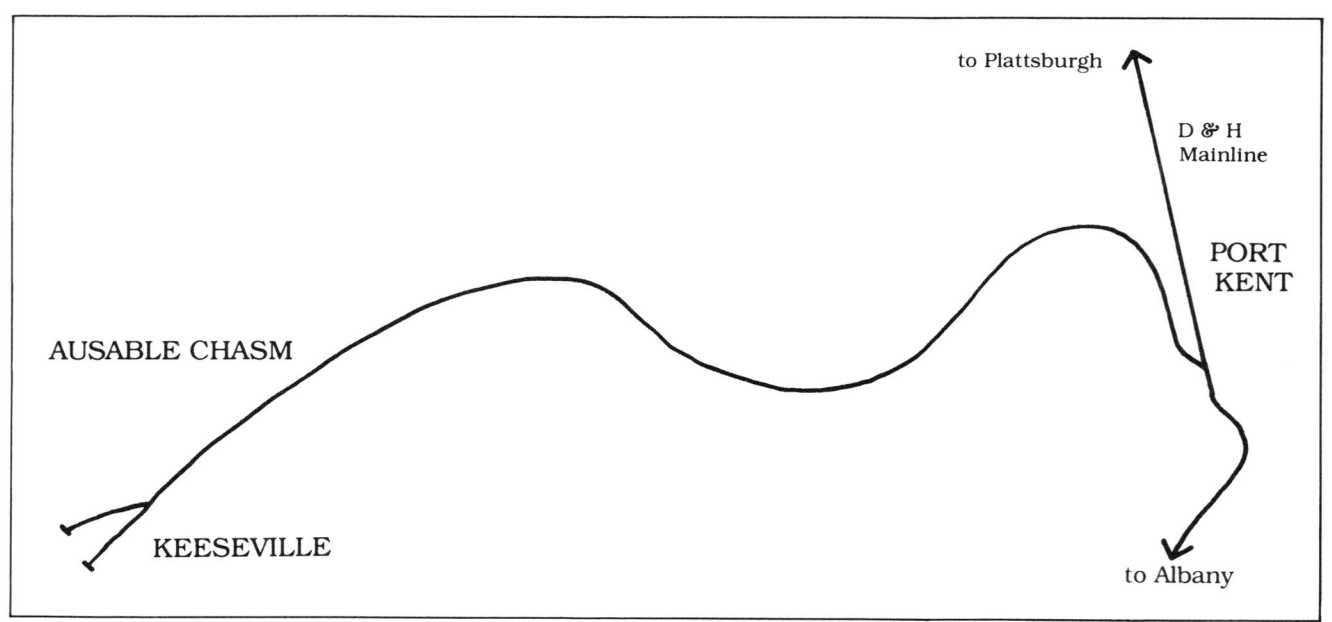

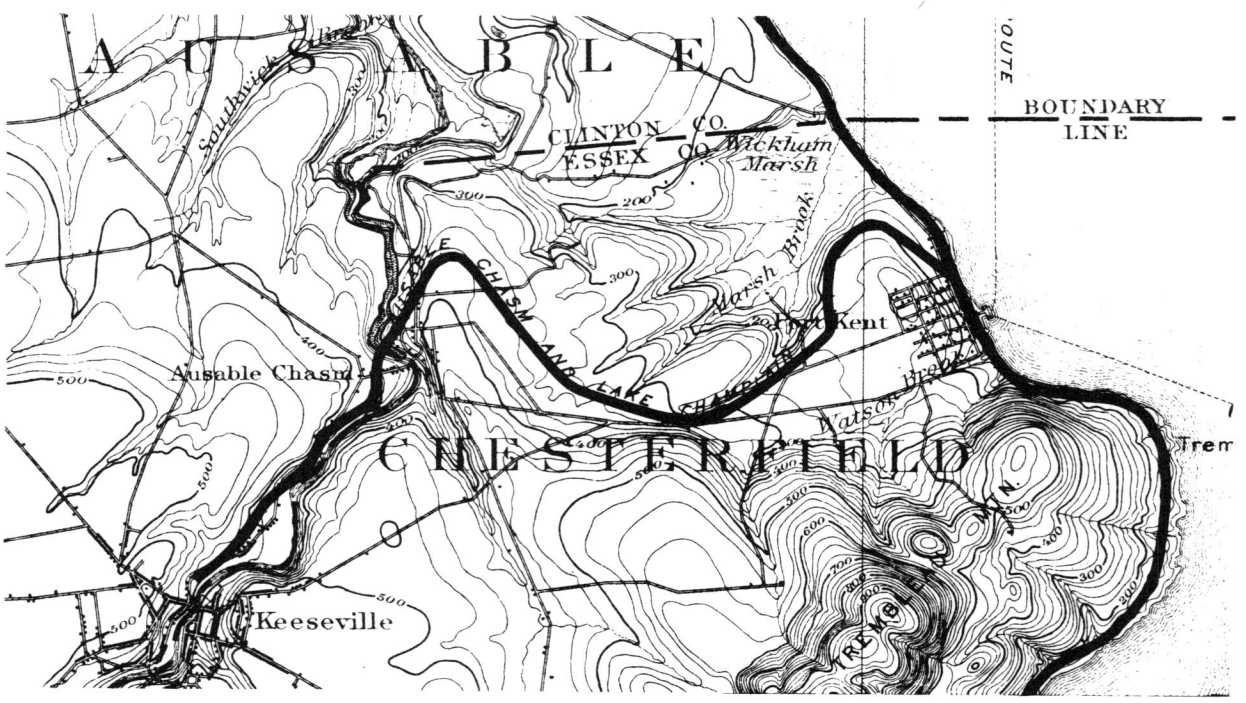

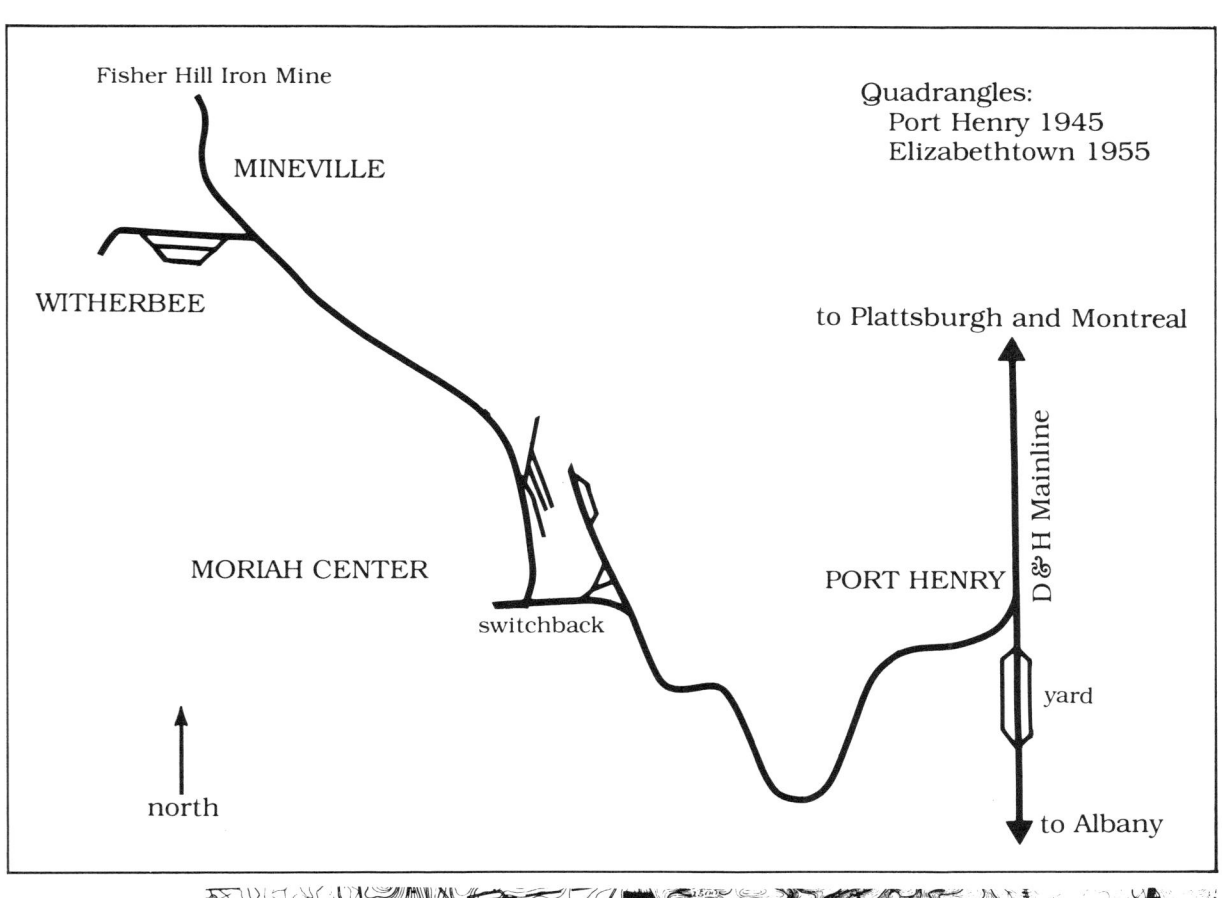

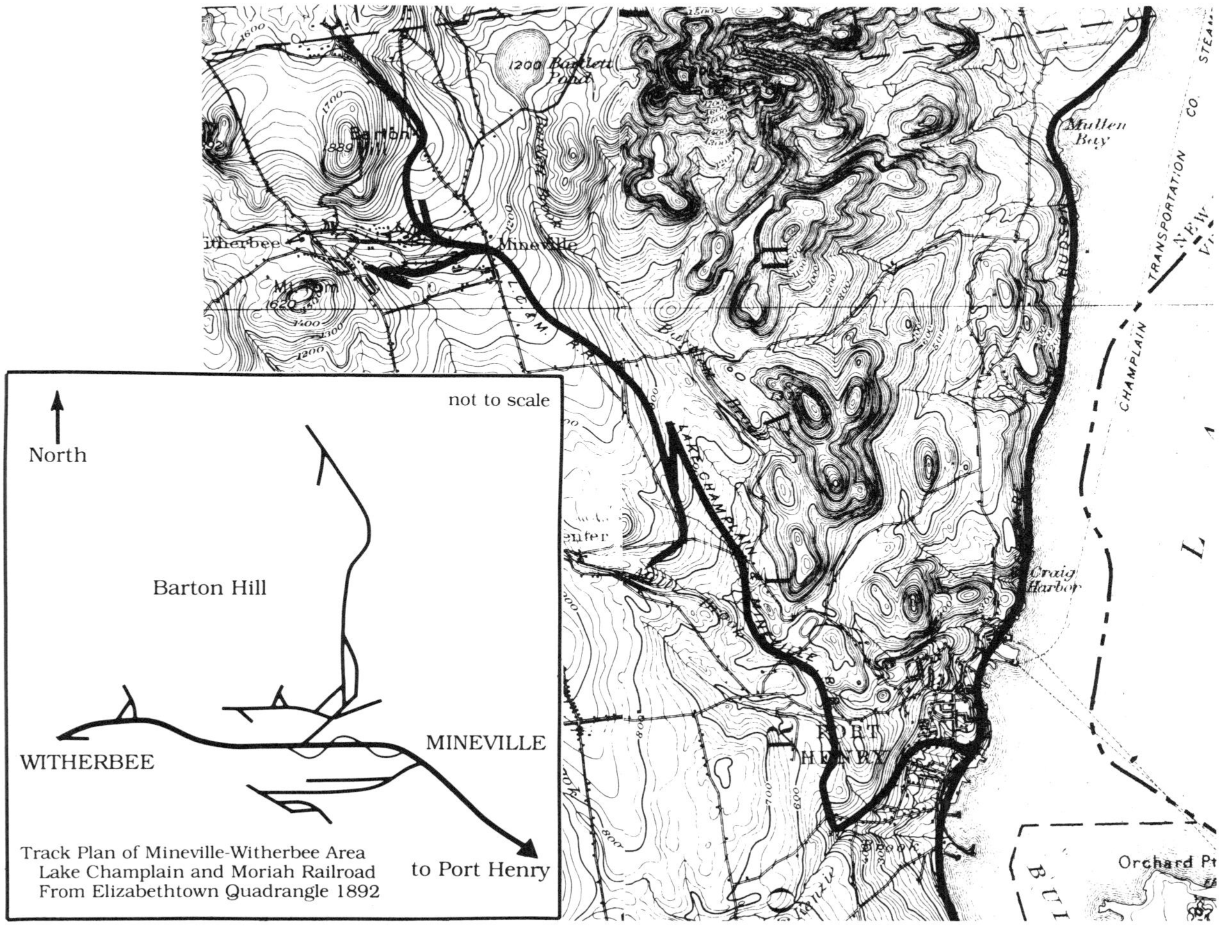

Fisher Hill Iron Mine
MINEVILLE
WITHERBEE
Quadrangles:
Port Henry 1945
Elizabethtown 1955
to Plattsburgh and Montreal
D&H Mainline
MORIAH CENTER
switchback
PORT HENRY
yard
north
to Albany

Mullen Bay
CHAMPLAIN TRANSPORTATION CO.
Craig Harbor
Orchard Pt
North
not to scale
Barton Hill
WITHERBEE
MINEVILLE
to Port Henry

Track Plan of Mineville-Witherbee Area
Lake Champlain and Moriah Railroad
From Elizabethtown Quadrangle 1892

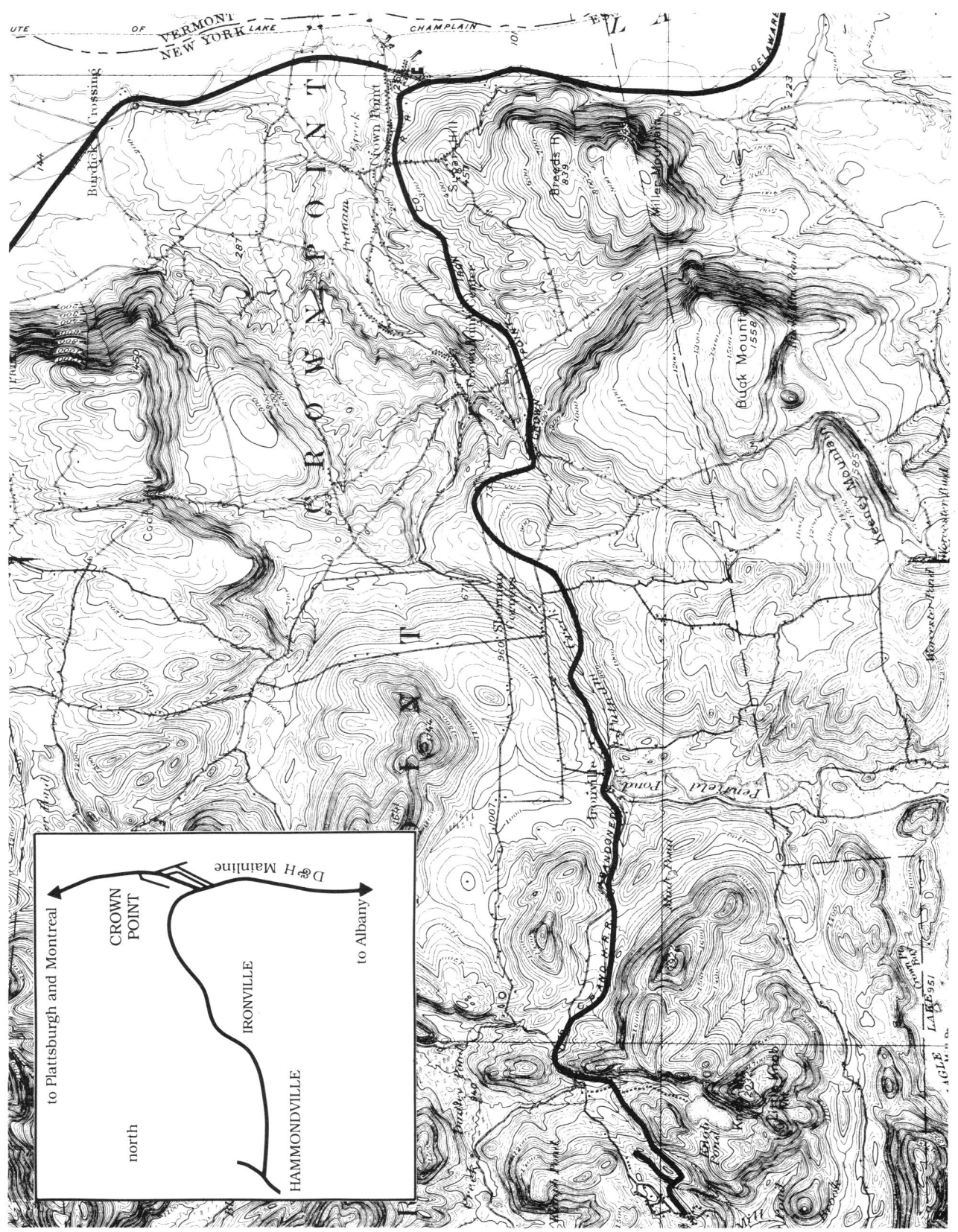

Palmer (1979) notes that the Lake Champlain and Moriah Railroad closed in 1968. Moravek (1981) offers that the mines closed in 1971. Hyde (1974, p. 154) says that the mining "operation is now shut down, but that the pumps which keep water from flooding the mines are kept running, with the thought that operations may possibly be resumed at some future date". This has not happened as of 1984.

Part IV — Crown Point Iron Company's Railroad

Unlike the previously discussed branches off The D&H Railroad mainline, much detail and a considerable number of photographs are available concerning this short line. The information summarized below comes primarily from Allen (1973), although Shaughnessy (1967) and Hyde (1974) also discuss the Crown Point Iron Company. The purpose of this railroad was to connect the iron mines at Hammondville and the separator forges at Ironville (Irondale) with the blast furnaces at Crown Point on Lake Champlain. Surveying occurred during the winter of 1872-1873, with construction in 1873, and service beginning in January, 1874. The whole line, with thirteen miles of main track and an additional seven of sidings and spurs, was three foot narrow gauge. Hence, interchange with The D&H Railroad at Crown Point was impossible, although dual-gauge tracks served the blast furnaces and yards.

A 1300 foot elevation change existed between Crown Point and the summit west of Ironville (milepost 8), a grade approximately as steep as the Moriah and Lake Champlain's. Over the twenty year life of the line, some four 2-6-0 Mogul locomotives were in service plus a standard-gauge 0-4-0 switcher in the Crown Point Yard. Allen (1973) informs us that there were about one hundred four-wheel single-truck ore cars, one combine, two cabooses, three boxcars, six flat cars, and three tool cars. Fortunately, the uphill runs were with empty ore cars! The line closed in July and August of 1893, partly due to the opening of the Mesabi Iron Range in Minnesota, which caused the decline of nearly all Adirondack mines.

Allen (1973) presents eleven photos of the Crown Point Railroad, Hyde (1974) has one, Mohr (1974) has one, and Shaughnessy (1967) has seven. Some of the photos occur in more than one publication.

A description, quite detailed, of the abandoned Crown Point Line will be found in the Inventory of Abandoned Railroad Rights of Way, published by the New York State Department of Transportation's Real Property Division in 1974.

Part V — The Adirondac(k) Company's Railroad to North Creek

Construction:

Much detail on this line is presented in Hochschild (1961) and Shaughnessy (1967, Chapter 6, pp. 114–133). It was the first railroad to penetrate to the interior of the Adirondack Mountains, construction having begun in 1865. One aim was to serve the iron mines at Sanford Lake (first realized in 1944!) and another to cross the Adirondacks to connect with the Great Lakes shipping at Ogdensburg. By December 1, 1865 (Hochschild), trains terminated at Wolf Creek, Thurman in 1869, Riverside in 1870, while it was not until early 1871 that the first trains arrived in North Creek (Shaughnessy, pp. 121 & 296). One part of the Adirondack Company's contract was for completion of sixty miles of track from Saratoga Springs, where the line originated. North Creek was at 57.2 miles, so that a 2.8-mile long extension was built past North Creek station and not used (until 1944!). The leading figure in the construction of this line was Dr. Thomas C. Durant; he was to the North Creek Line as Hurd was to The New York and Ottawa Railroad and Webb was to The New York Central Railroad's Adirondack Division.

In 1889 the Adirondack Company's Railroad was sold to The D&H Railroad (Hochschild, 1961, p. 12). In 1959, The D&H Railroad mainline was rerouted from downtown Saratoga Springs to the west edge of the City, thus shortening the North Creek Branch by about 0.6 mile; note the list of stations below and the mileage changes over time because of this relocation. Some of the minor mileage discrepancies might be due to station relocations, and possibly to straightening of curves, but this is only conjecture.

Saratoga Springs Junction, *0.0 mile, Elevation 300 feet.*

The Adirondack Company's Railroad shared the depot with the Rensselaer and Saratoga Railroad (later part of The D&H Railroad mainline). Station and junction were relocated in 1959. Photos occur in Shaughnessy, pages 114, 119, 361, 399, and 408 (1967).

AD Cabin, *1.1 miles in 1969.*

This point appears on the 1969 D&H Railroad Employees' timetable.

Greenfield, *6 or 7 miles in 1875. Elevation 600.*

This was a station from 1875 or earlier

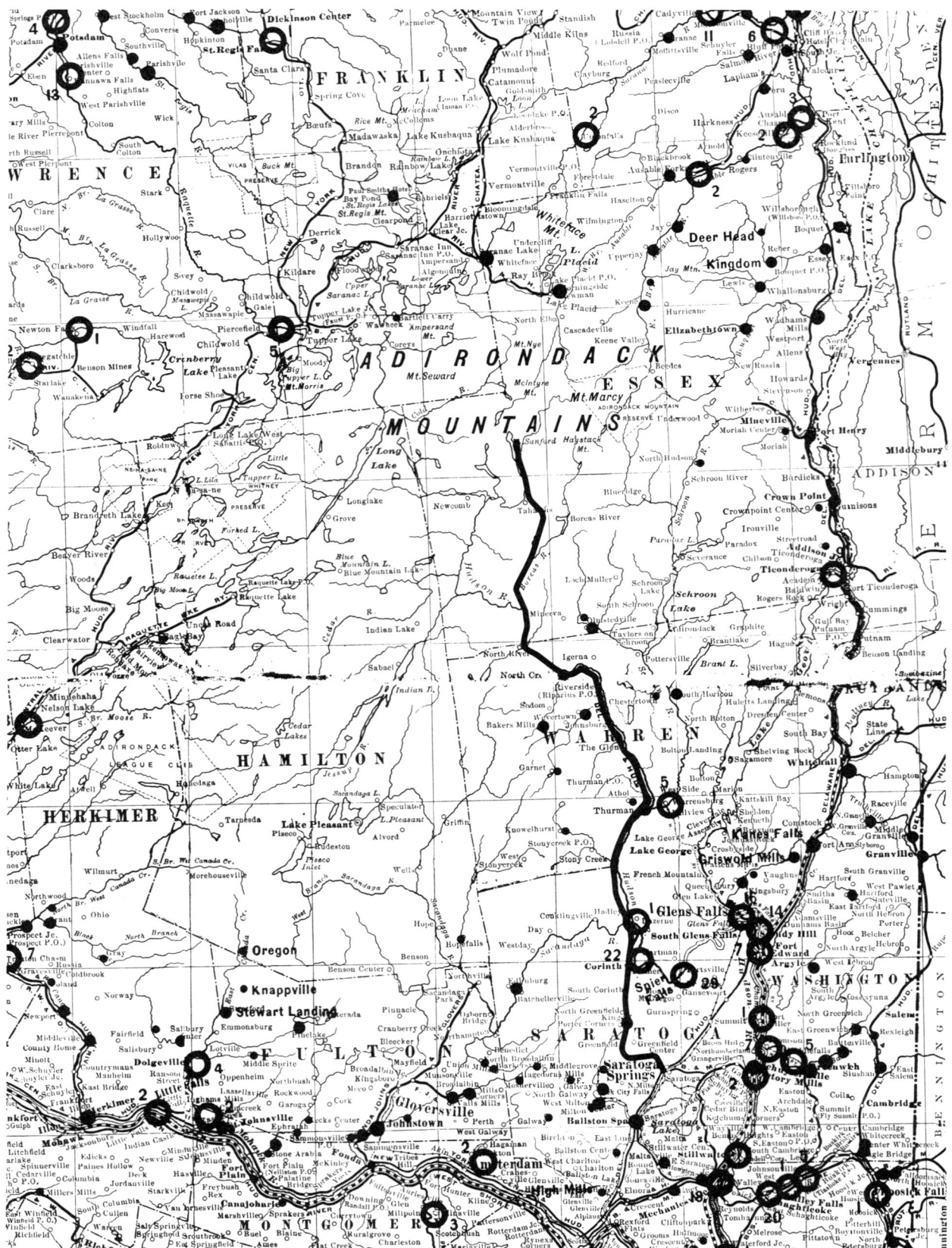

56

through at least 1927. It was no longer a stop in 1933.

Kings, *10 miles in 1875, 9.2 miles in 1969. Elevation 600.*

This was a station from 1875 or earlier through at least 1927, but no longer a station in 1933.

South Corinth, *13 miles in 1875, 12.4 miles in 1969. Elevation 620.*

This was a station from 1875 or earlier through at least 1933, but no longer a station in 1943. Trains met here in 1875, 1888, 1908, and 1912, requiring a passing siding.

Corinth (Jessup's Landing), *17 miles in 1875, 16.3 miles in 1969. Elevation 641.*

This was a station from 1875 or earlier through 1948 and probably later. It was originally called Jessup's Landing in 1890, but Corinth in 1896. There was a siding here in 1871 (Shaughnessy, 1967, p. 122) and a photo appears in the same reference on page 397.

Hadley (Lake Luzerne), *22 miles in 1875, 21.3 miles in 1969. Elevation 640.*

This was a station from 1875 or earlier through 1948 and probably later. Photos in Shaughnessy, 1967 (pp. 128, 130, and 354) are of the high truss bridge over the Sacandaga River just south of the station. The siding at the station, shown in Shaughnessy, (p. 131) was used in 1875 for meets. The 1900–1903 Luzerne Quadrangle indicates a two-track spur at Hadley, heading down toward a dam on the Hudson River just above its confluence with the Sacandaga River.

In 1875, there were stagecoach connections for Conklingville and the Sacandaga Valley, and omnibuses for the hotels at Luzerne. In 1912, there was an auto stage for Conklingville, Day, West Day, Edinburgh, and Batchellerville.

Quarry Switch (Wolf Creek), *25 miles in 1875. Elevation 630.*

Trains met here in 1888, requiring a passing siding. Wolf Creek Station, operating in 1912, 1916, and in 1927 was either here or nearby.

Stony Creek, *30 miles in 1875, 28.9 miles in 1969. Elevation 604.*

This was a station from 1875 or earlier through 1948 or later. Photos in Shaughnessy (1967) on page 128 show station and siding, and on page 131 the bridge over Stony Creek. Trains met here in 1875.

Warrensburg Junction, *34.4 miles in 1969. Elevation 618.*

The 3.5-mile-long spur from here to Warrensburg was built in 1905 (Shaughnessy, 1967, p. 226).

Thurman, *36 miles in 1875, 34.6 miles in 1969. Elevation 618.*

This was a station from 1875 or earlier through 1948 or later. A photo of the station and siding appears in Shaughnessy (1967, p. 132). Trains met here in 1908 and 1912. Stages in 1875 departed for Warrensburg and coaches for Lake George. In 1912, a stage met trains for Warrensburg and another for Athol.

The Glen (Friends Lake), *44 miles in 1875, 42.9 miles in 1969. Elevation 749.*

This was a station from 1875 or earlier through 1948 or later. Trains met here in 1875 and in 1948 requiring a passing siding. This siding is shown in Shaughnessy (1967, p. 132); other photos of nearby sites are on pages 126 and 133. In 1912, carriages left The Glen for Friends Lake.

Washburn's Eddy.

This was never a station but appeared on a map in Hochschild (1961, p. 7) dated to 1882.

Riverside (Riparius Station), *50 miles in 1875, 48.9 miles in 1969. Elevation 885.*

This was a station from 1875 or earlier through 1948 or later. A photo of the station and siding occurs in Shaughnessy (1967, p. 126). In 1875, coaches met trains for Chestertown, Pottersville, and the steamboats on Schroon Lake; stages met trains for Weavertown and Johnsburgh. In 1888, Tally-Ho coaches departed for Schroon Lake and Pottersville. In 1908, stages met trains for Schroon Lake. In 1912, one stage headed for Pottersville and Schroon Lake, a second headed for Chestertown, Horicon, and Brant Lake, and a third headed for Johnsburgh.

North Creek, *57.2 miles in 1875, 56.5 miles in 1969. Elevation 1028.*

This was a station from early 1871 until cessation of passenger service in 1956. Photos in Shaughnessy (1967) showing the station and yard appear on pages 121, 133, 196, 312, 314, and 418. Theodore Roosevelt here became the 26th President of the United States on September 14, 1901 (Shaughnessy, pp. 196 and 199); an exhibit of this event occurs as a scale model at the Adirondack Museum at Blue Mountain Lake. The pages

312 and 314 photos in Shaughnessy depict special ski trains, begun in March of 1934 by The D&H Railroad, at North Creek near the New York State ski center at Gore Mountain. A photo or North Creek station also occurs in Hochschild (1961, p. 10). Miller (1956) presents a photo near North Creek.

Stagecoach connections here were numerous. In 1875, stages departed for Minerva, North River, Indian River (Jacksons), and Cedar River Falls (Wakely's). Conveyances operated from Indian Lake to Blue Mountain Lake, and from Minerva to Newcomb, Long Lake, and Tahawus. In 1888, Tally-Ho coaches ran to Blue Mountain Lake with additional stage and boat connections there. In 1908, stages ran to Blue Mountain Lake. In 1912, stages departed for North River, Indian Lake, and Blue Mountain Lake to Long Lake; stages also ran to Olmsteadville, Minerva, Alden Lair, and Newcomb.

"Milepost 60", *Elevation 1037.*

Here, 2.8 miles beyond North Creek (measured in 1871), the track terminated from 1871 through 1944 — in the middle of nowhere! When the line was built from Saratoga Springs in the late 1860s, the contract specified a line precisely 60 miles long.

Boreas River Gorge.

A photo appears in Shaughnessy (1967) on page 354.

Sanford Lake (Tahawus), *90 miles in 1969. Elevation 1740.*

The National Lead Company and the Defense Plant Corporation (a federal agency) began constructing an extension out of North Creek in 1941–1942. The first train to reach the ilmenite (titanium ore) mines at Sanford Lake was on June 19, 1944 (Shaughnessy, 1967, pp. 296, 353–355 with photos), pulled by a diesel. The extension totalled about 33 miles, and the line to these mines still runs in 1984.

The *New York State Conservationist* in 1972 reported that the New York State Department of Environmental Conservation protested the sale of the line from North Creek to Sanford Lake; the protest postponed the sale from the Federal Government to the National Lead Company.

References on the geology of these mines include Stephenson (1945), Hochschild (1962, "The MacIntyre Mine —"), Hyde (1974, pp. 173–176, 193–196), and Jensen (1978, pp. 41 and 108).

Timetable Operation

In 1875, June 28, there were two trains each way daily accommodating passengers, one of them also carrying mail. A freight ran three round trips weekly between Saratoga Springs and North Creek.

An 1885 timetable in Hochschild (1961, p. 11) indicates two southbound passenger trains daily out of North Creek; obviously not all of this table is shown.

On June 25, 1888 (Gardner, 1975, p. 21), there were two round trips daily (one on Sunday), one of these carrying mail. A third round trip was put on beginning July 3 for the peak of the summer season. Meets were required.

As of October 5, 1890, there were two round trips daily. A single train was needed so that there were no meets between passenger trains as had occurred earlier. On October 3, 1896, service was very much like that of 1890, without Sunday trains.

On June 21, 1908, there were two round trips daily, but a third trip was added beginning July 6 for the summer season. Meets between passenger trains were then required. Only one train round trip ran on Sunday. As of August 27, 1912, three round trips with meets operated daily and one round trip on Sunday.

The schedule was such on September 24, 1916 (Gardner, 1975, p. 81) that a single train could make two round trips daily (none on Sunday) originating at North Creek. This type of operation was still extant on October 1, 1927.

In April 1933, January 1943, December 1947, and September 1948 there was one round trip daily (none on Sunday) originating at North Creek. But, during the summer of 1948, two trains were run daily (one on Sunday) to accommodate the seasonal crowds. Hochschild (1961, p. 8) notes that passenger service had run through the summer of 1956, and on a summer-only basis for the last several years.

One-way running times between Saratoga Springs and North Creek varied from two hours and forty-five minutes in 1875, to 2.5 hours in 1888, to about two hours from 1896 through 1948. In 1943, the shortest run was one hour and fifty minutes.

Equipment

Passenger locomotives were 4-4-0 Standard engines; abundant photographs occur in Hochschild (1961) and Shaughnessy (1967). Freight was hauled by Moguls. Later, after The D&H Railroad takeover, passenger locomotives were 4-6-0s (Ten Wheelers), with a photo of one appearing in Shaughnessy, page 397. In 1944, when the line to Tahawus opened, the first D&H Railroad diesels, Alco RS-2s, pulled the ore trains (Shaughnessy, pp. 354, 355).

Passenger cars of the Adirondack Company's Railroad consisted of an assortment of coaches, baggage-mail cars, and combines, well-documented in the Shaughnessy photos. As early as 1888 (Gardner, 1975, p. 22), drawing room cars and through sleeping cars from New York City were headed for North Creek. In 1908, parlor and sleeping cars were still running in the summers.

Shaughnessy (p. 125) describes the kind of traffic on the North Creek line: passengers were mainly headed to and from hotels, summer cottages, and children's camps. Freight included lumber, paper, tanned hides and tanbark, mineral products, and coal. After The D&H Railroad took over the line, typical D&H Railroad mainline cars and locomotives operated to North Creek.

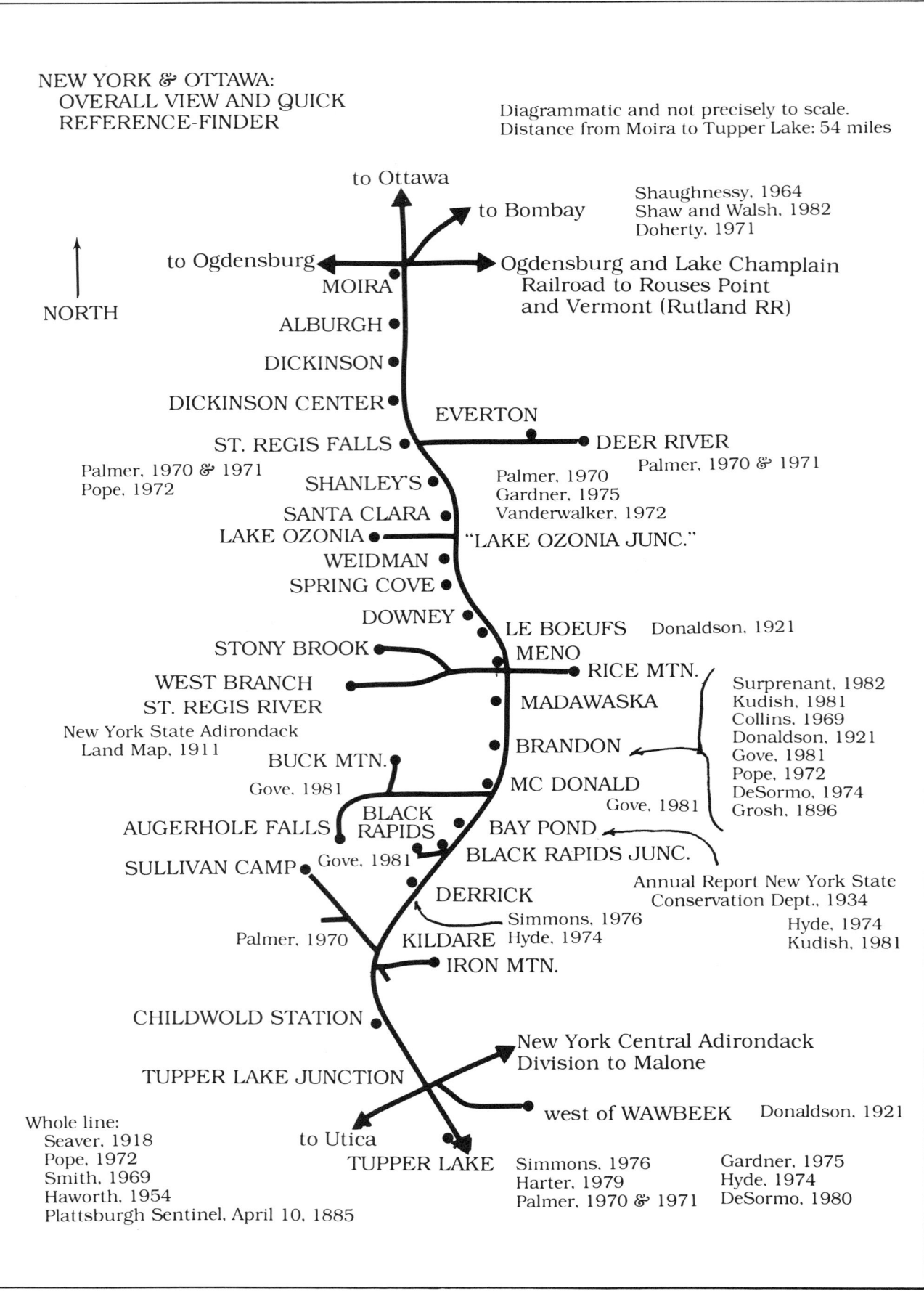

NEW YORK & OTTAWA:
OVERALL VIEW AND QUICK
REFERENCE-FINDER

Diagrammatic and not precisely to scale.
Distance from Moira to Tupper Lake: 54 miles

to Ottawa

to Bombay

Shaughnessy, 1964
Shaw and Walsh, 1982
Doherty, 1971

to Ogdensburg

NORTH

Ogdensburg and Lake Champlain
Railroad to Rouses Point
and Vermont (Rutland RR)

MOIRA

ALBURGH

DICKINSON

DICKINSON CENTER

EVERTON

ST. REGIS FALLS

DEER RIVER

Palmer, 1970 & 1971

Palmer, 1970 & 1971
Pope, 1972

SHANLEY'S

SANTA CLARA

LAKE OZONIA

"LAKE OZONIA JUNC."

Palmer, 1970
Gardner, 1975
Vanderwalker, 1972

WEIDMAN

SPRING COVE

DOWNEY

LE BOEUFS

Donaldson, 1921

STONY BROOK

MENO

RICE MTN.

WEST BRANCH
ST. REGIS RIVER

MADAWASKA

Surprenant, 1982
Kudish, 1981
Collins, 1969
Donaldson, 1921
Gove, 1981
Pope, 1972
DeSormo, 1974
Grosh, 1896

New York State Adirondack
Land Map, 1911

BRANDON

BUCK MTN.

MC DONALD

Gove, 1981

Gove, 1981

BLACK
RAPIDS

AUGERHOLE FALLS

BAY POND

SULLIVAN CAMP

Gove, 1981

BLACK RAPIDS JUNC.

Annual Report New York State
Conservation Dept., 1934

DERRICK

Simmons, 1976
Hyde, 1974

Hyde, 1974
Kudish, 1981

Palmer, 1970

KILDARE

IRON MTN.

CHILDWOLD STATION

New York Central Adirondack
Division to Malone

TUPPER LAKE JUNCTION

Whole line:
  Seaver, 1918
  Pope, 1972
  Smith, 1969
  Haworth, 1954
  Plattsburgh Sentinel, April 10, 1885

west of WAWBEEK

Donaldson, 1921

to Utica

TUPPER LAKE

Simmons, 1976
Harter, 1979
Palmer, 1970 & 1971

Gardner, 1975
Hyde, 1974
DeSormo, 1980

Chapter III

New York And Ottawa

"Adirondack Enterprises!
A New Route to the Wilderness!
Great Lumbering Industries!
The Boom that has Come to Brandon,
Brighton, and Waverly —
Will it be Permanent?

This newspaper quotation comes from the Plattsburgh *Sentinel* of April 10, 1885. John Hurd formed the Northern Adirondack Railroad Company on February 9, 1883 in order to timber the Adirondacks of Franklin County. Construction began on August 30, 1883 (Pope, 1972) at Moira, a station on The Ogdensburg and Lake Champlain (later part of The Rutland) Railroad. The new line was built to St. Regis Falls in late September, 1883, to Santa Clara in 1884, to Brandon in 1886, and terminated at Tupper Lake in late 1889.

On May 30, 1895, the Malone newspaper the *Palladium* stated that Hurd's bankruptcy forced him to sell the line (Pope, 1972). The railroad was reincorporated into The Northern New York Railroad; this was an unfortunate name, as The Ogdensburg and Lake Champlain Railroad had used the same name from 1848 to 1858. In 1897, the second Northern New York Railroad became the New York and Ottawa, as the line was extended northward from Moira toward the Canadian Capital. The bridge under construction over the St. Lawrence River at Cornwall collapsed on September 6, 1898, delaying the commencement of service to Ottawa until 1900. On December 12, 1906, The New York Central and Hudson River Railroad took over The New York and Ottawa Railroad, and the line became the Ottawa Division.

Service was suspended between Moira and Tupper Lake on May 6, 1937, (Doherty, 1971), and the rails and ties were removed in July of that year. The portion of the line from Helena (11 miles north of Moira) to Ottawa still operated one passenger train in each direction daily as late as April 25, 1948.

A description of the New York and Ottawa Railroad and its numerous logging branches will follow, on a station by station basis, beginning at Moira (milepost zero) and ending at Tupper Lake (milepost 54). In addition to the timber for the sawmills, Hurd's Railroad also carried hemlock bark (probably to the tannery at St. Regis Falls), cordwood to Montreal for fuel, and charcoal (Seaver, 1918, p. 535). Whereas Webb's Adirondack and St. Lawrence Railroad, built in 1892, cut a swath only 100 feet wide through the forest and was more tourist-oriented, Hurd's Railroad removed the forest along the right-of-way for several hundred feet on each side at least (Franklin County Historical Review, 1973, p. 57).

Station Descriptions

Moira, *0.0 miles. Elevation 370.*

It was from this point, on The Ogdensburg and Lake Champlain Railroad, where John Hurd began building his line southward in 1883.

Although The Ogdensburg and Lake Champlain Railroad lies outside the Adirondacks and thus is not included in this text, a brief chronology will be given here. Much information is available, the primary sources being Shaughnessy (1964), Doherty (1971), and Shaw and Walsh (1982). The O&LC was one of the first railroads to be built in northern New York, to connect the St. Lawrence River with Boston via northern New England.

1848–Northern New York Railroad construction began;

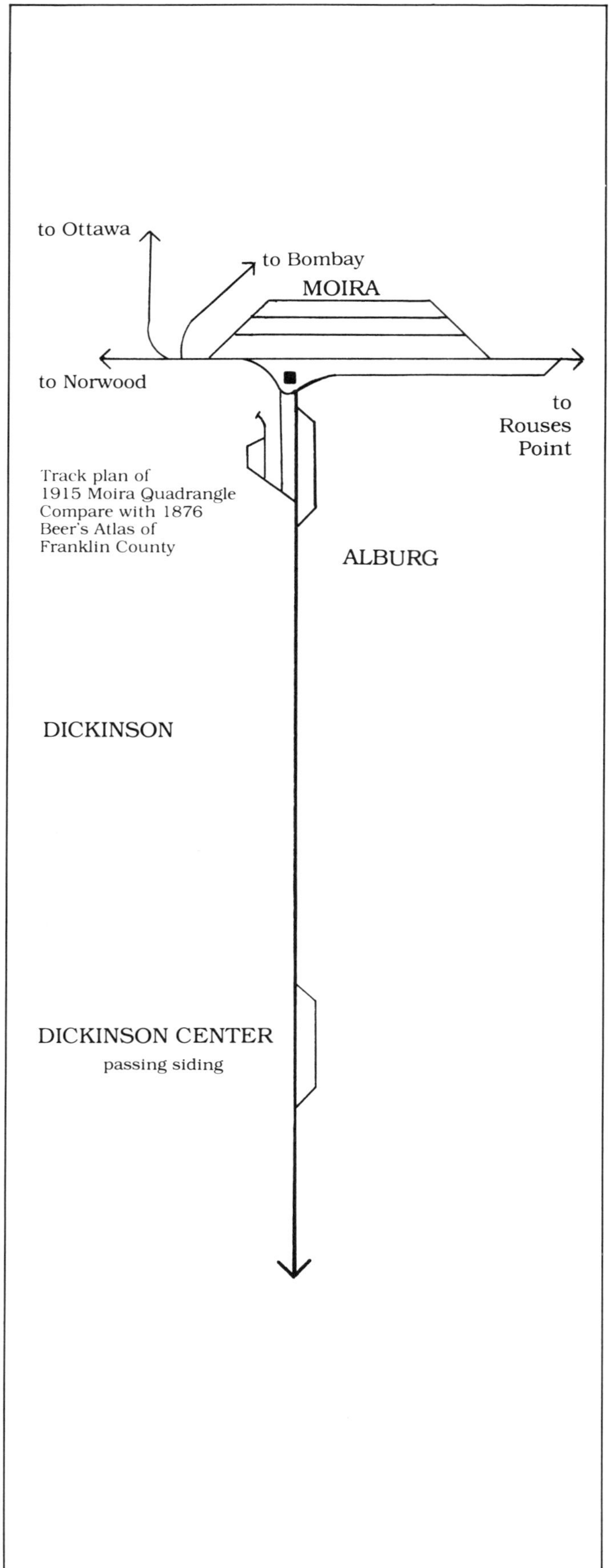

to Ottawa
to Bombay
MOIRA
to Norwood
to
Rouses
Point
Track plan of
1915 Moira Quadrangle
Compare with 1876
Beer's Atlas of
Franklin County
ALBURG
DICKINSON
DICKINSON CENTER
passing siding

Brushton
Moira
School No 5
Irish Corners
Alburg
East Dickinson
Potter School
Dickinson
Barnes Corners
Dickinson Center
School No 6

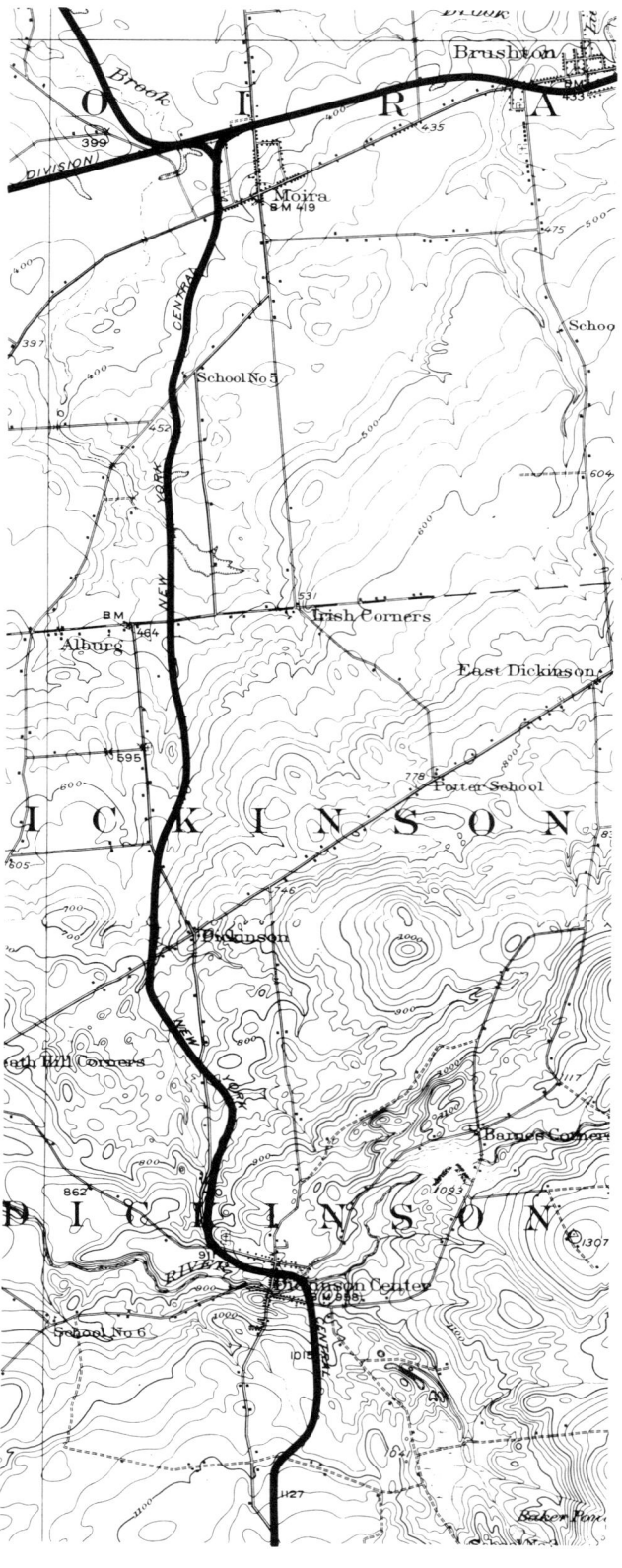

1850–first through train from Rouses Point on Lake Champlain to Ogdensburg on the St. Lawrence on September 20;

1858–Reorganization into The Ogdensburg Railroad;

1864–Reorganization into The Ogdensburg and Lake Champlain Railroad;

1870–Part of the Central Vermont System;

1898–Central Vermont System collapses on February 14;

1901–The O&LC Railroad becomes part of the The Rutland Railroad on September 27;

1953–Passenger service discontinued;

1963–Freight service discontinued.

Shaughnessy (1964), pages 59 through 68, offers much detail on The O&LC Railroad. The track plan on this page appears in Beer's 1876 Atlas of Franklin County, seven years before John Hurd started construction toward St. Regis Falls.

The track plan approximation is shown on the 1915 U.S.G.S. Moira Quadrangle (see page 131M), showing the junction between The O&LC Railroad and The New York & Ottawa Railroad. Both lines used the same station. The yards along The O&LC Railroad at Moira were about 0.5 mile long; the yard on The NY&O Railroad just south of the junction was about the same (0.5 mile) length. Haworth (1954) lists a roundhouse and a couple of saw mills at Moira.

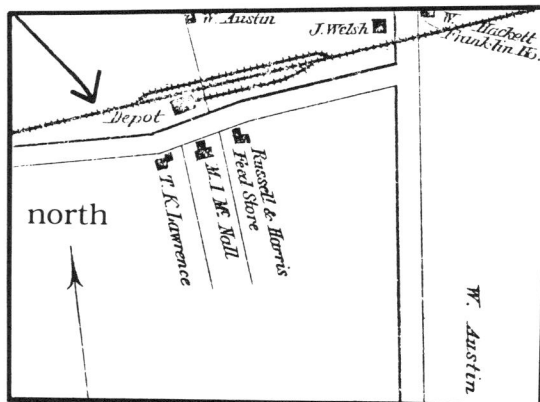

Moira in 1876, before construction of Hurd's Railroad. From Beers' Atlas of Franklin County. Note the Ogdensburg and Lake Champlain Railroad.

Alburgh, *3.2 miles. Elevation 490.*

This station is listed on a timetable of June 30, 1889.

Mosher (Dickinson), *5.5 miles. Elevation 690.*

This station is listed on timetables of August 10, 1896, and March 7, 1898.

Dickinson Center, *8.4 miles. Elevation 958.*

This station was in use throughout the life of the line. At least the timetables dated June 30, 1889 through June 28, 1936 list it. The 1919 U.S.G.S. Nicholville Quadrangle indicates a passing siding here 0.2 mile long. A photo of the Dickinson Center station with a train appears on the front cover of the Franklin Historical Review, Volume 6, 1969.

St. Regis Falls, *11.8 miles. Elevation 1256.*

St. Regis Falls was one of the largest forest product mill concentrations along The New York & Ottawa Railroad, with a variety of industries served by the railroad. A description of the first train into St. Regis Falls on September 25, 1883, rented from The Ogdensburg and Lake Champlain Railroad, will be found in Pope (1972). This train derailed!!

The 1919 Nicholville Quadrangle shows numerous sidings (see page 64), but it is difficult to determine from this Quadrangle which siding served which industry. A photo of the station is found in Palmer (1970) and of the yards (Palmer, 1971). The Nicholville Quadrangle also indicates a 0.35-mile long passing siding; this siding is verified by a timetable dated June 30, 1889, when two passenger trains, one northbound and the other southbound, met here. The yards at St. Regis Falls were, in total, according to the Quadrangle, 0.65 mile long.

The following industries at St. Regis Falls are listed as follows:

1. Several sawmills (at least some of which were bought by Hurd), a large tannery, and a box factory (Smith, 1969); a description in detail of a sawmill and box factory at St. Regis Falls will be found in the Plattsburgh *Sentinel,* April 10, 1885.
2. Freight house and Hotchkiss Lumber Company storehouse (Palmer, Feb. 1970).
3. Wooden two-stall engine house and a small repair shop until the large shops were completed in 1885 in Santa Clara (Palmer, 1970).
4. One sawmill was altered for making clapboards, lath, and broomsticks (Palmer, Feb. 1970).

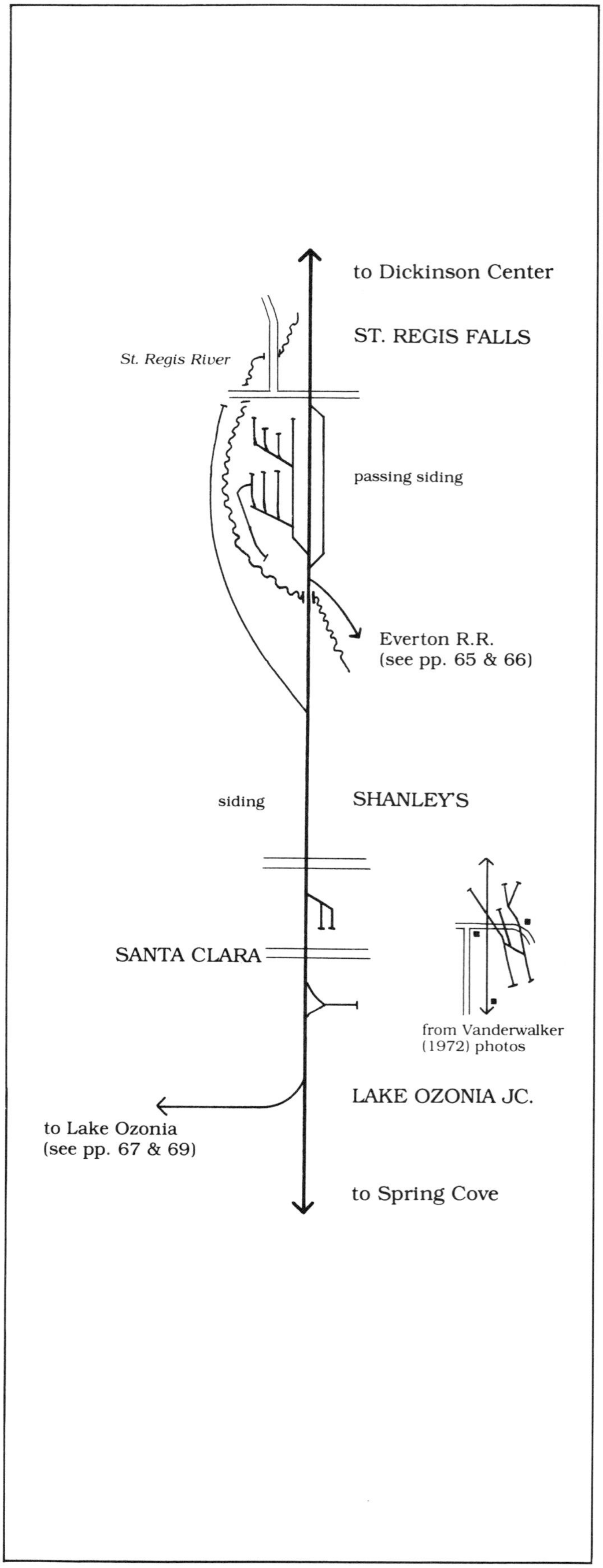

to Dickinson Center
ST. REGIS FALLS
St. Regis River
passing siding
Everton R.R.
(see pp. 65 & 66)
siding
SHANLEY'S
SANTA CLARA
from Vanderwalker
(1972) photos
LAKE OZONIA JC.
to Lake Ozonia
(see pp. 67 & 69)
to Spring Cove

St. Regis Falls
COOPERAGE
Palmer School
Little Clear Pond
Long Pond
Cheney Hill
Santa Clara
RIVER
Bearcove Hill
Alder

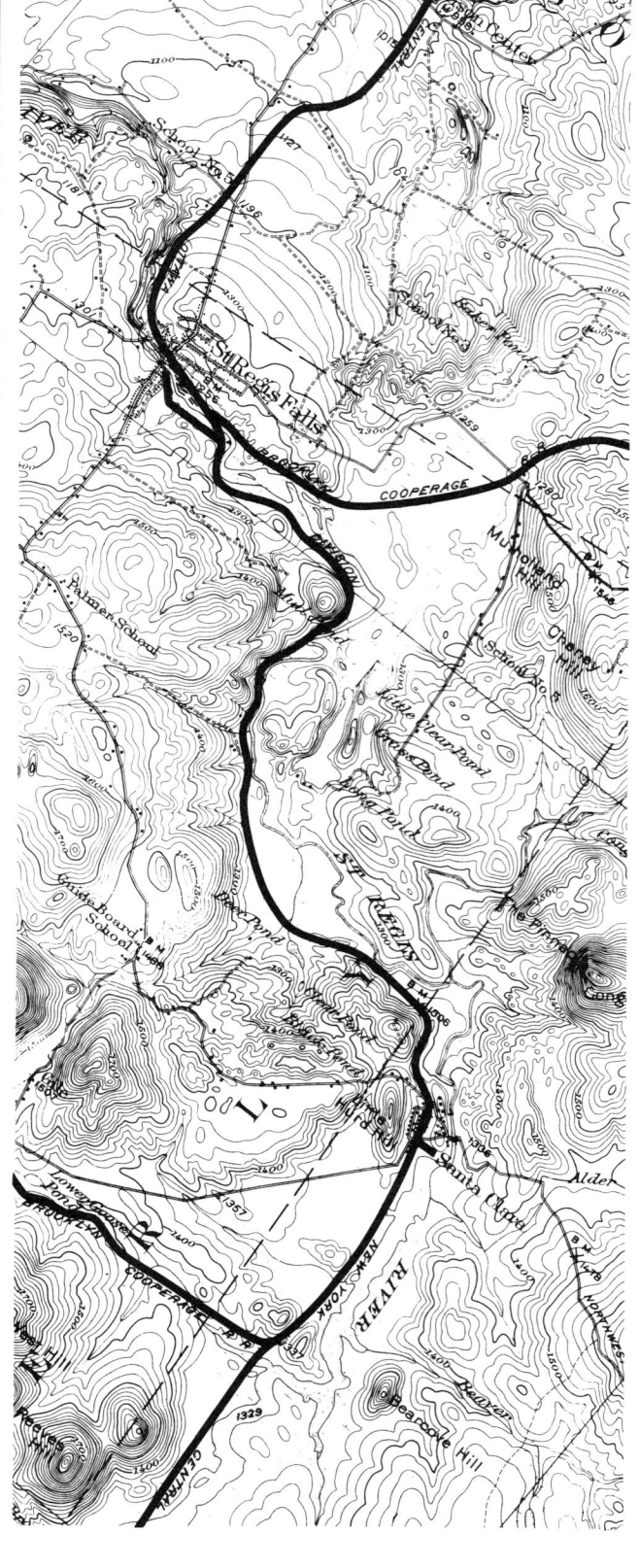

As of 1898, stagecoaches met the trains at St. Regis Falls for Lake Ozonia and Fernwood Hall. By 1909, Hotel Oneita had been added to the stagecoach schedules. The station was in service until abandonment, as the June 28, 1936 timetable still shows St. Regis Falls.

There is an air of mystery about the electric railway line which headed out of St. Regis Falls. At least, this writer has never seen any maps or photographs of the line, the only evidence being some notes (unpublished) of Palmer on file at the library of the Adirondack Museum at Blue Mountain Lake. Apparently, the Cascade Wood Products Company (Cascade Chair Company) built a five or six mile-long electric railway using two electric locomotives and thirteen cars to haul logs to St. Regis Falls. The Watson-Page Lumber Company later took over the line. No dates are given by Palmer, and somehow it is the impression of this writer that the line went to Lake Ozonia, but this is speculative.

Everton Railroad *(see map, page 66)*

Palmer (Feb. 1970) states that Macfarlane, Ross, and Stearns built, in 1886, a railroad from St. Regis Falls east six miles to Everton, where they had built two sawmills. The Malone *Palladium* of July 29, 1886 (page 2) confirms Everton Railroad construction as spring, 1886. Two years later, the line was sold to The Everton Railroad, which operated the mills and railroad only several more years — into the early or mid-1890s. The Everton Railroad is shown on the 1895 and 1898 Adirondack Land Maps published by the New York State Forest Commission. The March 7, 1898, New York and Ottawa timetable still lists connections with The Everton Railroad.

In 1904, Brooklyn Cooperage Company took over the abandoned Everton Railroad, but it is not clear in Palmer (1971) whether the tracks were still present or had to be relaid. Seaver (1918) does not offer a precise date for the Cooperage extension of the old Everton Railroad; perhaps the extension had been a gradual process over a number of years between 1904 and 1918. Seaver had predicted a closure of the Cooperage operation within a year or two of 1918, since most hardwood timber had been removed by then; the closure about 1920 is confirmed by Palmer (1970 and 1971).

The tracings of The Everton Railroad shown here are taken from two old 15-minute U.S.G.S Quadrangles, the 1919 Nicholville and the 1921 Santa Clara. Note the 0.2-mile long stub on the west bank of Pleasant Brook about 2 miles west of Everton. Also note that the Cooperage line terminated in 3 stubs at its east end along Deer River. The connection with The New York and Ottawa Railroad is at the east end of the yards at St. Regis Falls.

Shanleys, *15.0 miles. Elevation 1256.*

Shanleys is shown as a station on the early timetables (June 30, 1889, and August 10, 1896), but no longer on the March 7, 1898 timetable. The 1895 Adirondack Land Map also includes it, and Smith (1969) states that the Shanley and Alfred Lumber Company had mills there.

Santa Clara, *18.0 miles. Elevation 1330.*

In 1884, The NY&O Railroad reached Santa Clara, according to Palmer's notes; the shops and logging headquarters were moved here that year from St. Regis Falls. Palmer notes that by 1885, the line had been extended to a point eight miles south of St. Regis Falls (this would be equivalent to a point 1.8 miles south of Santa Clara), with another eight miles under construction. In other words, construction had reached beyond Meno by 1885.

A description of the construction and proposed construction as far as Brandon will be found in the Plattsburgh *Sentinel* of April 10, 1885. Much of the 75,000-acre Hurd and Hotchkiss tract south of St. Regis Falls (through Santa Clara) was still in first growth. The tract was about 13 miles wide around Santa Clara, and branch railroads were planned diverging 5 or 6 miles east and west to tap remoter areas near the borders of the tract. There is no evidence that these branches were ever built by Hurd and Hotchkiss, although Brooklyn Cooperage *did* build several in the Twentieth Century. Logs were to be skidded (dragged) by horses to railroad flat cars, rolled up onto the cars, transported by rail, and dumped into the river at Santa Clara, St. Regis Falls, or Everton. The minimum diameter for harvested trees was to be nine inches, with more than one-third of it pine, part birch and maple, and the remainder spruce.

In 1889, stagecoaches met the trains at Santa Clara for the Blue Mountain House Hotel, although Spring Cove became the stage connection site by 1896.

The track plan at Santa Clara is incompletely shown on the 1921 U.S.G.S. Santa Clara Quadrangle. Note the two stub sidings and the wye to turn engines and cars (map, page 64). A better reconstruction of the track plan is presented alongside of it (also on page 64), based on photos in Vanderwalker (1972) and Gardner (1975, page 10).

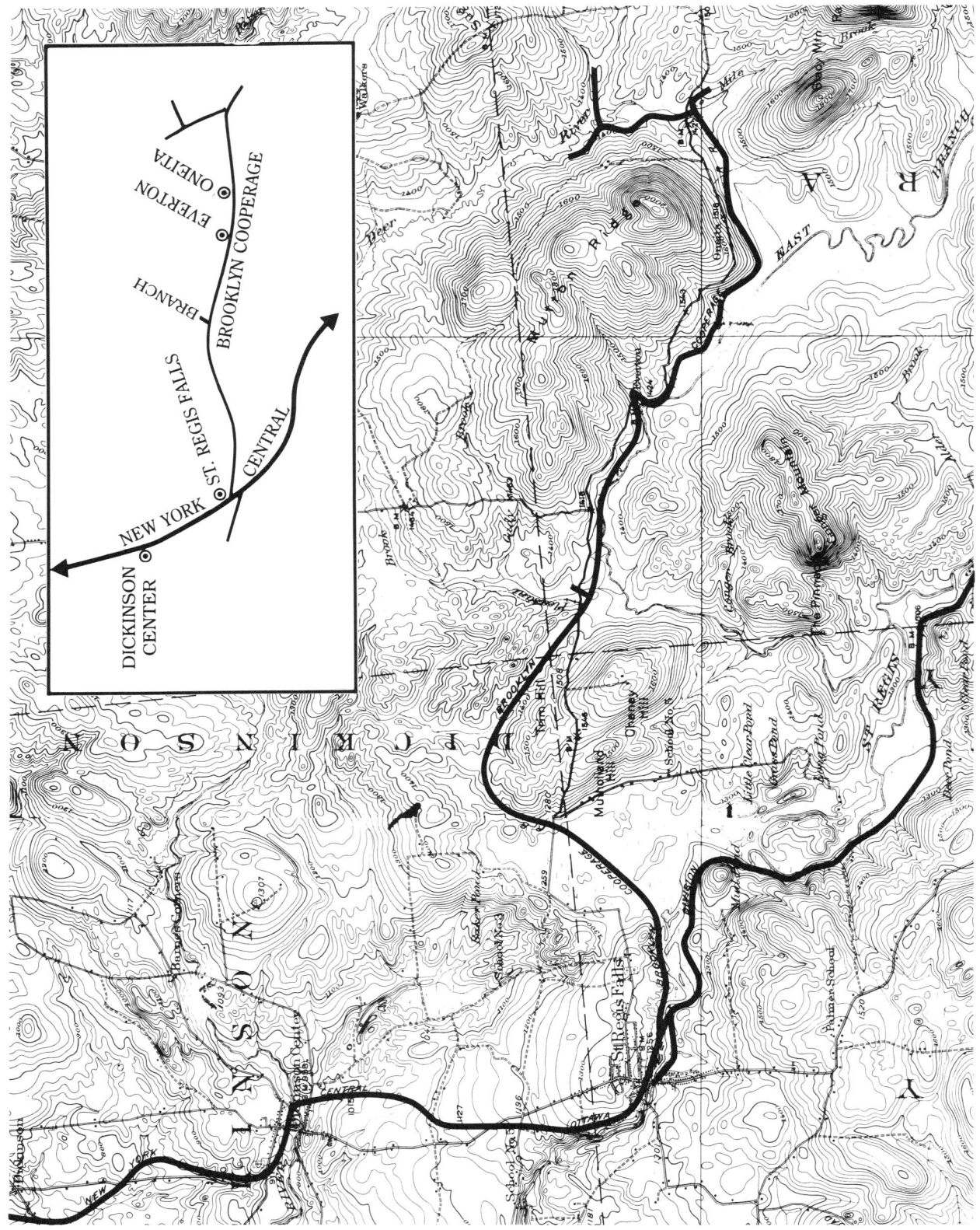

Santa Clara did not exist as a community until the railroad arrived. Here, Hurd established two sawmills, a chair factory, and a machine shop for the railroad (Seaver, 1918, p. 535); the shops burned in October, 1915 (Vanderwalker, 1972). Detailed descriptions of the two sawmills and railway station at Santa Clara will be found in the Plattsburgh *Sentinel* of April 10, 1885; shingles, lath, box stuff, broom handles, and pickets were being produced.

An interesting note in Seaver is that Hurd, along with former New York State Governor Alonzo B. Cornell, performed successful experiments in the Santa Clara shops in lighting passenger cars by electricity produced by the revolution of car wheels. When Hurd became bankrupt in 1895, the Brooklyn Cooperage Company acquired the mills at Santa Clara until they burned in November, 1903 (Seaver, 1918, p. 536).

The station at Santa Clara was still in service as late as June 28, 1936, and probably until abandonment the following May.

"Lake Ozonia Junction", *19.8 miles. Elevation 1337. Brooklyn Cooperage Line To Lake Ozonia*

The name "Lake Ozonia Junction" will not be found on any map nor on any timetable, as a station never existed here. I am introducing the name as a matter of convenience to label this junction, shown on the 1921 U.S.G.S. Santa Clara Quadrangle.

Palmer (1971) states that Brooklyn Cooperage built their line to Lake Ozonia from *Meno;* this must be an error, as the Lake Ozonia line joined the New York and Ottawa at a point only 1.8 miles south of Santa Clara.

The 1919 Nicholville and 1921 Santa Clara old U.S.G.S. 15-minute Quadrangles show the 8-mile long branch to Lake Ozonia (see map, page 69). Note five short stub tracks about midway along the branch and that the terminus at Lake Ozonia had four stub tracks. Palmer (1971) states that Brooklyn Cooperage pulled out of the Adirondacks about 1920, so that this Lake Ozonia branch, as well as the other Cooperage lines was abandoned about this time.

Weidman, *21.3 miles. Elevation 1334.*

Weidman is not listed on any timetable as a stop, but it is a place name on the 1920 and 1923 Adirondack Land Maps, published by the N.Y. State Conservation Commission.

Spring Cove, *22.2 miles. Elevation 1343.*

In 1896, 1989, and 1909, this was the Station for the stagecoach connection to the Blue Mountain House at the base of Azure Mountain. Spring Cove was already a station on the June 30, 1889 timetable, and existed as such through June 28, 1936 and probably through to abandonment a year later. Smith (1969) described charcoal kilns at Spring Cove where coke was made from hardwood timber and then shipped out by rail as fuel; a siding must have existed but its precise location has not been determined. Pope (1972) states that Hurd planned to build his line to Spring Cove by the winter of 1883–1884. A steep ascent then followed to:

Downey, *24.0 miles. Elevation 1520.*

The 1909 timetable lists this station.

LeBoeufs, *25.4 miles. Elevation 1590.*

Donaldson (1921, Volume II, pp. 137–140) states that this was the second point at which a railroad entered the Adirondack Park Blue Line; the first was the North Creek Branch of the Delaware and Hudson in 1871 (Hochschild, 1961). The Blue Line was located at LeBoeufs in 1886 when the NY&O arrived; today, the Blue Line is north of St. Regis Falls. A saw mill was established in 1886 along with the railroad. None of the timetables, however, list LeBoeufs as a station.

Meno, *27.0 miles. Elevation 1605.* **Brooklyn Cooperage Lines.**

Meno is listed as a station stop on the 1909 through 1936 timetables, but not on the earlier 1889, 1896, and 1898 timetables.

None of the U.S.G.S. Quadrangles shows the Brooklyn Cooperage branches out of Meno on The New York and Ottawa Railroad, but the 1911 and 1920 Adirondack Land Maps, published by the New York State Conservation Commission, do indicate two branches. These branches are reproduced here on page 72. One heads east out of Meno almost to the Town Line of Brighton, wrapping around the south and east base of Sugarloaf Mountain. The other heads west out of Meno, crosses the main branch of th St. Regis River, and ultimately follows Long Pond Outlet to the West Branch St. Regis River in St. Lawrence County. The 1909 Land Map does not yet show these branches.

I have tried on pages 70 and 71 to trace these two Cooperage branches on to the old 15-minute Santa Clara (1921) and Nicholville (1919) U.S.G.S. Quadrangles. The Quadrangles, as stated before, do not show the railroads, but there is some evidence on the maps to suggest trackage location. A trail is shown heading east out of Meno, for example, and terminating at Wolf Pond; this

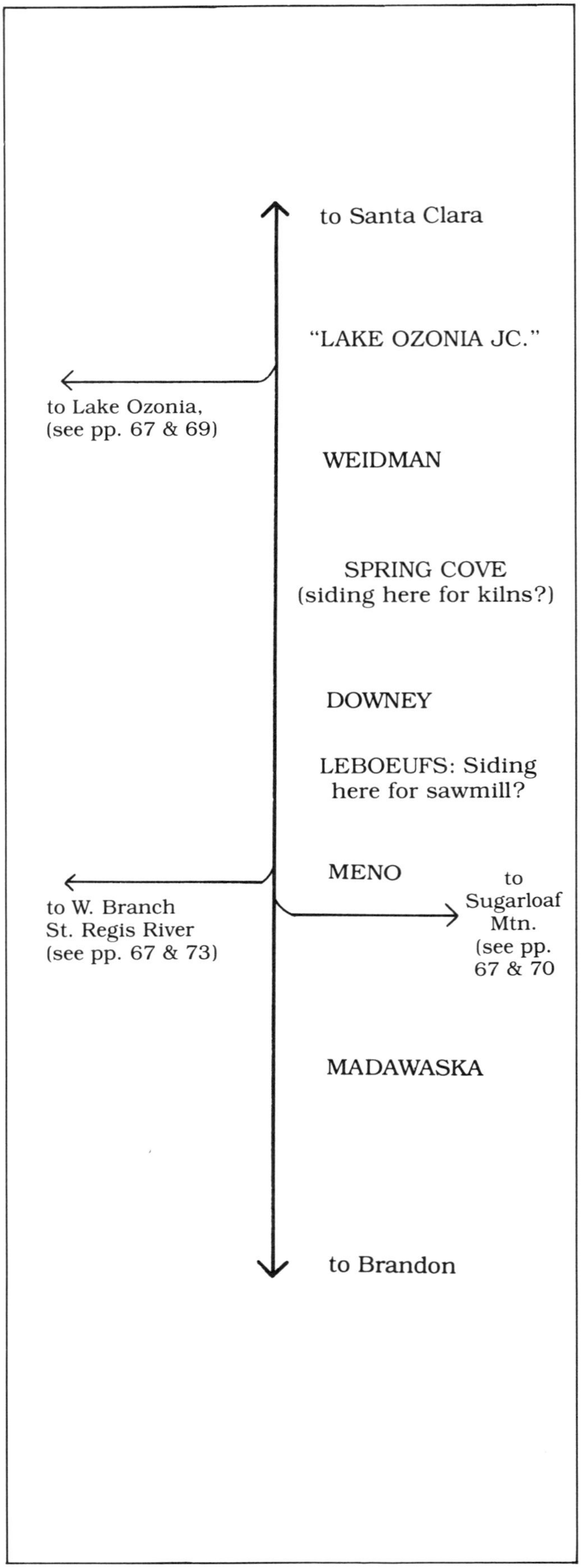

to Santa Clara
"LAKE OZONIA JC."
to Lake Ozonia, (see pp. 67 & 69)
WEIDMAN
SPRING COVE (siding here for kilns?)
DOWNEY
LEBOEUFS: Siding here for sawmill?
MENO
to W. Branch St. Regis River (see pp. 67 & 73)
to Sugarloaf Mtn. (see pp. 67 & 70
MADAWASKA
to Brandon

COOPERAGE R.R.
Bearcove Hill
West Hill
Reeves Hill
CENTRAL
Twin Brook
Spring Cove
Jennings Swamp
Downey
OTTAWA
Brook
Leboeuf Hill
Downey Hill
DIVISION
Hurd Hill
Grass Pond
Black Hill
Quebec
Meno
Madawaska
Madawaska Pond
Alder Bk.

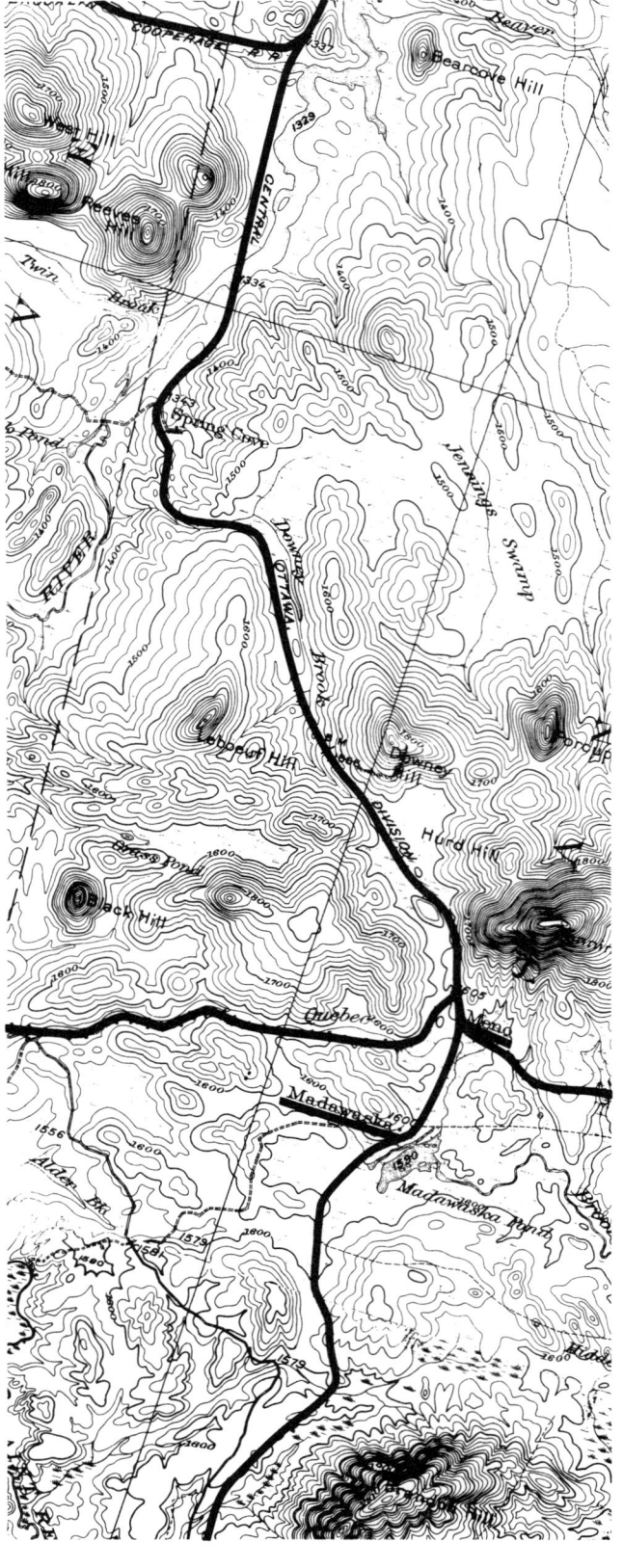

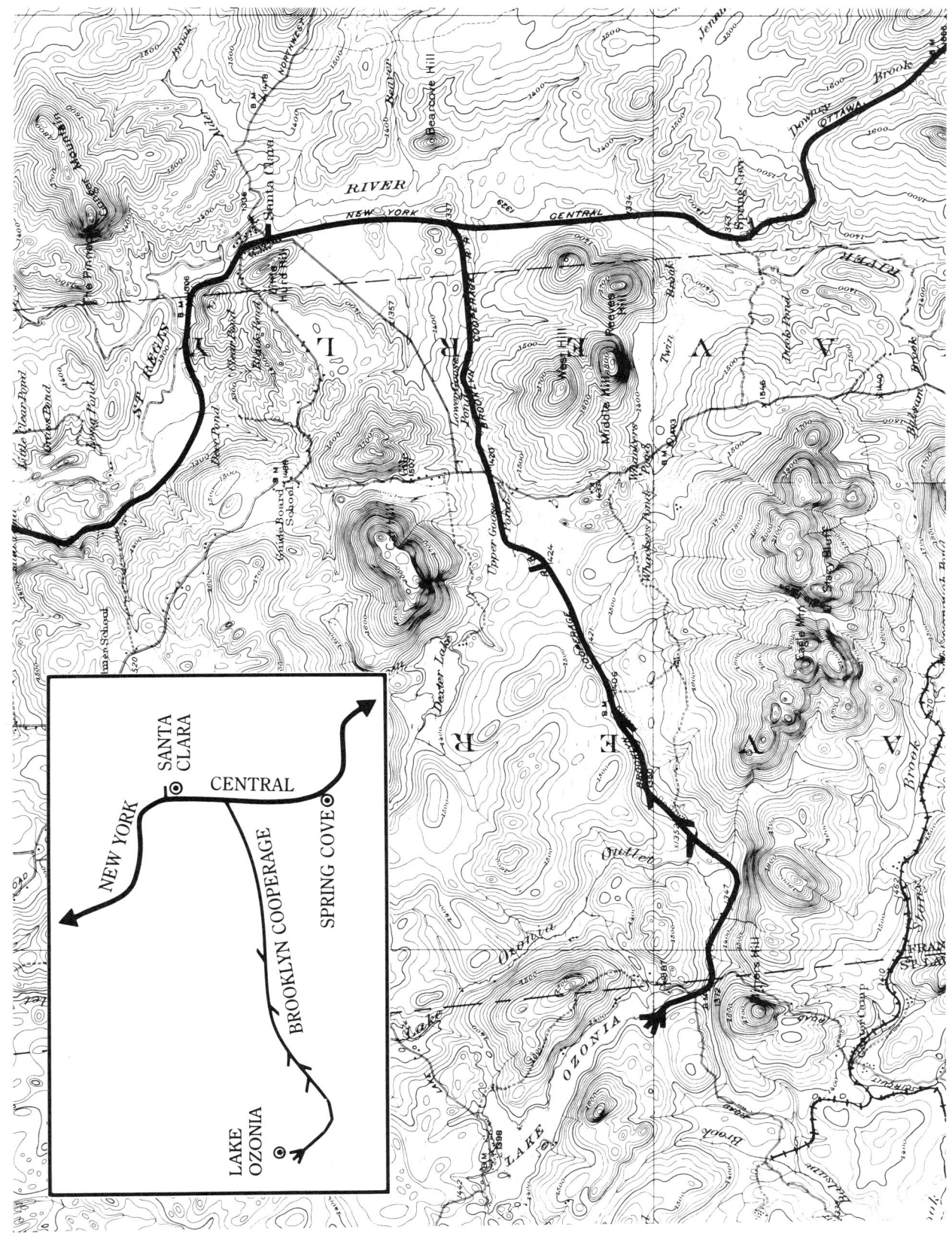

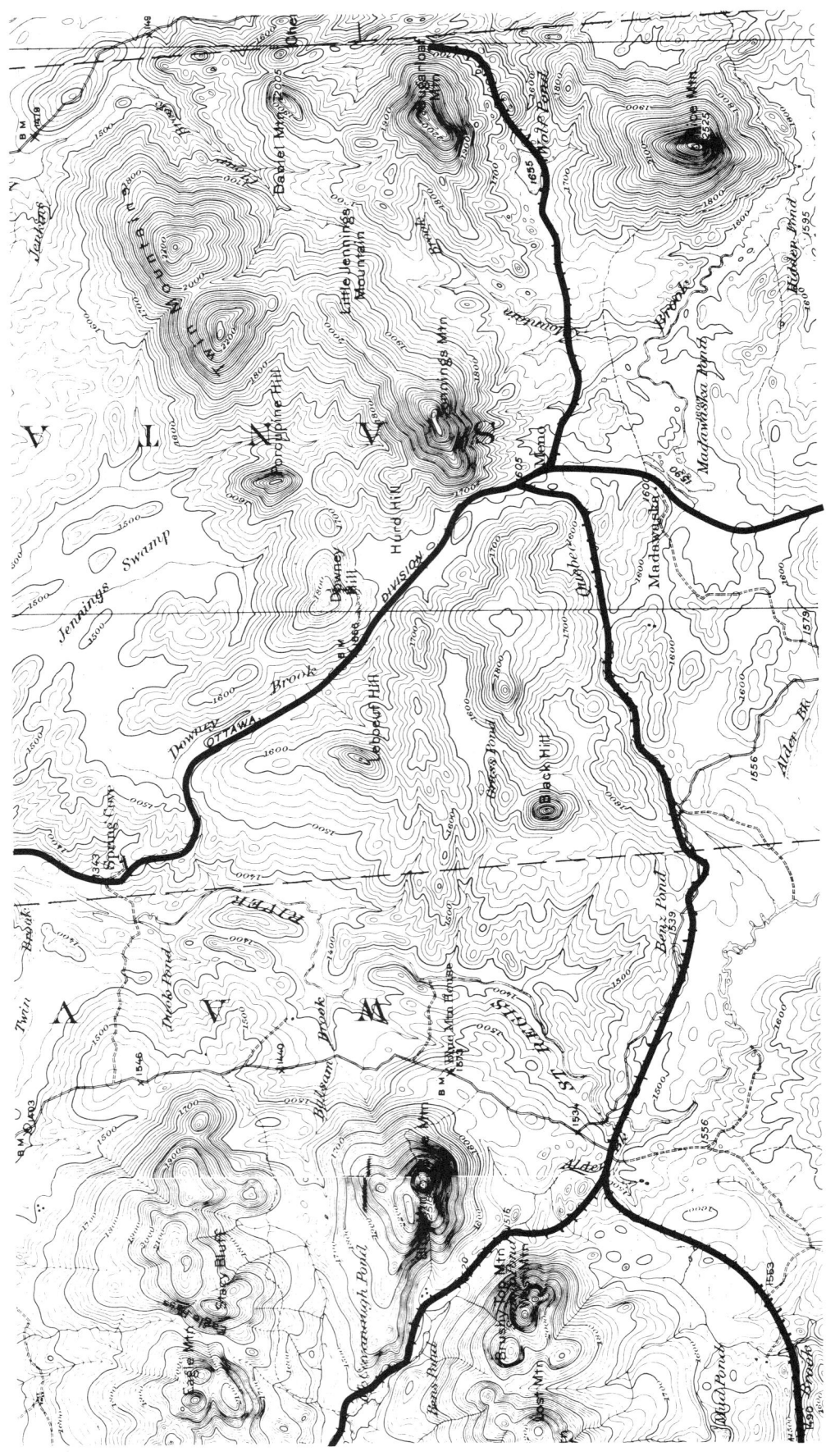

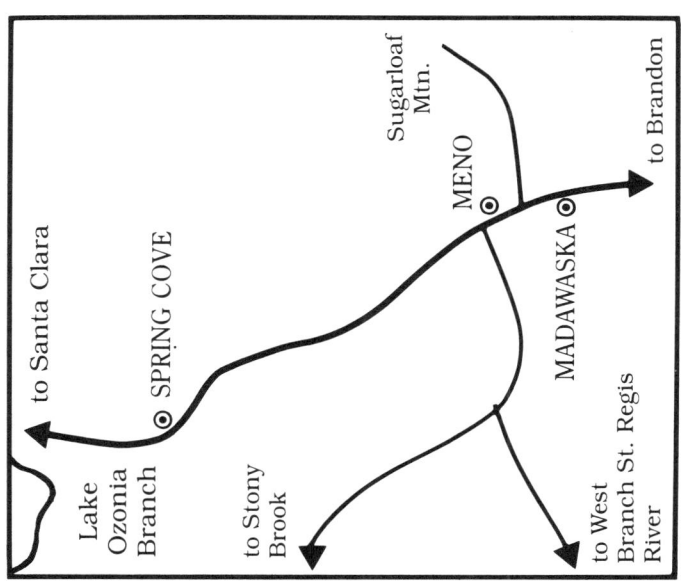

This page is
a continuation
of page 70.

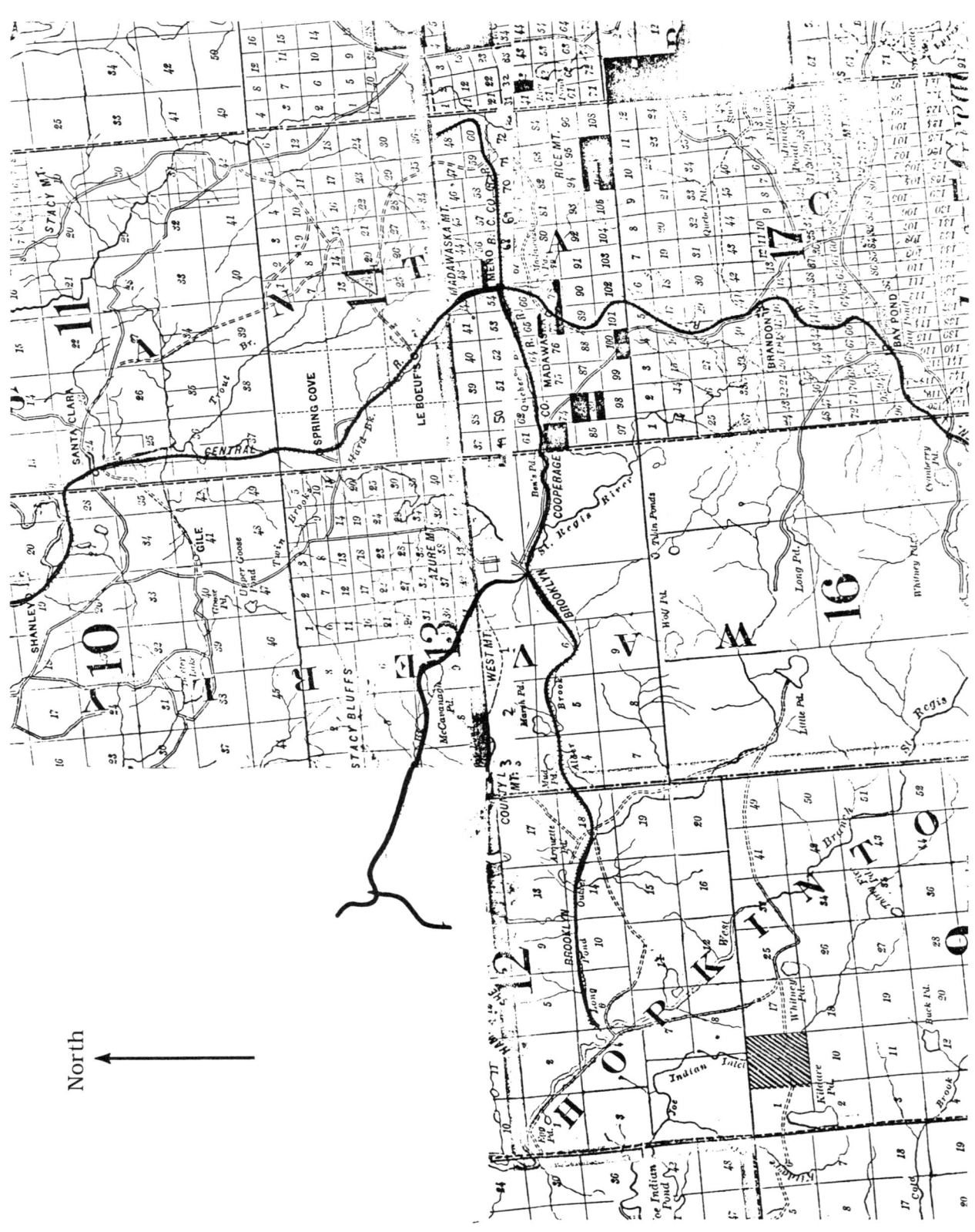

North ←

trail very likely follows the old railroad grade, but the grade continued past Wolf Pond to skirt Sugarloaf Mountain.

The Santa Clara 1921 Quadrangle shows a half-mile long stub track heading southwest out of Meno but abruptly terminating. This must be a remnant, in 1921, of the 1911 line which headed west to the West Branch St. Regis River. Note the tote road symbol on the Quadrangle further west along the south bank of Quebec Brook; this road must have followed the track. No more evidence occurs for the track location until the Nicholville 1919 Quadrangle; note the series of elevation bench marks following Alder Brook and Long Pond Outlet: 1553, 1490, 1469, 1444, 1432, 1423. Could these bench marks, often spaced a mile apart, been part of the survey for the Cooperage track? For what other reason would so many bench marks be placed out in the "middle of nowhere"?

A Franklin County Highway Map (year unknown, but probably published in the 1915–1920 era) indicates a railroad following Stony Brook and passing between Blue (Azure) and West Mountain. An examination of the 1919 Nicholville Quadrangle does NOT show the railroad, but it does show a trail along Stony Brook and passing between the two mountains. A series of elevation bench marks is here, too: 1516, 1520, 1470, 1462, and, in St. Lawrence County, 1410. "Center Camp" shown on the Quadrangle could have been a logging camp on the Cooperage. Note that the trail splits west of Center Camp with a stub to the north and the second to the south. This "Stony Brook" branch of the Cooperage must have connected with the branch to the West Branch St. Regis River just about where the Nicholville and Santa Clara Quadrangles adjoin; I have not found a map that indicates this connection.

Madawaska, *28.1 miles. Elevation 1600.*

This is a station indicated on the timetables from 1896 through 1936.

Brandon, *31.9 miles. Elevation 1603.*

Brandon was the largest community between Santa Clara and Tupper Lake, and was the temporary terminus of the railroad from July 6, 1886, when the first train arrived (Pope, 1972) to late 1889. The initial name of the station, as shown on the June 30, 1889, timetable was Paul Smith's Station, but by 1896 the name had already been changed to Brandon. For a short period, trains did not stop here, as stated in the July 3, 1902, Saranac Lake Daily *Enterprise.*

Brandon appeared as a stop on the timetable through June 28, 1936.

Patrick Ducey and John Torrent had purchased 28,000 acres in the Brandon area in December, 1881, or January, 1882 (Pope, 1972), in a tract adjacent to and south of the Hurd, Hotchkiss, and McFarlane Tract acquired in August, 1882. Ducey had begun building his sawmill on the St. Regis River where Hurd's railroad crossed it, the mill being completed by March of 1887 (Pope, 1972). By 1895, after Hurd's bankruptcy, Ducey's mill activity began to decline; the machinery and tools from this mill were bought from Ducey in April, 1897, by A. J. Norton and moved to St. Regis Falls (Pope, 1972).

Following closing of Ducey's sawmill, a series of dramatic shifts in land ownership occurred; these shifts are well documented in a number of publications (Donaldson, 1921; Collins, 1969; Pope, 1972; Gove, 1981; Surprenant, 1982). William Rockefeller began acquiring lands around Bay Pond and Brandon in 1898–1899. These were sold to Bay Pond, Inc. in 1923 (see the section below on McDonald and Bay Pond); in 1937, Bay Pond, Inc., sold the northern half of its tract centering around Brandon to the Ross Family, under whose ownership it is today. The southern half centering around Bay Pond was sold back to the Rockefeller Family in 1937.

Connections by stagecoaches to trains at Brandon were numerous. Concord coaches from Paul Smith's Hotel operated from 1886 to about 1906, when Paul Smith opened his own railway to Lake Clear Junction on the New York Central Adirondack Division. The 1889 timetable also indicates stage connections for the Meacham Lake House, the Saranac Lakes, and at Paul Smith's, a change of stage for Bloomingdale and Lake Placid. In the August 10, 1896, and 1898 timetables appeared advertisements for connections for Meacham Lake and McColloms. DeSormo (1974) offers detailed accounts of the hotels at Meacham Lake, McColloms, and Paul Smiths, as well as Gardner (1975, p. 9).

The 1902–1903 U.S.G.S. St. Regis Quadrangle shows a passing siding east of the main track and north of the Paul Smiths-Azure Mountain highway crossing; the siding is about 0.2 mile long, next to the station. Collins (1969) offers a village street map plus a photo of the station with a freight siding. Since Brandon was the terminus for The NY&O Railroad for three years, it would be interesting to find any old maps that indicated the means of turning engines: either a wye, loop, or turntable. Also, was there a siding into Ducey's mill?

Two publications concerning Brandon which must be mentioned are those of Grosh

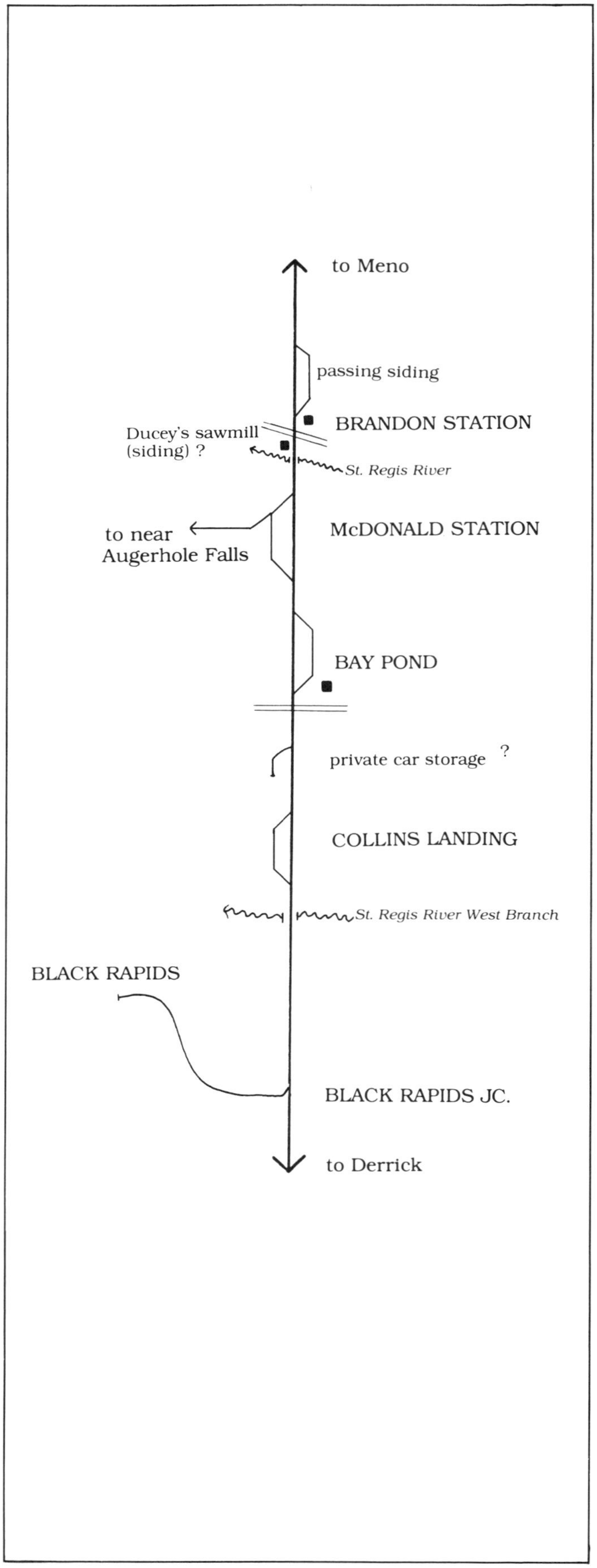

to Meno
passing siding
BRANDON STATION
Ducey's sawmill
(siding) ?
St. Regis River
to near
Augerhole Falls
McDONALD STATION
BAY POND
private car storage ?
COLLINS LANDING
St. Regis River West Branch
BLACK RAPIDS
BLACK RAPIDS JC.
to Derrick

Brandon
Mud Pond
RIVER
Bay Pond
Cranberry Pond

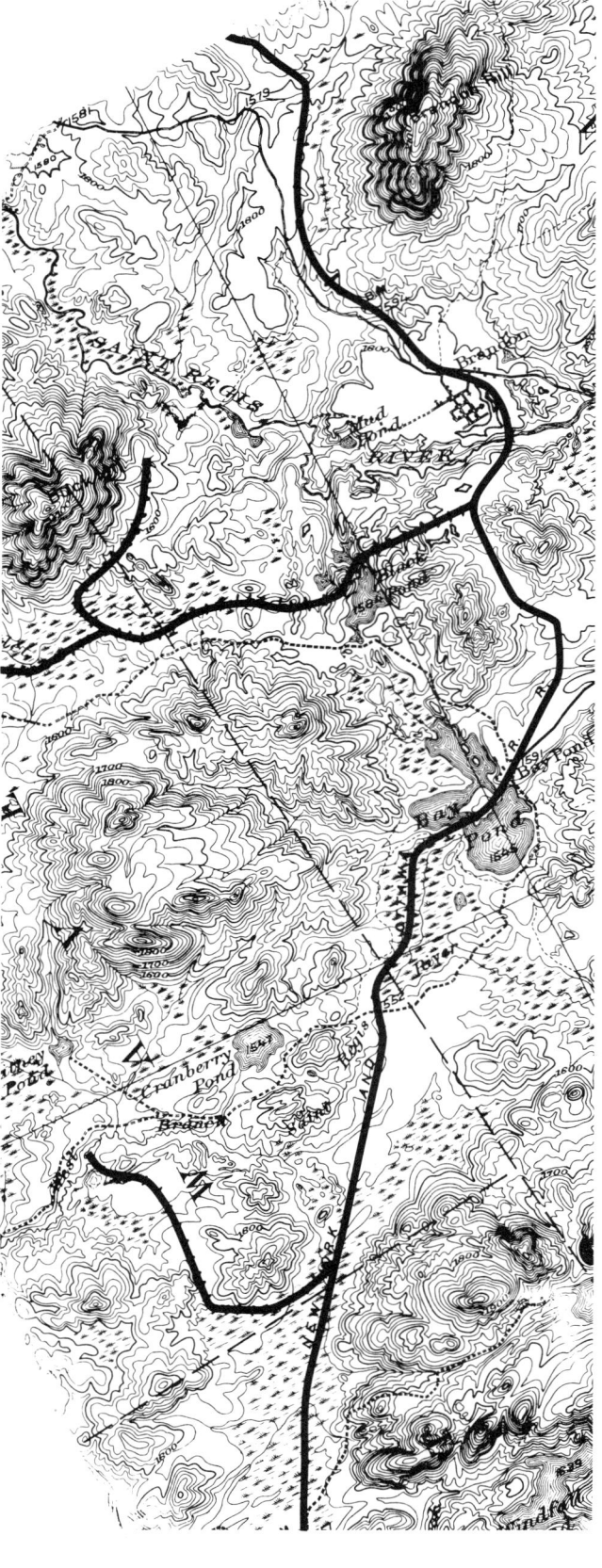

(1892–1896) and Surprenant (1982). Reverend Grosh kept a diary of his activities during the close of the Ducey era; these are unpublished and may be found at the library of the Adirondack Museum at Blue Mountain Lake.

Surprenant's *Brandon: Boom Town to Nature Preserve* (1982) is the most complete and up-to-date compilation on the history of Brandon.

The area from Brandon southward past McDonald Station burned in 1903, about the worst forest fire year in Adirondack history (Suter, 1903; Schmidt, 1916). On these sandy glacial outwash plains, the fires can be severe and the forest very slow to regenerate; stumps of white pine logged during the Ducey era (1887–1895) are still apparent (Kudish, 1981).

Tyler (1968, pp. 35–37) describes special Sunday church trains run by Hurd from Brandon to Santa Clara and Tupper Lake.

McDonald, *33.0 miles. Elevation 1611.* **Bay Pond, Inc.**

Gove (1981) offers a comprehensive history of Bay Pond, Inc., which built a logging railroad west from McDonald in 1924 to a point on the West Branch St. Regis River below Augerhole Falls. John N. McDonald had been a partner in the Mac-a-Mac Corporation operations at Brandreth (see p. 97) on the New York Central Adirondack Division). Bay Pond, Inc. bought the Rockefeller Tract in 1923, and it was about this time that McDonald became listed as a station. Photos of Bay Pond operations appear in Gove (1981) and in Hyde (1974, pp. 46 and 47). Note the Oval Wood Dish Company spur around the southeast base of Buck Mountain (map, p. 76).

Since the 1922 U.S.G.S. 15-minute Childwold Quadrangle and the 1902–1903 St. Regis Quadrangles were printed before Bay Pond, Inc., the railroad is not shown on either Quadrangle. The Augerhole Falls 7½ minute Quadrangle, printed in 1970, indicates a jeep trail which follows the old railroad grade. I have traced the grade as best I could on to the older 1922 15-minute Childwold Quadrangle, presented here on page 76. Oddly, the 1953 15-minute St. Regis Quadrangle does not show any vestiges of the railroad, but the new 1979 metric St. Regis Mountain topographic map (7.5 by 15 minute) *shows* the old grade as a jeep trail. Even the Oval Wood Dish spur around Buck Mountain is indicated!

Bay Pond, Inc., operations continued until 1932 (Gove, 1981). The McDonald station is still listed in the 1936 timetable. In 1937, Bay Pond, Inc. sold the lands back to the

Rockefeller family, the same year that all service on the Ottawa Division terminated.

Bay Pond, *35.6 miles. Elevation 1590.*

Bay Pond appeared as a station as early as on the August 10, 1896, timetable, and as late as on the June 28, 1936, timetable. During the period 1899–1923, when the Rockefeller Family owned the tract, Bay Pond was a private station.

The 1902–1903 U.S.G.S. St. Regis Quadrangle indicates a passing siding east of the main track and just north of the station, 0.1 mile long. I have seen photographs of this siding taken in 1936 and now in the collection of Philip Delarm of Paul Smiths. By 1936, there still were freight cars on the siding, but it was no longer double-ended; the switch at the southwest end had been removed.

Sally Rockefeller Bogdanovitch (personal communication) recollects having heard that an additional siding existed on an island in Bay Pond (the Pond itself) at about milepost 36.0, west of the main track for holding private cars; certainly there is space today where a siding could have been, but I have not found a map or a photo showing such a siding.

Gove (1981) indicates a passing siding at the southwest end of Bay Pond (the Pond itself) at about milepost 36.6 which he calls Collins Landing. This siding dates back to the Bay Pond, Inc. era (1923–1937), and not to the two Rockefeller eras (1899–1923, and 1937–present).

Hyde (1974) presents photos of logging trains at Bay Pond on pages 46 and 47 of her text. Refer to the section on McDonald above for detail on Bay Pond, Inc.

Palmer's notes at the Adirondack Museum Library suggest many logging spurs radiating from the Bay Pond area, but no map pinpoints their location. Perhaps Palmer is referring to the branches described in the above McDonald section and in the following Black Rapids Junction section below.

It was during the Bay Pond, Inc. era (1923-1937) that the 1934 fire burned the region from Bay Pond southwestward downstream along the West Branch St. Regis River and toward Derrick. See the Annual Report of the New York State Conservation Department for 1934 for details.

Black Rapids Junction, *38.6 miles. Elevation 1554.*

This Junction is listed on the 1896 and 1898 timetables only; it is also shown on the 1896 New York Central Railroad publication entitled *Health and Pleasure on America's*

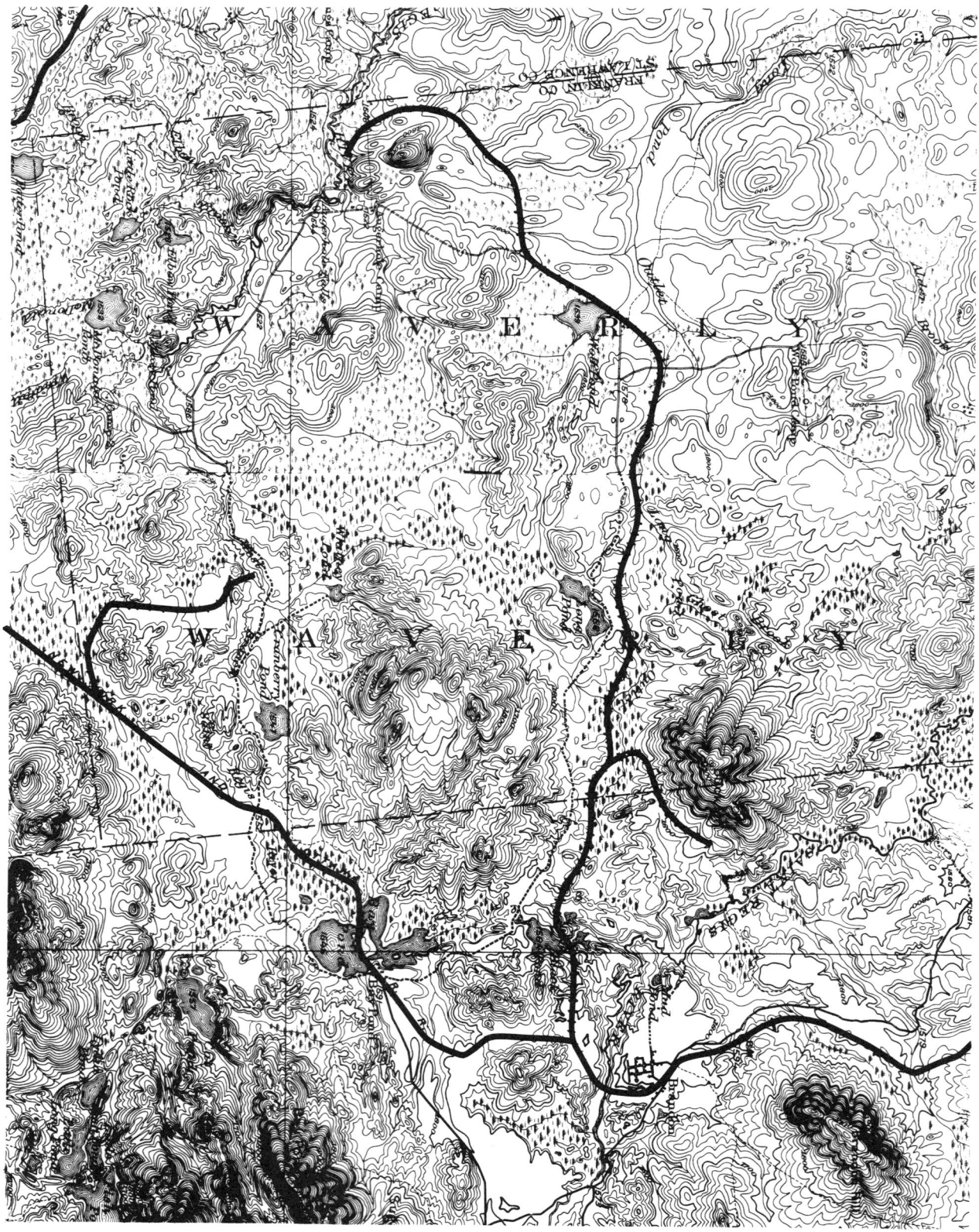

76

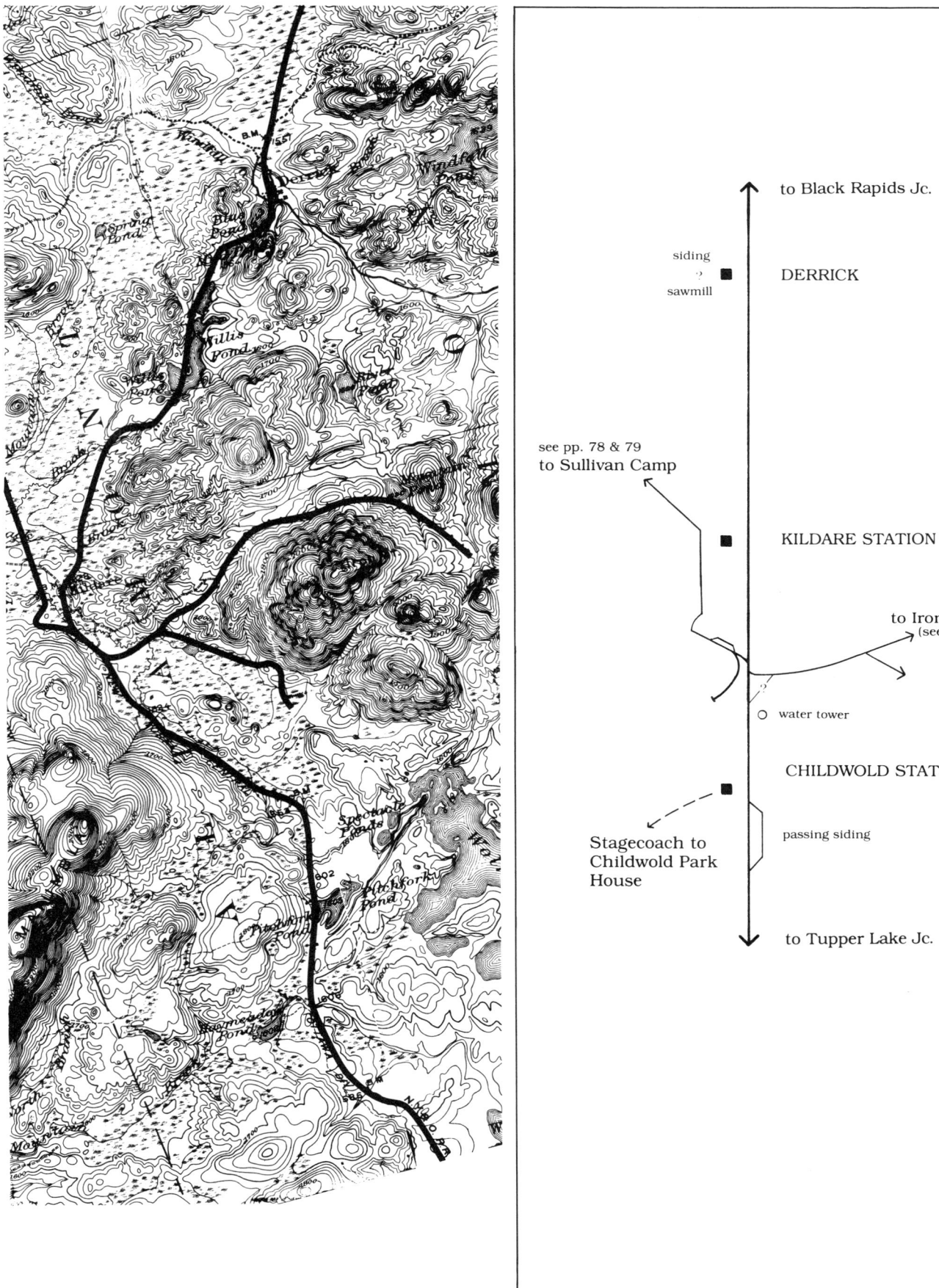

to Black Rapids Jc.

siding
      ■   DERRICK
sawmill

see pp. 78 & 79
to Sullivan Camp

    ■   KILDARE STATION

to Iron Mt.
(see p. 79)

○ water tower

CHILDWOLD STATION

  ■

Stagecoach to
Childwold Park
House

passing siding

to Tupper Lake Jc.

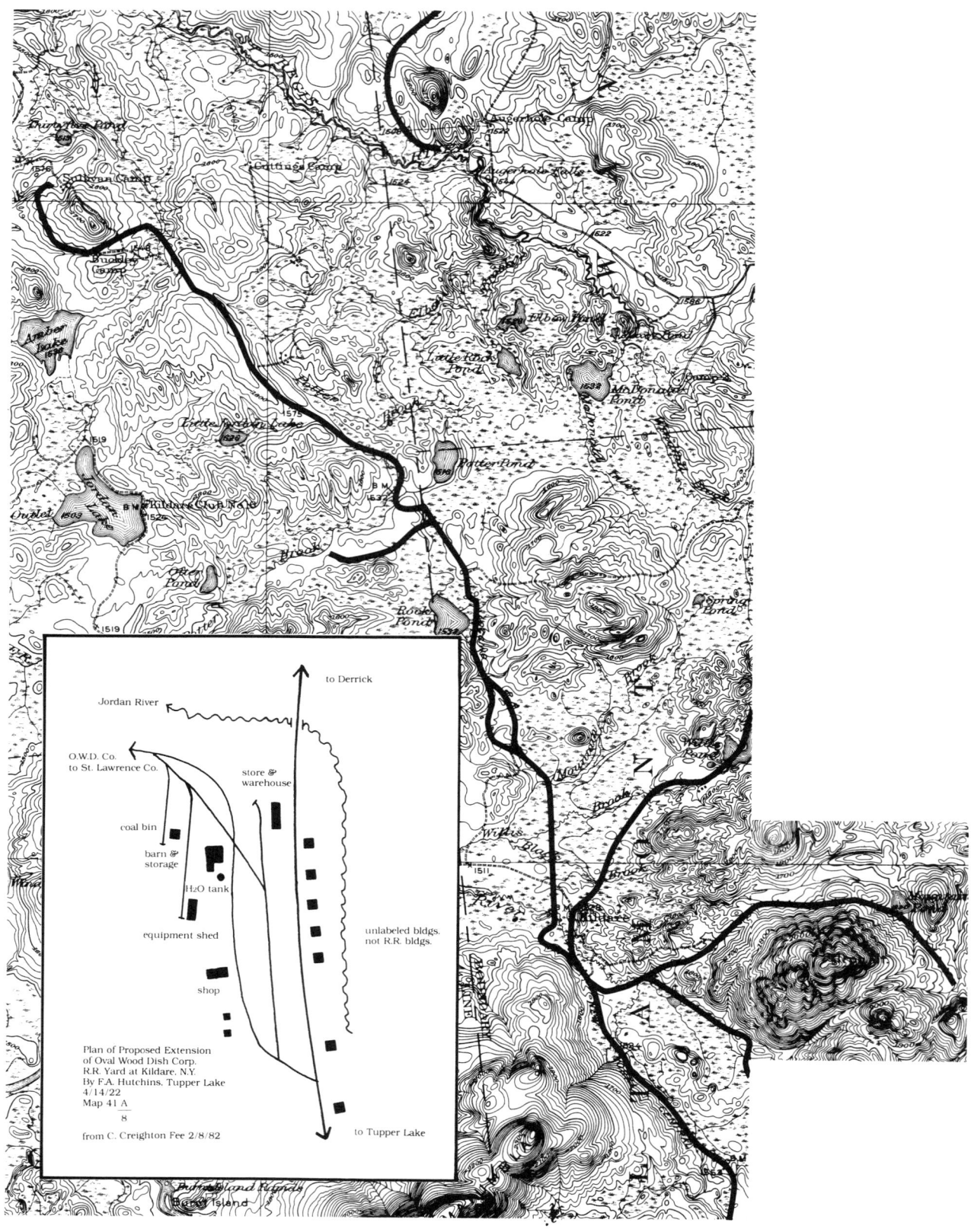

Jordan River

to Derrick

O.W.D. Co.
to St. Lawrence Co.

store &
warehouse

coal bin

barn &
storage

H2O tank

equipment shed

unlabeled bldgs.
not R.R. bldgs.

shop

Plan of Proposed Extension
of Oval Wood Dish Corp.
R.R. Yard at Kildare, N.Y.
By F.A. Hutchins, Tupper Lake
4/14/22
Map 41 $\frac{A}{8}$

from C. Creighton Fee 2/8/82

to Tupper Lake

Greatest Railroad, along with a short spur terminating at Black Rapids. This spur shows up as an unpaved road on the 1953 15-minute St. Regis Quadrangle, diverging from the New York and Ottawa right-of-way just north of the Waverly-Altamont Town Line. The spur had terminated at a jackworks on the West Branch St. Regis River (see map, page 74); I assume that this jackworks was Black Rapids.

Gove (1981) dates the Black Rapids spur to the Ducey era (1887–1895) when the Brandon sawmill was in operation. Hurd had planned an extension (Pope, 1972) of his railroad from Brandon to Tupper Lake in the summer of 1888. Although the line did not actually reach Tupper Lake until the end of 1889, it is likely that the railroad did reach the Black Rapids area by 1888 and that Ducey could make use of it.

Derrick, *40.9 miles. Elevation 1551.*

Simmons (1976, p. 110) mentions that this was the station for the connecting stage for Saranac Inn from 1888 to 1892. However, the 1896 and 1898 timetables do not call this station Derrick; the name is Willis Pond, after a body of water about a mile to the south. The 1909 timetable does use the name Derrick. Wallace's *Guide to the Adirondacks* (1894) lists the station as Blue Pond, after a body of water just south of Derrick Station. Apparently, there were frequent name changes here or even possibly minor station relocations. Derrick was still a station stop on September 9, 1929, but the April 26, 1936, timetable no longer shows a time when trains stopped there.

Hyde (1974, p. 32) describes Charles H. Turner's sawmill running here from about 1896 to about 1910. For several more years following, C. H. Elliott shipped out three carloads a week of mangle rolls for laundries, probably necessitating a siding just before World War I.

Kildare, *44.8 miles. Elevation 1528.*

Kildare Station is currently on exhibit at the Adirondack Museum in Blue Mountain Lake. It was a stop on the 1896 through 1936 timetables. From here, several logging railroads diverged, as shown on the 1922 U.S.G.S. Childwold Quadrangle (see maps on pp. 77 and 78).

Palmer (March, 1970) describes in detail how the Oval Wood Dish Company set up headquarters in Kildare in 1916, with construction of hardwood logging railroads beginning in 1917. At first, logging lines reached the southwest corner of Township 19 in Franklin County; about 1920, the line was extended north-northwest well into St. Lawrence County, with well over 30 miles of track including branches. The line terminated at Buckley and Sullivan Camps.

In 1926, according to Palmer (March, 1970), the Sisson White Company took over the logging railroad and removed the tracks about a year later. The logging branches off the main track to Sullivan Camp were used only about two years, then the rails removed and reused on more newly-constructed branches.

Professor C. Creighton Fee of Paul Smith's College let me examine a map he has drafted by F. A. Hutchins dated April 14, 1922. The map is entitled "Plan of the Proposed Extension of the Oval Wood Dish Corp., Railroad Yard at Kildare, New York." The map is sketched here on page 78.

Palmer's notes in the Adirondack Museum Library mention that Brooklyn Cooperage had a line running from a point one mile south of Kildare *west* to the Raquette River and back of the Kildare Club; I cannot find this Cooperage line on any map to locate it precisely.

The 1922 Childwold Quadrangle shows two additional branches heading east and southeast of Kildare. The easterly one continues onto the 1955 St. Regis Quadrangle where the grade is designated as abandoned, wrapping around the north slope of Iron Mountain. Palmer does not state whether these two lines belonged to Oval Wood Dish, Sisson White, or Brooklyn Cooperage; however, the *Inventory of Abandoned Railroad Rights of Way* (1974) published by the New York State Department of Transportation, states that the Iron Mountain branches belonged to Brooklyn Cooperage.

Childwold Station, *48.4 miles. Elevation 1602.*

The station is listed in the 1896 and 1909 timetables, but is gone by May 2, 1920. Stages from the Childwold Park House met trains here in 1896. This station must not be confused with Childwold Station established in 1892 on the New York Central Adirondack Division, some 6 miles to the southwest (see p. 99). The 1922 Childwold Quadrangle locates a passing siding just south of Pitchfork Pond, at 48.7 miles, about 0.2 mile long.

Tupper Lake Junction (Faust Post Office), *52.0 miles. Elevation 1550.*

The Village of Tupper Lake was almost non-existent until Hurd's Railroad reached the site with construction crews late in 1889. According to Simmons (1968, p. 32), the first train arrived on July 1, 1890. The Junction

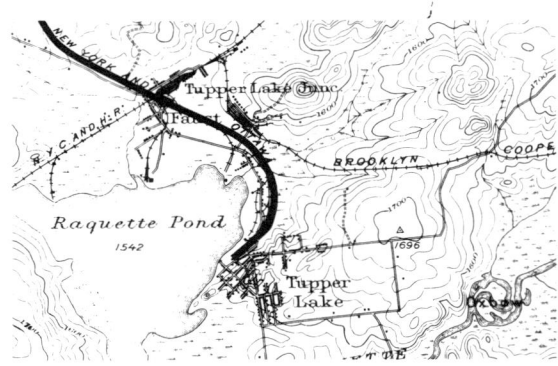

(Faust P.O.) developed a little later, as a result of the opening on July 15, 1892, of Webb's Adirondack and St. Lawrence Railroad which crossed Hurd's at this point. Photos of this junction occur in several publications including Gardner (1975, p. 29), Simmons (1976, pp. 146–149), and Harter (1979).

Palmer (1970) notes that the Oval Wood Dish Company later had a siding at Tupper Lake Junction, although, as stated above, logging operations were centered at Kildare, seven miles to the north; apparently, Oval Wood brought their logs from Kildare to the Junction with their own engines and flatcars via trackage rights over the Ottawa Division.

For Brooklyn Cooperage Company operations at Tupper Lake, refer to the section on the New York Central Adirondack Division,

with which the Cooperage connected (p. 103). Palmer (March, 1971) describes Brooklyn Cooperage operations at Tupper Lake.

Tupper Lake, *54.0 miles. Elevation 1550.*

Simmons (1976, p. 65) notes that Hurd's first railroad station, post office, and store were located temporarily, in 1890, on the site of the future Oval Wood Dish Company.

On a map dated May 24, 1899, in the Franklin County Clerk's Office in Malone, the depot is shown along Raquette Pond just north of Mill Street on the east side of the track. A 1935 map, also at the County Clerk's Office, shows the station also on the east side of the track but south of Mill Street. The track continued south of Wawbeek Avenue along Raquette Pond for several hundred feet.

In 1896, 1898, and 1909, the timetables indicate stage connections from the Hotel Wawbeek and other resorts on Upper Saranac Lake. The steamer "Altamont", run by the Tupper Lake Navigation Company, connected with the trains to serve resorts on Big and Little Tupper Lakes, including Tupper Lake House, Moodys, and Bog River Falls.

Simmons (1976, p. 143) states that closure of the Tupper Lake Station (not the Tupper Lake Junction Station) was in October, 1918, but the September 19, 1929, timetable still lists Tupper Lake as a station, along with Tupper Lake Junction. However, by the June

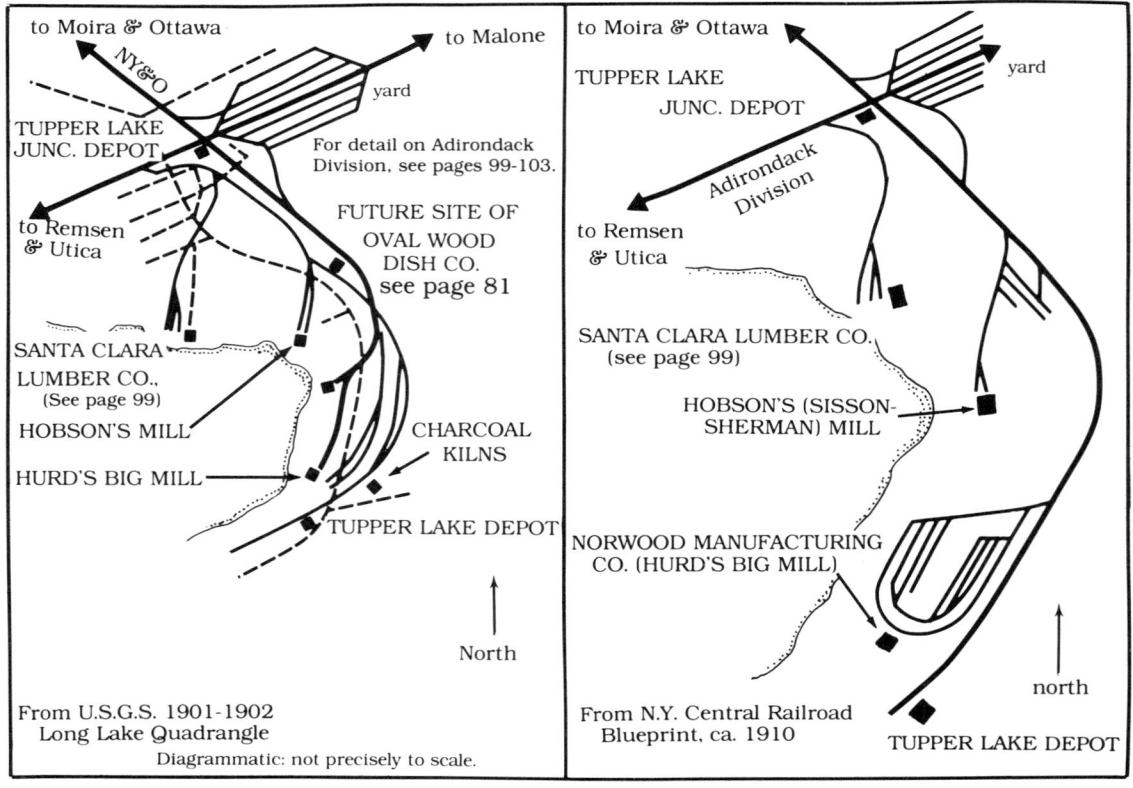

28, 1936, timetable, only the Junction is listed.

A map in Palmer (1970) indicates a proposed extension of the Northern Adirondack (Hurd's) Railroad southeastward from Tupper Lake up the Raquette River to Long Lake. Professor C. Creighton Fee states that this proposed line had been surveyed to the north end of Long Lake and graded a short distance out of Tupper Lake Junction; the May 24, 1899, map at the County Clerk's Office shows the proposed extension. The tracks were never placed on the grade because State Forest Preserve Land ahead blocked the plans; it had been hoped to eventually connect with the Delaware and Hudson at North Creek. I wonder whether the Brooklyn Cooperage line, built to near Wawbeek in 1900, used a portion of the proposed Long Lake grade to a point just east of Sunmount.

The number of wood products industries in the Tupper Lake area has been numerous, and the complexity increased further by the fact that many outfits changed owners several times; in reading different accounts published at different times, one realizes that not several industries were involved but only a single industry which had a different name each time! Those industries which were located directly along the New York and Ottawa line are presented in this chapter. Those industries, such as Brooklyn Cooperage, Santa Clara Lumber Mill, Champlain Realty Company, Tupper Lake Chemical, etc., which were located directly along the New York Central Adirondack Division, are presented in that chapter.

The primary reason for Hurd's Railroad reaching the shores of Tupper Lake (actually Raquette Pond) was the Big Mill, one of the largest of its time. Photos of the Mill appear in Simmons (1976, pp. 135, 136, and 137), including descriptions of its size and operations. It was built in 1890, when the railroad arrived on the site of what is now the Municipal Park grandstand (Simmons, 1976, p. 66). From Hurd's Big Mill, an aerial tramway was built across what is now Demars Boulevard to a series of charcoal kilns which were situated along the north side of Railroad Street (now Pleasant Avenue); these kilns are mentioned in Simmons (1976, p. 67), and in Hyde (1974), and are shown on the May 24, 1899, map at the Franklin County Clerk's Office in Malone. The tramway was nearly ⅛ of a mile long and carried wood chips and other waste from the sawmill to the kilns. A railroad siding served the kilns, presumably to haul away the charcoal. Simmons (1976, pp. 67 and 128) informs us that there was a succession of owners of the Big

Mill following Hurd's bankruptcy in 1895. They were:
(1) Shepard and Morse, operating it for about a year;
(2) Patrick A. Ducey (yes, the same of Brandon fame!), and several other owners for short periods (Simmons, 1968, p. 36);
(3) Norwood Manufacturing Company owned the Big Mill in 1900 (Simmons, 1976, p. 109) and in 1911 (photo, p. 135 in Simmons);
(4) Santa Clara Lumber Company bought the mill in 1913 (Simmons, p. 128) and ran it until 1926; it was torn down in 1930.

See the maps on page 80 for location of the Big Mill.

Howard H. Hobson's mill was the first built in Tupper Lake (Simmons, 1976, p. 67), a year or so earlier than Hurd's Big Mill, i.e., ca. 1889. The location (Simmons, p. 413) was on the shore of Raquette Pond where, later, Ohio Street and Michigan Avenue were built; a photo in Simmons (p. 135) shows this mill, roughly halfway between Hurd's Big Mill and Tupper Lake Junction. Hobson's Mill burned in 1894 (Simmons, p. 413) and was rebuilt by the A. Sherman Lumber Company (photo, Simmons, p. 137) in 1895. The Sherman Mill, known locally also as the Sisson Mill, operated until 1915 when sold to the Oval Wood Dish Company. A map of Tupper Lake Junction dated March 27, 1893, at the County Clerk's Office in Malone indicates a siding leading to this mill from the Adirondack and St. Lawrence Railroad (later, New York Central Adirondack Division), not The New York and Ottawa Railroad. However, a blueprint map of the Adirondack Division published by The New York Central Railroad about 1910 (available at the Franklin House of History in Malone) does show a spur of the Ottawa Division servicing the old Hobson Mill.

The Oval Wood Dish Company, in 1915, bought the old Hobson Mill from Sherman (Sisson), but began to construct a new facility across Demars Boulevard closer to the Ottawa tracks. Simmons (1976, pp. 65, and 150–166) offers much detail on this facility, which was completed in 1918. Oval Wood owned it until 1964, when Adirondack Plywood took over. In 1969–1970, Tupper Lake Veneer and Major Rod Limited replaced Adirondack Plywood as the operators. The huge warehouse, with interior railroad track, just northwest of the Oval Wood dish plant was also constructed in 1918, but burned in 1967. See the maps presented here locating Hobson's and Oval Wood industrial sites on p. 80. Hyde (1974, pp. 43 to 45) offers aerial photos of the Oval Wood Dish Company.

Palmer (1970) states that wood chips were converted into pulp and that hemlock bark was shipped by the ton to tanneries; the big tannery at St. Regis Falls no doubt received a large share of this tanbark. No specific locations in the Tupper Lake area are offered by Palmer for this wood chip and tanbark activity.

Timetable Operation

The June 30, 1889, timetable indicates two round trips daily between Moira and Paul Smiths Station (Brandon). The two arrivals were in the morning at Brandon and the two departures in the afternoon. Each train carried a Wagner Sleeping Car through to Grand Central Station in New York City; one car was routed via Vermont and the other via Watertown. Hence, connections were made at Moira with The Central Vermont Railroad (Ogdensburg and Lake Champlain). In addition, two more round trips occurred each day between Santa Clara and Moira, both leaving Santa Clara in the early morning and returning there from Moira in the afternoon. Apparently, sleeping car service had been in operation since about the time that the Line opened. The Plattsburg *Sentinel* of April 10, 1885, states that already one sleeper was making a round trip daily routed via Norwood, and that a second was soon to be placed in service via Vermont. In 1885, the sleepers would have terminated at Santa Clara.

By August 10, 1896, one round trip daily was scheduled between Moira and Tupper Lake, leaving Tupper Lake in the morning and returning there in the evening. These trains no longer carried sleeping cars, probably because of through sleeping car service to Paul Smith's Station (Gabriels) on the New York Central Adirondack Division which opened July 15, 1892. Sleeping cars were still running, however, in and out of Moira on The Central Vermont Railroad via New England. In addition, there was a mixed train (passenger and freight combined) running between Santa Clara and Moira, leaving Santa Clara in the afternoon and returning from Moira late in the evening.

The March 7, 1898, timetable shows no major change from the 1896 'table, except the discontinuation of Sunday service.

By March 1, 1909, there were two round trips daily between Tupper Lake and Ottawa, except Sunday. Departures from Tupper Lake were early morning and afternoon, while arrivals were near noon and evening. Two trains were involved, each making one round trip daily, meeting in Canada both

times. Connections were made at Tupper Lake with the Adirondack Division.

On June 23, 1912, and on September 22, 1914, the schedules were very similar to that of 1909.

However, by May 2, 1920, the number of trains operating between Tupper Lake and Moira in each direction was one, as it had been in 1896. It left Tupper Lake early in the morning and returned in the evening, except Sunday, but unlike that in 1896, it was routed through to Ottawa. In addition, one round trip daily except Sunday operated between Santa Clara and Ottawa, leaving Ottawa in the morning and returning there in evening. The date of abandonment of the afternoon departure from Tupper Lake was early in 1918, according to Simmons (1976, p. 143); this would substantiate my belief that the cutback must have occurred between 1914 and 1920. Simmons also notes that in October, 1918, passenger service was abandoned between Tupper Lake (uptown) and Tupper Lake Junction (Faust); the timetables date this abandonment between 1929 and 1936.

By September 27, 1925, the Santa Clara-Ottawa train had been reduced to Moira-Ottawa, operating one round trip daily except Sunday.

The June 27, 1926, timetable, along with that of June 24, 1928, September 29, 1929, April 26, 1936, and June 28, 1936 all show essentially the same service as in 1925: one round trip daily except Sunday between Tupper Lake and Ottawa with an additional round trip daily except Sunday between Moira and Ottawa. This service must have continued until abandonment. Simmons (1976, p. 141) notes that one freight train worked the whole line three times weekly in 1936, and that the last train (passenger) left Tupper Lake on May 6, 1937. Simmons, p. 142, proceeds to describe the track removal. However, the New York Central timetables of April 25, 1948, still show one round trip daily between Helena and Ottawa.

Equipment

Passenger locomotives on The New York and Ottawa Railroad were the American Standard 4-4-0 type. The cover of the Franklin (County) Historical Review (1969) shows engine 790 at Dickinson Center, while Vanderwalker (1972) shows engine 786 (? — number unclear in photo) at Santa Clara, and Palmer (February, 1970) shows engine 789 (? — number unclear in photo) with a combine (combination baggage-coach car) at St. Regis Falls. An illustration in the June 30, 1889, timetable depicts a 4-4-0 type locomotive and a mail-baggage car at Santa Clara.

Palmer's notes at the Adirondack Museum state that there were twelve locomotives on the line, all originally New York Central engines built between 1880 and 1890. There were seven 4-4-0s, one 4-6-0, three 2-6-0s, and one 0-6-0.

Haworth (1954) recalls ten-wheelers (4-6-0s) on the line in its later years (1930s). If this is so, then the ten-wheelers replaced the earlier and smaller 4-4-0s of the Nineteenth Century.

The Brooklyn Cooperage Company, according to Palmer (March, 1971) used a variety of geared locomotives, mostly Shays and Climaxes, which were slow but powerful logging engines; they could ascend steep grades and hold back heavy loads on steep down grades. Palmer includes a photo of a Climax at work with a Barnhart steam log-loader crane on the flat cars.

The Oval Wood Dish Company operated two Heisler 63-ton geared locomotives (Palmer, March, 1970) around Kildare. Simmons (1976) shows a photo of one of these on page 134. Oval Wood also had 65 standard flat cars for transporting logs to Tupper Lake (Simmons, 1976, p. 135 photo).

Bay Pond, Inc., in Gove's 1981 article, ran two rod locomotives (as opposed to geared locomotives) since there were no steep grades. One was a 2-6-0 Mogul type, while the second, used as a pusher at the rear of the train, is of an unknown type. Gove (1981) offers photos of the Bay Pond engine as does also Hyde (1974, pp. 46 and 47).

The 1889 timetable advertises that the American Express Company had offices at all stations on The Northern Adirondack Railroad. Also, an agent was located at the Paul Smith's Station (Brandon) in summer handling checked baggage. Hence, baggage and express cars were on the coach trains. There is no evidence that these cars were switched at Tupper Lake or Moira from or to the Adirondack Division or Ogdensburg and Lake Champlain, respectively, with the exception perhaps of private cars.

In 1889, as has been described in the section on Timetable Operation (page   ), through Wagner sleeping cars operated from Moira to and from Paul Smith's Station, but this service probably was stopped on or about July 15, 1892.

The Plattsburgh *Sentinel* of April 10, 1885, reports that Hurd's line had two 46-ton locomotives, one 36-ton locomotive, two pony engines, and that the cars are "neat, substantial, and as good as will be found anywhere." A telegraph line was built from Moira to Brandon.

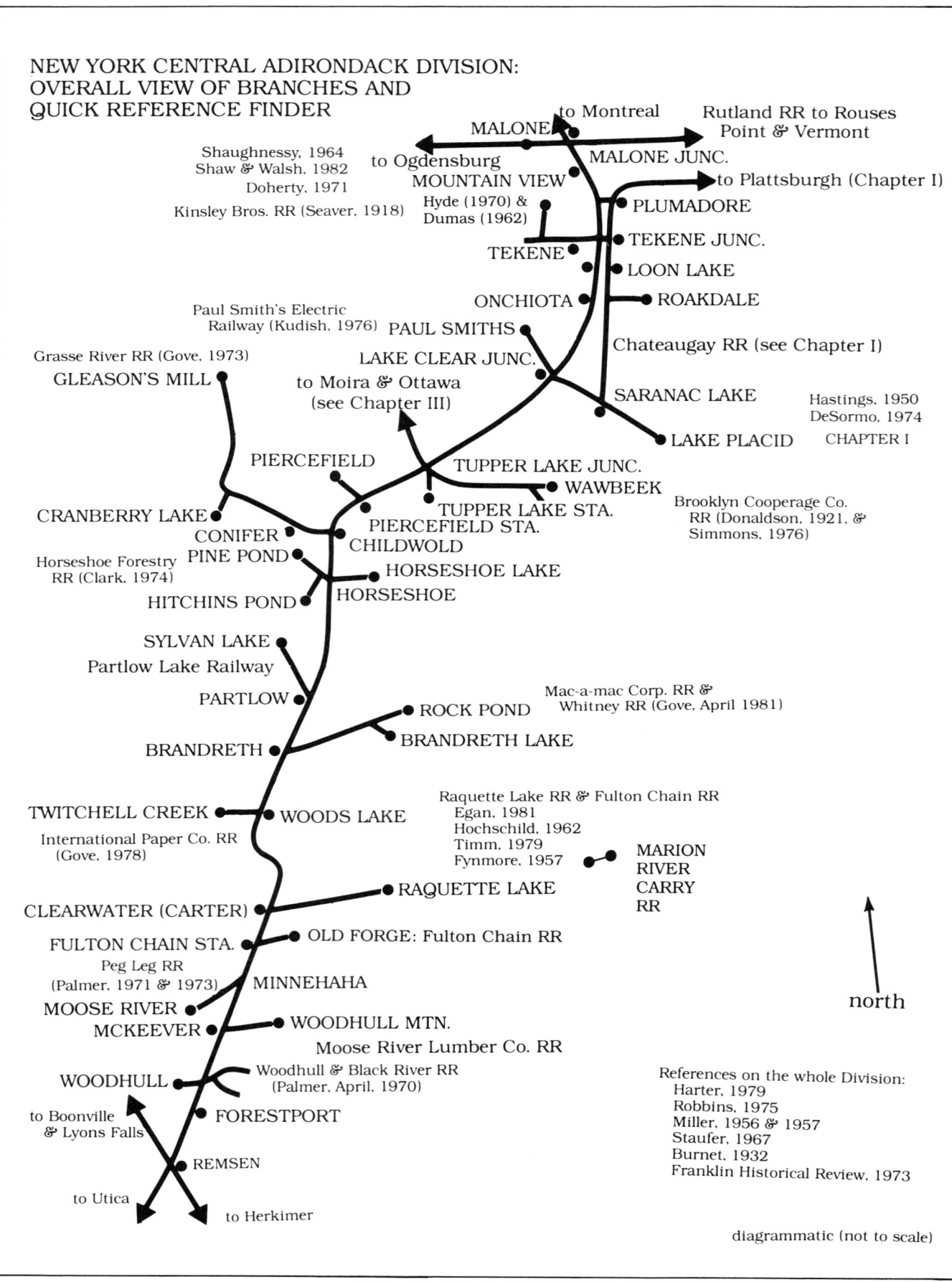

NEW YORK CENTRAL ADIRONDACK DIVISION:
OVERALL VIEW OF BRANCHES AND
QUICK REFERENCE FINDER

to Montreal   Rutland RR to Rouses
MALONE   Point & Vermont

Shaughnessy, 1964   MALONE JUNC.
Shaw & Walsh, 1982   to Ogdensburg
Doherty, 1971   MOUNTAIN VIEW   to Plattsburgh (Chapter I)
Kinsley Bros. RR (Seaver, 1918)   Hyde (1970) &   PLUMADORE
                                   Dumas (1962)
                              TEKENE   TEKENE JUNC.
                                        LOON LAKE
                          ONCHIOTA   ROAKDALE
Paul Smith's Electric
Railway (Kudish, 1976)   PAUL SMITHS
                      LAKE CLEAR JUNC.   Chateaugay RR (see Chapter I)
Grasse River RR (Gove, 1973)   to Moira & Ottawa
GLEASON'S MILL   (see Chapter III)   SARANAC LAKE   Hastings, 1950
                                                                   DeSormo, 1974
                                              LAKE PLACID   CHAPTER I
            PIERCEFIELD
                          TUPPER LAKE JUNC.
                                        WAWBEEK
CRANBERRY LAKE   TUPPER LAKE STA.   Brooklyn Cooperage Co.
        CONIFER   PIERCEFIELD STA.   RR (Donaldson, 1921, &
PINE POND   CHILDWOLD   Simmons, 1976)
Horseshoe Forestry   HORSESHOE LAKE
RR (Clark, 1974)
HITCHINS POND   HORSESHOE

SYLVAN LAKE
Partlow Lake Railway
        PARTLOW
                    ROCK POND   Mac-a-mac Corp. RR &
                                   Whitney RR (Gove, April 1981)
BRANDRETH   BRANDRETH LAKE

                        Raquette Lake RR & Fulton Chain RR
TWITCHELL CREEK   WOODS LAKE   Egan, 1981
                                Hochschild, 1962
International Paper Co. RR   Timm, 1979
(Gove, 1978)   Fynmore, 1957   MARION
                                                     RIVER
                                                     CARRY
                          RAQUETTE LAKE   RR
CLEARWATER (CARTER)
FULTON CHAIN STA.   OLD FORGE: Fulton Chain RR
Peg Leg RR
(Palmer, 1971 & 1973)   MINNEHAHA   north
MOOSE RIVER
MCKEEVER   WOODHULL MTN.
            Moose River Lumber Co. RR
                                               References on the whole Division:
WOODHULL   Woodhull & Black River RR   Harter, 1979
            (Palmer, April, 1970)   Robbins, 1975
        FORESTPORT   Miller, 1956 & 1957
to Boonville   Staufer, 1967
& Lyons Falls   Burnet, 1932
            REMSEN   Franklin Historical Review, 1973

to Utica   to Herkimer

                                               diagrammatic (not to scale)

Chapter IV:

New York Central Adirondack Division

Introduction

So much material is available on the Adirondack Division and its branches that all I will attempt to do in this Chapter is to locate the trackage and supply dates of operation. The dates stated for stations refer only to passenger service; freight service continued on the Adirondack Division until 1960 or 1961 to Malone, to 1965 to Gabriels, and 1972 to Lake Placid.

Construction of the Adirondack Division began in 1891, with crews working northward from Remsen and southward from Malone. Partial service opened in July, 1892, between Remsen and Fulton Chain Station, and between Malone, Childwold Station and Saranac Lake. Through trains from Herkimer to Malone commenced service on October 24, 1892.

The various branches were built and closed at different times; these dates are available in the text describing each branch. Some of the branches are precisely located on the topographic quadrangles printed by the United States Geological Survey, while other branches have been drawn in on the quadrangles by the authors in the following publications: Palmer, 1971 and 1973 on the Peg-Leg Railroad; and Clark, 1974, on Horseshoe Forestry. Still other branches appear on maps drawn by authors but not on topographic quadrangles (Gove, 1978, on Woods Lake; Gove, 1981, on Brandreth; Gove, 1973, on Grasse River Railroad; Palmer, 1970, on the Black River and Woodhull Railroad); in this third case, I have approximated these branches on the topographic quadrangles so

that the reader should not expect absolute accuracy.

Mileages are from Herkimer, not Utica, to agree with contemporary mileposts. Elevations are in feet taken from U.S.G.S. Quadrangles.

Station Descriptions

Remsen, *27.67 miles from Herkimer. Elevation 1172 feet.*

Remsen at one time was a busy junction point with railroads coming in from four directions: Herkimer, Utica, Boonville, and Malone. Harter offers the details of construction (pp. 1–33, 287–289). First to arrive in Remsen was the Utica and Black River Railroad which was built from Utica to Boonville, later to become part of the Rome, Watertown, and Odgensburg Railroad and extended north to Carthage. Harter does not date the construction of the Utica and Black River Railroad, but Hochschild (1962) in his Real and Phantom (p. 9) offers an 1866 map with the line already in place.

The Herkimer, Newport, and Poland Railroad was built as a narrow gauge, reaching Poland in 1882. In June of 1891, it was standard-gauged by Dr. Webb, and extended to Remsen to connect with the Utica and Black River.

Shortly after, in 1892, the Adirondack and St. Lawrence Railroad opened to Fulton Chain Station and then to Malone. When the New York Central Railroad took over the Adirondack and St. Lawrence Railroad on May 1, 1893, the trains to the Adirondacks were rerouted via the old Utica and Black

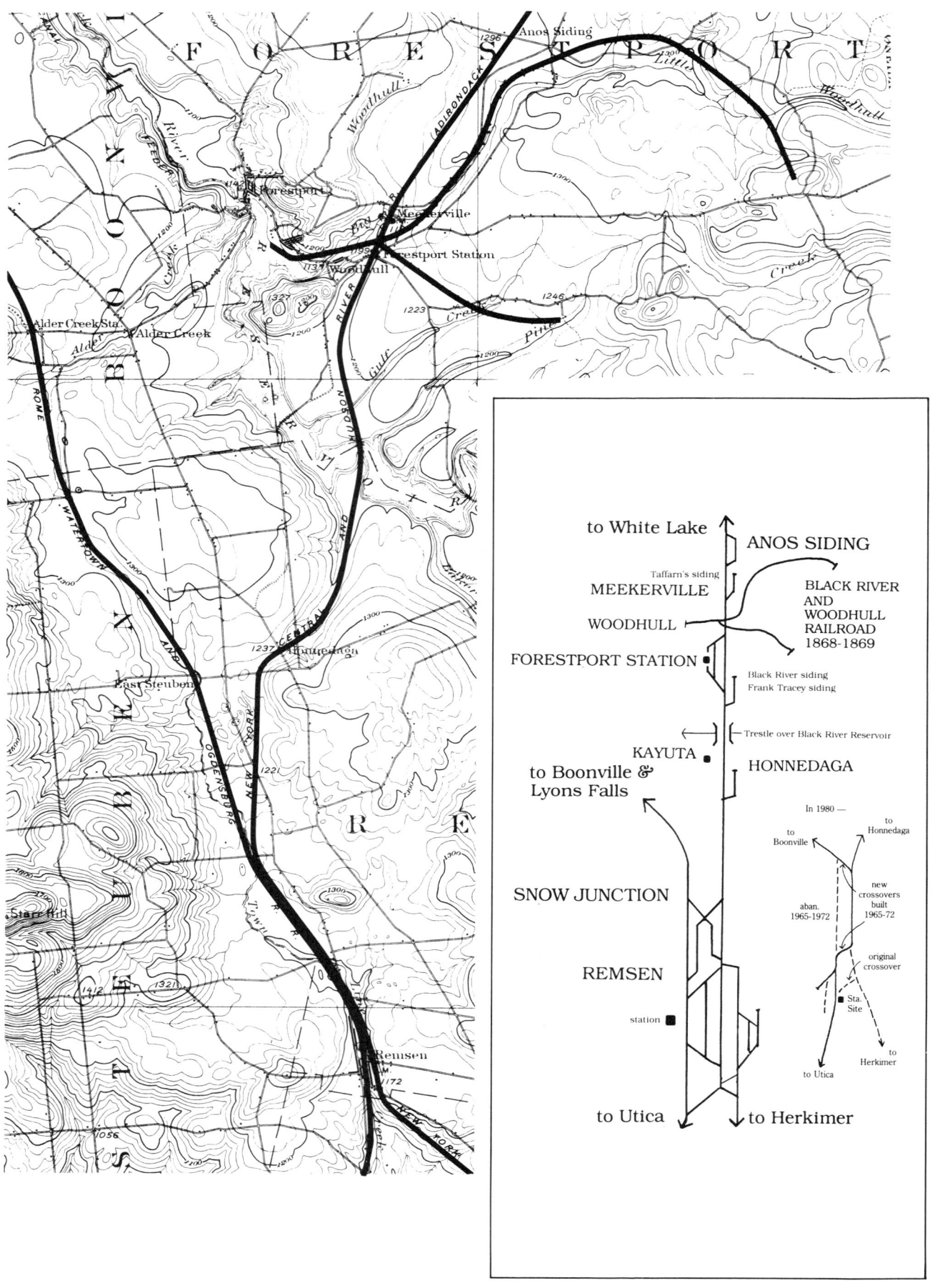

to White Lake
ANOS SIDING

Taffarn's siding
MEEKERVILLE
WOODHULL

BLACK RIVER
AND
WOODHULL
RAILROAD
1868-1869

FORESTPORT STATION

Black River siding
Frank Tracey siding

Trestle over Black River Reservoir

KAYUTA
HONNEDAGA

to Boonville &
Lyons Falls

In 1980 —

to Honnedaga

to Boonville

new
crossovers
built
1965-72

aban.
1965-1972

SNOW JUNCTION

original
crossover

REMSEN

Sta.
Site

to
Herkimer

station

to Utica

to Utica
to Herkimer

River Railroad. Eventually, the Herkimer-Remsen line was abandoned between Remsen and Poland in 1943. The station at Remsen was in service from before 1866 through 1958.

Photos of Remsen are common. Harter has several on pages 170–172. Gardner's photo page 49 is the same as Harter's on page 170. Gardner offers two additional photos on pages 55 and 60.

The track plan presented is from a New York Central Railroad track schematic ca. 1910. The more modern one is from my own observations made in 1980. Conrail still runs the line from Utica to Boonville and Lyons Falls.

A water tower was located in Remsen in 1910 and 1913. The employees' timetables list two passing sidings: the siding east of the station held 12 forty-foot cars in 1910 and in 1913, and 70 forty-four-footers in 1939. The siding north of the station on the west held 40 cars in 1913.

Snow Junction, *about 29 miles from Herkimer. Elevation 1210.*

The Adirondack Division and Lyons Falls Branch of The New York Central Railroad ran parallel for nearly two miles north out of Remsen. To eliminate the duplicate trackage, The New York Central Railroad removed a portion of the Lyons Falls Branch trackage sometime between 1965 and 1972. The new junction was called Snow.

Honnedaga, *31.66 miles. Elevation 1237.*

This station was in service from 1893 through 1914. From 1915 through 1925, it was called Delavan, and from 1926 to 1928, Desmond. By 1929, the station had closed. Harter spells it "Delevan" although the timetables list it as "Delavan". A stub siding, east of the main track and heading north, existed here at one time.

Kayuta, *33.45 miles. Elevation ca. 1190.*

Kayuta operated as a station from 1912 through 1940, although a photo in Harter (p. 174) shows that it was no more than a flag-stop shelter. Just north of the shelter was the trestle (Harter photo, p. 175) over the Kayuta Reservoir — actually, the Black River dammed up at Forestport.

The remains of a former siding at about milepost 34.5, east of main track and heading north, is still in evidence. An old New York Central Railroad track schematic called it Frank Tracey Siding, while Harter calls it Tracy's Spur and moves it south of Kayuta (p. 279); Harter also lists Black River Siding.

Forestport Station, *35.37 miles. Elevation 1199.*

This station operated from 1893 through 1956. The Buffalo Head Hotel was located here. A stagecoach connected Forestport Station with Woodhull (½ mile to the west) and Forestport (1½ miles to the west). A passing siding on the west existed with a stub in both directions on either side of the Station. The siding held 37 forty-foot cars in 1910, 47 cars in 1913, and 40 forty-four foot cars in 1939. The same photo of the Station appears in Gardner (p. 97) and in Harter (p. 174).

Palmer's article (April, 1970) entitled "Wooden Rails in the Wilderness," describes the Black River and Woodhull Railroad. It operated in 1868 and 1869 (possibly into the early 1870s), and was abandoned long before The New York Central Railroad Adirondack Division opened at Forestport Station in 1892. The rails of this line, 13 miles long, were made of wood and only horses pulled the cars (never locomotives!) loaded primarily with logs for the sawmills. Palmer offers a map of the Black River and Woodhull, which I have imposed upon the Remsen topographic Quadrangle as precisely as possible.

Meekerville, *About 36 miles. Elevation 1199.*

This was never a station but only a small community along the track. A New York Central Railroad track schematic indicates here Taffarn's Siding, east of main track and heading north (stub-ended).

Anos, *38.03 miles. Elevation 1296.*

Only the 1910 New York Central Railroad timetable lists this as a stop. The 1897 Remsen Quadrangle indicates Anos Siding 0.15 mile long on the east, stub-ended and heading north; my observations in 1980 reveal that this siding was double-ended. Harter lists "Boonville Sand" here.

A series of sidings occurred between Anos and White Lake. Harter lists Pit Four at 39.70 miles, Johnson (or Johnston) Siding at 39.81 miles, and Nichols Mills at 39.94 miles. One of these, on the east side and stub-ended north, shows on the 1897 Remsen Quadrangle, between the Woodhull and Bear Creek trestles; the elevation here is 1347. A New York Central Railroad track schematic ca. 1910 indicates Pit Four (sand), Johnson Track, and Lo Fountain (see map, page 88).

White Lake (Woodgate), *42.50 miles. Elevation 1417.*

From 1892 through 1920, this station was called White Lake, but by 1925 the name was

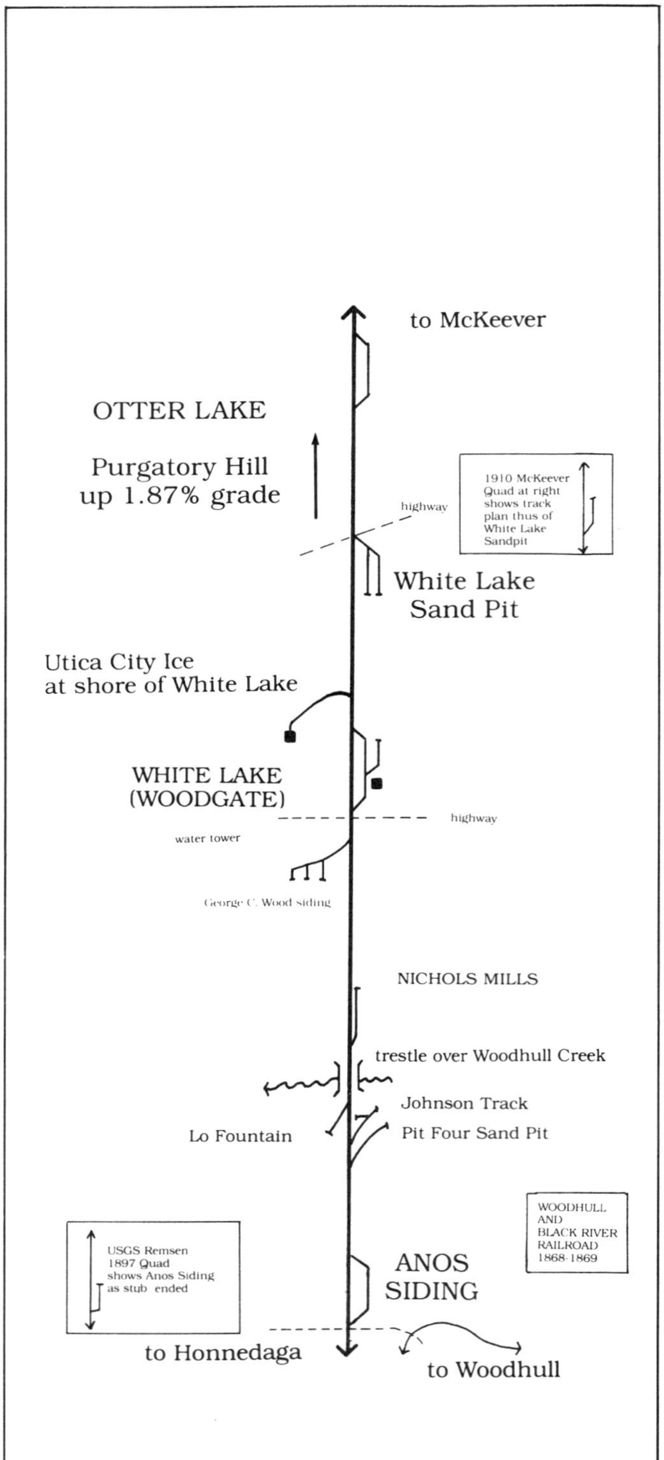
to McKeever
OTTER LAKE
Purgatory Hill
up 1.87% grade
highway
1910 McKeever Quad at right shows track plan thus of White Lake Sandpit
White Lake Sand Pit
Utica City Ice at shore of White Lake
WHITE LAKE (WOODGATE)
highway
water tower
George C. Wood siding
NICHOLS MILLS
trestle over Woodhull Creek
Johnson Track
Lo Fountain
Pit Four Sand Pit
WOODHULL AND BLACK RIVER RAILROAD 1868-1869
USGS Remsen 1897 Quad shows Anos Siding as stub ended
ANOS SIDING
to Honnedaga
to Woodhull

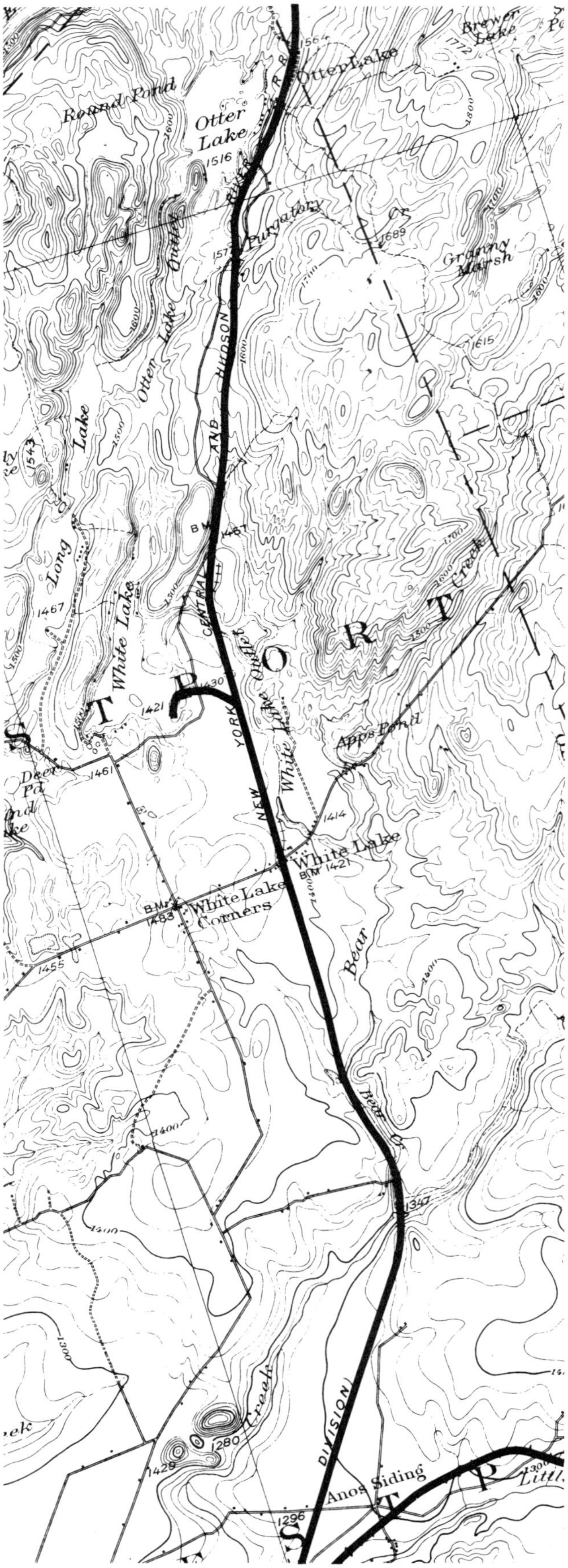
Round Pond
Otter Lake
Otter Lake
Brewer Lake
Purgatory
Granny Marsh
Otter Lake Outlet
NEW YORK CENTRAL AND HUDSON RIVER R.R.
Long Lake
White Lake
White Lake Outlet
Apps Pond
Deer Pd
White Lake
White Lake Corners
Bear Creek
Creek
DIVISION
Anos Siding

changed to Woodgate. Service was suspended here in 1957. Harter presents a photo on page 178. A 1910 New York Central Railroad track schematic shows the George C. Wood siding (see map, page 88) southwest of the station. At the station were two stubs heading north, one of them probably the remains of a passing siding which held 27 forty-foot cars in 1910, 58 of them in 1913, and 49 forty-four foot cars in 1939. A water tower was located here in the 1910 to 1913 era.

Between White Lake and Otter Lake, Harter lists (p. 280) Utica City Ice and White Lake Sand Pit.

Purgatory Hill began at about milepost 44 and ended at about milepost 46. Harter (p. 180) states the grade as 1.87%.

Otter (Otter Lake), *47.57 miles. Elevation 1551.*

This station was in service from 1893 through 1958. Harter (p. 178) and Gardner (p. 39) present the same photo. The 1958 McKeever Quadrangle indicates a siding 0.3 mile long on the east. This siding held 34 forty-foot cars in 1910, 35 of them in 1913, and 25 forty-four foot cars in 1939.

McKeever, *49.15 miles. Elevation 1538.*

The passenger station operated from 1893 through 1957. Harter (p. 179) shows the station with two trains passing, plus a photo of the bridge over the Moose River just north of the Station.

The 1910 McKeever Quadrangle gives us a picture of the operations by showing us the location of the 3½-mile-long Moose River Lumber Company spur to Woodhull Mountain. Palmer has notes on this Company at the Adirondack Museum Library. A New York Central Railroad track schematic ca. 1910 gives us the track plan (see page 186M). A passing siding in 1910 held 30 forty-foot cars; in 1913, 32 cars; and in 1939, 39 forty-four foot cars.

Nelson (Nelson Lake), *52.19 miles. Elevation 1620.*

This station was in service from 1910 through 1940. Although the 1903 Scarborough Map shows it, the 1905 New York Central Railroad timetable does not. A short passing siding existed here on the west side, holding 45 forty-foot cars in 1910 and 46 in 1913. It was gone by 1939.

Minnehaha, *53.75 miles. Elevation 1683*

This station first appears on the 1903 Scarborough Map and continues to be listed through 1948. The C. R. Snell siding diverged here about 1910.

Palmer's 1971 article (reprinted 1973) on the earlier Fulton Chain or "Peg Leg" Railroad centers on this area. Photos appear on page 42 and 56 of the 1971 article and on pages 151 and 155 of the 1973 reprint. The line was built in 1888 and ceased running on July 1, 1892, when Webb's Adirondack and St. Lawrence Railroad was completed to Fulton Chain Station. The "Peg Leg" Railroad was eight miles long and, like the Black River and Woodhull Railroad, had wooden rails. Palmer offers great detail on the locomotive and operations. The "Peg Leg" ran during the summer months only to bring passengers from the Boonville-Port Leyden area to the Fulton Chain of Lakes; from Minnehaha, they boarded a steamboat to Old Forge. The "Peg Leg" also carried some freight, especially during construction of the Adirondack and St. Lawrence Railroad.

Onekio, *55.01 miles. Elevation 1740.*

Onekio was a station from 1904 through 1913.

Fulton Chain Station (Thendara), *57.93 miles. Elevation 1712.*

The Fulton Chain Station was the terminus of the Adirondack and St. Lawrence Railroad temporarily from July 1, 1892, through October 24, 1892, when the first through train ran from Herkimer to Malone. On June 27, 1920, the name was changed to Thendara (Harter, p. 183) which remained the station name through 1965. When the Adirondack Railway operated in 1979 and 1980, Thendara was the site of the headquarters and shops.

At Thendara, a 2.21-mile-long branch was constructed in 1896 (Harter, p. 290) to Old Forge. The branch was called the (second) Fulton Chain Railroad, and it ran until July 11, 1932. See also Hochschild (1962, "Life & Leisure in the Adirondack Backwoods," p. 33) for details, and page 117 in this work for service.

A track plan of Fulton Chain Station about 1910 is presented on page 90, with a contemporary 1980 map alongside. The New York Central Railroad employees' timetables list a passing siding here accommodating 74 forty-foot cars in 1910, 76 of them in 1913, and 73 forty-four foot cars in 1939; this siding was west of the main track. The Adirondack Railway in 1980 added a stub siding off the passing siding to store equipment, in addition to that which The Penn Central Railroad had abandoned here in 1972.

Photos of the Thendara and Old Forge

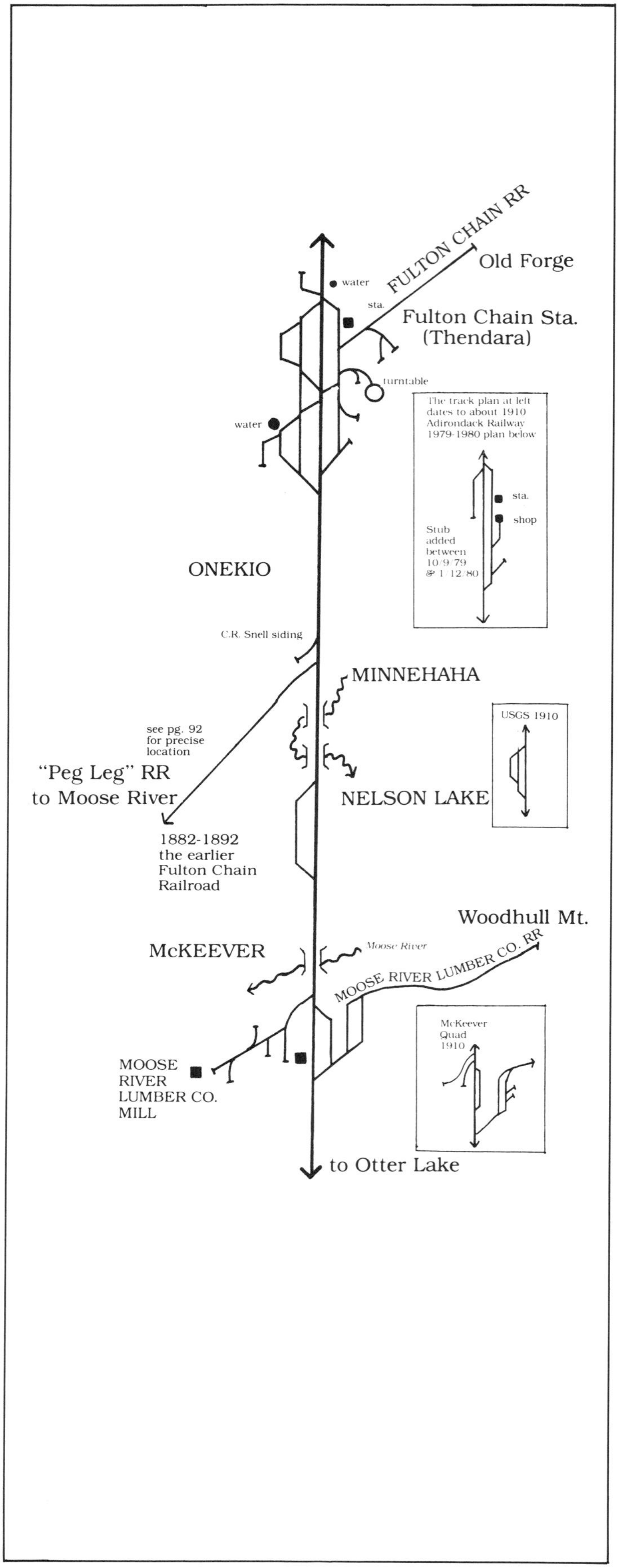

FULTON CHAIN RR
Old Forge
water
sta.
Fulton Chain Sta.
(Thendara)
turntable
water
The track plan at left dates to about 1910 Adirondack Railway 1979-1980 plan below
sta.
shop
Stub added between 10/9/79 & 1/12/80
ONEKIO
C.R. Snell siding
MINNEHAHA
see pg. 92 for precise location
"Peg Leg" RR
to Moose River
USGS 1910
NELSON LAKE
1882-1892 the earlier Fulton Chain Railroad
Woodhull Mt.
Moose River
McKEEVER
MOOSE RIVER LUMBER CO. RR
MOOSE RIVER LUMBER CO. MILL
McKeever Quad 1910
to Otter Lake

Indian
Brook
Nelson Lake
SOUTH
McKeever
HERKIMER

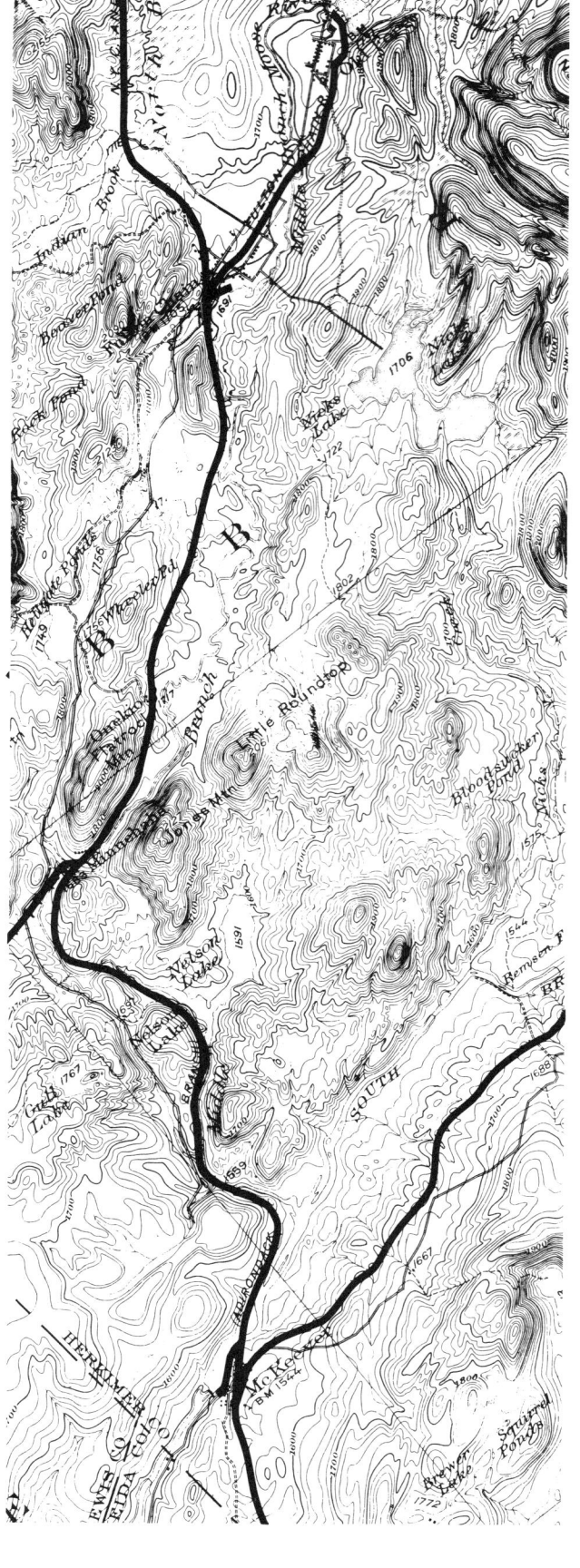

area abound: Harter, pages 188 & 262; Gardner, Pages 23, 39, 40, 75; Hochschild (1962) "Life & Leisure in the Adirondack Backwoods," page 35; DeSormo (1974), page 108.

A water tower was located here in 1910, 1913, and 1958. Both the Fulton Chain and Raquette Lake Railways were acquired by The New York Central Railroad in 1917 (Hochschild, 1962, Life & Leisure in the Adirondack Backwoods, p. 97).

Moulin, *60.66 miles. Elevation 1748.*

Moulin is shown on 1912 and 1914 timetables only, although a 1904 map also locates it. Slightly north of milepost 62 was the W. D. DeCamp Siding (shown on The New York Central Railroad track schematic, ca. 1910); Harter (p. 280) calls it Lotus Siding. There were two stub tracks on the west side of the main track heading south.

Clearwater (Carter Station), *64.12 miles. Elevation 1752.*

On July 11, 1900, the Raquette Lake Railway opened (Harter, p. 291; and Hochschild, 1962, Life & Leisure, pp. 38 and 97), connecting with the Adirondack Division at this point. Harter also notes that Clearwater Station appeared in the 1899 timetables while the Raquette Lake Railway was under construction. The junction was first named Clearwater, but the name was changed to Carter Station on June 23, 1912 (Harter, p. 186).

A passing siding holding 46 forty-foot cars was here in 1910, holding 51 of them in 1913, and gone by 1939. The Raquette Lake Railway had two short sidings; one was south of the station on the east side holding 8 forty-foot cars in 1910 and 10 cars in 1913. The second siding was north of the station on the west side of the main track and held 18 forty-foot cars in 1910 and 22 cars in 1913. Detail on the Raquette Lake Railway will be found on page 117.

Adirondack Division service continued at Carter Station through 1956.

Big Moose, *69.31 miles. Elevation 2034 or 2035.*

This station, located at the highest point on the line, was in service from 1893 through 1965. Harter (p. 180) describes the 1.11% grade from Clearwater to Big Moose which often caused problems. At the summit near Big Moose Station was a double passing siding on the east (only one siding left in 1980); the siding, according to Employees' timetables, held 35 forty-foot cars in 1910 and 1913, and 27 forty-four foot cars in 1939. A wye

existed north and west of the station in 1913, possibly to turn pusher engines coming up from Clearwater.

At Buck Pond, just north of milepost 70, the Champlain Realty Company (a division of International Paper) had a siding for loading pulpwood on to railroad cars as a part of the Woods Lake operation (see below).

Photos of Big Moose occur in Harter (p. 189), Gardner (p. 94), Hochschild (1962, "Adirondack Railroads Real and Phantom," p. 11).

At 71.7 miles was the Twitchell Creek Bridge (Harter photo p. 199). At 72.7 miles was the spot where the last spike was driven on October 12, 1892, completing the Adirondack and St. Lawrence Railway between Herkimer and Malone.

Woods (Woods Lake), *73.47 miles. Elevation 1875 or 1882.*

This station was in service from 1895 through 1953. A passing siding held 64 forty-foot cars in 1910, 65 cars in 1913, and 54 forty-four foot cars in 1939. The Champlain Valley Realty Company, a division of International Paper Company, built a three-mile-long logging railroad from the passing siding westward down to Twitchell Creek about 1916. Gove (1978) offers full details on this operation including photos. The railroad ceased running about 1926 and the rails were pulled up about 1932. The Buck Pond siding near Big Moose was also linked with this operation.

Beaver River, *77.69 miles. Elevation 1692.*

From 1893 through 1965 this was a stop on the railroad, although supplies were brought in to the Hotel here by the Adirondack Railway in 1979 and 1980. The existing passing siding (1980) is on the east; it held 30 forty-foot cars in 1910, 37 in 1913, and 29 forty-four foot cars in 1939. A stub south of the siding headed northeast down to a gravel pit before 1914. Harter has photos of Beaver River on pages 190 and 191, including the Stillwater Reservoir crossing between mileposts 78 and 79. A water tower was located at Beaver River in 1910 and 1951, and probably all the years in between. The original station burned in 1940 (Harter, p. 190) while the Norridgewock Hotel, adjacent to the station, burned in 1914.

Little Rapids, *80.24 miles. Elevation 1689.*

Elevations for this station range from 1685 to 1721!! It was in service from 1893 through 1959.

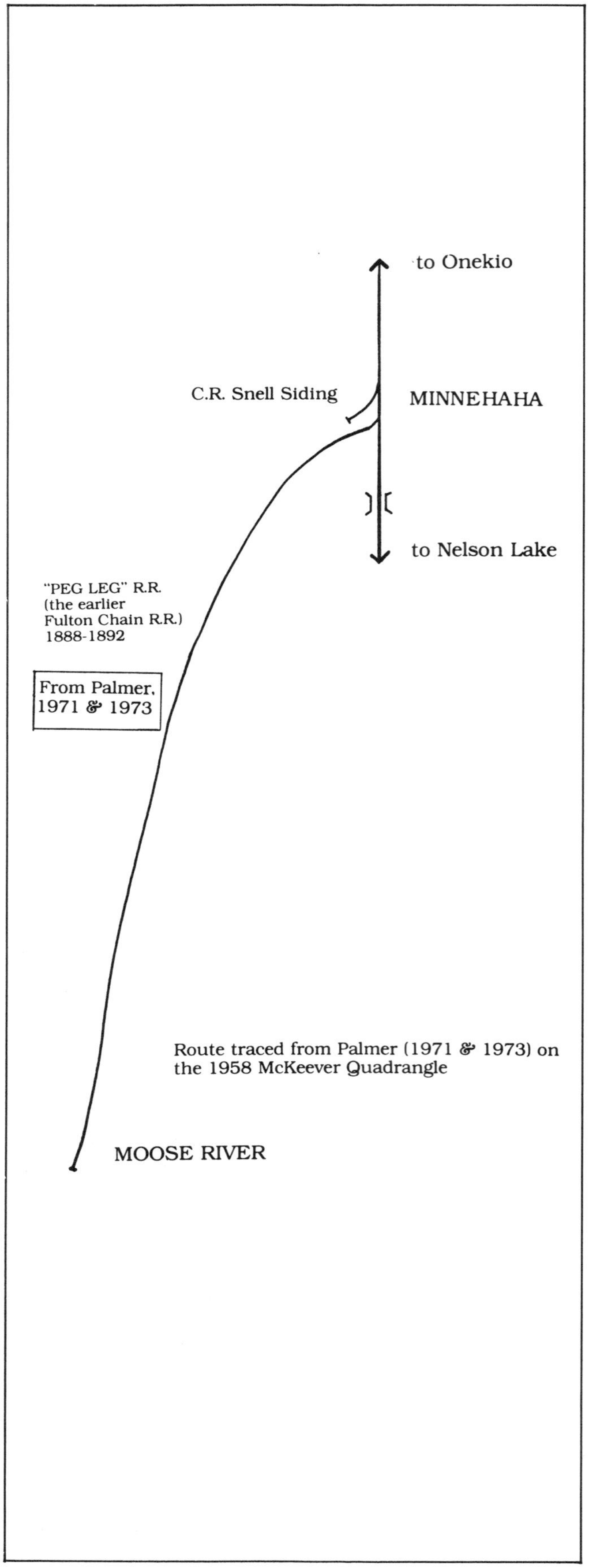

to Onekio
C.R. Snell Siding
MINNEHAHA
to Nelson Lake
"PEG LEG" R.R.
(the earlier
Fulton Chain R.R.)
1888-1892
From Palmer,
1971 & 1973
Route traced from Palmer (1971 & 1973) on
the 1958 McKeever Quadrangle
MOOSE RIVER

Nelson Lake
HERKIMER
LEWIS CO
ONEIDA CO
McKeever
RIVER
Round Pond
Otter Lake
1516
1767

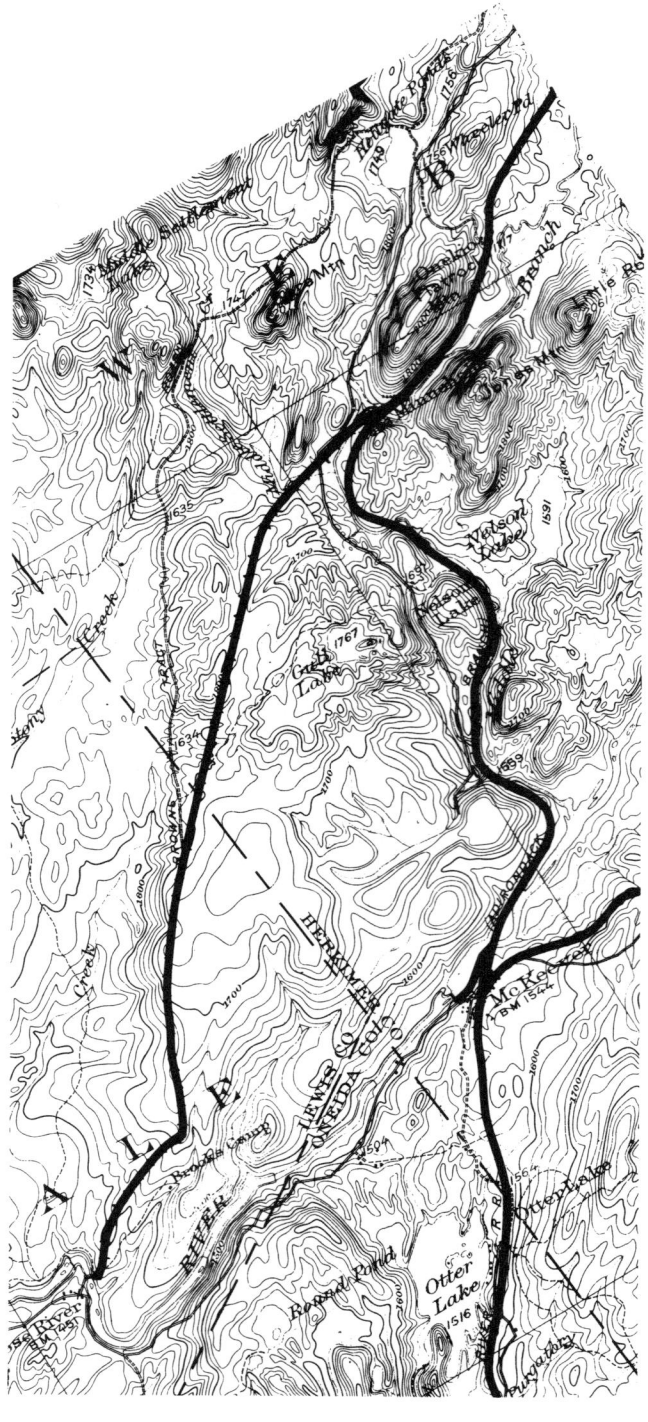

Woods Lake
Razorback Pond
Snake Pond
NEW YORK CENTRAL
Twitchell Creek
Buck Pond
Big Moose
Little Independence Pond
River
Diamond Pond
Independence Lake
Clearwater (Carter Sta.)
Clear Pond
Little Safford Lake
North Rondaxe
West Lake
Bald Mountain
Branch Moose
First
Second Lake
STEAMBOAT ROUTE

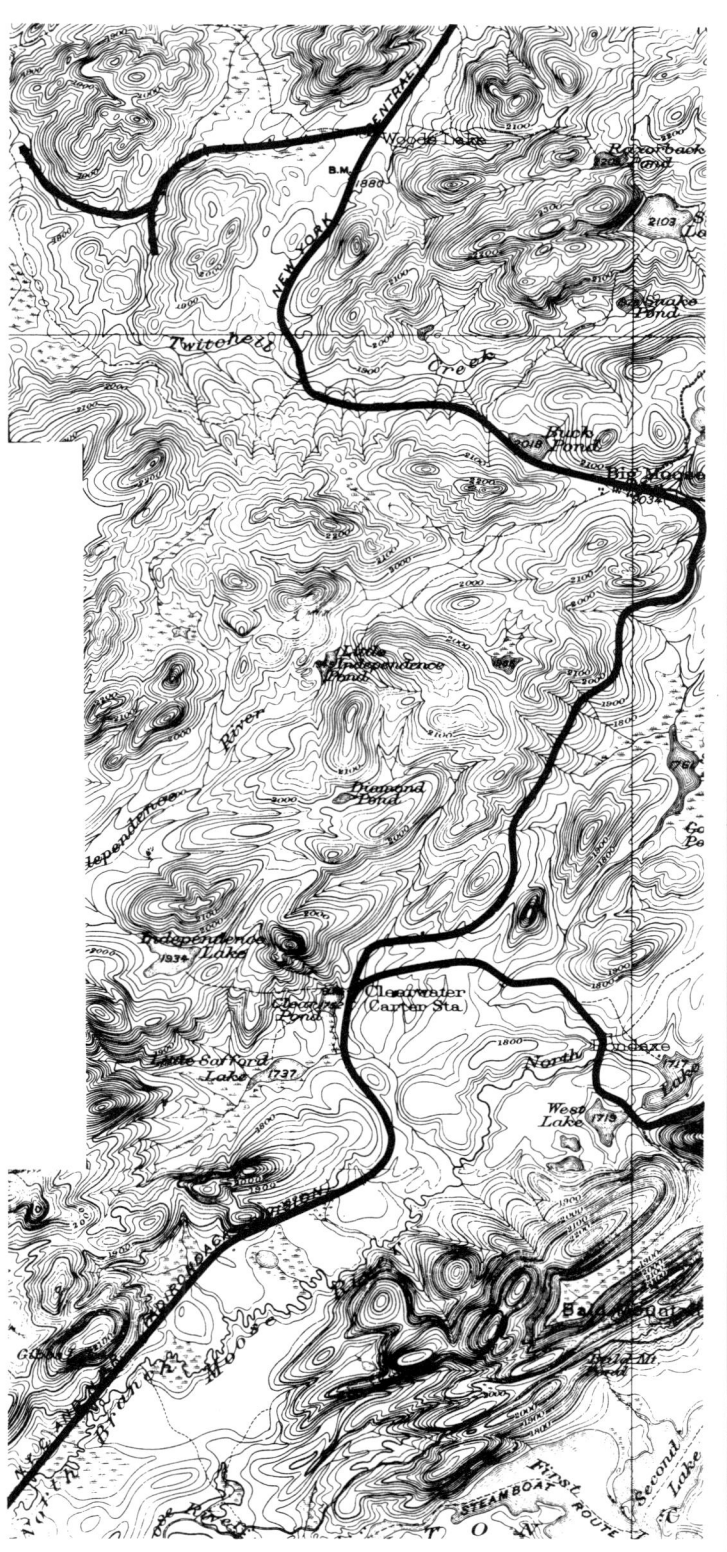

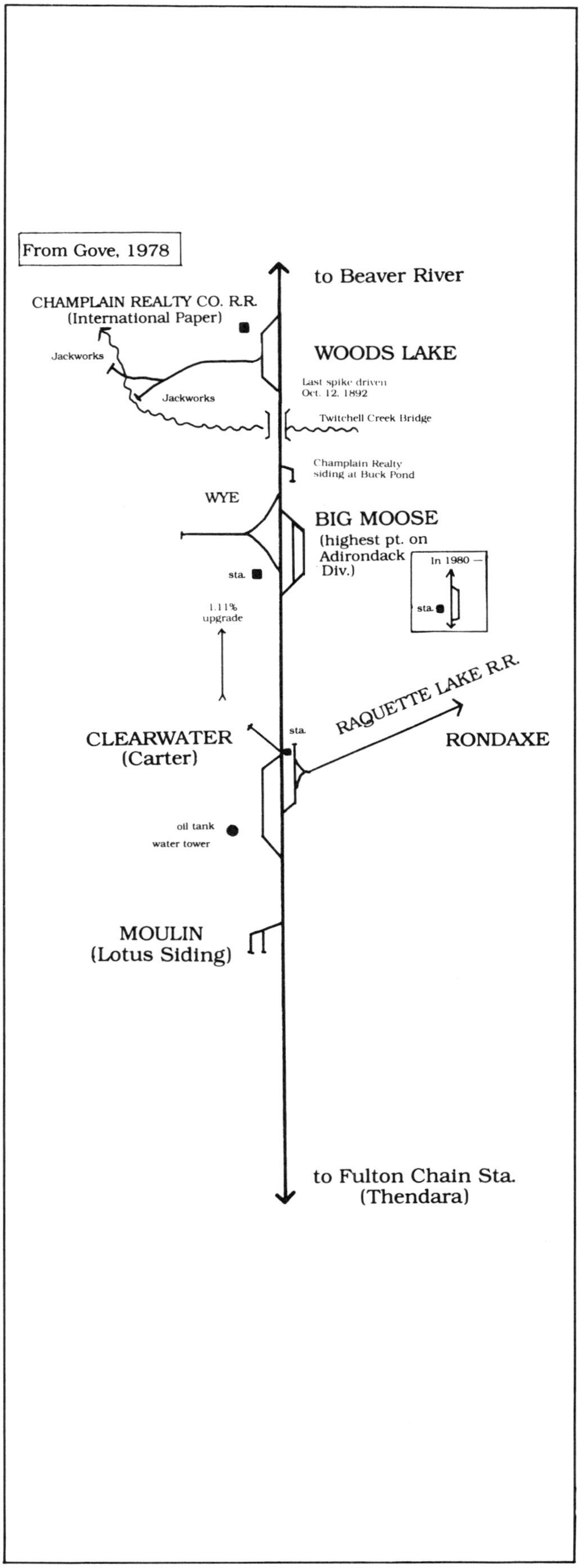

From Gove, 1978
to Beaver River
CHAMPLAIN REALTY CO. R.R.
(International Paper)
Jackworks
Jackworks
WOODS LAKE
Last spike driven
Oct. 12, 1892
Twitchell Creek Bridge
Champlain Realty
siding at Buck Pond
WYE
BIG MOOSE
(highest pt. on
Adirondack
Div.)
sta.
In 1980
sta.
1.11%
upgrade
RAQUETTE LAKE R.R.
sta.
CLEARWATER
(Carter)
RONDAXE
oil tank
water tower
MOULIN
(Lotus Siding)
to Fulton Chain Sta.
(Thendara)

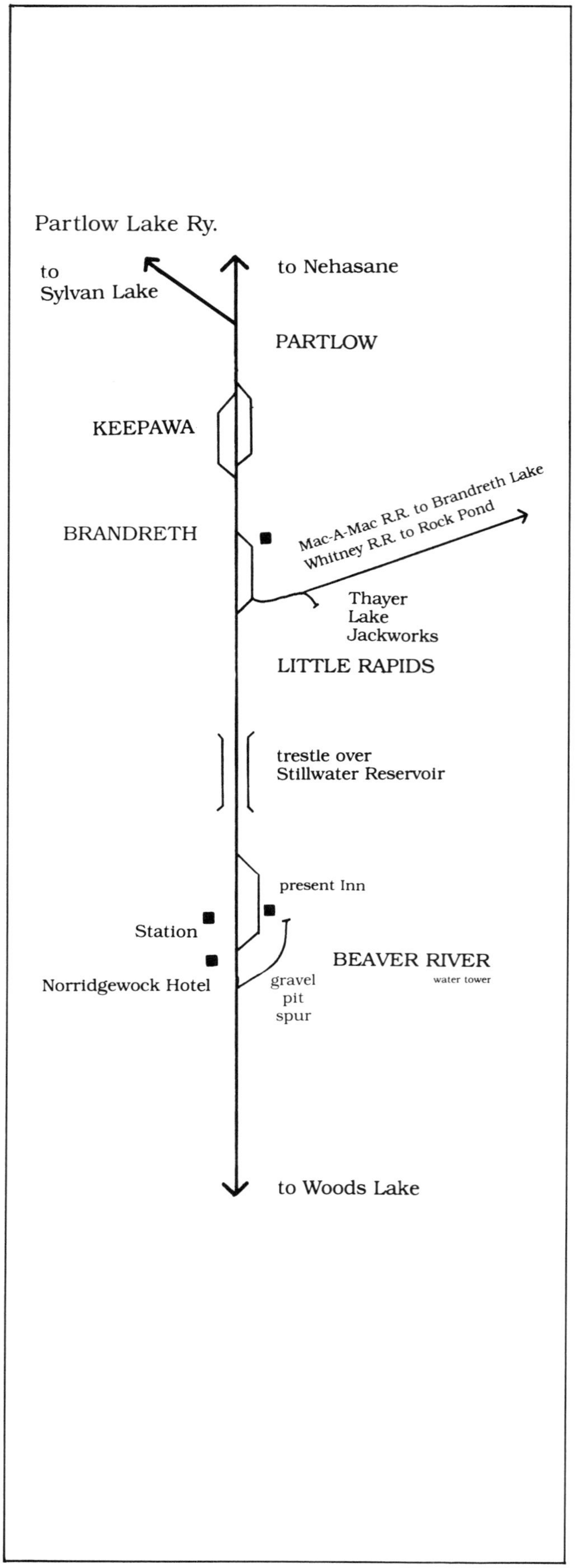

Partlow Lake Ry.
to Sylvan Lake
to Nehasane
PARTLOW
KEEPAWA
BRANDRETH
Mac-A-Mac R.R. to Brandreth Lake
Whitney R.R. to Rock Pond
Thayer Lake Jackworks
LITTLE RAPIDS
trestle over Stillwater Reservoir
present Inn
Station
BEAVER RIVER
water tower
Norridgewock Hotel
gravel pit spur
to Woods Lake

KEEPAWA
ADIRONDACK
DIVISION
Rose Pond
Beaver River
Twitchell Mt.
Razorback Pond
Oswego Pond

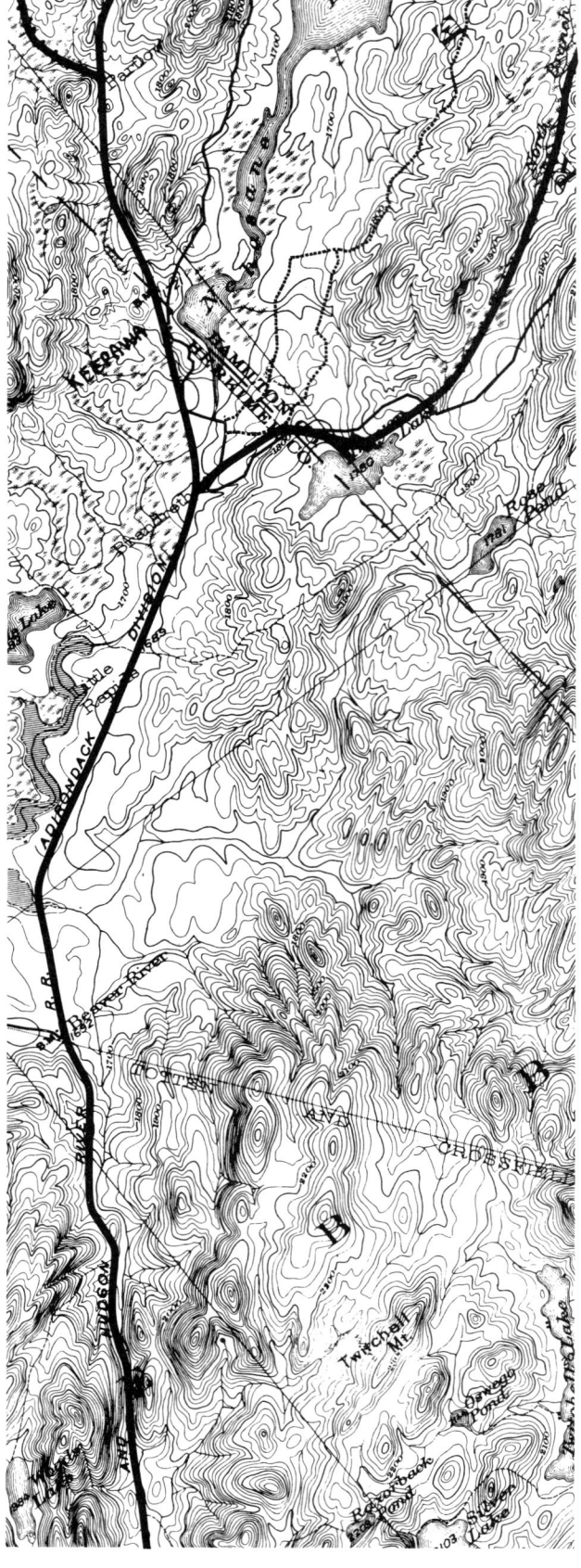

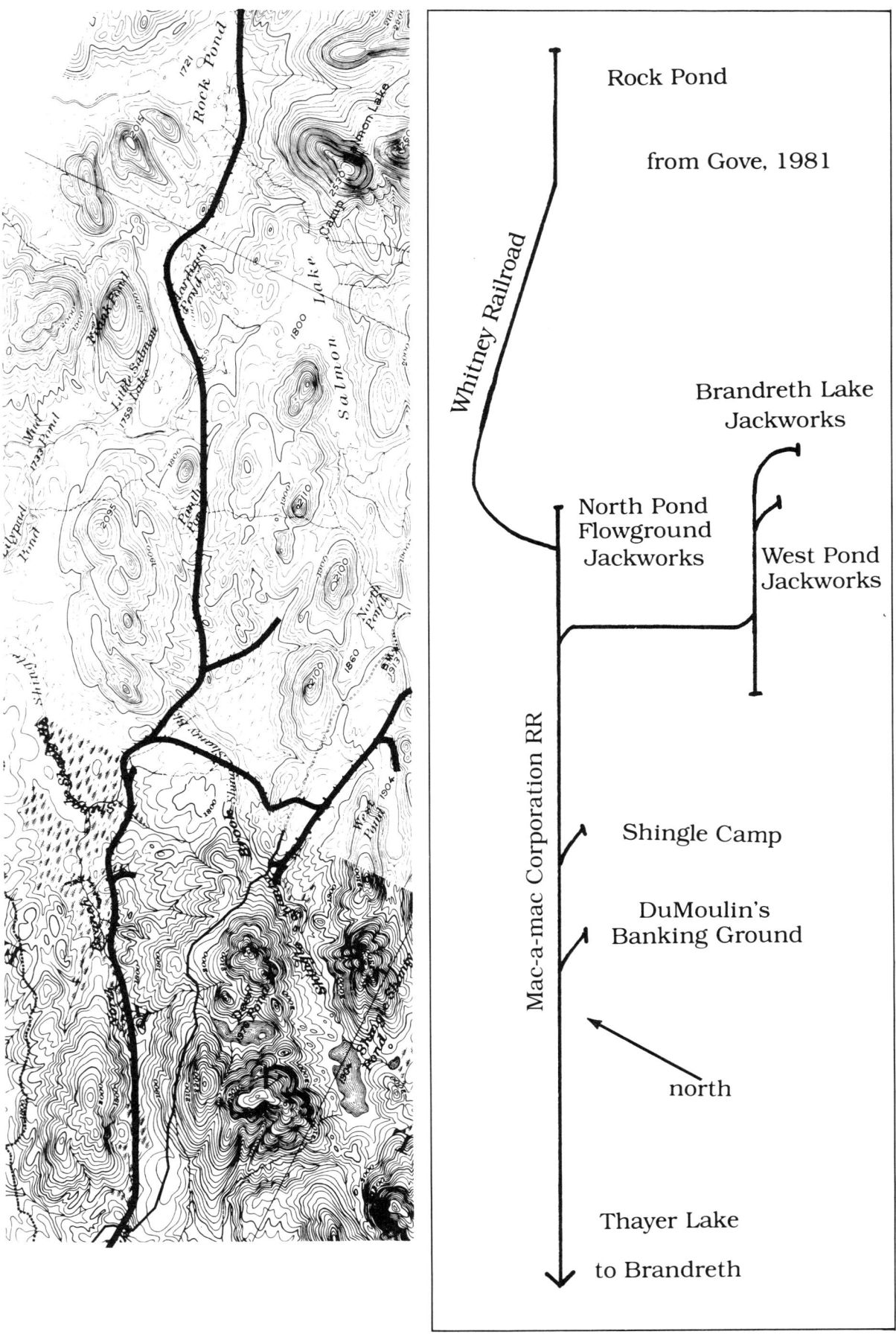

Rock Pond

from Gove, 1981

Whitney Railroad

Brandreth Lake
Jackworks

North Pond
Flowground
Jackworks

West Pond
Jackworks

Mac-a-mac Corporation RR

Shingle Camp

DuMoulin's
Banking Ground

north

Thayer Lake

to Brandreth

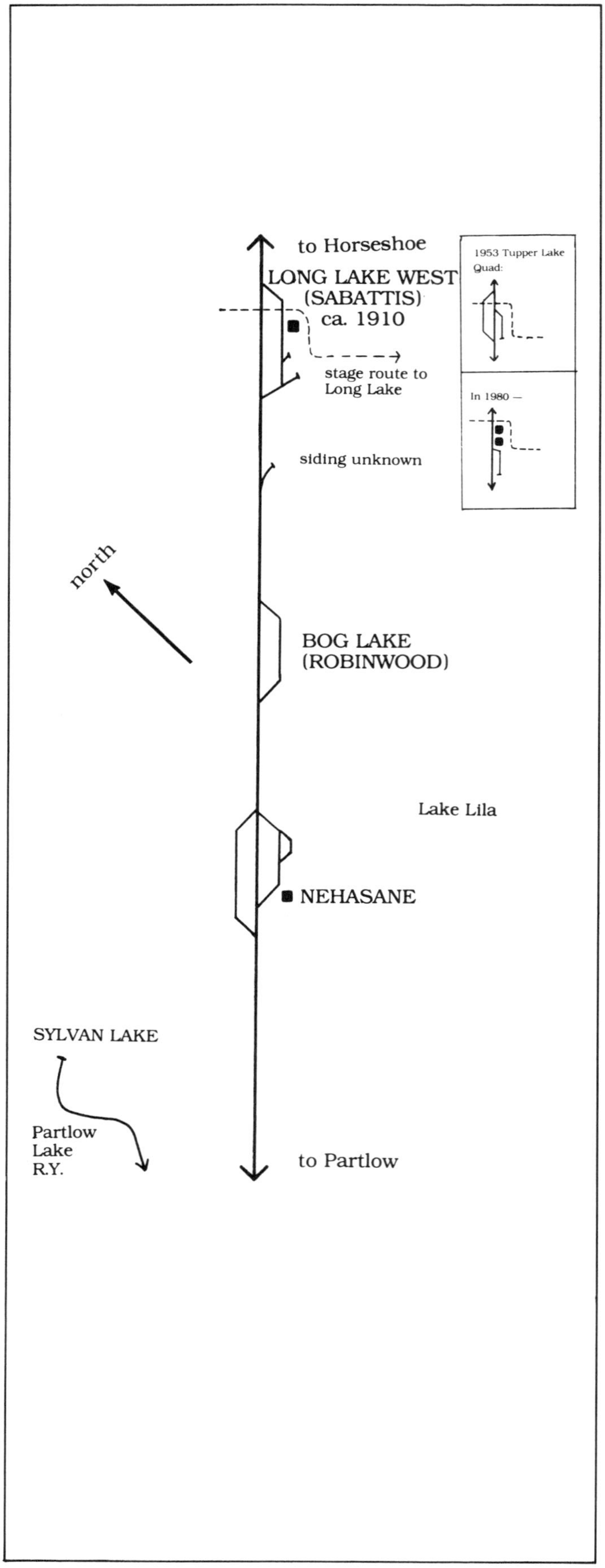

to Horseshoe
LONG LAKE WEST
(SABATTIS)
ca. 1910
stage route to
Long Lake
1953 Tupper Lake
Quad:
In 1980 —
siding unknown
north
BOG LAKE
(ROBINWOOD)
Lake Lila
NEHASANE
SYLVAN LAKE
Partlow
Lake
R.Y.
to Partlow

ST. LAWRENCE CO
HAMILTON CO
Bog River
Bog Lake
Robinwood
Clear Pond
Third Pond
Second Pond
First Pond

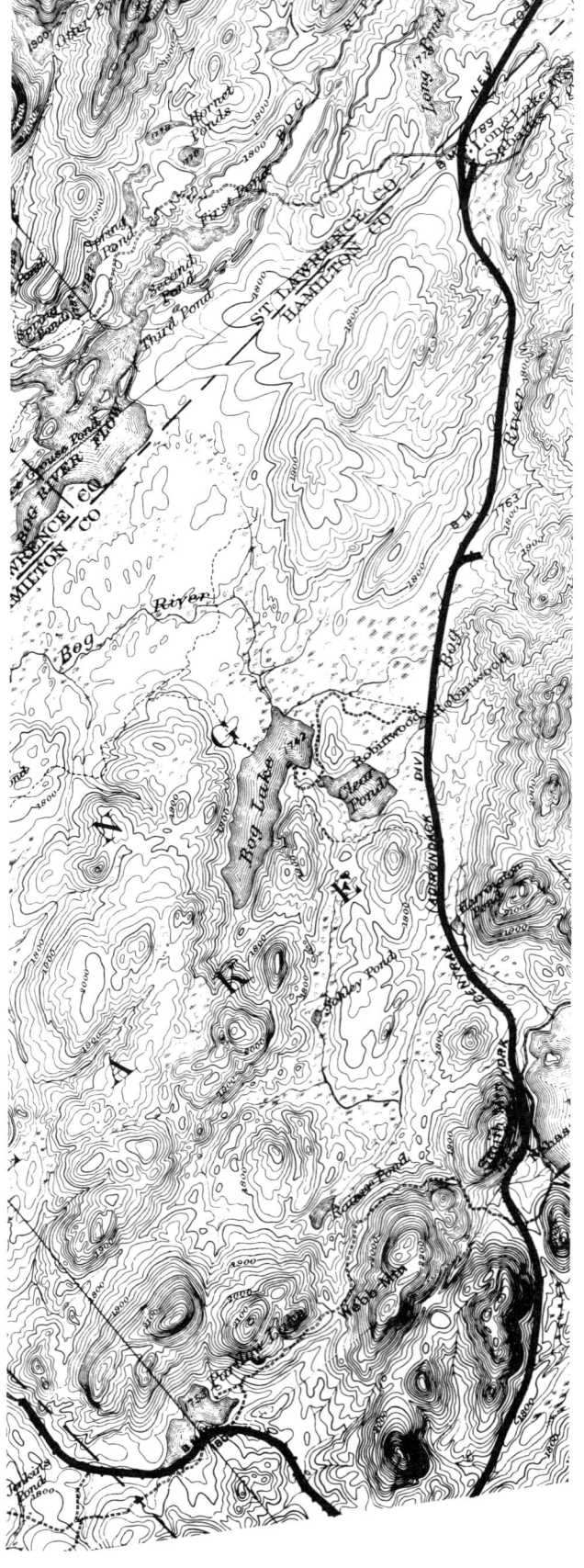

Brandreth (Brandreth Lake), *81.37 miles. Elevation 1690.*

The earliest evidence I have for this station is on a 1900 New York Central Railroad map, the latest a 1965 timetable. Gove (April, 1981) notes that the Brandreth Lake Station opened in 1895 for people with nearby summer homes. From Brandreth Station, the Mac-a-Mac Corporation built a logging railroad eastward to Brandreth Lake in 1912, primarily for pulp. Gove (April, 1981) offers a whole article on the line, which ran until 1920, well-illustrated with photos. Harter includes photos, too, on pages 198 and 199.

In 1936, Whitney Industries, Inc. relaid track from Brandreth Station to a point short of North Pond Flowground, upon the former Brandreth line. At this point, Whitney built a new right-of-way east to Rock Pond for mostly hardwood logging, trains ran only until 1939. The 1953–1954 Raquette Lake Quadrangle shows the abandoned right-of-way of the Whitney Railroad.

Keepawa, *82.77 miles. Elevation 1721.*

This station was in service from 1910 to 1939. Here were two passing sidings, one on each side of the main track. One of them held 27 forty-foot cars in 1910, 28 such cars in 1913, and was abandoned by 1939. Keepawa was the station for those who operated Webb's private park.

Partlow (Pulpwood P.O.), *84.27 or 84.32 miles (Was the station moved?). Elevation 1730.*

This was a junction point for the Partlow Lake Railway which headed north to Sylvan Lake, 5 miles. Partlow station was used for lumbering operations and appears on timetables from about 1900 through 1905. These operations were on Webb's private park.

Nehasane, *87.82 miles. Elevation 1787 or 1788.*

Harter (p. 200) states that there were three stations within Nehasane Park (Webb's private landholding): Keepawa, Partlow, and Nehasane. Nehasane was Webb's private station for his nearby estate on Lake Lila; it appears on the timetables from 1893 through 1965. The New York Central Railroad track schematic ca. 1910 indicates two sidings on the east, but on-site observations in 1980 suggest more room and more evidence for sidings on the west of the main track. Wherever the major siding was located, it held 31 forty-foot cars in 1910, 34 such cars in 1913, and 21 forty-four foot cars

in 1939. The station house still stood in 1980. Photos are in Harter (pp. 202–205, and 210).

Bog Lake (Robinwood), *90.89 or 90.92 miles. Elevation 1756.*

There is some confusion here. Harter lists (p. 282) Bog Lake at 90.7 miles and Robinwood as a different place at 90.89. The timetables lead one to believe that it was *one* flagstop with a name change. The station was first in service in 1893 as Bog Lake, became Robinwood between 1905 and 1908, and was listed through 1959. A passing siding was located here holding 16 forty-foot cars in 1910 and 17 such cars in 1913; it was gone by 1939.

An examination of the 1903–1904 Tupper Lake Quadrangle at about milepost 91.8 reveals a small stub siding on the east, heading north 0.15 mile to a building. The function of this siding is a mystery.

Long Lake West (Sabattis), *94.78 miles. Elevation 1788 or 1789.*

My earliest evidence of this station is on a 1900 New York Central Railroad map. Harter (p. 209) notes that the name was changed from Long Lake West to Sabattis on June 26, 1923, the station being in service until 1965. The New York Central Railroad employees' timetables list a passing siding accommodating 60 forty-foot cars in 1910, 62 such cars in 1913, and 41 forty-four foot cars in 1939. The 1903–1904 and 1953–1954 Tupper Lake Quadrangles show a change of track plan during the half-century; the two plans are illustrated on the maps.

Photos occur in Harter (pp. 205, 210, 211). Robbins (pp. 27 and 29) includes photos of Sabattis but amazingly calls the station Brandreth!

This was the station for Long Lake, hence the name. Stagecoach connections ran between Long Lake West, Little Tupper Lake, and Long Lake.

Horse Shoe (American Legion), *99.91 miles. Elevation 1738.*

Here is another name-change station! This time, the station was originally called Horse Shoe (a variety of spellings in Harter, p. 282) and dates to 1893. The name change to American Legion occurred between 1947 and 1948, and the station remained in service through 1965. Passing siding data are 65 forty-foot cars in 1910, 61 such cars in 1913, and 52 forty-four-foot cars in 1939. A water tower was here in the 1910 to 1913 era.

From Horse Shoe Station, Abbot Augustus Low built his Horseshoe Forestry Company Railway, well described in Clark (1974). The

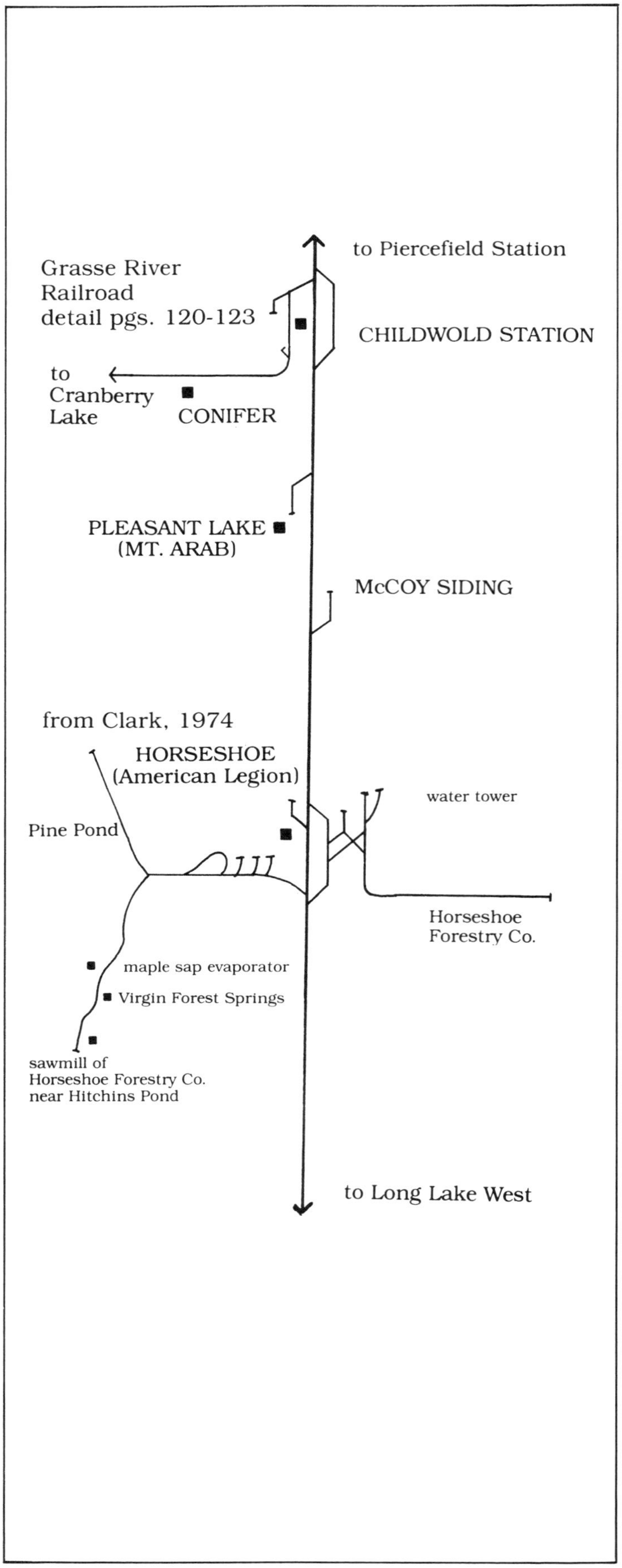
to Piercefield Station
Grasse River
Railroad
detail pgs. 120-123
CHILDWOLD STATION
to
Cranberry
Lake
CONIFER
PLEASANT LAKE
(MT. ARAB)
McCOY SIDING
from Clark, 1974
HORSESHOE
(American Legion)
water tower
Pine Pond
Horseshoe
Forestry Co.
maple sap evaporator
Virgin Forest Springs
sawmill of
Horseshoe Forestry Co.
near Hitchins Pond
to Long Lake West

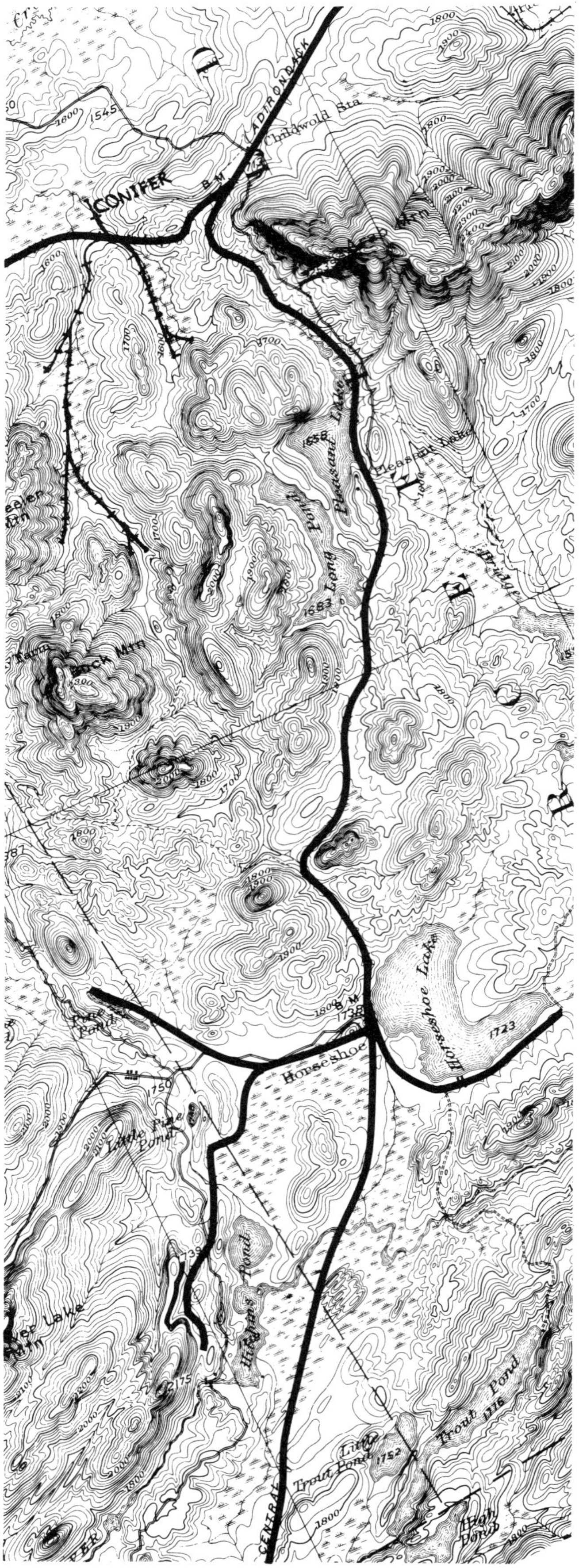
CONIFER
ADIRONDACK
Childwold Sta
Pleasant Lake
Long Pond
Horseshoe Lake
Horseshoe
Trout Pond
Little Trout Pond
CENTRAL

Railway, with three branches off the New York Central, was built in 1897 and ran to shortly after the 1908 fire removed much of the remaining timber. By 1911, the Railway had ceased completely. The branch to Hitchins Pond served a combination of uses: sawmill, maple sap and bottled spring water carrier. The sawmill also included box, stave, and heading (barrel) mills.

DeSormro (1974) has a photo of a wreck at Horseshoe (p. 115).

Pleasant Lake (Mt. Arab), *104.01 miles. Elevation 1676.*

Yet another name-change station! Pleasant Lake first appears in the timetables in 1912. The name was changed to Mt. Arab between 1920 and 1925, the station closing in 1958. A photo occurs in Gardner (p. 75). The track schematic ca. 1910 indicates a short stub siding on the west heading south.

Harter lists McCoy Siding (p. 282) as at milepost 103.14, but the New York Central track schematic (ca. 1910) shows it at about 102.5. It was on the east, stub-ended north.

Childwold Station, *106.75 or 106.76 miles. Elevation 1713.*

This station was in service from 1892 through 1959. From July through October, 1892, it was the temporary terminus of the Adirondack and St. Lawrence Railroad being built southward from Malone. It served the nearby Childwold Park House hotel, but should not be confused with the New York and Ottawa station some 6 miles to the northeast which also, via another stage route, served the same hotel.

A passing siding here held 40 forty-foot cars in 1910, and in 1913, and was extended by 1939 to hold 46 forty-four foot cars.

See page 123 on the Grasse River Railroad which connected here.

Piercefield Station, *109.23 miles. Elevation 1673 or 1674.*

The earliest evidence I have for this station is a New York Central 1900 map, and the last a 1940 timetable. A passing siding was located here, some 920 feet long in 1910, 1000 feet in 1913, and gone by 1939. A photo of the station occurs in Harter (p. 211). A 1.4-mile-long spur ran northwest down to the Raquette River and the hamlet of Piercefield; here, the International Paper Company had a mill which was already running when the 1903–1904 Tupper Lake Quadrangle was printed, and was still running in 1931. The 1938 New York State Adirondack Land Map published by the Conservation Department no longer shows the spur.

Underwood, *112.0 or 112.3 miles. Elevation 1550.*

We turn to Simmons (1976) to give us the details of the activities at Underwood (pp. 79 and 80 with photo on 88). George Underwood in 1898 and 1899 built a pulp rossing plant (to remove the bark of pulpwood) at the west bank of the Raquette River near the railroad bridge. The plant ran until 1909, shipping the debarked pulp to the International Paper Company mill at Piercefield. Simmons notes that Underwood worked for the Champlain Realty Company, a subsidiary of International Paper; the site was used as a jackworks at a later time, but Simmons offers no dates for this.

Tupper Lake Junction (Faust Post Office), *113.64 miles. Elevation 1556.*

This busy station was in service from 1892 through 1965. The Northern Adirondack Railroad, built by John Hurd in 1889–1890, predated the Adirondack and St. Lawrence built by William Webb by about 2½ years. The two railroads crossed here at Tupper Lake Junction. Webb's Road was taken over by the New York Central in 1893 and Hurd's in 1906 (the latter becoming the Ottawa Branch), so that one railroad then operated both lines. For details on the New York and Ottawa, which operated until 1937, see Chapter III, pages 60 to 83. Although passenger service terminated on the Adirondack Division on April 24, 1965, Tupper Lake Junction Station was not demolished until 1975. In the earlier years, the Station was served by stagecoaches for Tupper Lake Village (two miles), the Wawbeek Lodge, Rustic Lodge, and the Waukesha.

Those industries along the New York and Ottawa are described in Chapter III (pp. 60 to 83): Hurd's Big Mill later operated by Norwood, the Hobson Mill later operated by Sherman and Sisson, and the Oval Wood Dish Company. Only those industries served directly by the Adirondack Division will be described in the section below.

At milepost 113, about ⅔ of a mile southwest of the Tupper Lake Junction Station, was a spur leading to a jackworks on Raquette Pond, across the River from Underwood. It is present on both the 1901–1902 and 1955 Long Lake Quadrangles, but had been abandoned before the Penn Central ceased operations in 1972.

Moving further northeast along the Adirondack Division, we find the spur leading to the Santa Clara Lumber Company Mill, also on Raquette Pond. The spur crossed Main Street twice, once by the Station and again at a diagonal near Water Street. It followed Poplar Street to the Mill, which was built in

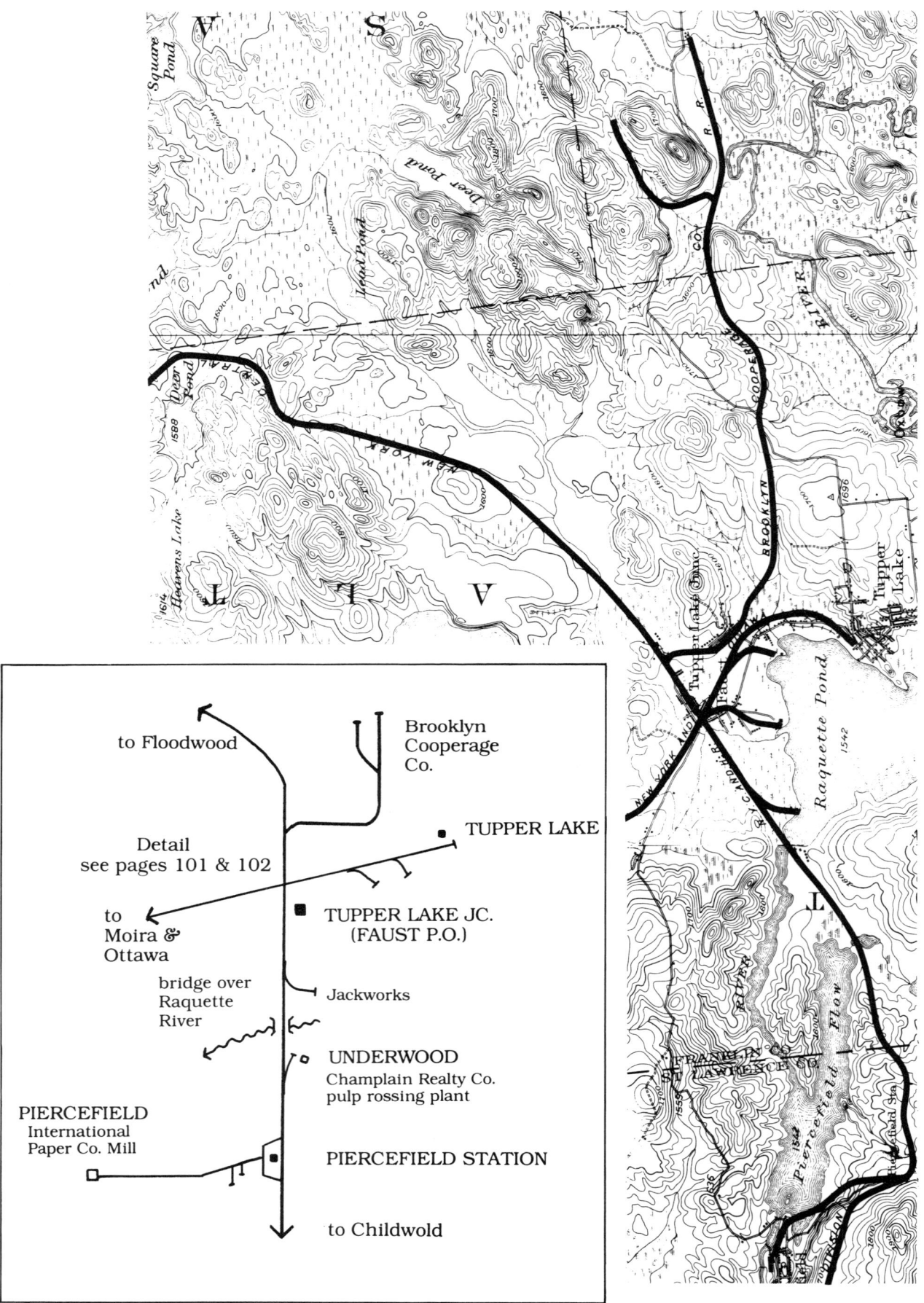

to Floodwood

Brooklyn
Cooperage
Co.

Detail
see pages 101 & 102

TUPPER LAKE

to
Moira &
Ottawa

TUPPER LAKE JC.
(FAUST P.O.)

bridge over
Raquette
River

Jackworks

UNDERWOOD
Champlain Realty Co.
pulp rossing plant

PIERCEFIELD
International
Paper Co. Mill

PIERCEFIELD STATION

to Childwold

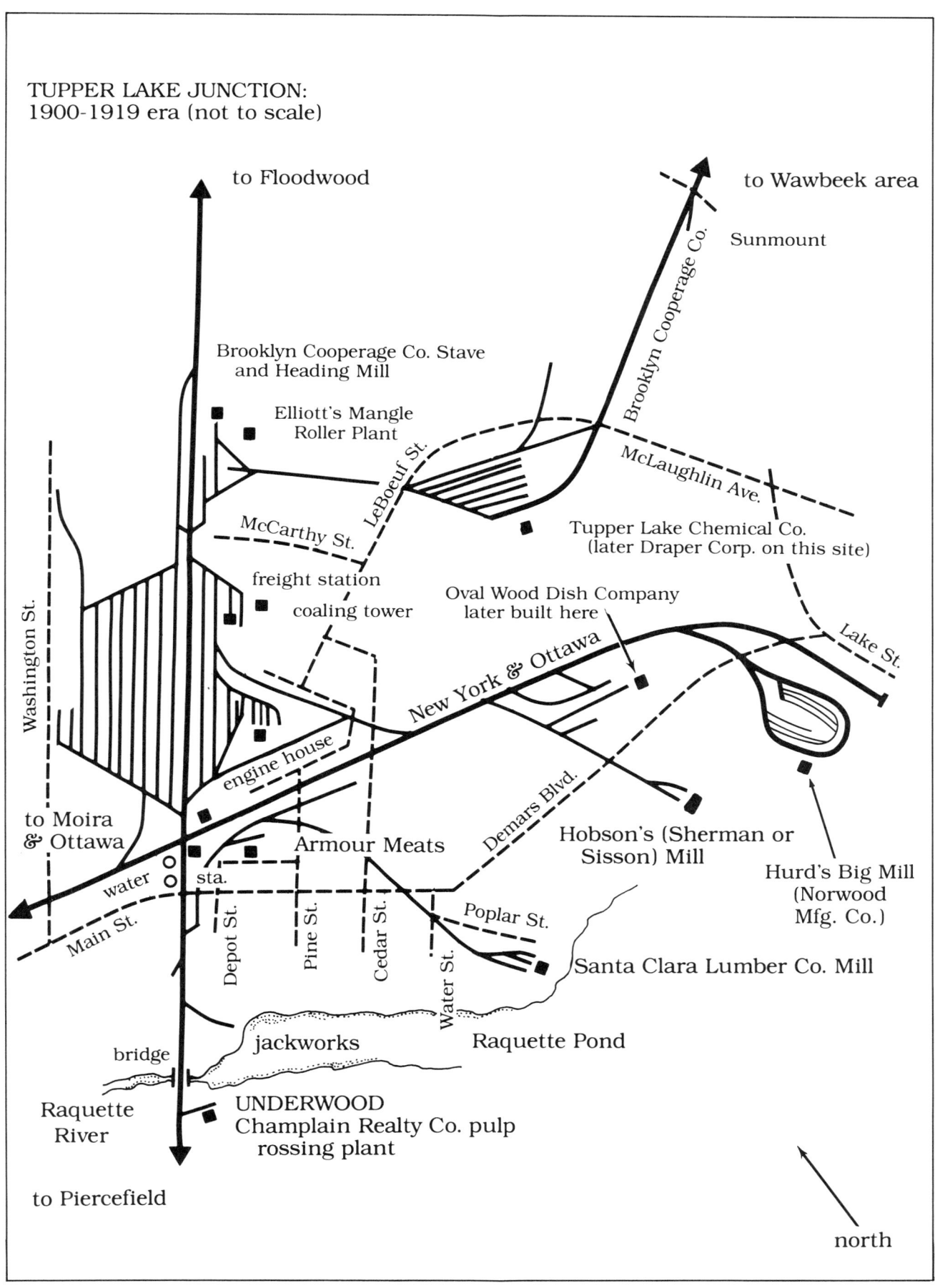

TUPPER LAKE JUNCTION:
1900-1919 era (not to scale)

to Floodwood

to Wawbeek area

Sunmount

Brooklyn Cooperage Co. Stave
and Heading Mill

Elliott's Mangle
Roller Plant

Brooklyn Cooperage Co.

McLaughlin Ave.

LeBoeuf St.

McCarthy St.

Tupper Lake Chemical Co.
(later Draper Corp. on this site)

freight station

coaling tower

Oval Wood Dish Company
later built here

New York & Ottawa

Lake St.

Washington St.

engine house

to Moira
& Ottawa

Demars Blvd.

Hobson's (Sherman or
Sisson) Mill

Hurd's Big Mill
(Norwood
Mfg. Co.)

water

sta.

Armour Meats

Main St.

Depot St.

Pine St.

Cedar St.

Water St.

Poplar St.

Santa Clara Lumber Co. Mill

bridge

jackworks

Raquette Pond

Raquette
River

UNDERWOOD
Champlain Realty Co. pulp
rossing plant

to Piercefield

north

101

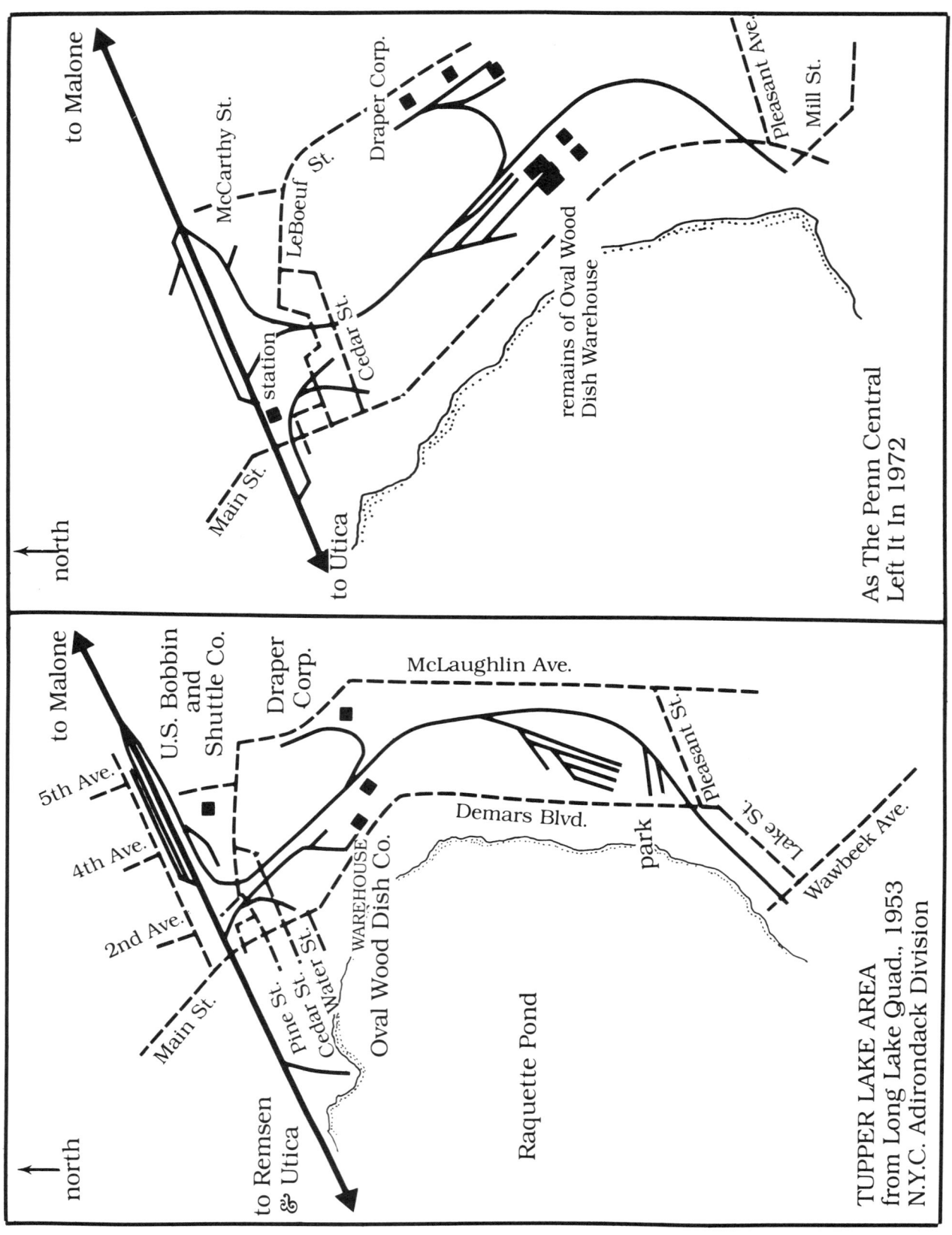

to Malone

north

McCarthy St.

LeBoeuf St.

Draper Corp.

station

Cedar St.

Main St.

to Utica

remains of Oval Wood
Dish Warehouse

Pleasant Ave.

Mill St.

As The Penn Central
Left It In 1972

to Malone

north

U.S. Bobbin
and
Shuttle Co.

Draper
Corp.

McLaughlin Ave.

5th Ave.

4th Ave.

2nd Ave.

Main St.

to Remsen
& Utica

Pine St.

Cedar St.

Water St.

WAREHOUSE

Oval Wood Dish Co.

Demars Blvd.

park

Pleasant St.

Lake St.

Wawbeek Ave.

Raquette Pond

TUPPER LAKE AREA
from Long Lake Quad., 1953
N.Y.C. Adirondack Division

102

1899 and ran until 1913 (Simmons, 1968, p. 36). The Santa Clara Mill, like the Underwood Mill, was a pulp rossing plant, removing the bark from the pulpwood. Simmons says that the spur connected with the New York and Ottawa at Cedar Street, but the track plans indicate that this spur connected more directly with the Adirondack Division; switching from one line to the other must have been easy, however. A short stub off the Santa Clara Mill spur but near the Station served the Armour Meats Plant (Simmons, 1976, p. 81 and photo, p. 86). Several other industries (Tupper Lake Supply, Texaco & Mobil) used this spur (cut back later to just beyond Cedar Street) until the Penn Central abandoned service in 1972.

Past the Junction and Station to the northeast were the yards and servicing facilities, stretched out along the Adirondack Division for 0.4 mile to McCarthy Street. Many photos of these facilities exist: Harter, pages 218, 219, 256, 302; Miller, page 19; Staufer, pages 71 and 215; Gardner, page 29; Simmons, pages 86, 134, 135, 146–149, 164–166, and 336. Seaver (1918, p. 138) describes the railroad machine shops, probably connected with the engine house already in existence by 1910. The house had four tracks serving it, as is observable from Simmons' page 146 photo. This engine house, which sat in the middle of the wye, burned down on May 20, 1951 (Simmons, p 143–144) also destroying offices and a locomotive. In 1953, the remains of the engine house were razed; about the same time, along with dieselization, the fuel oil tanks, coal tower (which stood in the middle of the yard), and water tanks (at Main Street crossing near the Station) were removed. In the yard, freight trains were made up heading for Utica, Lake Placid, and Malone.

Southwest of McCarthy Street and on the southeast side of the yard was the U.S. Bobbin and Shuttle Company (Simmons, p. 311, photo, p. 321) built in 1948–1948 and running to 1953. Bobbin spools and shuttles were made for the textile industry, and were shipped to other plants for finishing. In 1960, Jamestown Adirondack Corporation took over the mill and made furniture parts until 1967 (Simmons, p. 312).

Northeast of McCarthy Street was the Brooklyn Cooperage Mill (Simmons, pp. 78, 79 with photo p. 88), built in 1900. The mill made barrel staves and headings, and operated until 1921. A seven-mile long logging railroad was built by Brooklyn Cooperage in May of 1900 east to near Wawbeek, with two branches (see map, page 100). Donaldson (1921, Volume II, pp. 202–207) describes the legal battle between the Brooklyn Cooperage Company and the then recently-formed New

York State College of Forestry at Cornell (yes, Cornell, not Syracuse!!) which shut down the railroad in 1904. The line split at its east end, with two branches, as shown on the 1901–1902 Long Lake and the 1902–1903 St. Regis Quadrangles; a portion of the south branch is presently occupied by State Highways 3 and 30 on a long, level stretch west of the Highway junction. The 1901–1902 Long Lake Quadrangle also indicates a small yard which Brooklyn Cooperage built near its stave and heading mill.

Brooklyn Cooperage later built a second mill (Simmons, p. 79) using the wood waste from the stave and heading mill to manufacture charcoal, wood alcohol, and acetate of lime; this second mill ran until 1915. Then, the Tupper Lake Chemical Company took it over and ran it until 1919. Palmer's unpublished notes at the Library at the Adirondack Museum state that the Tupper Lake Chemical Company had an industrial 0-4-0 steam switcher. In 1948–1949, the Draper Corporation, now part of Rockwell International, built a mill on the site of the former Tupper Lake Chemical Company, using the original stack; the Draper Mill has produced a variety of hardwood products since, including bobbin blanks for textile mills, lumber, bowling pin blanks, and furniture components (Simmons, 1976, pp. 310 and 311).

Adjacent to the Brooklyn Cooperage's stave and heading mill, Clayton Elliott, in 1915, built a mangle roller plant using materials that came from the Cooperage Mill. Mangle rollers are used for the smoothing and pressing of cloth, such as for bed sheets at laundries. Simmons (1976, p. 80) describes a narrow gauge railroad that connected the Cooperage Mill with the Elliott Plant. The latter shut down after 1921, and relocated to the site of Hurd's Big Mill on Demars Boulevard from 1924 through 1931.

Floodwood, *121.57 miles. Elevation 1585.*

This station first appears on an 1895 New York Central Map and the last timetable to list it is 1959. There is some confusion in the location of the station, as the 1910 through 1915 employees' timetables list the mileage from Herkimer as 121.57, while the 1939 employees' timetable lists the mileage as 121.84. Sometime in the 1920s and 1930s, could the station have been moved north 0.27 mile?

A passing siding did exist here on the west side, south of the station, but was removed probably also sometime in the 1920s or 1930s; the 1910 Track Schematic shows it. The passing siding held 60 forty-foot cars in 1910 and 57 of them in 1913; it was gone by 1939. The old 1902–1903 St. Regis Quadrangle in-

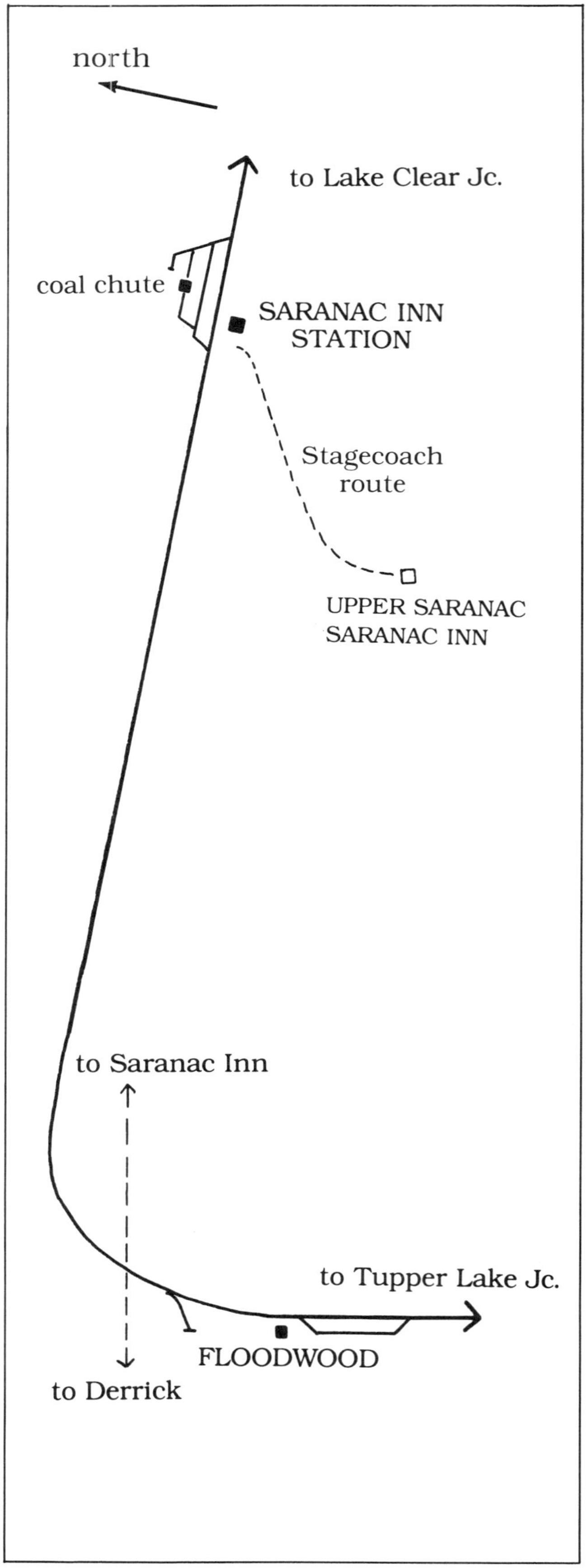

north
to Lake Clear Jc.
coal chute
SARANAC INN
STATION
Stagecoach
route
UPPER SARANAC
SARANAC INN
to Saranac Inn
to Tupper Lake Jc.
FLOODWOOD
to Derrick

Lake Clear
Upper Saranac
LAKE
Hoel Pond
Floodwood Pond
Middle Pond
Long
Rollins
Green
Markham Pt.
Moss Rock Pt.
Follensby Clear Pond
Whey Pond

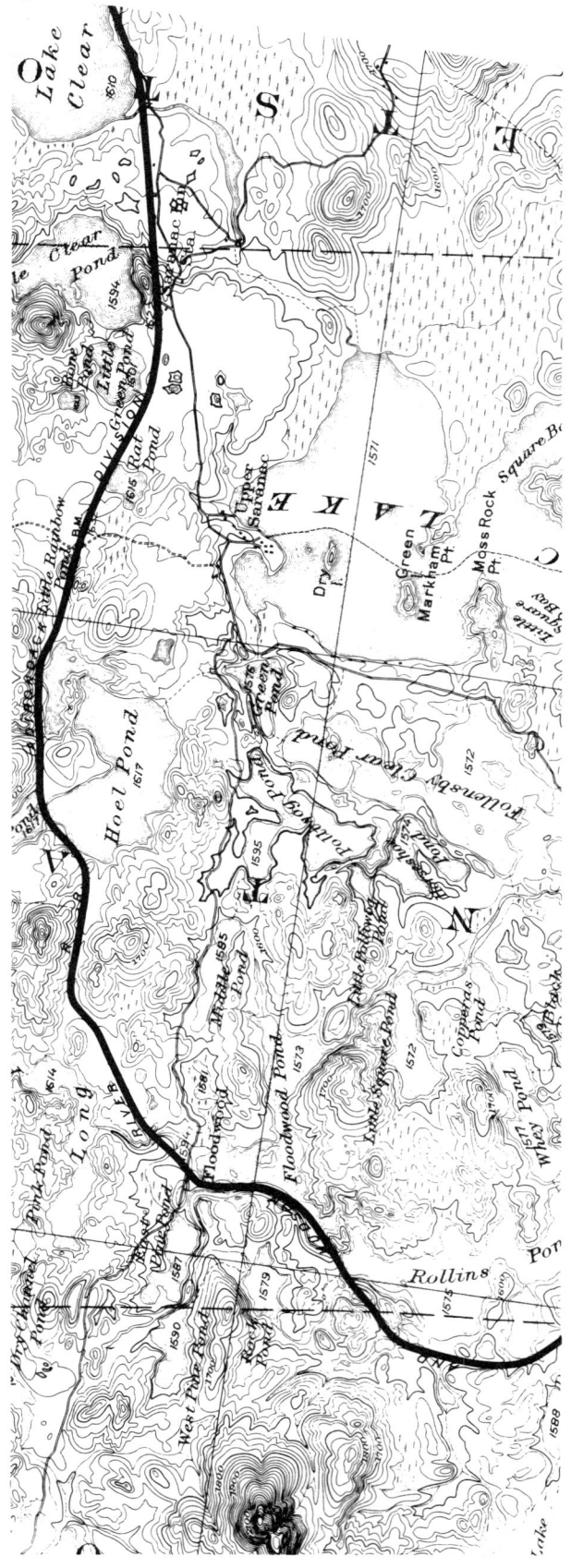

dicates a short stub on the west side, heading south at the old Derrick turnpike; this stub is about 0.1 mile long.

Saranac Inn, *128.56 miles. Elevation 1626.*

This station operated from 1892 through 1956. It replaced the Derrick Station on the New York & Ottawa Railroad as the nearest point on a railroad to the Saranac Inn hotel. Derrick Station was considerably further away (about 9 miles) when it opened in 1890; Saranac Inn station was only a two mile stage ride to the hotel.

Photos of Saranac Inn Station are plentiful. Harter includes them on pages 165, 166, 220, 221, 262, and 263 of his book. Staufer has a photo on page 73, but incorrectly names the station as Saranac *Lake*!!

A passing siding was located here west of the main track, plus a second double-ended team track and a stub (see map, p. 104). The main siding held 22 forty-foot cars in 1910 and 25 of them in 1913; it held 16 forty-four foot cars in 1939.

Lake Clear Junction, *131.68 miles. Elevation 1629 (496.6 meters).*

When this station opened in July 1892, it was called Saranac Junction, as here the Saranac Lake Branch departed from the Adirondack and St. Lawrence main track. The name was changed to Lake Clear Junction in 1893, and the station was in service through 1965. For detail on the branch into Saranac Lake and on the trackage rights over the Delaware and Hudson from Saranac Lake to Lake Placid, see Chapter I of this book, pages 37 to 44. The Branch to the D&H track was 5.82 miles long.

Photos of this Junction are abundant. Because Lake Clear Junction also served as a terminus for the Paul Smith's Electric Railway from 1906 through about 1930, I have catalogued photos of the Junction as part of the Paul Smith's Railway file (Kudish, 1976). Here is the list of photos:

Paul Smith's Electric Railway catalog number	Author and page number
1201	Kudish (1976), pp. 24 and 25.
1202	(unpublished)
1203	(unpublished)
1204	(unpublished: Alan Thomas photo
1205	(unpublished: Alan Thomas photo
1206	(unpublished: Alan Thomas photo
1207	(unpublished: Alan Thomas photo
1208	Harter, p. 225.
1209	Harter, p. 226.
1210	Harter, p. 221.
1211	Harter, p. 226.
1212	Harter, p. 226.
1213	Hastings, p. 23.
1214	Hastings, p. 24.
1215	Hastings, p. 24.
1216	Hastings, p. 24.

The State Highway 30 overpass just south of the Junction was built in 1929.

The track plan of Lake Clear Junction, as indicated in the New York Central schematic published about 1910, is shown here on page 106. Oddly, it conflicts somewhat with how the photos portray the junction, shown also on page 106. The Paul Smith's Railway electrified track was that track nearest the station. A wye was provided for turning engines that worked the Saranac Branch with connecting trains. A water tower was in the earlier years, 1910 and 1913, located south ot the wye, near what is now the Highway 30 overpass; later, the water tower was moved inside the wye.

The longest passing siding at the Junction in 1910 and 1913 held, according to an employees' timetable, 84 forty-foot cars, the longest siding on the Adirondack Division. In 1939, this siding held 63 forty-four foot cars.

The Paul Smith's Electric Railway operated from August 20, 1906 to about 1930; the date of closure is still in doubt although Collins (1977) says 1932. DeSormo (1974, p. 111) offers a photo of the Paul Smith's Electric Railway car, catalog #1405.

Passenger service from here north to Malone was abandoned in January, 1958, although service continued to Saranac Lake and Lake Placid out on the branch until April, 1965.

Gabriels (Paul Smith's Station), *136.69 miles. Elevation 1705.*

When the station opened on July 16, 1892, stagecoaches to and from Paul Smith's Hotel met the trains, so that the station was named "Paul Smith's Station." On August 20, 1906, when the Paul Smith's Electric Railway opened to Lake Clear Junction, stagecoaches no longer met trains at Paul Smith's Station, and the name was changed to Gabriels. The

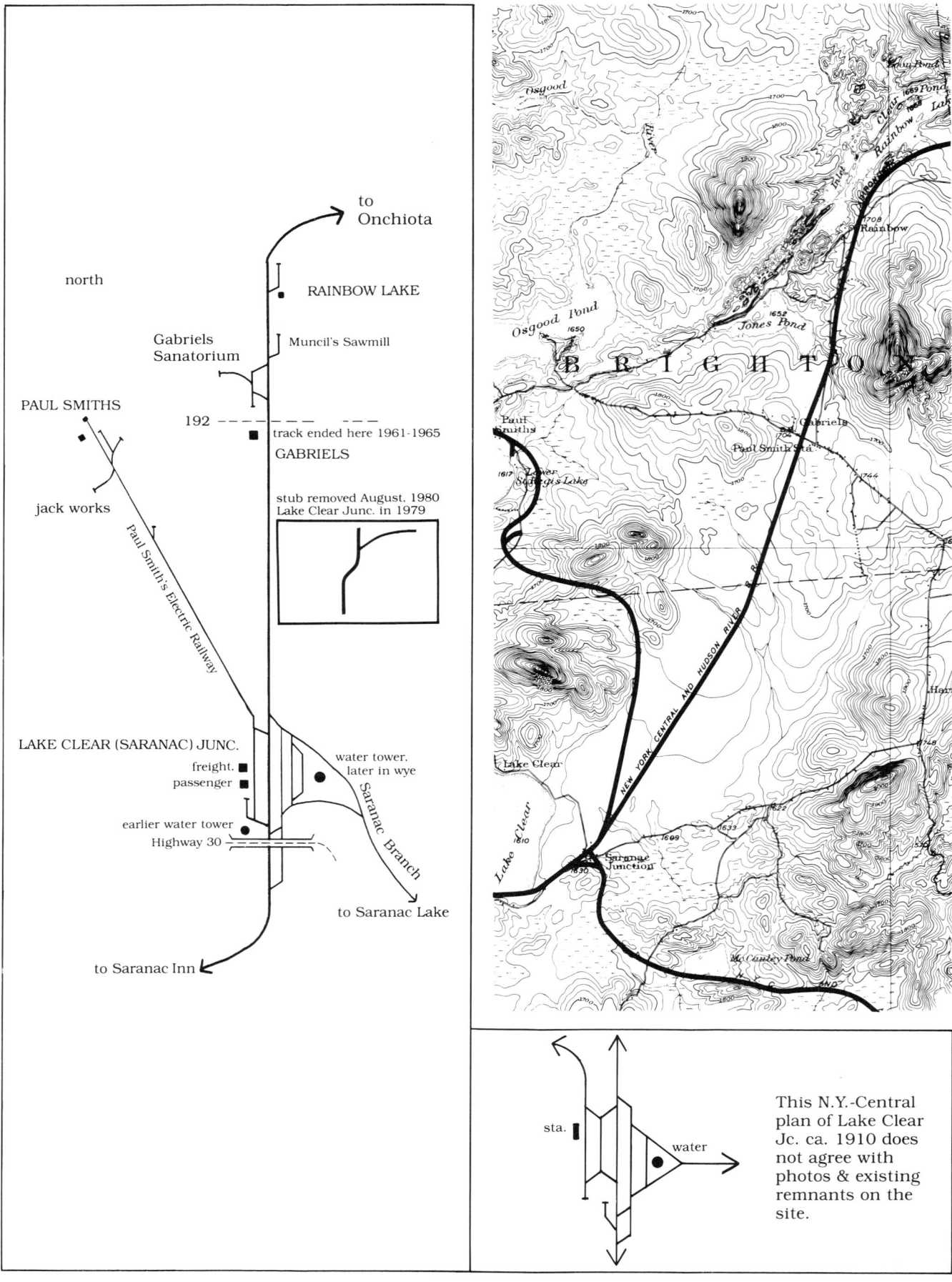

north

to
Onchiota

RAINBOW LAKE

Gabriels
Sanatorium   Muncil's Sawmill

PAUL SMITHS

192 ———————   track ended here 1961-1965

GABRIELS

jack works

stub removed August, 1980
Lake Clear Junc. in 1979

LAKE CLEAR (SARANAC) JUNC.

freight,   water tower.
passenger   later in wye

earlier water tower
Highway 30

to Saranac Lake

to Saranac Inn

Saranac Branch

Paul Smith's Electric Railway

sta.   water

This N.Y.-Central
plan of Lake Clear
Jc. ca. 1910 does
not agree with
photos & existing
remnants on the
site.

station burned on August 22, 1927, according to Collins (1977, p. 19), and was replaced by a smaller building until passenger service ceased in January 1958.

A passing siding on the west side already present in 1904 and north of State Highway 192, held 33 forty-foot cars in 1910 (employees' timetable), 34 forty-foot cars in 1913, and was abandoned by 1939. A stub curved north and west from the passing siding to bring in coal cars to heat the Sisters of Mercy Sanatorium. Ben Muncil's sawmill on the east side of the main track had a stub serving it heading north; an article in the *Plattsburg Press Republican* in May, 1982, by Bill McLaughlin, entitled "Changes Loom for Gabriels as Prison Nears," mentions that Muncil's mill was established about 1920, burned in 1948 and closed in the late 1950s. It has been said that potatoes and Christmas trees were shipped out in railroad cars from Gabriels, but no documentation of this has been found to date.

When freight service terminated between Lake Clear Junction and Malone in 1960 or 1961, the whole segment of track was removed except for five miles between Lake Clear Junction and Gabriels. The five-mile-long stub continued to be in use for delivery of materials for construction of dormitories at Paul Smith's College until April of 1965. By October 14, 1966, Niagara-Mohawk had not yet connected the high voltage transmission line (which followed the Adirondack Division grade from milepost 135 to Malone) to the poles which had just been installed. For more detail on the Gabriels area, see Collins (1977) and Kudish (1981).

The proximity of Gabriels to the Paul Smith's Electric Railway has urged me to catalogue all photos of the Gabriels Station as well:

Paul Smith's Electric Railway catalog number	Author and page number
1101	(unpublished)
1102	Published in an 1893 Paul Smiths Hotel Brochure
1103–1107	(unpublished: 1105–1107 by Charles Ballard

The overpass at milepost 137.7 over the Gabriels-Rainbow Highway was built in 1932.

Rainbow (Rainbow Lake), *139.19 miles. Elevation 1702 (518.6 meters).*

This station operated from 1893 through 1950. A stub siding on the east side heading south is shown on the Track Schematic, ca. 1910, by the New York Central. Photos in Collins (1977) show the station and the nearby Rainbow Lake House hotel, especially the photo which appears on the ninth (unnumbered) page in the picture section following page 118. Before 1893, the nearest railroad station to the Rainbow Lake House was Onchiota on the Chateaugay Railroad which opened in 1887.

Onchiota, *142.51 miles. Elevation 1710 (521.4 meters).*

Scarborough's 1903 map is the first evidence I have for this station, and the last is the 1957 timetable. A passing siding east of the main track in 1910 and in 1913 held 20 forty-foot cars; it was no longer in service in 1939. From this siding ran a spur heading south and east to the Roak (later Baker and Odell) sawmill at Oregon Pond. Oddly, this sawmill was served by two different railroads, the Adirondack Division and the D&H Chateaugay Branch (see Chapter I, pp. 35 and 36). At about 143.2 miles, the Adirondack Division crossed the Kushaqua Narrows on a viaduct about 25 feet high and built in 1904; a photo of this viaduct with double-headed steam appears on page 230 of Harter.

Lake Kushaqua (Stonywold), *144.50 miles. Elevation 1726.*

Here is another name-change station! From 1893 through 1953, the name was Lake Kushaqua, but it was changed to Stonywold in 1953. Passenger trains served this stop through 1957. Gardner (p. 94) has a photo of the station, while Harter (p. 230) includes photos of a freight train wreck about 3 miles north of Lake Kushaqua Station; he describes the wreck on page 228. The station building itself was moved in the summer of 1975 to a point just southwest of the intersection of New York State Routes 3 and 99, adjacent to the Pine Grove Restaurant.

The New York Central 1910 track schematic shows a siding on the west, but this was not a passing siding; rather, it served for coal deliveries to heat the Stonywold Sanatorium (later Whitefathers). A water tower in 1910 and 1913 stood at Lake Kushaqua.

At 146.1 miles, the Champlain Realty Company (a division of International Paper) had a stub on the west side heading south. At 146.21 miles, Harter lists a place called Morgan's Mills (p. 284).

Loon Lake (Inman Post Office), *148.76 miles. Elevation 1479.*

Operating dates were 1892 through 1957.

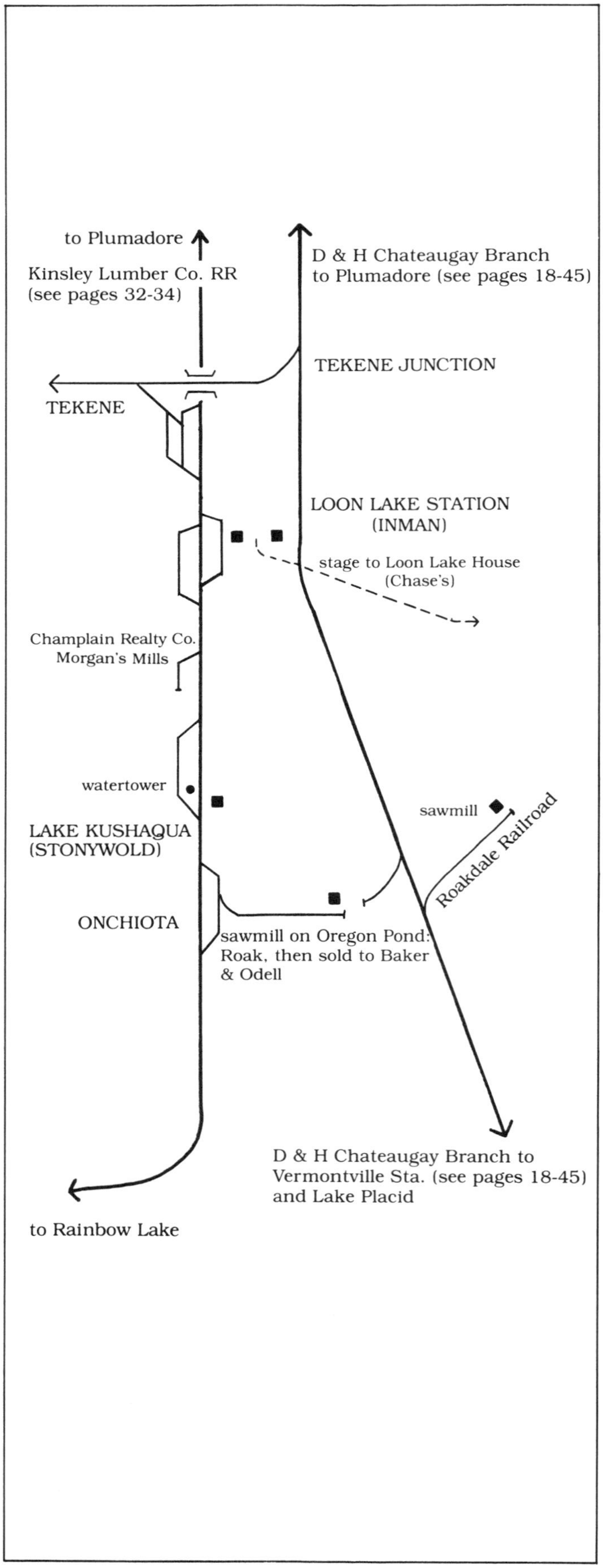

to Plumadore
Kinsley Lumber Co. RR
(see pages 32-34)
D & H Chateaugay Branch
to Plumadore (see pages 18-45)
TEKENE JUNCTION
TEKENE
LOON LAKE STATION
(INMAN)
stage to Loon Lake House
(Chase's)
Champlain Realty Co.
Morgan's Mills
watertower
LAKE KUSHAQUA
(STONYWOLD)
sawmill
Roakdale Railroad
ONCHIOTA
sawmill on Oregon Pond:
Roak, then sold to Baker
& Odell
D & H Chateaugay Branch to
Vermontville Sta. (see pages 18-45)
and Lake Placid
to Rainbow Lake

Duck Pond
Elm Pond
Tekene
Grass Pond
Porkbarrel Pond
Loon Lake Sta.
Mountain Pond
Lake Kushaqua
Little Hope Pond
Hope Pond
Buck Pond
Oregon Pond
Onchiota
Square Pond
Mud Lake

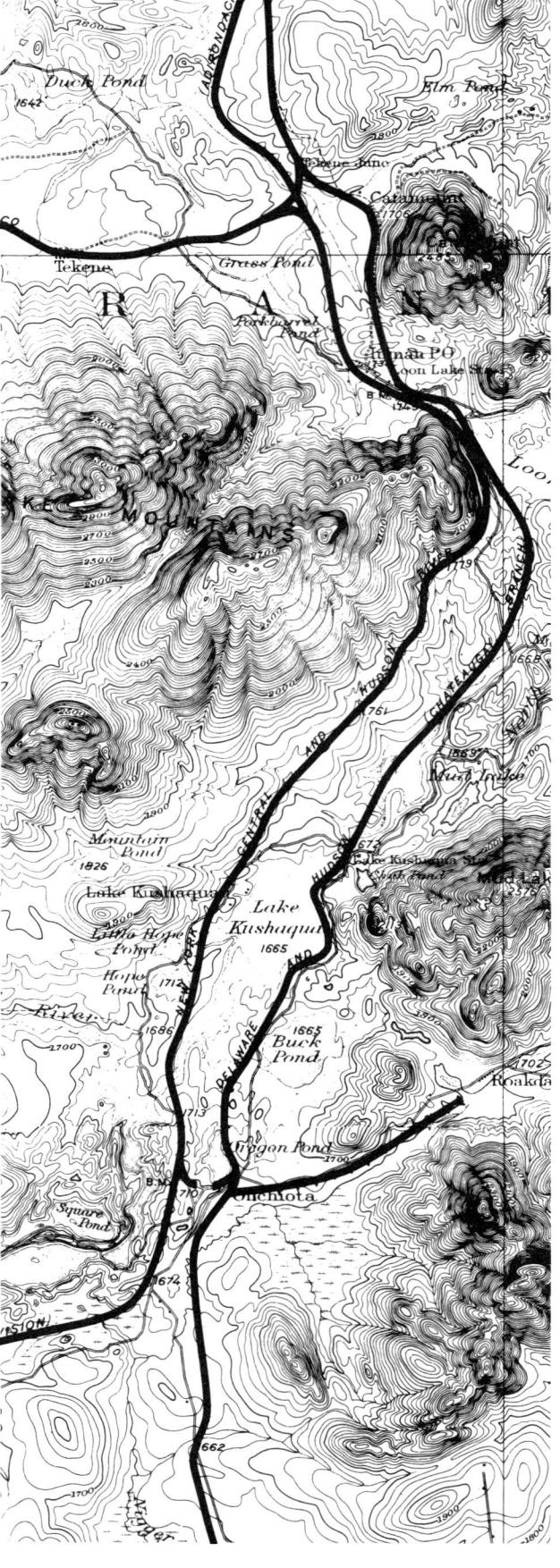

Across the highway was the Chateaugay Railroad's station of the same name, built 6 years earlier. Hence Loon Lake was a transfer point for passengers between the two lines as well as the connecting point for stagecoaches for the three-mile ride to Chase's Loon Lake House (see Chapter I, p. 35 for details).

The passing siding, west of the main track, held 20 forty-foot cars in 1910, 35 cars in 1913, and 26 forty-four foot cars in 1939. On the east of the main track, along the station, was a double-ended team track which could also serve as a second passing siding. Measurements in feet for the primary passing siding length were 800 feet in 1910, 1400 feet in 1913, and 1144 feet in 1939.

Tekene Junction, *150.13 miles. Elevation 1680.*

The fascinating history of Tekene Junction is presented in Chapter I, page 33. It was never a station, but rather a junction point for the Kinsley Lumber Co. logging railroad, built in 1898, and later sold to the Baker Brothers of Plattsburgh, operating to about 1904, 1905, or 1906. The Loon Lake Quadrangle, published in 1902–1906, incorrectly names this logging line as Brooklyn Cooperage! Seaver (1918) describes this logging railroad. A passing siding was located here on the west in 1910 with a capacity of 20 forty-foot cars; it held 30 cars in 1913, and was abandoned by 1939.

Plumadore, *153.48 miles. Elevation 1705.*

Plumadore was not a passenger station, but a passing siding did exist here on the west in 1910 with a capacity of 34 forty-foot cars and in 1913 for 35 cars. It was gone by 1939. In 1940, a connection was made here between the Adirondack Division and the D&H Chateaugay Branch so that D&H trains could be routed over New York Central tracks from here south to Saranac Lake via Lake Clear Junction; details are available in Shaughnessy (1967, p. 335) and in this volume (Chapter I, p. 31).

Little Bryants, *157.6 miles. Elevation 1508.*

On the 1902–1906 Loon Lake Quadrangle appears a short stub on the west, crossing the highway, heading north and barely 0.1 mile long. Yet the New York Central track schematic ca. 1910 indicates the stub on the east side heading south and attributes it to the Champlain Realty Company (a division of International Paper Company). Was the siding moved between 1906 and 1910?

Bryants Mill, *158.6 miles. Elevation 1506.*

The New York Central track schematic ca. 1910 shows a stub on the west heading north; yet Hyde (1970, p. 65) states that it was on the east side of the main track and ran down almost to the south end of Mountain View Lake. Two sawmills were located at Bryants, and there was even a loading siding parallel to the main track. Employees' timetables in my files do not list this siding. Hyde (1970, p 65) notes that the sawmills here closed in 1916, so that only firewood and pulpwood were shipped out, not lumber, after 1916.

Mountain View, *160.19 miles. Elevation 1498 or 1501.*

This station first appeared in the 1893 timetables and was in service through 1957. Much detail is available thanks to Hyde (1970), Harter, and Dumas (1962) with numerous photographs published:

Hyde (1970): pp. 63, 64, 65.

Harter (1979): pp. 231, 232, 233, 261. Photo on p. 231 is duplicated on the back jacket cover.

Dumas (1962): p. 11.

DeSormo (1974): p. 108.

Hyde (p. 64) states that initially, there was a siding to serve a lumber yard. When the lumber yard closed or declined, this siding was extended and converted into a passing siding. It was west of the main track and held 14 forty-foot cars in 1910, 15 of them in 1913, and had been abandoned by 1939. An additional stub was built to accommodate local freight on the east (Hyde, p. 64).

Hyde and Dumas both mention the fact that berry pickers would come up from Malone on the morning train on Sundays and head back down in the evening, sometimes necessitating extra coaches cut off here during the day.

Owls Head, *162.83 miles. Elevation 1526.*

This station operated from 1893 through 1957 and a photo of it occurs in Harter, page 232. A passing siding holding 34 forty-foot cars existed in 1910, 36 cars in 1913, and 26 forty-four foot cars in 1939. The Loon Lake Quadrangle, 1902–1906, indicates a passing siding on either side of the main track, plus two dead-end stubs on the east. A water tower was here in the 1910 to 1913 era. Owls Head was the summit of the long upgrade out of Malone.

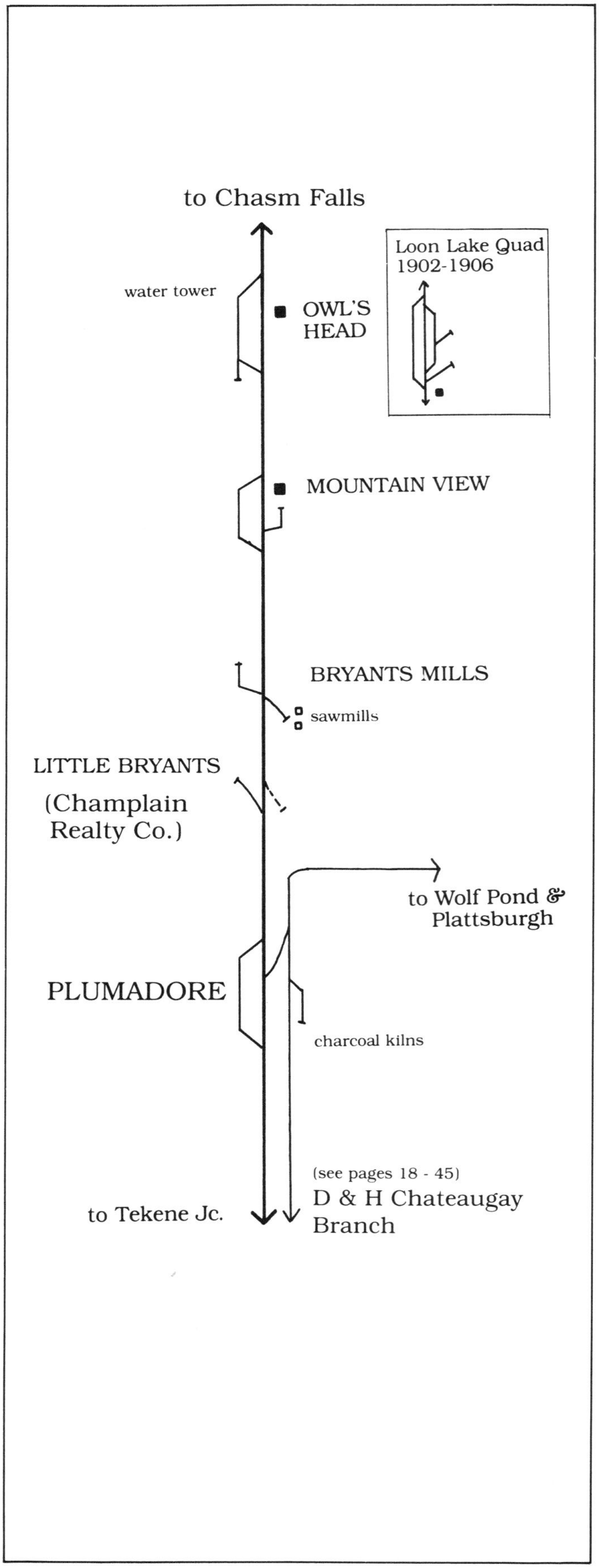

to Chasm Falls
Loon Lake Quad
1902-1906
water tower
OWL'S
HEAD
MOUNTAIN VIEW
BRYANTS MILLS
sawmills
LITTLE BRYANTS
(Champlain
Realty Co.)
to Wolf Pond &
Plattsburgh
PLUMADORE
charcoal kilns
(see pages 18 - 45)
D & H Chateaugay
Branch
to Tekene Jc.

Owls Head
Pinnacle
Fishpole
Pond
Owls Head
Pond
Owls Head
Ingraham
Stream
NEW YORK CENTRAL AND HUDSON RIVER
High
Falls
Indian
Lake
Mountain View
Barnesville
RIVER
Mountain
Lake
Barnes
Brook
Barnes
Pinnacle
Doctor
Hill
Deerfly Pond
Buck Ponds
Black Cat
Brook
Salmon
RANGE
1705
Plumadore

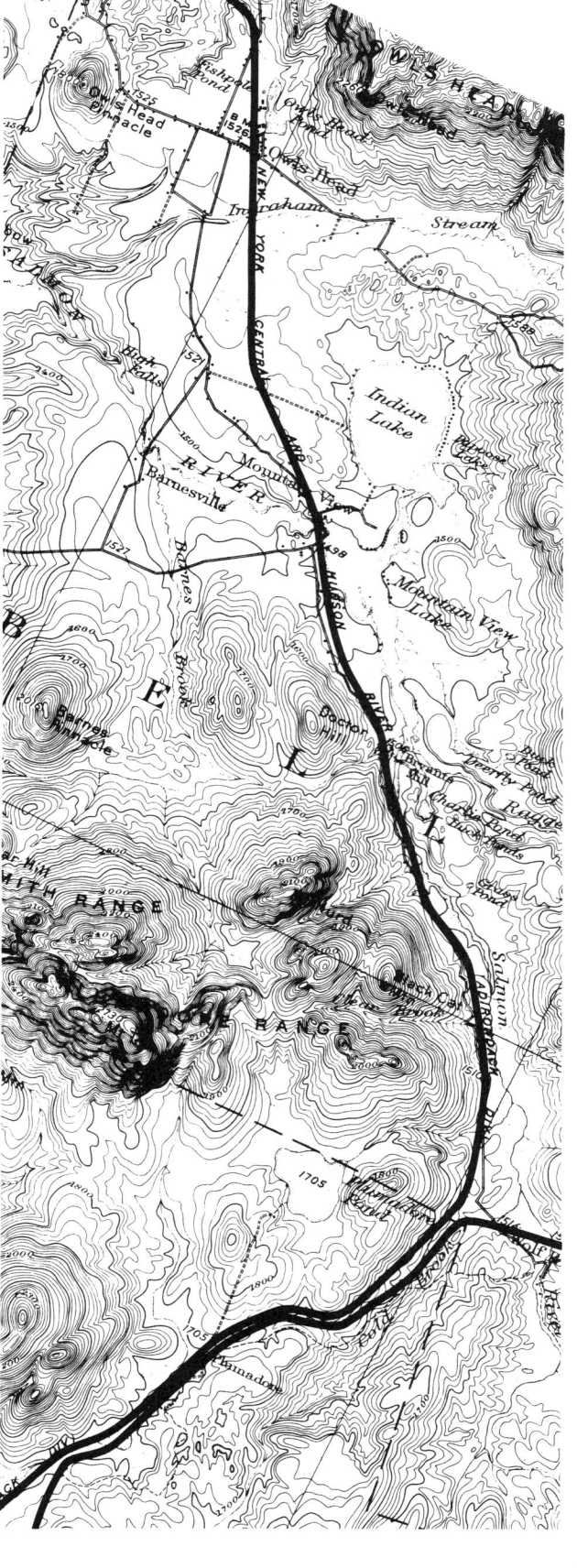

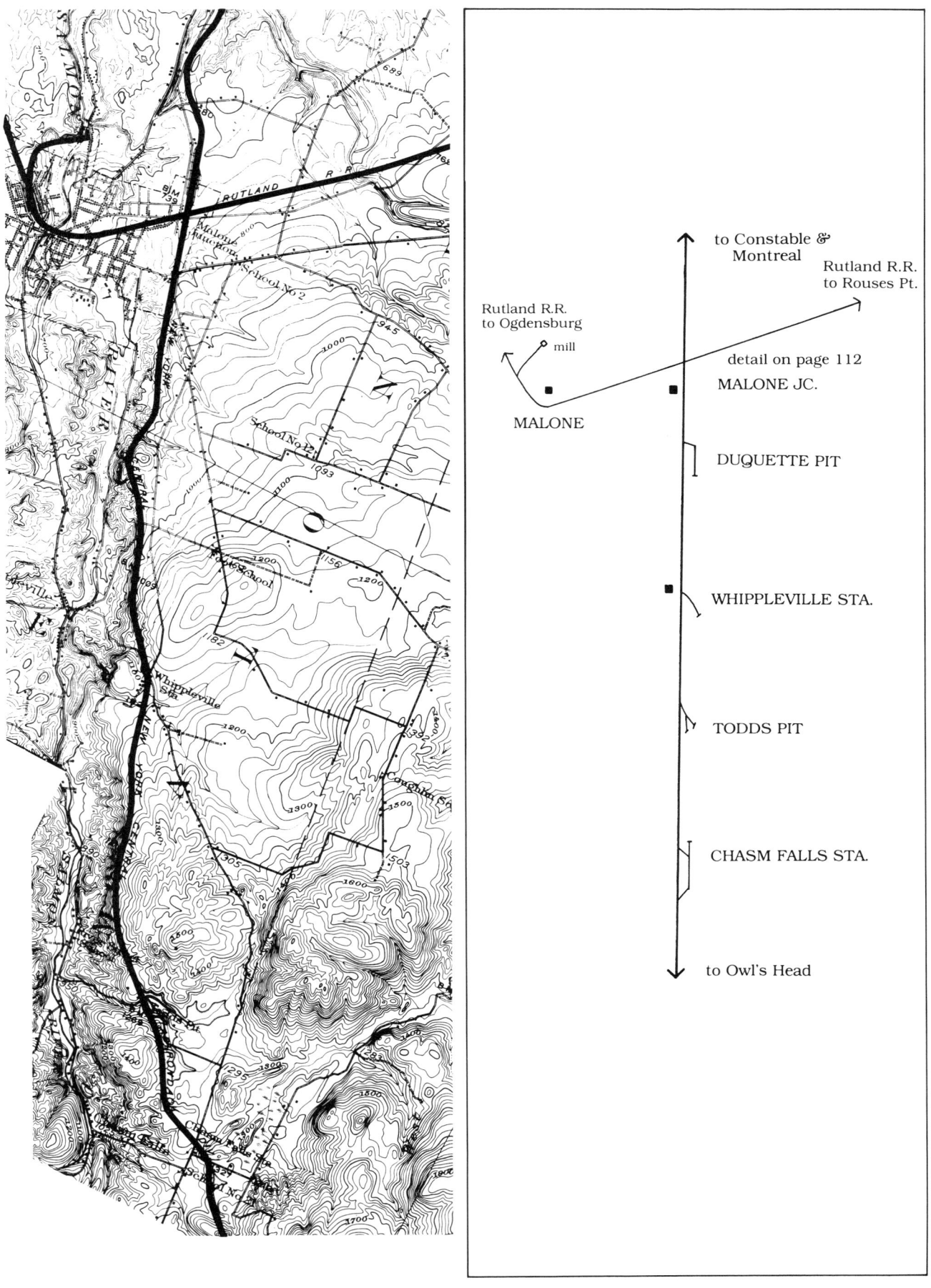

to Constable &
Montreal

Rutland R.R.
to Rouses Pt.

Rutland R.R.
to Ogdensburg

mill

detail on page 112

MALONE JC.

MALONE

DUQUETTE PIT

WHIPPLEVILLE STA.

TODDS PIT

CHASM FALLS STA.

to Owl's Head

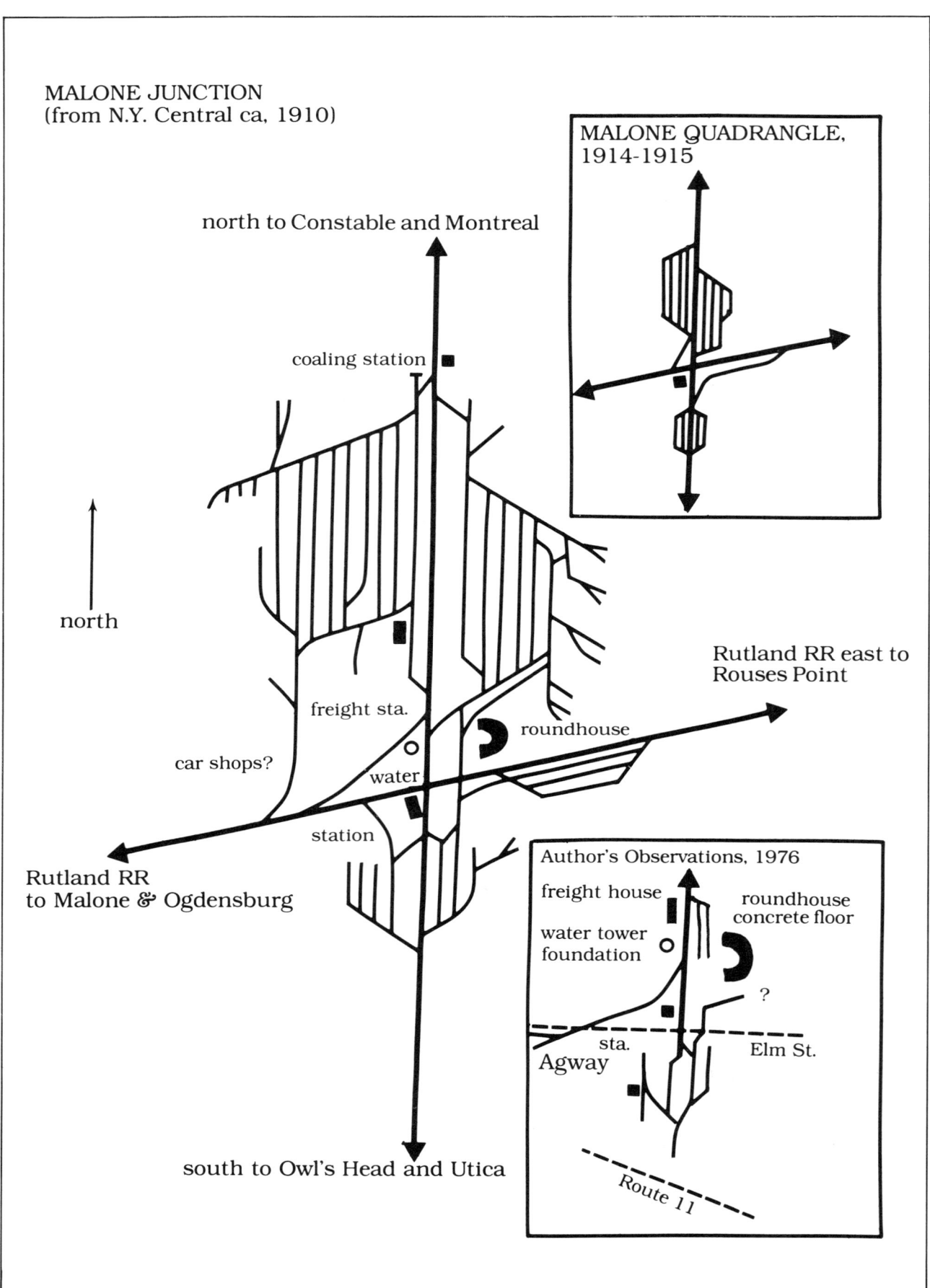

MALONE JUNCTION
(from N.Y. Central ca, 1910)

MALONE QUADRANGLE,
1914-1915

north to Constable and Montreal

north

coaling station

Rutland RR east to
Rouses Point

freight sta.

roundhouse

car shops?

water

station

Rutland RR
to Malone & Ogdensburg

Author's Observations, 1976

freight house

roundhouse
concrete floor

water tower
foundation

?

sta.

Elm St.

Agway

Route 11

south to Owl's Head and Utica

A photo of the Owls Head station after the tracks were removed in 1960 or 1961 appears in Dumas (1962, p. 11).

Chasm Falls, *165.51 miles. Elevation 1300.*

This station was in use from 1895 through 1936. Employees' timetables do not list sidings, but a dead-end stub 0.2 mile long on the east heading north is shown on the 1912–1913 Chateaugay Quadrangle. The New York Central track schematic ca. 1910 indicates a short passing siding plus a stub.

Todd's Pit, *166.52 miles. Elevation 1269.*

This was not a passenger station, but the employees' timetables of 1910 and 1913 do list it. The 1912–1913 Chateaugay Quadrangle shows a short stub on the east heading south, but the New York Central track schematic ca. 1910 denotes a double stub oriented this way. I wonder what kind of a pit this was, as I cannot find the information in my files; sand, gravel, or charcoal are the most likely possibilities.

Whippleville, *169.28 miles. Elevation 1112.*

Whippleville station appears on the passenger timetables from 1893 through 1936. The 1912–1913 Chateaugay Quadrangle denotes a short stub on the east heading south. The track schematic ca. 1910 agrees.

Duquette's Pit,

I cannot find any precise mileage for this pit, but Harter estimates it as two miles south of Malone Junction, or about 171.3. The Malone Quadrangle records an elevation of about 920 at this point along the track. Again, as at Todd's Pit, was this sand, gravel, or charcoal?

Malone Junction, *173.31 miles. Elevation 730.*

This is as far as we will go on the Adirondack Division, although the line continued north through Constable, crossed the Border and headed for Montreal. At Malone Junction were the connection with the Rutland or Ogdensburg and Lake Champlain (built in 1850 — see Chapter III, page 61), extensive yards, and servicing facilities. The Rutland's station in downtown Malone was a mile west of Malone Junction.

The station opened in 1892 and closed in 1957 for trains headed south. However, trains still continued to run between Malone Junction and Montreal in 1958. In earlier years, some Utica trains terminated here, but most headed through the Junction to Montreal.

Photos of the Junction are plentiful:

> *Harter, pages 164, 234 through 239, 255 through 261.*
>
> *Franklin Historical Review, 1973, pages 53 and 55.*
>
> *DeSormo (1974), pages 14 and 107. The latter page 107 photo shows construction in 1891 south out of Malone.*

A roundhouse was located in Malone Junction, north and east of the crossing of the two railroads. There were also a water tower in 1910, 1913 and 1958, fuel oil tanks, coaling station, car shops, and storage of snow plows. Shown on the maps on page 112 are the New York Central track schematic ca. 1910, the Malone 1914–1915 Quadrangle, and this writer's observations in April 1976.

Freight service ended sometime in 1960 or 1961 south of Malone, although such service persisted to the north from Canada until April, 1980, as part of Conrail.

Timetable Operations

New York Central Adirondack Division: Passenger Timetable Operation Run Numbers

FALL, WINTER, AND SPRING

Timetable Dates	Utica-Montreal		Utica-Malone	Connections at L. Clear	Utica- Lake Placid	Comments
4/23/93 (H)	47&44	21&36	61-63&62-64(F)	Saranac Lake only		Not yet open to Lake Placid
9/22/14 10/13/15	5&4	3&2	11&12	to Saranac Lake & Lake Placid		
5/20/20 to 5/25/28	5&4	3&2	11&6			
9/29/29	5&4	3&2	11&6			11&6 Sunday only to Montreal
9/25/32	5&4	3&2			11&6 to Saranac Lake only	
4/26/36	5&4	3&2	11&6			11&6 Sunday only to Montreal
9/24/39	5&4	3&2	11&6 to Nov. 15 only			#11 Sunday only to Montreal after 11/15
9/29/40 to 12/07/47	5&4	3&2	11 Sunday only			#6 discontinued, then #11 discontinued
9/30/51	5&4			105&104 Lake Clear to Lake Placid	3&2	Dieselization in Oct. '51
4/26/53	Termination of Utica-Montreal Service except for commuter trains between Malone & Montreal which ran through at least 4/27/58.					
12/6/53 to 5/13/57			5&4	105&104	3&2	
Jan. '58	Termination of Utica-Malone Service except for commuter trains between Malone & Montreal which ran through at least 4/27/58 but abandoned by 1962.					
4/27/58					163&162 165&164	Lake Clear connection discontinued
10/25/59 & in 1961	163&162 a Beeliner (Budd or RDC car)				163&162 165&164	
4/29/62 to 10/25/64	Day service discontinued				165&164	
4/24 or 4/25/65	Last passenger train Utica to Lake Placid; newspapers from that time disagree on the exact date.					

Odd number trains = northbound; **Even number trains** = southbound
H = In 1893, trains ran from and to Herkimer, not Utica.
F = Mixed trains. Passengers carried in caboose. See freight service operation.

New York Central Adirondack Division: Passenger Timetable Operation Run Numbers

SUMMER

Timetable Dates	Utica-Montreal	Utica-Malone	Connections at L. Clear	Utica-Lake Placid		Comments
7/15/92	Not completed through between Fulton Chain Station and Childwold Station until 10/24/92. One round trip daily between Malone and Childwold Station with branch to Saranac Lake. Two round trips daily between Remsen and Fulton Chain Station (Thendara).					
6/19/04	655&656 653&654	657&658 643&618	to Saranac Lake and Lake Placid			685&690 mixed (see freight operation)
7/18/05	655&656 653&654	657&658 643&618		659&630		
6/19/10 and 6/23/12	5&4 3&2 11&12	7&6	with 5&4, 3&2,11&12 to Saranac & L. Placid	9&10 1&8		six trains each way daily south of L. Clear
6/22/13	5&4 3&2 11&12	7&6	↓	1&10	9&8 to Tupper only	
6/27/26	5&4 3&2	11&6 7&12 / 11 Sunday only to Montreal	to Saranac Lake & Lake Placid with Malone & Montreal trains at Lake Clear Junction. No connections necessary on through trains to Saranac Lake or Lake Placid.	15 & 10	1 to Saranac L. only	
6/24/28	5&4 3&2	11&14–16 7&12		15 & 10 / 6 / 16	9&8 to Tupper only / 1 to Saranac L. only	seven north-bound and eight south-bound trains daily
6/28/36	5&4 3&2	11&6		17&10 15 Fri. only	9&8 to Tupper only	
7/19/42	5&4 3&2 11 Sun. only			13&14 155 Fri. only		
6/13/48	5&4 3&2 except Sunday 11 Sun. only			15 Sat. only 16 Sun. only		
6/18/50	5&4 3&2			15 Fri. only 16 Sun. only		
Between 1950 and 1965, summer and winter service was essentially the same.						

Odd-numbered trains are northbound; **even-numbered trains** are southbound.

The fall, winter, and spring timetable consisted basically of three trains daily each way through 1939 between Utica and Malone. After 1939, service declined. Summer service included the three trains daily each way but there were additional runs as well: Until through 1913, a 4th round trip went to Montreal daily; Until through 1942, a 5th round trip daily served Lake Placid, although by 1948 this supplemental run only ran weekends; Through 1946, a 6th round trip ran daily but terminated in Saranac or Tupper Lake, not Lake Placid, at times.
1928 seems the peak summer regards number of runs.

Supplemental Local Service between Remsen and Fulton Chain Station (Thendara)

Timetable Dates	Northbound Run Numbers			Southbound Run Numbers		
	Daily	Except Sunday	Sunday only	Daily	Except Sunday	Sunday only
6/19/04	655	607	677		656&674	678
6/18/05		607&661	677		656&674	678
6/19/10	15	19	77		16 & 18	78
6/14/12 and 6/22/13		71&79	73		70 & 76	78

Freight Service: New York Central Adirondack Division

In 1893, 1904, 1905, the timetables show mixed trains, i.e., freight trains carry passengers in caboose cars. Northbound trains are odd-numbered while southbound trains are even-numbered.

    4/23/93:   ##61 and 62 except Sunday Herkimer to Tupper Lake.
                  ##63 and 64 except Sunday Tupper Lake to Malone.
    6/19/04 & #690 Saturday only Malone to Tupper Lake.
    6/18/05:   #685 Sunday only Tupper Lake to Malone.

My early timetables do not show freight-only trains. Note how Tupper Lake was the terminal for freight trains, even into more recent times.

On June 19, 1910, freights ran six days a week, Sunday the day most often skipped, but some runs were skipped on Monday mornings.

    ##81 and 80, way freight, Remsen to Tupper Lake.
    ##83 and 86, freight, Remsen to Tupper Lake.
    ##91 and 90, way freight, Tupper Lake to Malone.
    ##97 and 98, way freight, Malone to Adirondack Junction (Quebec).
    ##85 and 82, freight, Malone to Adirondack Junction (Quebec).

On October 13, 1915, freight service was the same with this change: trains ##85–82 were extended southward from Malone to Tupper Lake. Thus, there were two freights daily each way between Tupper Lake and Malone, as there were south from Tupper Lake to Remsen.

Hastings (1950) notes a midday freight working the Lake Placid yard at that time (1950), originating in Tupper Lake. Through the 1950s, the through daily freight between Utica and Montreal was known as the "Banana Train" because of a significant portion of its cargo (Thomas Kyle, personal communication). The last freight from Lake Clear to Malone ran in 1960, although a stub from Lake Clear to Gabriels existed until April of 1965 so that materials for building of dormitories at Paul Smith's College could be brought in by rail.

When passenger service ended on April 24 or 25, 1965, there was one freight round-trip per week between Remsen and Lake Placid. When I arrived in Saranac Lake in the fall of 1971, the freight came once every two weeks until the Penn Central abandoned service in April of 1972.

Equipment Of The New York Central Adirondack Division

Since the Adirondack Division of the New York Central connected with the mainline at Utica, it was easy for nearly every conceivable type of New York Central locomotive (except the very heaviest) and cars to run on the Utica-Montreal line. Great detail of the Adirondack and St. Lawrence's roster of locomotives is presented in Harter (1979, pp. 303–305) and in Palmer's notes at the Adirondack Museum; this line ran only a year or so from 1892 until The New York Central Railroad took it over.

Hastings (1950), Stauffer (1967), Harter (1979), and Robbins (1975) show a variety of engines and rolling stock. In the Nineteenth Century, the most common passenger locomotive was the 4-4-0 or American Standard type, Class C on the New York Central. These were replaced by the slightly larger Class F-2 Ten-wheelers (4-6-0) around the turn of the century. By 1913, still heavier Pacifics (Class K, 4-6-2) were already in service, and were the mainstay of such service until dieselization in October, 1951. Passenger trains during the diesel era (1951 to 1965) were pulled by Alco RS-2 road switchers.

Freight locomotives were mainly the smaller Moguls (2-6-0, Class E), and larger Consolidations (2-8-0, Class G-2). In the later years, Class K-3 Pacifics handled the freights, while similar K-11s handled the passenger. Dieselization took place between 1949 and 1952, and the predominant freight engines were also Alco RS-2 road switchers in service until the Penn-Central abandoned the Division in 1972. On occasion, Alco road engines type FA and FB hauled the through freights from Utica to Montreal.

Switchers in yard service during the steam era were the 0-6-0 Class B-10.

Seely (1928) describes the equipment used by the Adirondack and Ottawa Divisions for fighting forest fires: five flat cars bearing each a 7000-gallon water tank and pump with hose.

Webb's combination locomotive and private inspection car, the "Nehasane" is shown in Robbins (1975, pp. 24 and 26).

Most passenger trains carried mail, baggage, and express cars in addition to coaches. The day trains included diners or at least some kind of food service, while the night trains included sleepers. In 1892, when the line opened, Wagner Palace Sleeping Cars were advertised. Most of the cars operating on the Adirondack Division were standard older heavy weight cars, even through the diesel era; on occasion a light-weight streamlined sleeper with round roof would sneak into a train consisting of the older standard cars.

Shorter Railroads Connecting With The Adirondack Division

Fulton Chain Railway *(Fulton Chain or Thendara to Old Forge, 2.3 miles).*

New York Central timetables of September 10, 1910, and July 9, 1919, indicate four round trips daily and two on Sunday. The June 14, 1912, timetable shows six round trips daily, three on Sunday. The shortest running and connecting time one-way was ten minutes for the 2.3 miles. The Official Guide for Spring, 1933, has a note that the Fulton Chain Railway was being operated for freight only at that time. Palmer (1979) states that the Fulton Chain Railway was abandoned in 1932.

Paul Smith's Electric Railway

The present author, in preparing his 1976 article on this line, used a number of original conductor's trip reports as well as New York Central timetables showing connections. In Summer season, five round trips were made daily, while in Fall, Winter, and Spring there were two round trips daily. The line opened August 20, 1906, with steam; it became electrified probably later that year or the next year. The date of closure is dubious, probably between 1930 and 1932.

The Raquette Lake and Marion River Carry Railways

At Clearwater (Carter Station) on the Adirondack Division, the Raquette Lake Railway was built in 1899 heading east, and opened for the Summer season on July 11, 1900.

The Raquette Lake Railway was 17.89 miles long, and Harter (pp. 280–281) lists the following intermediate points: Rondaxe, 2.49 miles; Summit, 4.48 miles; Minnowbrook, 5.55 miles; Bald Mountain, 5.7 miles; Fair View, 7.2 (1900 N.Y.C.R.R. Employees' Timetable lists 7.00) miles; Skensowane, 8.06 miles; Eagle Bay, 9.14 miles; Uncas Road, 12.14 miles; Raquette Lake, 17.89 miles.

The track plan shown here on page 119 is taken from map #153 of the Adirondack Museum Library, dated October, 1899, when the terminus was under construction. In 1910 and 1913, a water tower was located at Raquette Lake Station. Service terminated on the Raquette Lake Railway on September 30, 1933, although this short line (eventually a branch of the New York Central) was abandoned officially on February 27, 1932 (Harter, p. 292).

One point of interest was the Marion River Carry Railroad, the shortest standard-gauged railroad in the world, according to Miller (1956) at 0.87 mile. It was possible to travel from the Raquette Lake Railway Station to Blue Mountain Lake by boat, except for the rapids on the Marion River which the Carry Railroad was built to bypass. The Railroad opened in 1900 for the Summer season, along with the Raquette Lake Railway. The Marion River Carry Railroad locomotive now on exhibit at The Adirondack Museum went into service in May, 1900, after serving formerly on the New York City elevated lines. Hochschild (1962, Life & Leisure in the Adirondack Backwoods, p. 42) notes a sawmill at the Carry run by W. W. Durant and shows a photo on page 49. Freight cars were ferried by barge from Raquette Lake to Blue Mountain Lake using the intermediate Carry Railroad (photos in Hochschild, pp. 51, 86). On September 15, 1929, the Marion River Carry Railroad closed (Harter, p. 292).

Photographs of the Clearwater-Raquette Lake-Marion River Carry area abound: Harter, pages 94, 95; Hochschild's Life and Leisure —, pages 39, 49, 51, 55, 80, 86, 92, 93; Timm (1979); Egan (1981), pages 40, 42; Fynmore (1957), page 36; Miller (1956), page 18; DeSormo (1974), page 180. Timetables and maps appear in Hochschild's Life and Leisure — pages 63, 54, 34 and in Adirondack Railroads Real & Phantom, page 14.

The following New York Central timetables show two round trips daily on the Raquette Lake Railway with one on Sunday: June 19, 1910; September 10, 1910; June 14 and 23, 1912; June 27, 1915; July 19, 1919; and on an undated timetable, possibly June 26, 1921. The June 19, 1910 timetable is an employees' and indicates that the trains were running mixed, that is, with both freight and passenger cars combined on the same train. Running times one way for the 17.89 miles between Clearwater (Carter) and Raquette Lake ranged from 60 minutes to 100 minutes.

On September 22, 1914, only one round trip operated daily with none on Sunday; this might have been a reduced non-Summer schedule. By September 29, 1929, one mixed train made one round trip only on Mondays, Wednesdays, and Saturdays. The October 1, 1932, timetable announces that service had

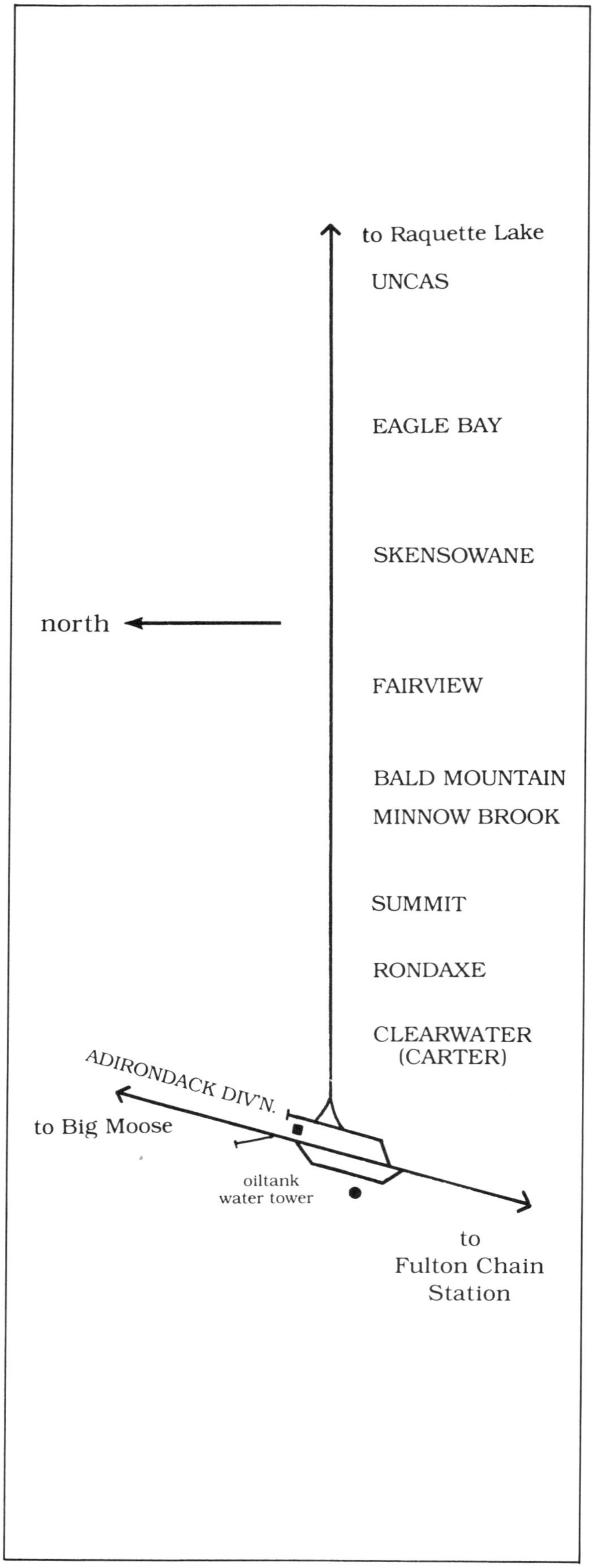

to Raquette Lake
UNCAS
EAGLE BAY
SKENSOWANE
north
FAIRVIEW
BALD MOUNTAIN
MINNOW BROOK
SUMMIT
RONDAXE
CLEARWATER
(CARTER)
ADIRONDACK DIV'N.
to Big Moose
oiltank
water tower
to
Fulton Chain
Station

Rocky Point
Eagle Bay
Cedar
Lake
Fourth
Moss
Lake
Bald Mountain
Rondaxe
North
West Lake
Clearwater
(Carter Sta.)

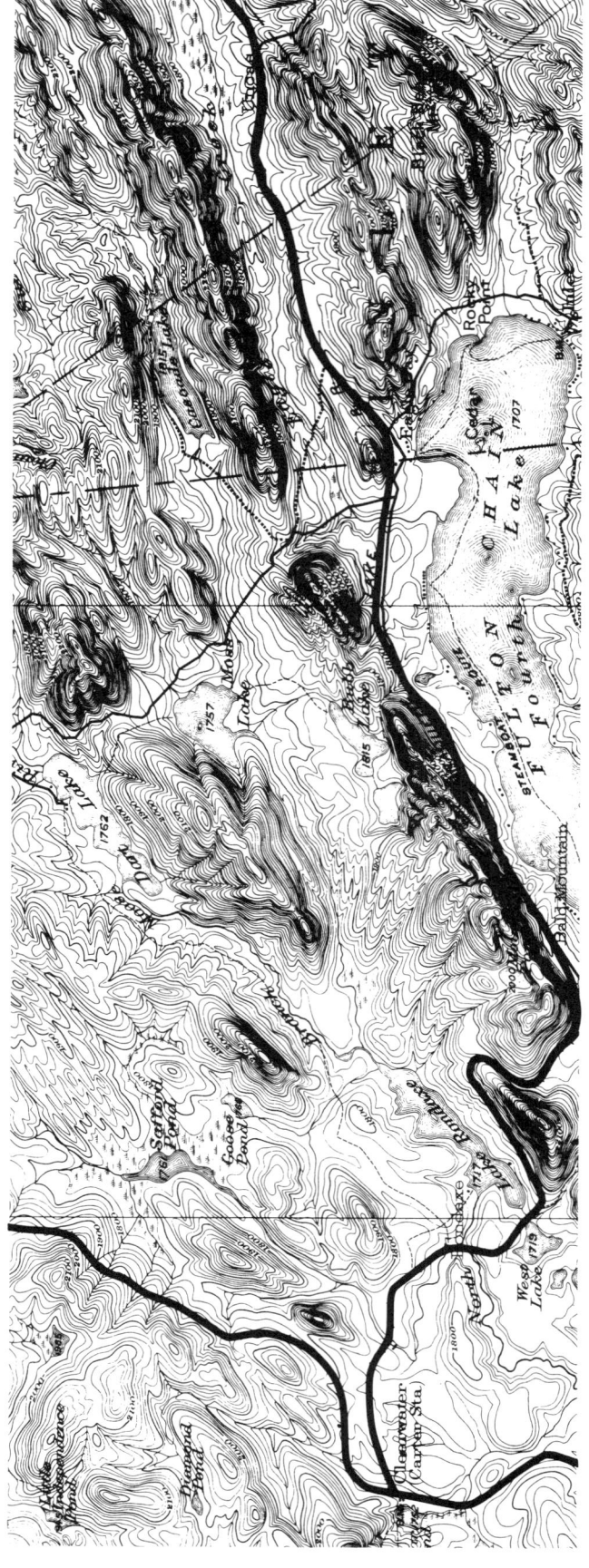

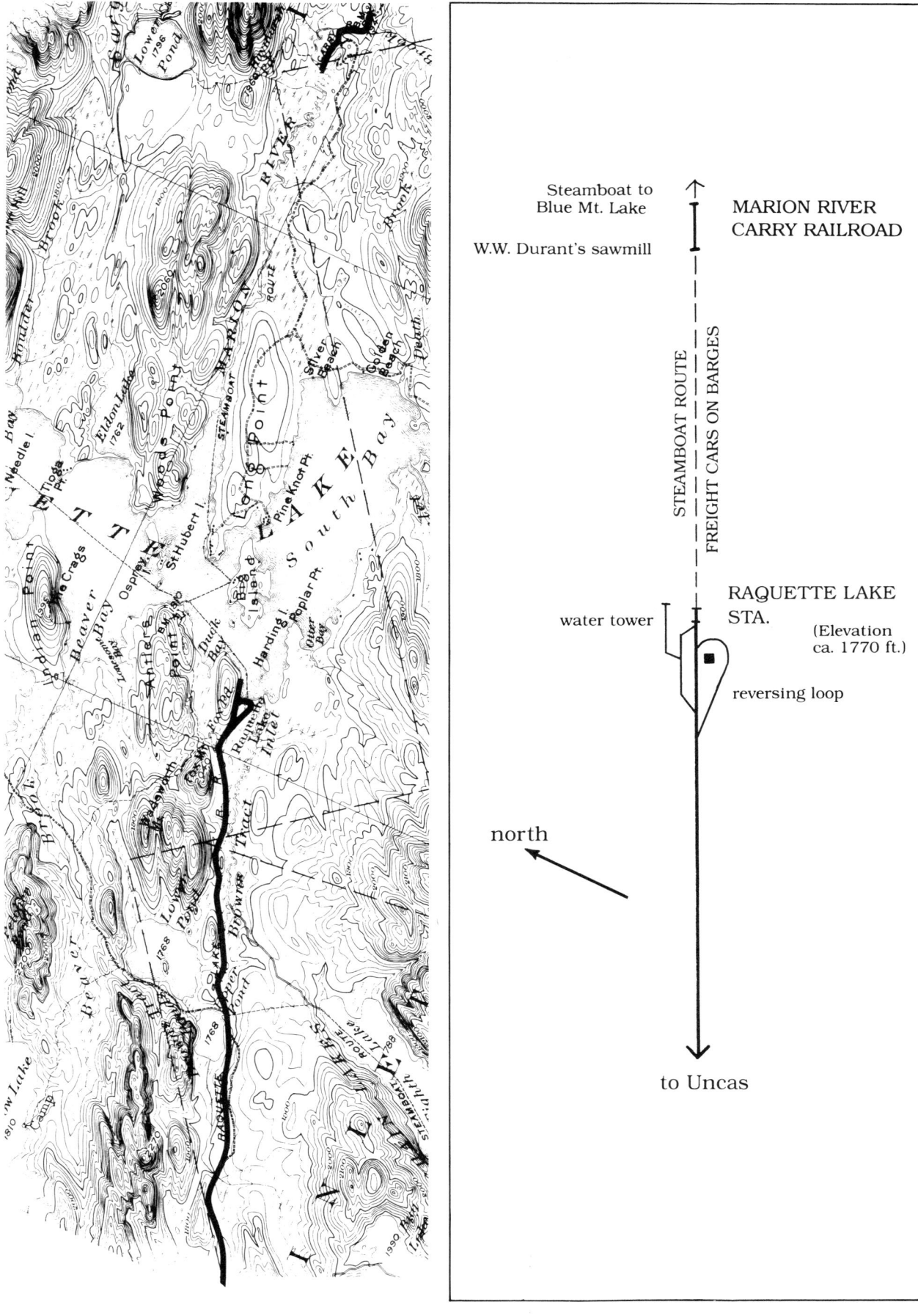

Steamboat to
Blue Mt. Lake

W.W. Durant's sawmill

MARION RIVER
CARRY RAILROAD

STEAMBOAT ROUTE

FREIGHT CARS ON BARGES

water tower

RAQUETTE LAKE
STA.

(Elevation
ca. 1770 ft.)

reversing loop

north

to Uncas

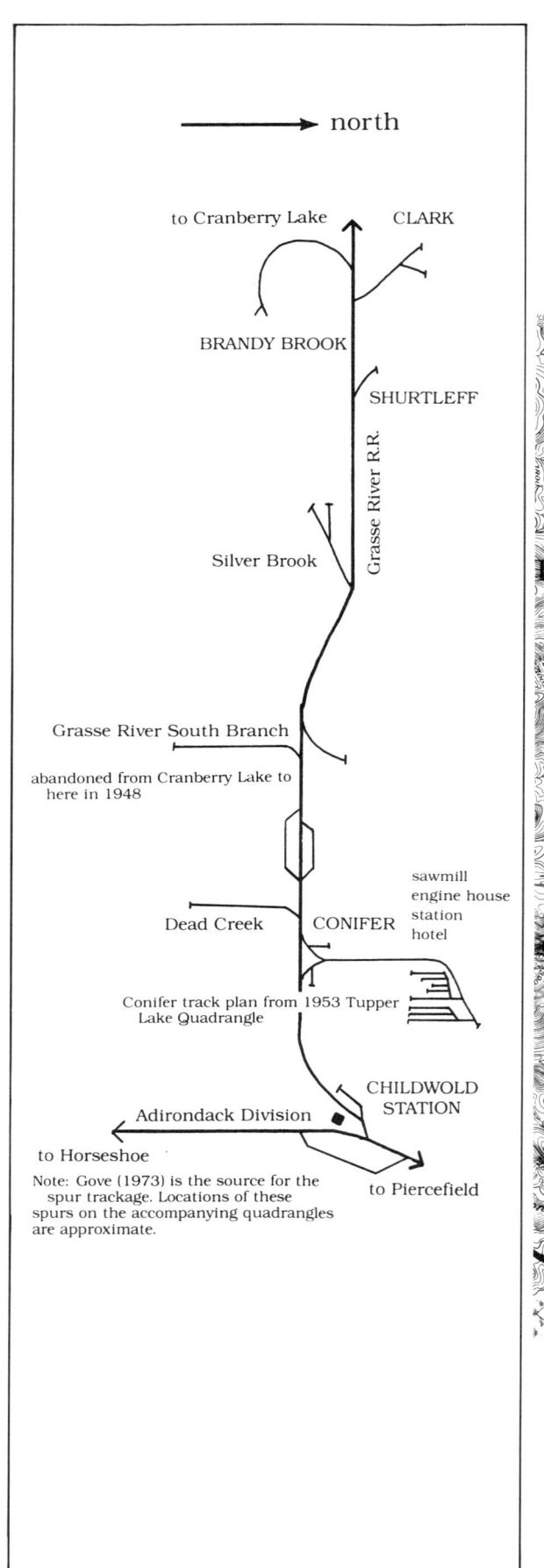

north

to Cranberry Lake   CLARK

BRANDY BROOK

SHURTLEFF

Grasse River R.R.

Silver Brook

Grasse River South Branch

abandoned from Cranberry Lake to
here in 1948

Dead Creek   CONIFER

sawmill
engine house
station
hotel

Conifer track plan from 1953 Tupper
Lake Quadrangle

CHILDWOLD
STATION

Adirondack Division

to Horseshoe

to Piercefield

Note: Gove (1973) is the source for the
    spur trackage. Locations of these
spurs on the accompanying quadrangles
are approximate.

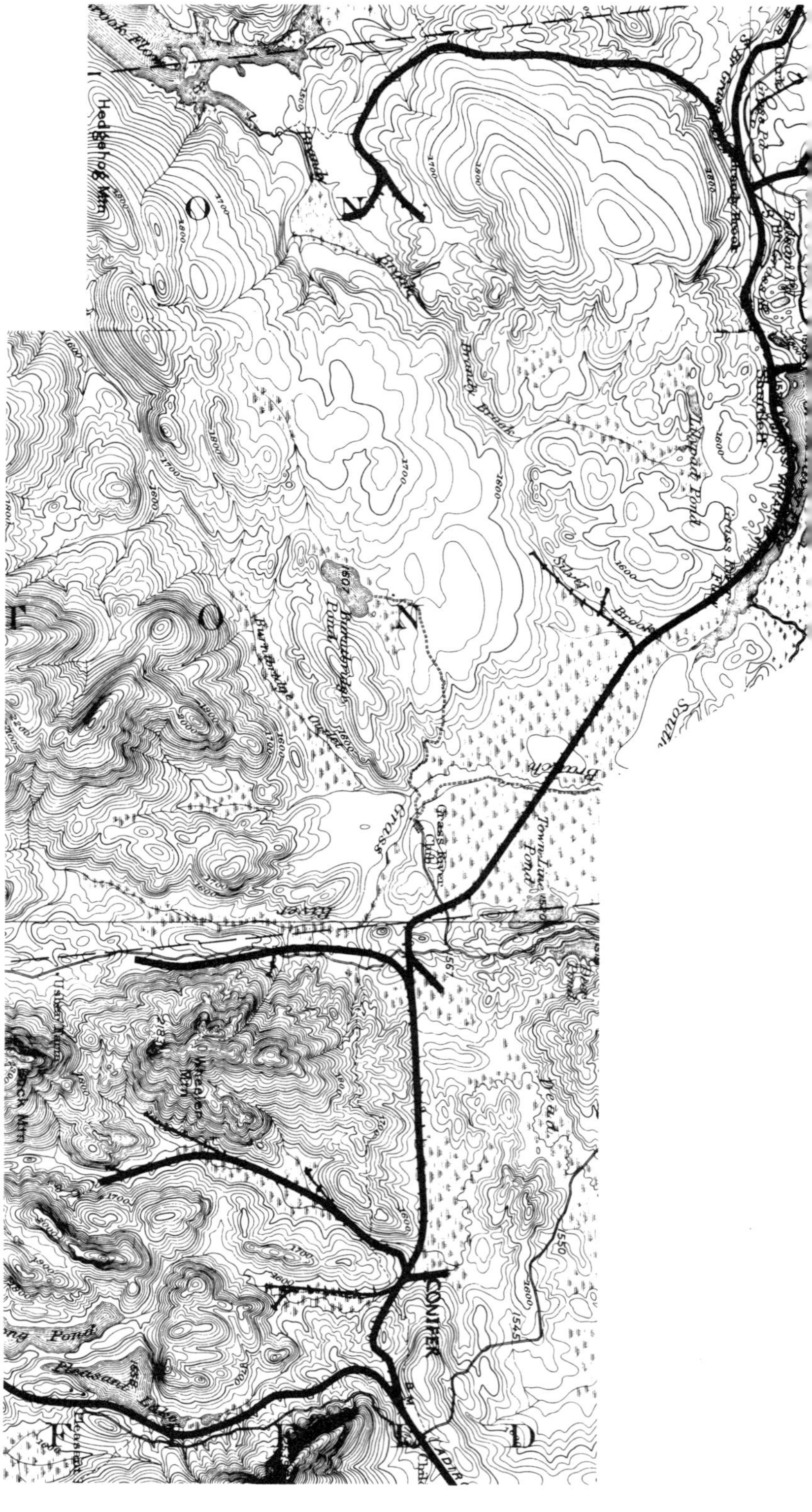

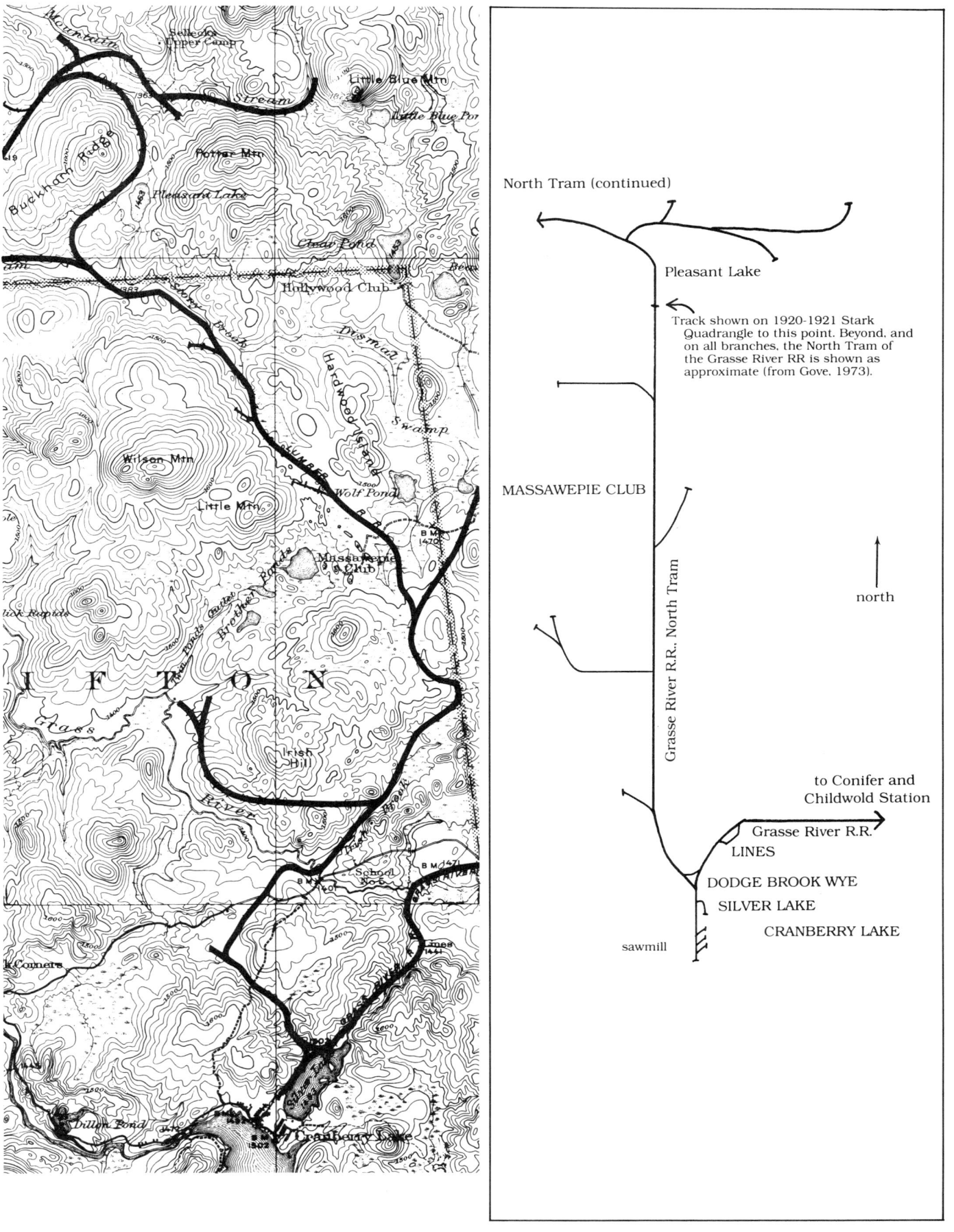

North Tram (continued)

Pleasant Lake

Track shown on 1920-1921 Stark
Quadrangle to this point. Beyond, and
on all branches, the North Tram of
the Grasse River RR is shown as
approximate (from Gove, 1973).

MASSAWEPIE CLUB

Grasse River R.R. North Tram

north

to Conifer and
Childwold Station

Grasse River R.R.
LINES

DODGE BROOK WYE

SILVER LAKE

CRANBERRY LAKE

sawmill

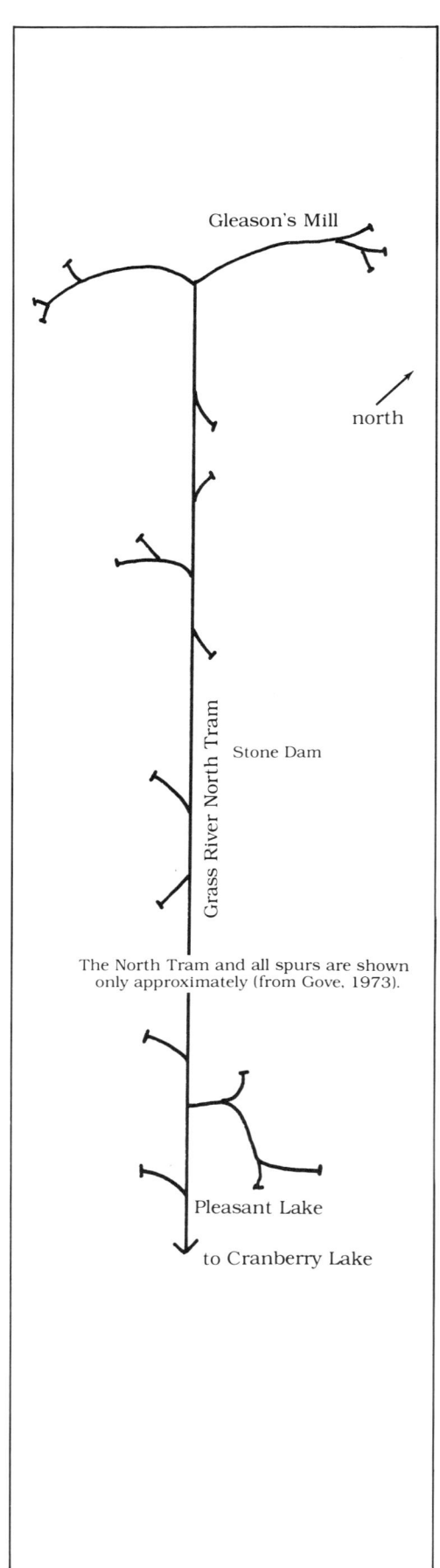

Gleason's Mill
north
Grass River North Tram
Stone Dam
Pleasant Lake
to Cranberry Lake

The North Tram and all spurs are shown only approximately (from Gove, 1973).

The Stillwater
Gulf
Alder
Brook
Deerskin
Creek
Grass
Blue
Webb Creek
Big
Brook
Buckhorn Ridge

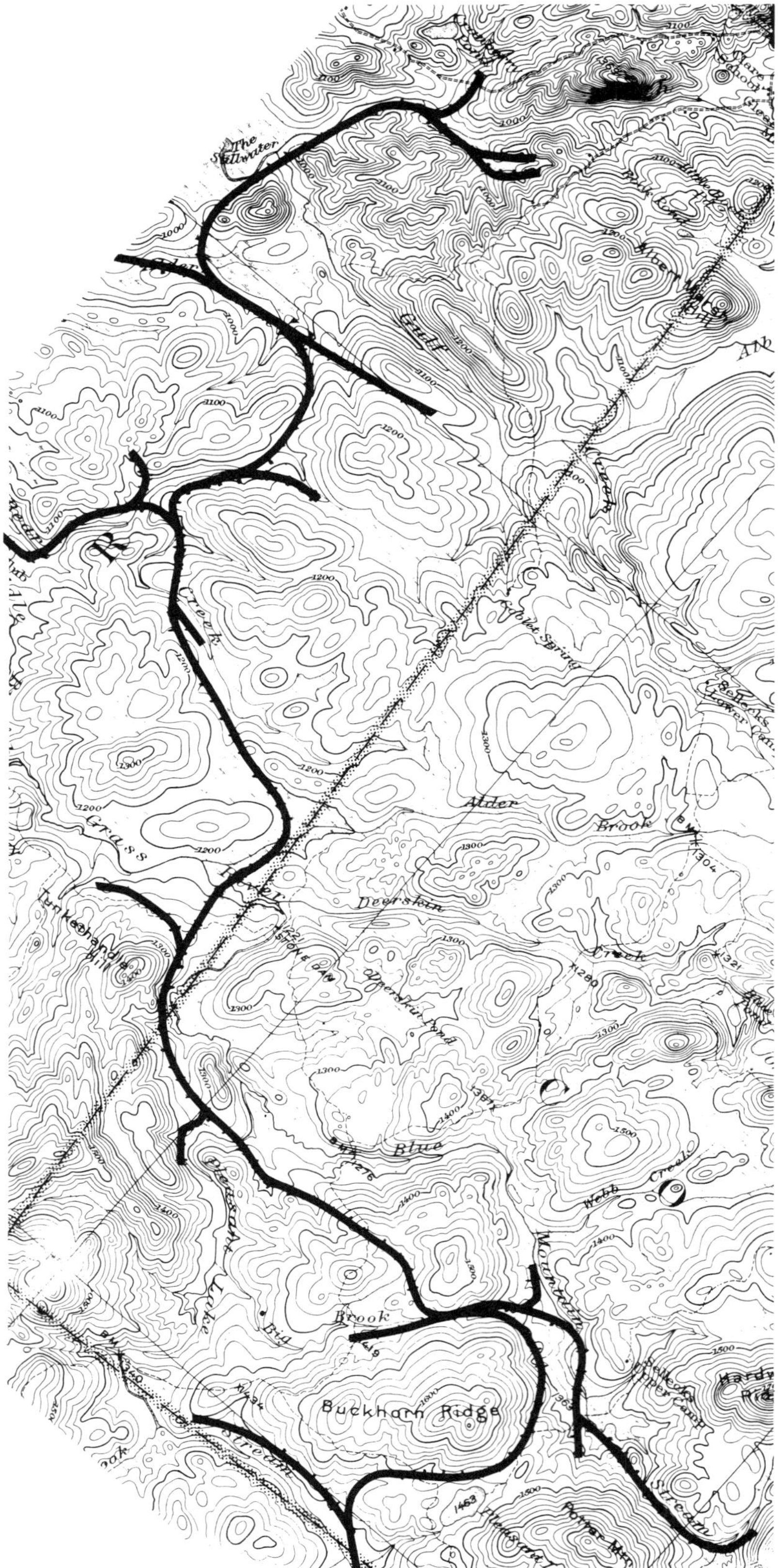

been discontinued from that day through June 15, 1933, operating thus during the Summer season only. Palmer (1979) notes that the Raquette Lake Railway was abandoned in 1934.

The Grasse River Railroad

At Childwold Station, the Grasse River connected with the New York Central Adirondack Division from 1913 to 1957. The primary source for The Grasse River Railroad is Gove (1973) who also offers much detail on the various locomotive power. William L. Sykes and his Emporium Forestry Company built a sawmill at Conifer in 1911, and in 1913 built a railroad 1.2 miles long to it from Childwold Station. The railroad offices and shops were also located in Conifer. A rapid extension of the railroad then ensued, with nearly 14 miles of track laid to Cranberry Lake during the same year, 1913. A sawmill at Cranberry Lake was constructed and many logging spurs were built (see map on pages 120, 121, 122 modified from Gove's map).

Passenger service began in 1915 with one combine car coupled to the locomotive, but after 1916 various rail motor cars were used. A list of stations, indicated on Grasse River Railroad timetables, is as follows:

0.0 mile.	Childwold Station.
1.2 miles.	Conifer.
4.0 miles.	Grasse River Club.
6.1 miles.	Silver Brook Junction. 1922 and 1923 timetables only.
9.0 miles.	Shurtleff's.
11.0 miles.	Brandy Brook. 1930 and 1932 timetables only.
12.0 miles.	Clark's.
13.8 miles.	Lines. Not shown on timetables, but appears on U.S.G.S. 1920–1921 Stark Quadrangle.
15.1 miles.	Dodge Brook Wye. Not shown on timetables, but named in Gove (1973).
16.0 miles.	Cranberry Lake.

Mileages are from the 1933 spring Official Guide.

Summer service on the June 25, 1922, and June 29, 1930, timetables reveals two round trips daily between Childwold and Cranberry Lake, with two additional shuttle round trips daily between Childwold and Conifer. No service operated on Sunday. Additional evening runs operated on Mondays and Fridays only during July and August between Childwold and Cranberry Lake.

The Fall/Winter/Spring schedule of September 30, 1923, indicates two round trips daily between Childwold and Cranberry Lake without the additional shuttle trains. No service operated Sundays. By September 25, 1932, the Conifer-Childwold shuttles were reinstated in addition to the two daily (except Sunday) round trips between Childwold and Cranberry Lake.

Running time between Childwold and Cranberry Lake ranged from 50 minutes non-stop to well over 1½ hours when meal stops at Conifer were included.

Shortly after arrival at Cranberry Lake in 1913, the Emporium Forestry Company began building the North Tram, connecting with the Grasse River Railroad at Dodge Brook Wye. By 1920–1921, when the Stark Quadrangle was published, the North Tram had been completed almost to Pleasant Lake; it was extended later, with many lateral spurs, nearly to Gleason's Mill (about 30 miles from Dodge Brook Wye). Spur construction occurred until 1937.

Gove (1973) notes that pulpwood was brought out on the Grasse River to Childwold, and then run the 2½ miles on The New York Central Railroad trackage to Piercefield Station. From here it was brought down the Piercefield spur to the International Paper Company pulp mill in the late 1920s and until 1931.

The North Tram was abandoned in 1945, and the segment of track between Cranberry Lake and Conifer abandoned in 1948. It was not until November, 1957, that the last 1.2 miles were torn up between Conifer and Childwold.

Photos of the Grasse River Railroad occur in great numbers throughout Gove, and also in Harter (1979, pp. 110 and 111), Simmons (1976, p. 366), and Hyde (1974, p. 40).

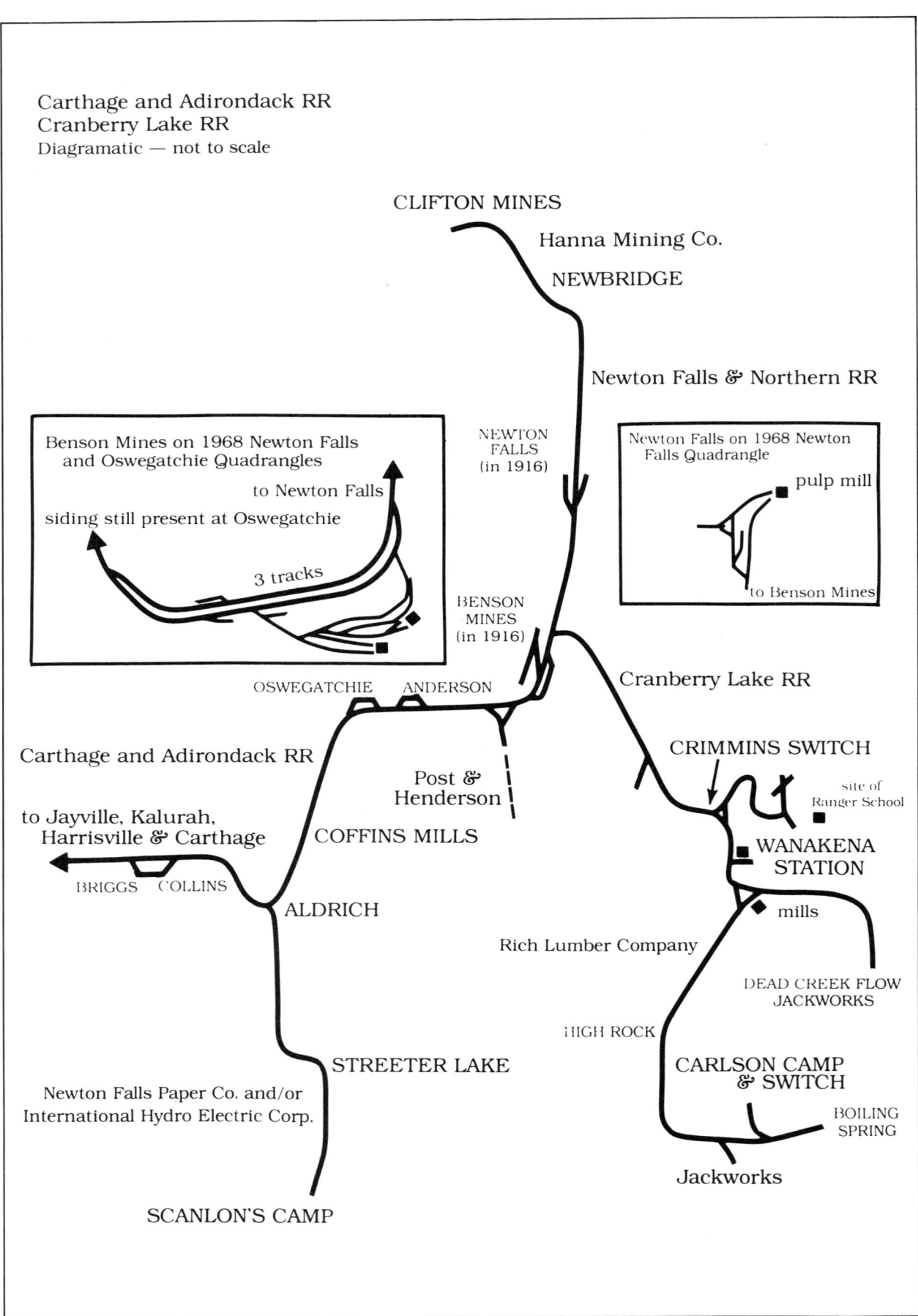

Carthage and Adirondack RR
Cranberry Lake RR
Diagramatic — not to scale

CLIFTON MINES

Hanna Mining Co.

NEWBRIDGE

Newton Falls & Northern RR

NEWTON FALLS (in 1916)

Benson Mines on 1968 Newton Falls and Oswegatchie Quadrangles

to Newton Falls

siding still present at Oswegatchie

3 tracks

Newton Falls on 1968 Newton Falls Quadrangle

pulp mill

to Benson Mines

BENSON MINES (in 1916)

OSWEGATCHIE   ANDERSON

Cranberry Lake RR

Carthage and Adirondack RR

CRIMMINS SWITCH

site of Ranger School

Post & Henderson

to Jayville, Kalurah, Harrisville & Carthage

COFFINS MILLS

WANAKENA STATION

BRIGGS   COLLINS

ALDRICH

mills

Rich Lumber Company

DEAD CREEK FLOW JACKWORKS

HIGH ROCK

STREETER LAKE

CARLSON CAMP & SWITCH

Newton Falls Paper Co. and/or International Hydro Electric Corp.

BOILING SPRING

Jackworks

SCANLON'S CAMP

Chapter V

Carthage & Adirondack Railroad and Cranberry Lake Railroad

Carthage and Adirondack Railroad

This Railroad was built from Carthage on the Rome, Watertown, and Ogdensburg Railroad eastward into the Adirondacks, and was soon to become the Carthage and Adirondack Branch of The New York Central Railroad. The tenth Annual Report of the New York State Board of Railroad Commissioners (1893), page 152, states that the line was chartered March 28, 1883, and opened to Jayville on January 1, 1887. It was extended to Oswegatchie in February, 1889, and to the Little River iron ore beds (Benson Mines) August 22, 1889. Later, the line was built to Newton Falls, then to Newbridge, and ultimately to Clifton Mines. The purpose was to transport wood products, pulp and paper, and the products of the iron mines at Benson and Clifton. A list of stations from the Spring, 1933, Official Guide to the Railroads follows, with some additional mileages estimated. I have not been able to obtain detail between Carthage and Kalurah.

0.00 – Carthage. Elevation 742 feet. Junction with Rome, Watertown, and Ogdensburg Railroad.

4.91 – Rogers. In this area were also Clearwater, Wilma, and Karter.

The elevation of Karter was 884.

7.55 – North Croghan. Elevation 880.

9.83 – Natural Bridge. Elevation 839. The U.S.G.S. 1/250,000-scale topographic sheet "Ogdensburg" published in 1961 shows a spur heading north out of Natural Bridge about four miles to a quarry located about a mile east of the hamlet of Lewisburg.

11.43 – Rock. Elevation 857. Several additional quarry spurs are shown in this vicinity on the 1912–1916 Lake Bonaparte Quadrangle.

13.1 – Diana. Elevation 829.

14.23 – Fitzgerald. Elevation 820.

17.73 – Lake Bonaparte. Elevation 770.

20.62 – Harrisville. Elevation 809.

23.16 – Bacon or Backus. Elevation 894.

27.17 – Kalurah. Elevation 1080. Palmer (March, 1970) describes the Mecca Lumber Company, organized by Nellis, Amos, and Swift in 1903. A logging railroad 6 to 8 miles long was built from Kalurah south to the Scuttle Hole, where operations continued to about 1910. Initially, Kalurah was called Little Mill.

28.80 – Jayville. Elevation 1121. Palmer (March, 1970) states that Post &

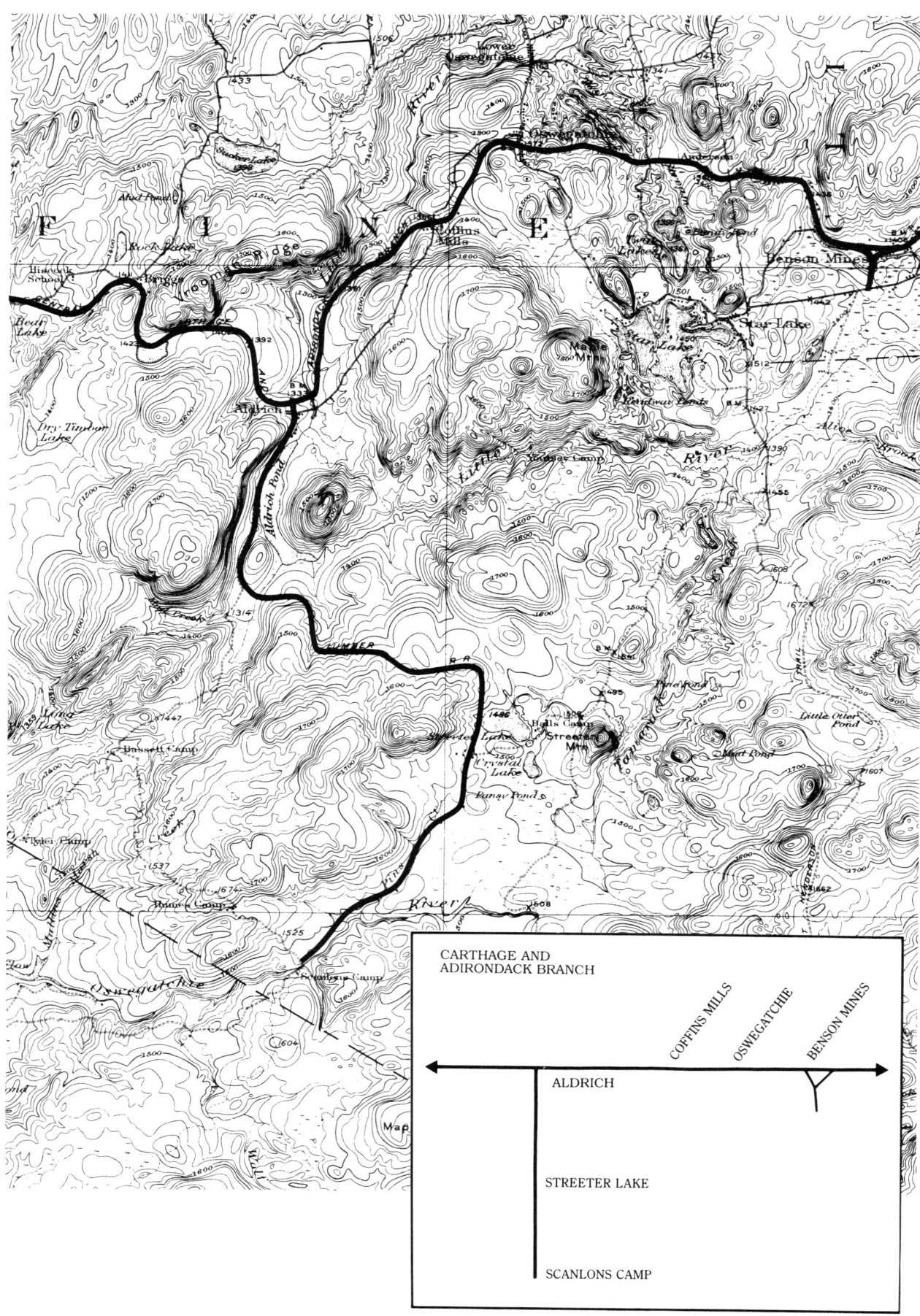

CARTHAGE AND
ADIRONDACK BRANCH

COFFINS MILLS

OSWEGATCHIE

BENSON MINES

ALDRICH

STREETER LAKE

SCANLONS CAMP

126

Henderson opened a sawmill at Jayville in the early 1890s.

The 1915 Oswegatchie Quadrangle shows a 0.3-mile long spur headed northwest at Jayville.

32.63 – Briggs. Elevation 1411. The maps in this Chapter begin here, on page 124. The Oswegatchie 1915 Quadrangle reveals a passing siding here 0.1 mile long.

33.0 – Collins.

35.04 – Aldrich. Elevation 1333. A photo of a sawmill at Aldrich appears in Palmer (March, 1970), with the caption: "Aldrich, a few miles west of Star Lake, was a busy place on the C&A branch of The New York Central Railroad. Prior to World War I, the Newton Falls Paper Company operated a logging railroad from there to Streeter Lake." I assume that the sawmill at Aldrich belonged to Newton Falls Paper Company. This logging railroad appears on the Oswegatchie Quadrangle, surveyed in 1915; the spur passes Streeter Lake and terminates at Scanlon's Camp about a half-mile short of the St. Lawrence-Herkimer County Line on the Middle Branch Oswegatchie River (see p. 126).

In 1974, the New York State Department of Transportation completed an *Inventory of Abandoned Railroad Rights of Way;* according to this *Inventory,* the approximately eight-mile-long spur had been built by International Hydro Electric Corporation to haul pulpwood. This conflicts with Palmer's statement that Newton Falls Paper Company built it; could there have been a corporate name change or sale? The date of abandonment and track removal, offered by the *Inventory* is 1922. We have no date of construction with any precision.

37.30 – Coffins Mills. Elevation 1366.

38.51 – Oswegatchie. Elevation 1372. The 1915 Oswegatchie Quadrangle shows a passing siding here ¼ mile long.

40.0 – Anderson. Elevation 1368. The 1915 Oswegatchie Quadrangle shows a passing siding here also ¼ mile long.

42.47 – Benson Mines. Elevation 1416. The operations of these iron mines are described in Hyde (1974, with

photo on p. 177), and the regional geological background presented by Buddington and Leonard (1962). Moravek (1981) notes that the Benson Mines shut down in 1977.

In addition to the iron mines, Palmer (March, 1970) notes that there was significant lumbering activity here supporting this notion with a photo. Post & Henderson, who earlier opened a sawmill at Jayville, established operations in the Benson Mines area with headquarters and a second sawmill. About 1905, Post & Henderson built a logging railroad south out of Benson Mines; examine the 1915 Oswegatchie Quadrangle on page 126, and you will note a wye at Benson Mines which looks like it was used to turn steam locomotives. I believe that this 0.4-mile-long wye was the remaining stub of Post and Henderson's logging spur!

At Benson Mines was the connection with the Cranberry Lake Railroad, described in the next section of this Chapter.

45.65 – Newton Falls, Elevation 1383. Sometime between 1895 and 1900 the C&A was extended to Newton Falls to serve the pulp mill. A New York Central 1895 map on page 55 of Harter (1979) does not yet show the Newton Falls extension, whereas a 1900 New York Central map does. Conrail still serves the Newton Falls Pulp Mill in 1984.

53 – Newbridge. Elevation 1237. Here again Palmer (1970, March) clarifies the complex history of an area. The Robert W. Higbie Lumber Company formed the Newton Falls and Northern Railroad on June 24, 1902, and built a line about seven miles long to Newbridge. It ran until November 14, 1919, when the company dissolved and the rails were removed. The abandoned right-of-way of this line is shown on the 1915 Oswegatchie Quadrangle and on the 1920 Stark Quadrangle as a trail with railroad survey benchmarks: 1443, 1458, 1354, and at Newbridge, 1237.

55.94 – Clifton Mines. Elevation 1200. Palmer to the rescue again (March, 1970)! The Hanna Mining Company during the early

NEW YORK CENTRAL
NEWTON FALLS
BENSON MINES
WANAKENA
HIGH ROCK
THE PLAINS

Newton Falls
Rocky Mtn
SWAMP
Chaumont Pond
Twin Mountain
CHAUMONT
NEW YORK CENTRAL
C L I F F
Lost Pond
Muskrat Pond
Heath Pond
Little River
Sunny Pond
State Ranger School
Wanakena
River
Inlet
F I N E
Otter Pond
High Rock
Oswegatchie
Dead Creek
Roundtop Mtn
Griffin Rapids
Boiling Spring
THE PLAINS
Glasby Creek
High Falls

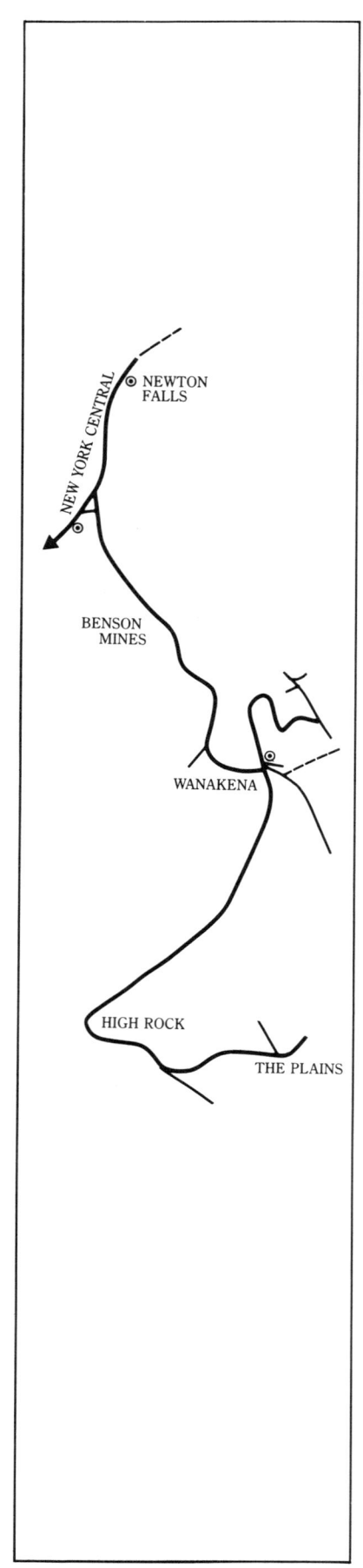

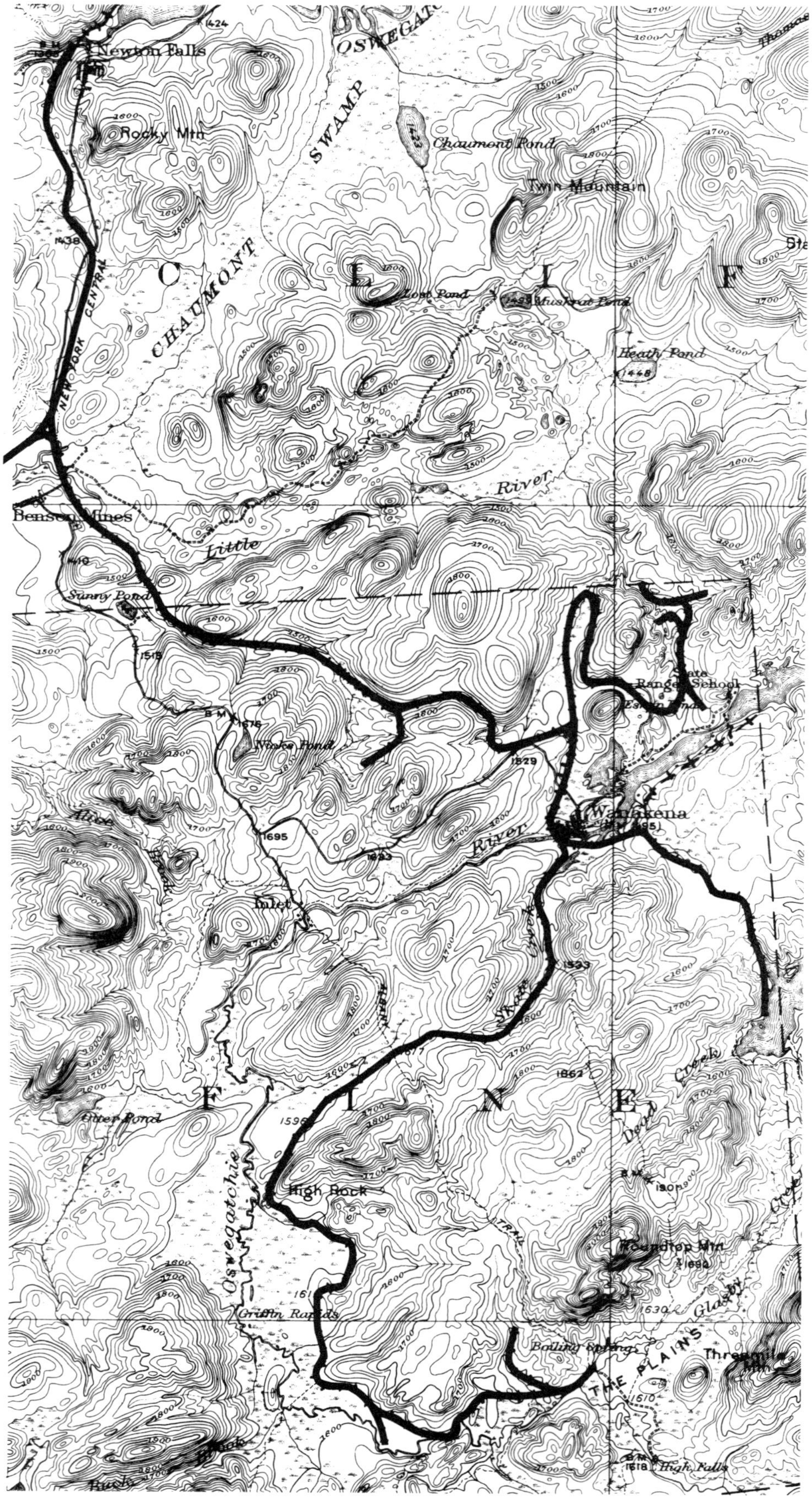

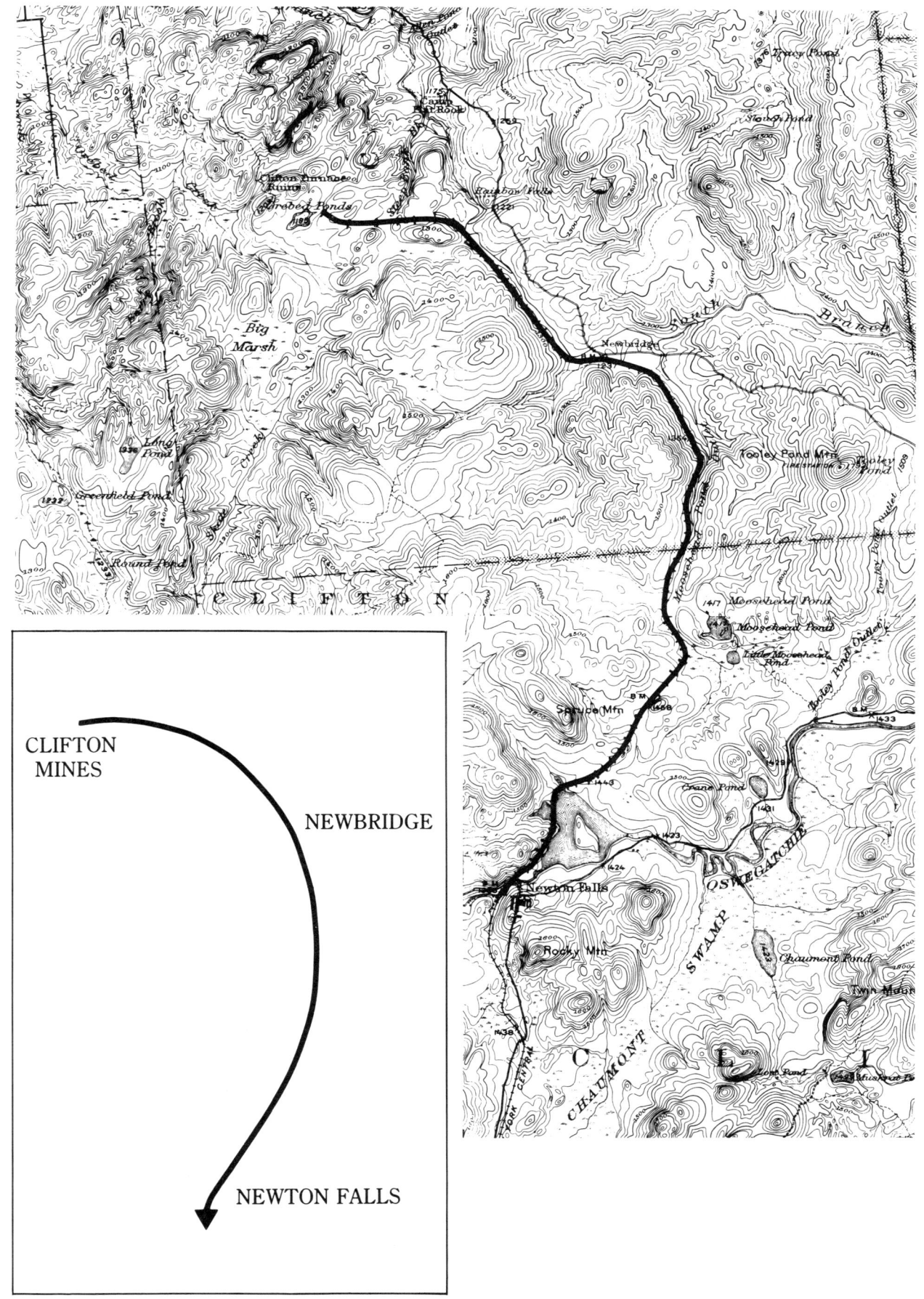

CLIFTON
MINES

NEWBRIDGE

NEWTON FALLS

1940s relaid track on the bulk of the old Newton Falls & Northern grade between Newton Falls and Newbridge; then they built nearly 3 miles of new trackage into Clifton Iron Mines. Palmer (1979) indicates that the date of abandonment of this 10.04-mile long mining extension (total to Newton Falls) as 1955. The only map I have showing the railroad into Clifton Mines is a 1956 publication entitled "Bulletin 1072, Plate 9, Map of New York State Showing Mineral Occurrences," published by the U.S.G.S.

A railroad had been built into Clifton Mines at a much earlier date and from a very different direction, according to Palmer and Thomas (1969). The Clifton Iron Company Railroad was surveyed in 1866 and opened January 1, 1868. Beginning at DeKalb Junction (East DeKalb) on the Rome, Watertown, and Odgensburg, the line with wooden rails was built 23½ miles to the southeast with stations at Marshville, Stalbird, Grant's Crossing, Silverhill, DeGrasse P.O. (Monterey), and Clarksboro. Clarksboro was the residential village, located about 1½ miles north of the mines and blast furnaces. A fire on September 4, 1869, destroyed much of the equipment, and operations were suspended. A chimney, 160 feet tall, built about 1867, was not torn down until 1942, when the Hanna Mining Company reopened the mine.

A photo of the Carthage & Adirondack appears in Gardner (1975, p. 29), showing a mail train near Harrisville on April 6, 1907. The train consists of one 4-4-0 locomotive, two mail cars, and three coaches.

A New York Central System timetable, dated June 23, 1912, pages 11 and 12, indicates two trains each way daily between Carthage and Newton Falls. One train could have easily made two round trips. The Cranberry Lake Railroad provided connections to Wanakena, two each way daily.

By January 2, 1933, and July 19, 1942, the New York Central System timetables reveal a single round trip daily, except Sundays, originating at Carthage.

The Annual Report of the New York State Board of Railroad Commissioners (1893), pages 153—158 offers details on equipment, income, and operating costs.

Cranberry Lake Railroad

The primary published source on this short line is Gove (1973) who offers great detail and a superb map showing locations of the logging spurs. These spurs have been traced onto U.S.G.S. 15-minute quadrangles and presented here on page 128. Palmer also has notes at the Adirondack Museum on the Cranberry Lake Railroad.

Six miles of common carrier railroad (including passenger and freight service) between Benson Mines and Wanakena, plus about 15 miles of logging trackage were built. The Cranberry Lake line was chartered on February 24, 1902, and opened officially on May 18, 1903. Benson Mines station became a union station, shared jointly by the Cranberry Lake and the Carthage and Adirondack. Passenger service was provided by a 2-8-0 locomotive, a combine, and a coach, making two round trips daily on June 23, 1912, according to a New York Central System timetable, pages 11 and 12. Connections were made at Benson Mines with trains running between Newton Falls and Carthage.

The sawmill in Wanakena was constructed in 1903 and ran until 1910, while the last mill to close, in 1912, was the mill making heading for barrels. Gove also notes a whipbutt mill (for buggy whips), a shoe last factory, and a veneer mill. The Rich Lumber Company, which ran all these mills and the logging railroad, was served by two Shay locomotives, a Barnhart log loader, 20 flat cars, 27 log cars, speeders, and fire-fighting cars stationed at the engine house in Wanakena (Gove, 1973). Due to the exhaustion of merchantable timber and the forest fires of 1908, the Cranberry Lake Railroad ran only until 1914, with the rails removed in 1917. Hence the Cranberry Lake Quadrangle, surveyed in 1916 and 1919, does not show the Line; I have sketched it in as best as possible on the map on page 128. Notice that the present New York State Highway 3, for about 3 miles out of Benson Mines, follows the abandoned Cranberry Lake Railroad. Another reason why the Cranberry Lake Line closed is due to competition of the newly-opened Grasse River Railroad at the east end of Cranberry Lake in 1913.

The 1909 New York State Adirondack Land Map, published by the Forest, Fish, and Game Commission, indicates that the Cranberry Lake Railroad extended downstream along the southeast bank of the Oswegatchie River from Wanakena to the Clifton-Fine Town Line, opposite the Ranger School. Gove (1973) does not indicate this, and I have drawn the extension as a dashed line on the map on page 128.

Addendum

After this manuscript went to press, additional information on the Delaware and Hudson Chateaugay and Ausable Branches was obtained. James Bailey, Plattsburgh City Historian, brought my attention to Delaware and Hudson Railroad Company maps, dated June 30, 1916 (and with more recent revisions) in the Clinton County Real Property Tax Office. The maps are of the Chateaugay Branch in Clinton County from Plattsburgh to Twin Ponds, and of the entire Ausable Branch. Instead of revising the text and maps, I have decided upon this Addendum. The information and maps presented in Chapter I and in Part I of Chapter II are correct, but lack only the detail of the Addendum. Note that the Addendum maps are not to scale; obtain precise mileages from Chapter I and Part I of Chapter II.

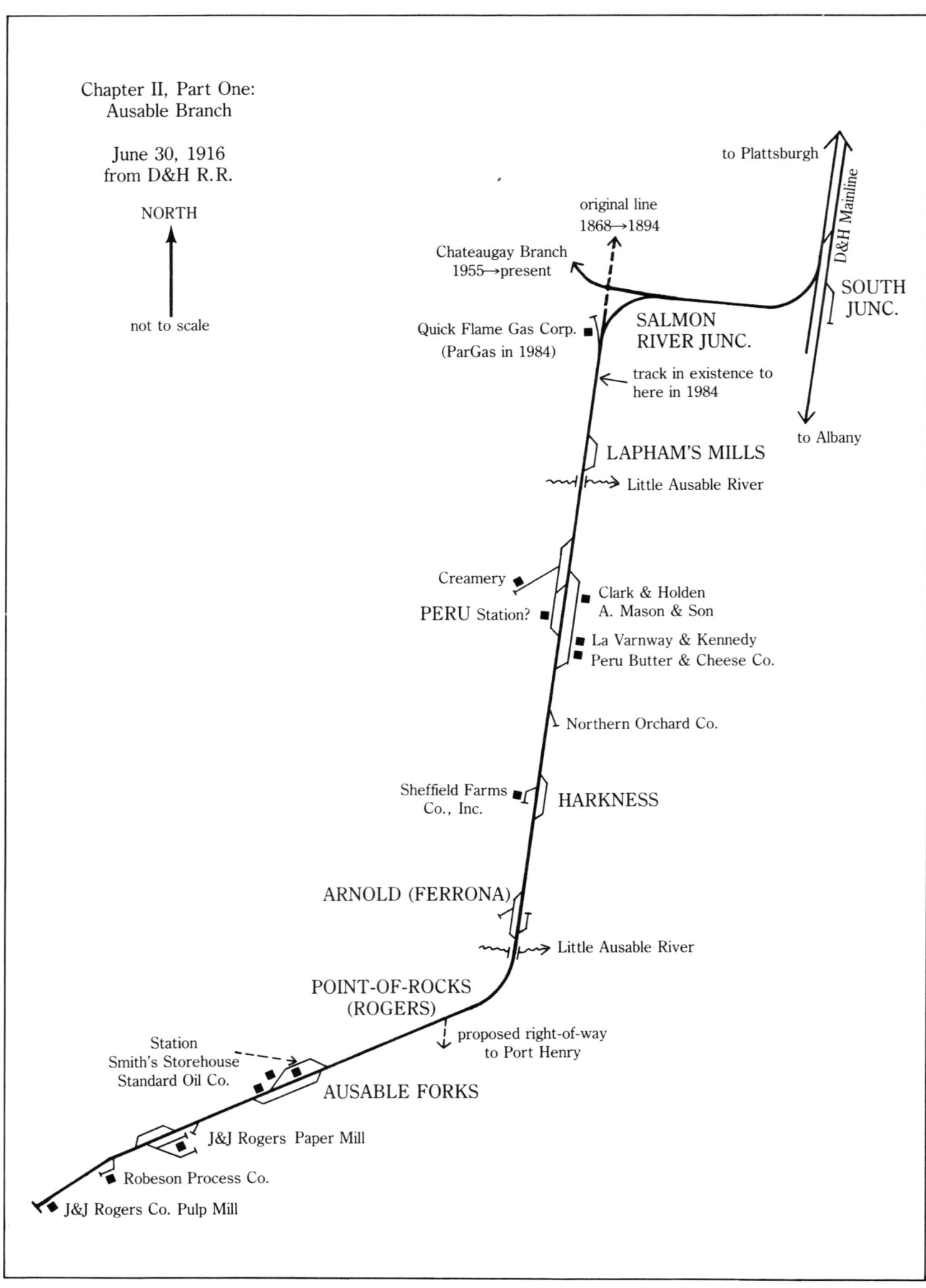

Chapter II, Part One:
Ausable Branch

June 30, 1916
from D&H R.R.

NORTH

not to scale

to Plattsburgh

original line
1868→1894

Chateaugay Branch
1955→present

D&H Mainline

SOUTH
JUNC.

Quick Flame Gas Corp.
(ParGas in 1984)

SALMON
RIVER JUNC.

track in existence to
here in 1984

to Albany

LAPHAM'S MILLS

Little Ausable River

Creamery

Clark & Holden
A. Mason & Son

PERU Station?

La Varnway & Kennedy
Peru Butter & Cheese Co.

Northern Orchard Co.

Sheffield Farms
Co., Inc.

HARKNESS

ARNOLD (FERRONA)

Little Ausable River

POINT-OF-ROCKS
(ROGERS)

proposed right-of-way
to Port Henry

Station
Smith's Storehouse
Standard Oil Co.

AUSABLE FORKS

J&J Rogers Paper Mill

Robeson Process Co.

J&J Rogers Co. Pulp Mill

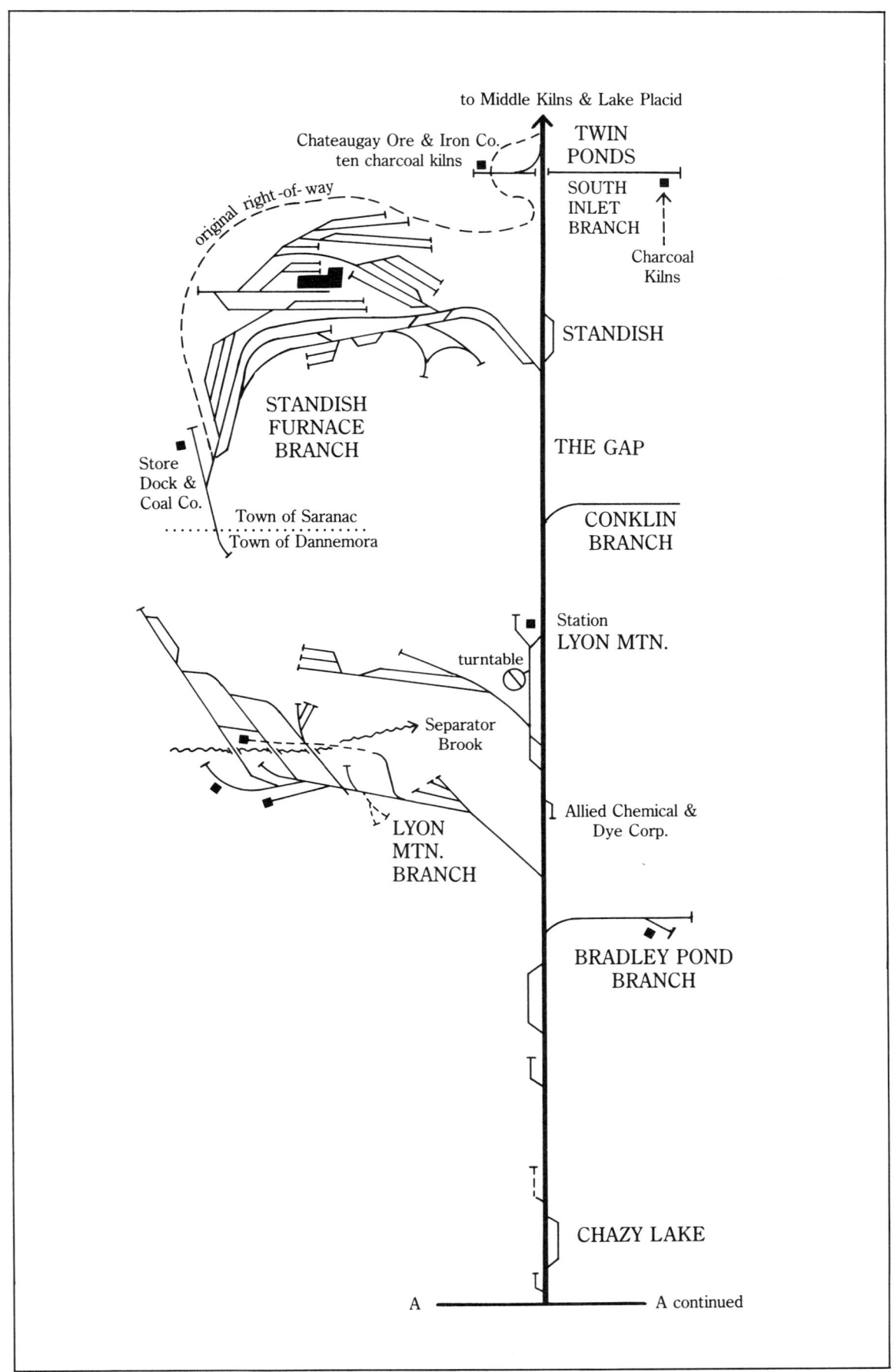

to Middle Kilns & Lake Placid

Chateaugay Ore & Iron Co.
ten charcoal kilns

TWIN
PONDS

SOUTH
INLET
BRANCH

Charcoal
Kilns

original right-of-way

STANDISH

STANDISH
FURNACE
BRANCH

THE GAP

Store
Dock &
Coal Co.

CONKLIN
BRANCH

Town of Saranac
Town of Dannemora

Station
LYON MTN.

turntable

Separator
Brook

Allied Chemical &
Dye Corp.

LYON
MTN.
BRANCH

BRADLEY POND
BRANCH

CHAZY LAKE

A   A continued

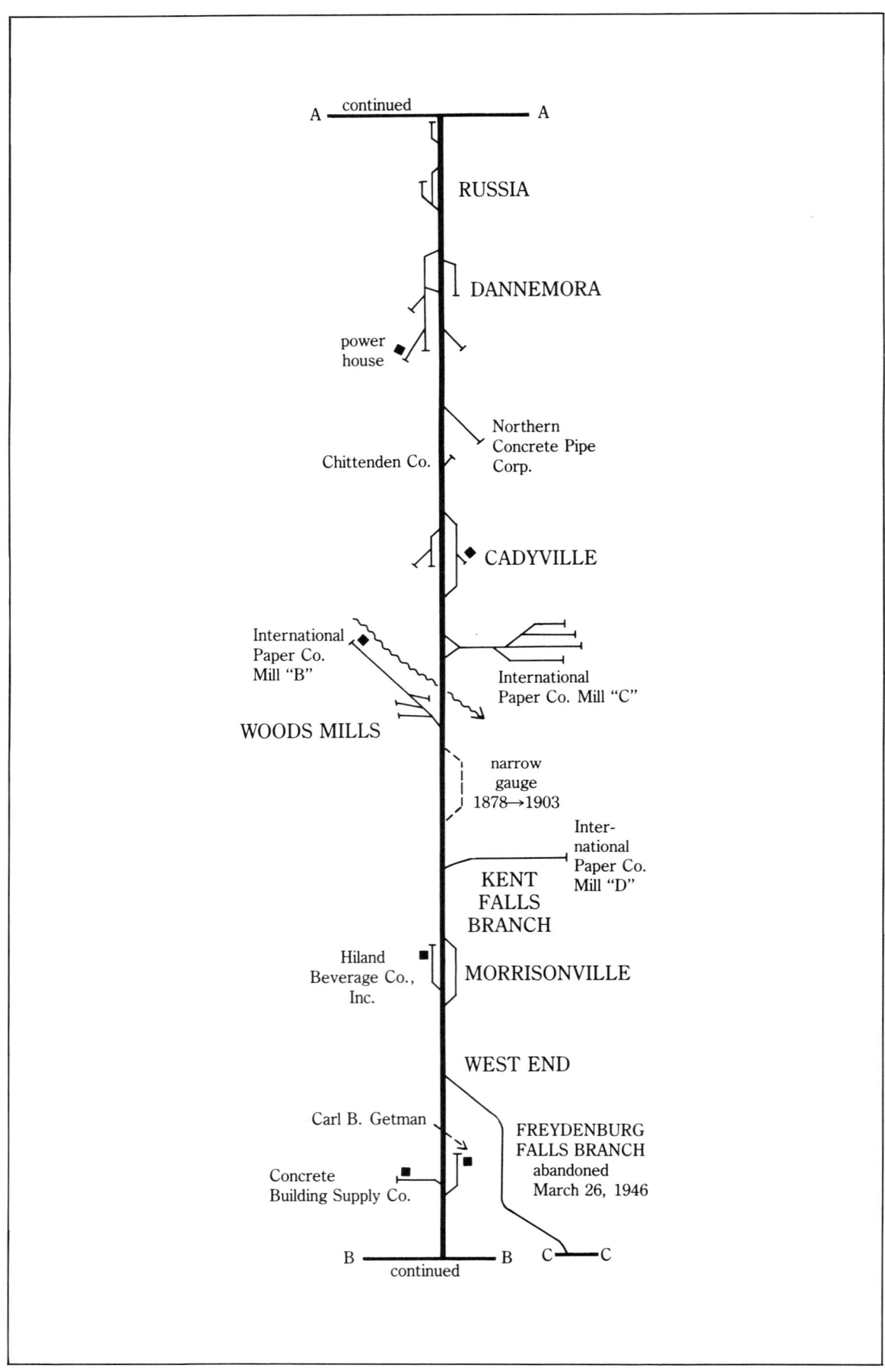

A —— continued —— A

RUSSIA

DANNEMORA

power
house

Northern
Concrete Pipe
Corp.

Chittenden Co.

◆ CADYVILLE

International
Paper Co.
Mill "B"

International
Paper Co. Mill "C"

WOODS MILLS

narrow
gauge
1878→1903

Inter-
national
Paper Co.
Mill "D"

KENT
FALLS
BRANCH

Hiland
Beverage Co.,
Inc.

MORRISONVILLE

WEST END

Carl B. Getman

FREYDENBURG
FALLS BRANCH
abandoned
March 26, 1946

Concrete
Building Supply Co.

B —— continued —— B   C —— C

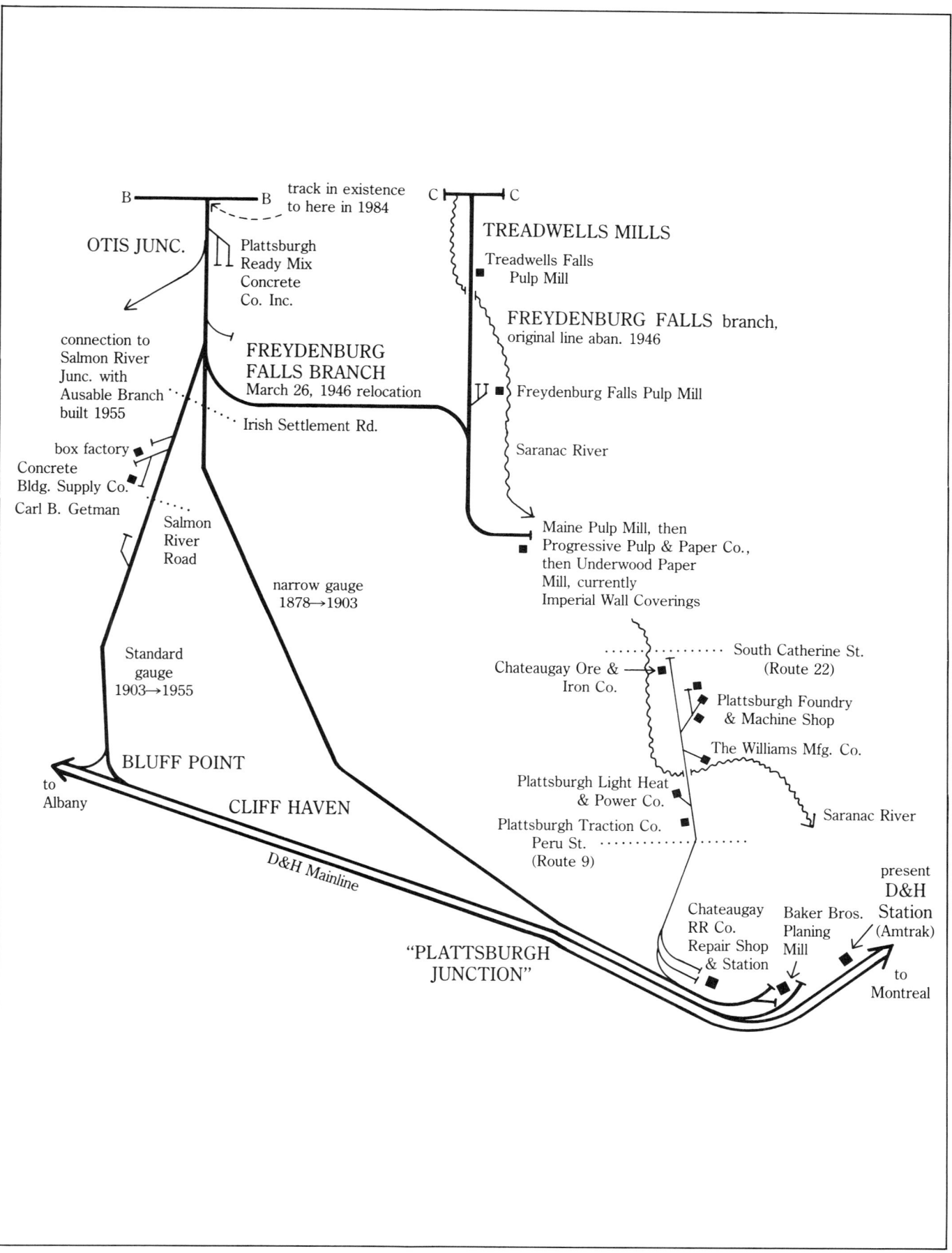

B — B   track in existence to here in 1984

OTIS JUNC.

Plattsburgh Ready Mix Concrete Co. Inc.

connection to Salmon River Junc. with Ausable Branch built 1955

FREYDENBURG FALLS BRANCH
March 26, 1946 relocation

Irish Settlement Rd.

box factory
Concrete Bldg. Supply Co.
Carl B. Getman

Salmon River Road

narrow gauge
1878→1903

Standard gauge
1903→1955

BLUFF POINT

to Albany

CLIFF HAVEN

D&H Mainline

"PLATTSBURGH JUNCTION"

C — C

TREADWELLS MILLS

Treadwells Falls Pulp Mill

FREYDENBURG FALLS branch, original line aban. 1946

Freydenburg Falls Pulp Mill

Saranac River

Maine Pulp Mill, then Progressive Pulp & Paper Co., then Underwood Paper Mill, currently Imperial Wall Coverings

Chateaugay Ore & Iron Co.

South Catherine St. (Route 22)

Plattsburgh Foundry & Machine Shop

The Williams Mfg. Co.

Plattsburgh Light Heat & Power Co.

Saranac River

Plattsburgh Traction Co.
Peru St. (Route 9)

Chateaugay RR Co. Repair Shop & Station

Baker Bros. Planing Mill

present D&H Station (Amtrak)

to Montreal

135

Bibliography

Adirondack Company's Railroad (North Creek Line) Pamphlets in Saranac Lake Library A235, 2 through 6.

Adirondack Directory, 1910–1911. Map published by McDonald & Foy of Saranac Lake Directory. Village map shows track plan. In Saranac Lake Free Library A235D. Also S522 pamphlet and P176 pamphlet.

Adirondack Mountain Club. 1958. *Adirondack Bibliography.** Railroads on pp. 183–187, and in the addition to original edition on pp. 66 & 67.

> * a list of books, pamphlets, and periodical articles published through the year 1955. Dorothy A. Plum, chairman, and Lynette L. Scribner.

Allen, Richard S. *The Crown Point Iron Company's Railroad.* 1973. IN Rails of the North Woods, pp. 175–194. Published by North Country Books, Lakemont (now Sylvan Beach), New York.

Baker, Sarah, 1970. *The Saranac Valley,* published by the author in two volumes. Volume II contains industries and railroads.

Beers, D. G. & Co. 1876. *Atlas of Franklin County, New York.* Philadelphia. Reprinted by B & E Printers, Inc., Churchville, New York, 1977.

Belcher, C. Francis. 1980. *Logging Railroads of the White Mountains* (New Hampshire). Appalachian Mountain Club. Boston, 242 pages, paperback.

Board of Railroad Commissioners, State of New York, Tenth Annual Report, for the fiscal year ending June 30, 1892, Volume II. James B. Lyon, State Printer, Albany, 1893.

> Page 152: Carthage and Adirondack
> Page 293: Keeseville, Ausable Chasm & Lake Champlain
> Page 305: Lake Champlain and Moriah
> Page 374: New York & Canada (D&H to Montreal)
> Page 468: Northern Adirondack (Hurd's)
> Page 477: Ogdensburg & Lake Champlain

Buddington, Arthur Francis, and B. F. Leonard. 1962. *Geology of the St.Lawrence Magnetite District, Northwest Adirondacks.* U.S.G.S. Professional Paper #376.

Burnett, Charles H. 1932. *Conquering the Wilderness: The Building of the Adirondack and St. Lawrence Railway.* Published privately in 1932. Saranac Lake Free Library B964.

Clark F. Mark. 1974. *The Low Dynasty.* The Quarterly, official pub'n. of the St. Lawrence County Historical Assn. January, 1974, pp. 9–15 and front cover.

Cootey, Hoit, and Hoy. 1973. *The Story of the Iron Works at The Forge (Chateaugay Lake).* Franklin Historical Review, 1973, Volume 10, pp. 31–37.

Collins, Geraldine.
> *Brandon – Ghost Town of Franklin County.* 1969. Franklin Historical Review, Vol. 6, pp. 22–28.
> *The Brighton Story.* 1977. North Country Books, Lakemont, N.Y.

Delaware and Hudson Railroad.
> *1973 Map.*
> *Delaware and Hudson Railroad: A Century of Progress, 1823–1923.* Published 1925 by J. B. Lyon Co., Albany. Saranac Lake Free Library D343. Pp. 624–630 on the Chateaugay Railroad.

DeSormo, Maitland.
> *The Heydays of the Adirondacks.* 1974. Adirondack Yesteryears, Inc., P.O. Box 209, Saranac Lake, New York.
> *Summers on the Saranacs.* 1980. Adirondack Yesteryears, Inc. Printed by the George Little Press, Burlington, Vt. Includes hotels on Lower and Upper Saranac Lakes (even Wawbeek and Saranac Inn), RR connections at Saranac Lake, and Tupper Lake.
> *The Three Macs of McColloms.* Franklin Historical Review, 1968, Volume 5, pp. 19–26.

Doherty, Lawrence. 1971. *Railroad History of Franklin County.* Franklin Historical Review 1971, pp. 6–22. Mostly on the Rutland.

Donaldson, Alfred L. 1921. *A History of the Adirondacks*. The Century Company, N.Y. Volume 2, pp. 131–141 on railroads and entry on Brooklyn Cooperage to Wawbeek.

Dora, Donna and Mildred Keough, editors. 1977. *A Past To Remember, A Future to Mold: Saranac Lake, New York*. Women's Civic Chamber, Saranac Lake. 96 pp.

Dumas, Eleanor L. 1962. *End of an Era*. The Quarterly, official publication of the St. Lawrence County Historical Association. Concerns the abandonment of the NYC Adirondack Division at Mountain View.

Egan, Patrick. 1981. *The Marion River Railroad*. Adirondack Life. Jan.-Feb. 1981, pp. 40–43.

Franklin Historical Review, 1973, pp. 49–61. *Dr. Webb's Adirondack Railroad*. Excerpts from New York Herald June 1, 1897.

Fynmore, Jim. 1957. *Relics of 1890 Travel in the Central Adirondacks*. North Country Life, Fall, 1957.

Gallagher, D. 1937. *Origin of the Magnetite Deposits at Lyon Mountain, New York*. N.Y. State Museum Bulletin #311.

Gardner, Ed. 1975. *Adirondack Vistas*. Harbor Hill Books, P.O. Box 417, Harrison, N.Y. 10528. Ed Gardner's address in 1975: 2 Garden Avenue, Mountain Top, Pa. 18707.

Gove, William. Articles in the Northern Logger and Timber Processor:
William L. Sykes and The Emporium —
Part I: is in Pennsylvania.
Part II: *The Emporium Forestry Co. of New York and the Grasse River Railroad*. Sept. 1970, pp. 10–13, 32, 33.
Part III: *Latter Days*. Dec., 1970, pp. 12, 13, 32, 35, 38.
The Adirondack's Shortest Logging Railroad.
June, 1978, pp. 16, 17, 30, 31, and 33. (Concerns International Paper Co. at Woods Lake).
The Mac-a-Mac Railroad of Brandreth. April, 1981, pp. 10–12, 40–42, 44.
John McDonald's Railroad at Bay Pond. September, 1981, pp. 6, 7, 8, 38, 39, 40.
Rich Lumber Company, chapter in Rails in the North Woods, pp. 11–33, 1973, published by North Country Books, Lakemont, N.Y. (now Sylvan Beach, N.Y.).

The Grasse River RR article, in addition to being published in 3 installments in the Northern Logger, was reprinted in 1973 as a chapter in Rails in the North Woods, pp. 69–110, published by North Country Books, Lakemont (now Sylvan Beach), N.Y.

Grosh, Reverend Esta E. 1896. Unpublished manuscript at the Adirondack Museum, Blue Mountain Lake. Concerns Brandon-Keese's Mills-McColloms area. Ministry at Santa Clara & Brandon 1892-1896.

Harter, Henry A. 1979. *Fairy Tale Railroad: The Mohawk and Malone from the Mohawk, through the Adirondacks, to the St. Lawrence — the Golden Chariot Route*. North Country Books, Sylvan Beach, N.Y.

Hastings, Philip R. 1950. *Pacifics to Placid*. Trains (magazine), September, 1950, pp. 22–26.

Haworth, James A. 1954. *Wilderness Railroad*. North Country Life. Spring, 1954. Pp. 20–22. (on the N.Y. & Ottawa)

Hochschild, H. K.
Dr. Durant and his Iron Horse (North Creek line). 1961. Adirondack Museum.
Adirondack Railroads Real and Phantom. 1962. Published by Adirondack Museum.
Life and Leisure in the Adirondack Backwoods. 1962. Published by Adirondack Museum.
The MacIntyre Mine — from Failure to Fortune. 1962. Published by Adirondack Museum.

Hough, Franklin B., Dr. 1853. *A History of St. Lawrence and Franklin Counties, New York*. Originally published 1853 in Albany, New York. Reprinted by Regional Publishing Company, Baltimore, 1970.

Hoy, Ralph L. (editor). 1973. *The Story of the Iron Works at "The Forge"*, from a tape recording of an interview with Roy I. Cootey by Edward G. Hoit in 1972. Franklin Historical Review, 1973, pp. 31–37. Vol. 10.

Hyde, Floy Salls.
Adirondack Forests, Fields, and Mines. 1974. North Country Books, Lakemont, N.Y. (now Sylvan Beach, N.Y.).
Water Over the Dam at Mountain View in The Adirondacks. 1970. Chapter IV, pp. 55–66 on N.Y. Central Adirondack Division. Published by the author and printed by Vail-Ballou Press, Binghamton, N.Y.

Jensen, David E. 1978. Minerals of New York State. Ward Press, Rochester, New York. Pages 41 and 108 on MacIntyre Mine.

Kudish, Michael.
Paul Smith's Flora. 1975.
Paul Smith's Flora II. 1981. Both published by Paul Smith's College.
Paul Smith's Electric Railway. Franklin Historical Review. 1976, pp. 20–31.

Lamy, Margaret W. 1965. *You Can't Get There From Here By Rail Any More*. N.Y. Times. Sunday, July 18, 1965, Section 10, pages xx1 and xx7. On abandonment of passenger service on the NYC Adirondack Division.

Lindsey, James. 1958-1959. *The Fish Car.* New York State Conservationist Dec. 1958-Jan. 1959, p. 31. State fish hatchery RR car.

Lobeck, Armin K. 1956, 1964. *Things Maps Don't Tell Us.* The Macmillan Company, New York.

Lodge, Donald E. 1972. *The Freight Carloadings Market on the Lake Placid Branch.* SUNY Plattsburgh Technical Assistance Center.

Miller, Roland B. 1956, 1957. *Iron Horses in the Adirondacks.* New York State Conservationist.

    Part I, October-November, 1956, pp. 18 & 19.

    Part II, April-May, 1957, page 9.

    Photo of Marion River Carry locomotive appears on page 37 of December-January, 1955-1956.

Mohr, William A. 1974. *Delaware & Hudson.* Adirondack Life, Spring 1974, pp. 15-20 (on Westport Station).

Moravek, J. R. 1981. *Iron Mining and Smelting: Ghost Towns and Forgotten People.* Manuscript from Dept. of Geography, SUNY, Plattsburgh. Sept. 1981.

Newspapers:

    Plattsburgh Sentinel 4/10/1885 on NY & Ottawa

    Malone Palladium 5/30/1885 on NY & Ottawa

New York Central Railroad.

Health and Pleasure on America's Greatest Railroad, 1896, New York Central Railroad's 4-Track Series:

    #5 (1896) in Saranac Lake Free Library N573.

    #2 (1893).

    #6 (1903) entitled "The Adirondack Mountains."

These show fares, hotel accommodations, stage connections, excursions, even running times, but no timetables. Maps are very general and of small scale.

New York State *Conservationist* magazine. February-March, 1972, page 36, and June-July, 1972, page 36. Unsigned articles are entitled "Commissioner Protests Sale of Railroad" and "Tahawus Railroad Sale Postponed", respectively.

New York State Conservation Commission *Adirondack Maps:* 1909, 1911 (for Brooklyn Cooperage lines at Meno), 1920, 1923.

New York State Conservation Commission *Annual Reports:*

    for 1934: Bay Pond fire.

    for 1893, volume II (Appendix): includes granting of charters to railroads in the Adirondacks on pages 245-293, but through 1887 only. Deals mainly with the North Creek Line and proposed lines that were never built.

New York State Department of Transportation. 1974. *Inventory of Abandoned Railroad Rights of Way.* Published by Real Property Division in Regions by counties:

    Region #1 — Albany, Saratoga, Rensselaer, Schenectady, Greene, Washington, Warren, Essex;

    Region #2 — Fulton, Hamilton, Herkimer, Madison, Montgomery, and Oneida;

    Region #7 — Clinton, Franklin, Jefferson, Lewis, and St. Lawrence.

New York State Agricultural Manual, arranged by counties. Ca. 1922. Compiled by Edith Van Wagner. Department of Farms and Markets, Division of Agriculture, Bulletin #133. Albany.

Nielsen, Wally "Caboose." 1970. *Walking the Railroad or Trompin' the Tracks.* The ETM Log, Autumn 1970. Abandoned Railroads in New York State as of 1969.

Official Guide to the Railways. Published monthly by the National Railway Publication Company, New York, New York.

Palmer, Richard F. *Logging Railroads in the Adirondacks*, a four-part series in the Northern Logger and Timber Processor:

    Part I: *John Hurd — a Man with a Dream.* February, 1970, pp. 28, 29, 47.

    Part II: March, 1970, pp. 14, 15 (includes Oval Wood Dish Company and Benson Mines area).

    Part III: *Wooden Rails in the Wilderness.* April, 1970, pp. 26, 27, 47 (includes the Black River & Woodhull RR near Forestport).

    Part IV: *Brooklyn Cooperage Operations.* March, 1971, pp. 16, 17, 26.

Peg-Leg Railroad, a chapter in Rails in the North Woods, pp. 149-157, published in 1973 by North Country Books, Lakemont, N.Y. (now Sylvan Beach, N.Y.). This article was also printed in the Northern Logger, April, 1971, pp. 14, 15, 37.

Richard Palmer has unpublished notes on file at the Library of the Adirondack Museum in Blue Mountain Lake.

The Abandoned Railroads in New York State. This is a typed manuscript (unpublished) given to Michael Kudish on the Adirondack Railway inaugural run, 10/9/79, by the author.

Iron Horse is Dead. On file at Saranac Lake Free Library. Syracuse Herald-American, Stars Magazine, Sunday 4/18/65, pp. 3 & 12. Pamphlet P176 f pam.

Adirondack Train has Last Toot. Syracuse

Herald-American, Sunday 11/7/65 in Empire Magazine, pp. 9–11. Excursion by Central NY Chapter of National RY Hist. Soc. in Sept. '65, from Syracuse to Tupper Lake. Saranac Lake Free Library pamphlet p176a f pam.

Palmer, Richard and John Thomas. 1969. *Wooden Rails in the Wilderness*. The Quarterly: Publication of the St. Lawrence County Historical Association.
    Part I, April, 1969, volume 14, #2, pp. 3, 11–14, 22.
    Part II, July, 1969, volume 14, #3, pp. 11, 14, 22.
    Part III, Oct., 1969, volume 14, #4, pp. 11 and 14.

Pierce, Harry H. 1953. *Railroads of New York: A Study of Government Aid, 1826–1875*. Harvard Univ. Press. Syracuse E.S.F. Moon Library, Robin Hood Coll'n. HE 2771 .N5P61.

Pope, Connie. 1972. *Brandon — A Legendary Ghost Town*. York State Tradition. Summer, 1972. Pp. 37–47.

Robbins, Stephen A. 1975. *A Second Chance for the Adirondack Division?* Adirondack Life, Spring, 1975, pp. 24–29.

Rochette, Frank. 1937. *Frogs Croaked Sole Greeting*. D&H Bulletin, February 1, 1937. Chateaugay Railroad.

Scarborough's New Railroad, Post Office, Township and County Map of New York with distances between stations. 1903, The Scarborough Company, Boston, Mass.

Seaver, Frederick J. 1918. *Historical Sketches of Franklin County*. J. B. Lyon Company, Albany.

Seely, S. A. 1928. *A Mountain Railroad Arms Against Fire*. American Forests, July, 1928.

Shaughnessy, James.
The Rutland Road. 1964. Howell North, Berkeley, Calif.
Delaware and Hudson. 1967. Howell North, Berkeley, Calif.

Shaw, Robert B. and Stephen G. Walsh. 1982. The Quarterly, Official publication of the St. Lawrence County Historical Association. *Along the "Lower Route": A History of the Northern Railroad,*
    Part One, Vol. 27, #1, pp. 7–13.
    Part Two, Vol. 27, #2, pp. 15–20 (Ogdensburg & Lake Champlain).

Simmons, Louis J.
Mostly Spruce and Hemlock: Historical Highlights of Tupper Lake and the Town of Altamont. 1976. Printed by Vail-Ballou Press, Inc., Binghamton, N.Y.
Tupper Lake. 1968 Franklin Historical Review. Pp. 27–41. Volume 5.

Smith, Nelda Young. 1969. *John Hurd's Railroad*. Franklin Historical Review, Vol. 6, pp. 29–32.

Smith, H. P. 1885. *History of Essex County*. D. Mason & Co., publishers. At Saranac Lake Free Library, behind main desk, 974S.

Staufer, Alvin F. 1967. *Steam Power of the New York Central, Volume I, 1915–1955*. Published by the author, 3186 Stony Hill Road, Medina, Ohio, 44256.

Stephenson, Robert C. 1945. *Titaniferous Magnetite Deposits* of the Lake Sanford Area, New York. New York State Museum Bulletin 340. Albany.

Surprenant, Neil. 1982. *Brandon: Boom Town to Nature Preserve*. Published privately by Ross Park.

Suter, H. M. *Forest Fires in the Adirondacks in 1903*. Circular #26, Bureau of Forestry, U.S. Dept. Agriculture, Washington, D.C.
    See also: New York State Conservation Commission, Karl Schmitt, Forester. *Fire Protection Map of the Adirondack Forest, 1916*. J. B. Lyon Co., State Printers.
    Annual Report of the Forest Commission, State of New York, for the Year 1891. Contains map entitled Great Forest of Northern New York. James B. Lyon, State Printers. Shows areas burned through 1891.

Timm, Ruth. 1979. *Profile of Raquette Lake: The Era of the Railroad and the Steamboat*. Boonville Herald, April 18, 1979, page 10.

Tyler, Helen Escha.
In Them Thar Hills: Folk Tales of the Adirondacks, 1968.
    Printed by Currier Press, Saranac Lake. Chapters:
    "A Train's Last Run," pp. 14–17. Roakdale.
    "The Gospel Train", pp. 35–37. Church trains run by John Hurd to Tupper Lake and Santa Clara from Brandon.
    "Moving Day — 1917," pp. 21–25. A family uses the siding at Bloomingdale Station en route to Moriah (Port Henry) via Plattsburgh, chartering a boxcar.
Early Days in Franklin. 1969. Franklin Historical Review Vol. 6, pp. 16–21 (Vermontville and Franklin Falls).

United States Geological Survey — 15 minute topographic quadrangles. When two years are connected by a hyphen below, the first year is the year of survey or aerial photo, and the second year is the year of publication. Many quadrangles have been resurveyed and republished decades after the originals. Normally, there is a lapse of several years between time of survey or photo and year of publication.

Ausable 1893–1903, Ausable Forks 1953.

Big Moose 1900–1903, 1953–1954.

Chateaugay 1912–1913.

Childwold 1919–1920.

Cranberry Lake 1916–1919.

Dannemora 1911; 1954.

Elizabethtown 1892; 1955.

Lake Luzerne 1900–1903; 1947–1955.

Lake Placid 1893–1894; 1942–1953.

Long Lake 1901–1902; 1955.

Loon Lake 1902–1906.

Lyon Mountain 1911.

Malone 1914–1915.

McKeever 1910; 1958.

Moira 1915.

Newcomb 1953–1954.

Nicholville 1919.

North Creek 1895–1897; 1942–1958.

Old Forge 1892–1898; 1954.

Oswegatchie 1915–1916.

Paradox Lake 1895; 1942–1947. 1895 surveyed, 1897 edition, reprinted 1930, as map #215 of Saranac Lake Free Library.

Plattsburgh 1893; 1939–1956.

Port Henry 1945.

Raquette Lake 1899; 1953–1954.

Remsen 1897.

Russell 1919.

Saint Regis 1902–1903; 1953–1955.

Santa Clara 1921.

Santanoni 1952–1953.

Saranac 1902; Saranac Lake 1953–1955.

Stark 1920–1921.

Thirteenth Lake 1953–1954.

Ticonderoga 1894.

Tupper Lake 1903–1904; 1953–1954.

United States Geological Survey — publications other than topographic 15-minute quadrangles:
  Map of New York State Showing Mineral Occurrences. Bulletin 1072, Plate 9, 1956.
  Ogdensburg map. 1/250,000 scale series. 1961. 100-foot contour.

Vanderwalker, Mrs. David B. 1972. *Town of Santa Clara: A Pictorial History.* Book One. Published by Santa Clara Town Historian.

Wakefield, Manville B.
  Coal Boats to Tidewater. 1965 and 1971. Wakefair Press, Grahamsville, N.Y. 12740. History of the Delaware and Hudson Canal in Pennsylvania and Southeastern New York.
  To the Mountains by Rail. 1970. Wakefair Press, Grahamsville, N.Y. Printed by the Intelligencer Printing Co., Lancaster, Pa. Typesetting by Batsch Company of Camp Hill, Pa. History of the Sullivan County segment of the New York, Ontario and Western Railway.

Wallace's Guide to the Adirondacks. 1898. Contents on RRs:
  New York and Ottawa — Moira p. 175, Brandon p. 182, Tupper Lake p. 183. Adirondack and St. Lawrence mileages, pp. 185, 104, 422, 425.
  Ausable Branch, p. 230.
  Chateaugay RR, p. 231.
  Paul Smiths, pp. 237, 243.
  Bloomingdale stages, p. 246.
  Saranac Lake, p. 247.

Weitzman, David. 1980. *Traces of the Past: A Field Guide to Industrial Archaeology.* Charles Scribner's Sons, New York. 229 pp. Chapter 1 "Mirrors of Rust", pp. 3–40, is on railroads.

Index

In this Index, entries of certain topics are listed together under the general topic name, instead of many separate entries arranged alphabetically and thus scattered. The purpose here is twofold: to avoid duplication, and to make the Index more useful for researchers. The general topics are: HOTELS, MINES, FOREST PRODUCTS, FOREST PRODUCT INDUSTRIES, RAILROAD CARS AND LOCOMOTIVES.

145